TESTOSTERONE
INC.

TESTOSTERONE
INC.

TALES OF CEOs GONE WILD

CHRISTOPHER BYRON

WILEY

JOHN WILEY & SONS, INC.

Published by John Wiley & Sons, Inc., Hoboken, New Jersey.
Published simultaneously in Canada.

For general information on our other products and services, or technical support,
please contact our Customer Care Department within the United States at
800-762-2974, outside the United States at 317-572-3993 or fax 317-572-4002.

Wiley also publishes its books in a variety of electronic formats. Some content that
appears in print may not be available in electronic books.

For more information about Wiley products, visit our web site at www.wiley.com.

Library of Congress Cataloging-in-Publication Data:
Byron, Christopher.
   Testosterone inc. : tales of CEOs gone wild / Christopher Byron.
      p. cm.
   Includes bibliographical references.
   ISBN 0-471-42005-0 (cloth)
   1. Chief executive officers—United States—Case studies.   2. Welch,
Jack, 1935–   3. General Electric Company—Management.   I. Title.
   HD38.25.U6B973   2004
   658.4′2—dc22

                                        2004003667

Printed in the United States of America.

10   9   8   7   6   5   4   3

CONTENTS

ACKNOWLEDGMENTS

The primary research material for this book is the public record of the four business figures who are the book's principal focus: Jack F. Welch Jr. of General Electric; Ronald O. Perelman of Revlon; Leo D. Kozlowski Jr. of Tyco International; and Albert J. Dunlap Jr. of Sunbeam. Each of these men has declined the opportunity for interviews for this book.

As gathered and digested for this narrative, the public records of these individuals consist, at latest count, of more than 15,000 individual documents. They range from the U.S. Securities and Exchange Commission annual 10K filings of the companies they headed, to the various land records, property deeds, divorce files, financial statements, court records, and police reports created at one point or another by and about the individuals themselves.

To bolster this material and help with its interpretation and analysis, interviews were requested from roughly 120 individuals, both in the United States and abroad, and of that total approximately 90 responded favorably. Many of the resulting interviews concerned topics that the interviewees were uncomfortable discussing for quotation, and their identities have not been revealed in these pages. The same is true for various individuals who put their professional careers in jeopardy to share with us information that they judged to be matters of importance to the public and about which we otherwise would not have known.

This book makes use of extended footnotes, presented where they are most accessible (on the pages of the actual narrative) to aid readers who may wish to explore the topics discussed in the narrative more deeply. They are offered, in a sense, as a "story within a story," and are intended to entertain as well as inform. Additional research materials are footnoted to the narrative sentences based on them and are numerically listed, by chapter, at the back of the book.

Six people—five of them women—have done the real and arduous work in bringing this book into being, and without any one of them, *Testosterone Inc.* would not exist. So I would like at the outset to thank, with the deepest love I know how to express, the woman who not only conceived of the idea for this book, but came up with its title and organized the resulting research. She is my wife Maria, who gave me every funny joke—and the inspiration for every sigh—in its pages.

I likewise wish to thank my research colleague, Donna Bertaccini, whose relentless pursuit of the facts on this project kept her working through months of eighteen-hour days, pursuing dozens of interviews, hundreds of leads, and thousands of pages of documents, without voicing so much as a single complaint.

To my editor, Pamela van Giessen, goes my heartfelt gratitude for continuing to believe in this book when even the author seemed to be going crazy. I am grateful as well for the work of the extraordinary and many talented Heather Florence, who saved me from myself more than once in all this. And to the person without whom no one would even be returning my calls, what else can I say but, Praise God Almighty, my agent is Joni Evans.

PROLOGUE

The only truly happy people are married women and single men.

—H. L. Mencken

The thing everyone noticed first was the eyes, and he dressed to bring out their best. The eyes—pale blue and riveting—with the cerulean blue Sea Island cotton shirt and the cashmere blue blazer.

The height he couldn't do much about, though in time he had learned how to make it work for him: Never enter the room alone. Always be flanked by taller men, this way your very shortness becomes a statement, the way it did for Al Pacino in *Godfather II*. A little man flanked by big men automatically becomes big himself—big, powerful, and in control. And the closer one got the more one could see where the control really lie. It was in the eyes. The eyes of Jack Welch.

Donald Trump too had blue eyes, and he also wore a uniform to bring out their maximum intensity. He had shortcomings that included a bad scalp reduction to cover his bald spot, which sometimes made it seem as if his face were positioned just ever-so-slightly too high on his head. But Trump was tall, and he had no trouble entering a room alone, or with a "top model" girlfriend at his side. Yet when he did, it wasn't Melania Knaus that the crowd noticed first, it was the clothes on the man next to her—the $10,000 superfine wool Brioni hand-tailored Italian suits, the gold and enamel cuff links, the tassled loafers. In his way, Trump was as much a piece of performance art as was the decorative object at his elbow, and for that matter, as was the man long at the helm of GE with his gang.

In fact, they all were exercises in performance art—Mort Zuckerman with his clown-sized Don Diego cigars and the jokes about having his tombstone inscribed to read "At Last He Sleeps Alone;" Richard Scrushy and his custom-built sloop the Chez Soiree; WorldCom chairman Bernie Ebbers and his 132-foot yacht, the Aquasition; Steve Case and his Dockers ads. From Jack Welch with his glamour cache as the head of the NBC television network, to Ron Perelman with his trophy wives and his Revlon, Inc., ticket of admission to the Oscars, to Dennis Kozlowski and his 134-foot custom-built racing yacht, the Endeavor, and Al Dunlap and his chainsaw—these were the men who became the heroes of the greatest bull market of the twentieth century.

By and large, America's late century heroes of business were almost entirely male, almost entirely white, and almost entirely middle-aged. And scarcely had the bull market run its course than adulation turned to derision and the merciless sword of public retribution began claiming its victims.

What exactly was it that caused so many men, at the very apogee of their power and acclaim—with the world at their feet and their dreams in the stars—to do as Ron Perelman did at the peak of his fame as the czar of the American cosmetics industry, and turn his private life into tabloid headlines through a divorce proceeding that featured allegations of out of control serial womanizing?

And what caused Dennis Kozlowski of Tyco International, Inc., to help himself to the corporate treasury to spiff up his company-paid pied-a-terre on Manhattan's East Side with gold lamé shower curtains in the loo? Or stirred Al Dunlap to pretend that an entire period of his professional career had never occurred?

Or, to dial down the question to the heart of the matter, what was it that caused the chairman and CEO of the ultimate American corporation of them all, GE—the premier industrial company of the last 100 years, and for all anyone knew, the next one hundred to come—to walk on stage in the fifth act of a career that seemed to be arcing toward business immortality, and admit to the world that he'd had it with the wife (and just after the prenup had expired!) and thereupon make a public spectacle of himself at the feet of an odd woman from Boston who liked to boast of her sexual exploits with CEOs? Why do men do things like that?

The answer lies not in their stars but in their skivvies. Both males and females produce the hormone testosterone in roughly equivalent amounts until approximately the 144th month of life, at which point testosterone levels in males simply shoot off the chart. These dramatically elevated levels of testosterone in the male body in turn initiate the many physiological changes by which little boys, if left free of any encumbering encouragements toward socialization, will almost inevitably develop into wild teenage animals—an outcome only rarely seen among women, whose adult levels of testosterone are usually no more than about 5 percent that of males.

A lot of what defines contemporary American politics flows from such facts. They invite one to argue, for example, that although Hewlett Packard's Carleton Fiorina and Yahoo's Terry Semel are both CEOs, Terry Semel (being a male) is actually twenty times the man that Carleton Fiorina is because (her name notwithstanding) Carly is a woman.

From such quarrels, Americans have erected such mighty edifices as the Equal Employment Opportunity Commission and Title IX of the United States Code—though for most of human history, societies have dealt far more directly, and permanently, with the more extreme expressions of male misbehavin' by simply attacking the problem at its source. The first known use of castration as social policy appears in on the walls of tomb paintings in Egypt, 4,450 years B.C., and in the grand sweep of things can be said to have continued as a form of social control in even relatively civilized cultures up until virtually the day before yesterday—or at least the fifteenth century.

Yet though civilization no longer tolerates such barbaric practices, the task of channeling male energy into socially useful activity remains, as ever, one of civilization's core challenges. And the effort is never more effectively pursued than when the behavior of men is yoked most convincingly to the value systems of self-restraint, decency, and respect for the rights of others—in particular women, whose rights as human beings are constantly at risk when male behavior is at its worst (even when the women may arguably be said to bring it on themselves.)

For most of American history, the leaders of big business and Wall Street seemed able to control themselves in these matters—at least when it came to their deportment in public.* Yet in the blowout decade of the twentieth century, things changed, and with the sap of prosperity rising on Wall Street as never before in the country's history, American business began to pulse with a new kind of public figure: The Celebrity CEO. And as the money grew, and

---

*One exception: a turn of the century New York businessman named Harry K. Thaw, who caught the public eye after living a life of such relentless and open debauchery that he wound up moving into his own suite of rooms in a Manhattan brothel. From there it was a matter of mere time and opportunity before Thaw was making headlines by gunning down the country's most famous architect, Stanford White, during a dinner theater performance atop Madison Square Garden. The resulting trial revealed that that both men had shared a common interest in Thaw's wife, a Lolita-like starlette named Evelyn Nesbit, who had satisfied White's own quirky sense of entertainment by dressing in little girl's clothes and licking a lollypop while swinging on a velvet-roped swing in an elegant "playroom" in White's mansion.

along with it the fame, the behavior of CEOs gone wild began to seep into the news, and at times even to dominate it.

At one point or another in the Great Bull Market, Jack F. Welch Jr., the chairman and CEO of the General Electric Co.; Ronald O. Perelman, the chairman of the Revlon Corporation; Leo D. Kozlowski Jr., the chairman and CEO of Tyco International, Inc.; and Albert J. Dunlap Jr., the chairman of Sunbeam Corp. were all lionized in the press and celebrated by the public as larger than life figures—true heroes of American culture. In some cases, the praise, such as for Welch's financial helmsmanship of GE, was warranted, too. Yet in the end, each in turn suffered ridicule and rebuke—and in the case of Kozlowski and Dunlap, even worse—when internal guidance systems of all four men regarding what is decent behavior and what is not, simply failed them.

Ultimately, the Great Bull Market and the crash that followed is the same ageless and timeless story that has been repeated by poets and storytellers from Homer to Tom Wolfe. It is the story of men and women—and of power, lust, greed and betrayal—in the ever-changing, yet eternally changeless interaction between flesh, blood, and the hormone testosterone.

Does a man today react any differently than any man ever did, when, like Mozart's Salieri, he yearns to write the symphony he believes to lie buried within him, yet somehow lacks the ability to call it forth—when from his earliest memories onward the driving force in his life has been some combination of thickening muscles, penile erections, and dominance, aggression, and power . . . at the culmination of which he discovers that his children think he's a jerk, his wife wants him to retire and spend more time with her sitting in the den holding hands, and nothing he has ever done has prepared him for the moment when that muscle twitch in the chest turns out to be more than just a bench-press cramp from the gym? Does he agree, upon reflection, that perhaps a slice of quiche might have been a better choice after all rather than 30 years of roast beef end-cuts and golf? Or does his gaze linger after the departing waitress (or stewardess, or McKinsey & Co. partner) with the tailored silhouette and no VPL (as in Visible Panty Lines), and think, "Hey, am I the boss around here or what . . . ?" and thereupon summon the trumpet call to ruin and the ten-year siege of Troy?

What follows is the story of four men and their companies during a time when all stock prices rose, all business leaders were heroes, and all days were forever morning in the olive groves of Elysium. Then, as night at last descended and Agamemnon gave his daughter for a fair wind to battle, did he possibly suppose his wife would slay him in his bath while the headlines read, "Greeks Meet Resistance At The Gates Of Troy"?

Of such pathos do we now know the story of these men—and indeed, of American business itself—in the runaway bull market of the 1980s and 1990s. In Greek tragedy, the heroes are eventually undone by a fatal flaw that dooms them all. As Yeats thus tells us, in the most astonishing rape scene ever told:[1]

> *A sudden shudder in the loins engenders there,*
> *The broken wall, the burning roof and tower,*
> *And Agamemnon dead.*

This is their story told yet again, an American Iliad, in the dream decades that came to naught.

1

"IS THAT A GUN IN YOUR POCKET, OR ARE YOU JUST HAPPY TO SEE ME?"

In the Year of Our Lord 1692, it came to a group of men reeling from the ravages of too many New England winters that salvation by a vengeful God could best be assured by offering, into the bosom of eternal bliss, an assortment of teenage girls.

Thus did the town of Salem, Massachusetts, stake out its claim to tragic notoriety for that moment in its history when the Devil, accompanied by an outbreak of small pox and a band of marauding Indians, helped the manly elders of the village pronounce a group of young women to be witches and have them hanged.

So, mindful of Karl Marx's maxim that history's second comings have a habit of morphing from tragedy into farce for the return engagement, it seems somehow fitting that 243 years after the Salem witch trials came to an end there should appear on the Registrar of Births for the Commonwealth of Massachusetts an infant destined to emerge, over the following seven decades, as the world's most famous business leader of his time as well as one of the most sociosexually conflicted public figures the town of Salem, Massachusetts, has produced since the witch trials themselves: the future chairman and CEO of General Electric (GE), John Francis Welch Jr.

To understand Welch and his entanglements with women, it helps greatly to know the circumstances of his upbringing, which are evoked, if only vaguely, in his best-selling business world memoir, *Jack: Straight from the Gut.* It is doubtless a testament to the public's intense fascination with the man that his memoir, which had the great misfortune of going on sale on the morning of September 11, 2001, leaped quickly onto the *New York Times* nonfiction best-seller list anyway, eventually selling a total of 800,000 copies in hardcover.

Though some reviewers criticized the memoir for lacking depth and personal insight,[1] Welch's feelings about himself and his life are evident on every page, often revealed through what he chose *not* to say about himself as opposed to what he chose to reveal. We are constrained to take the author at his word when he writes of himself, at the age of sixty-five, "Truth is, deep down, I've never really changed much from the boy my mother raised in Salem, Massachusetts."[2]

From the perspective of six decades and the approach of old age, *Jack: Straight from the Gut* summons a childhood rich in the generational promise of America itself—of hard-working fathers and loving mothers, sandlot baseball after school, and summers in the bleachers at Fenway Park.

But there is more in these pages than the hallelujah choir of Walt Whitman and Hart Crane; we hear as well the deeper murmur of mom and the Holy Ghost, and it is in the missing notes of that dirge that we find Jack Welch's true melody.

"She was the most influential person in my life," Jack writes of his mother, Grace Andrews Welch, who worked as a bookkeeper to supplement the income of her husband, and Jack's father, John Welch Sr., a second-generation Irish American, who worked as a conductor on the Boston & Maine (B&M) Railroad. "Grace Welch taught me the value of competition, just as she taught me the pleasure of winning and the need to take defeat in stride," Jack informs us.[3] But it is strange, even unsettling, to be invited to share in such sentiments since, for all their apparent sincerity and ardor, there is little in the book to convey the warmth and love that Welch says he felt radiating from his mother. There is not even a physical description of the woman, nor anything to illuminate a lifetime of her personal history. She is simply urged upon us, as a kind of Ur-figure from the Land of Future Greatness. Reflected in the mirror of her son's sensibilities, there is eerily no reflection of Grace Welch at all.

In place of that reflection, we encounter a Welch family mythology. It is Jack's version of how he grew up, complete with an evocation of the joy and fulfillment he found living across the street from a cemetery and a factory in Salem's working-class North End.

For a fifteen-year-old boy hanging with his mates in front of the corner candy store, life is what it is, and joy can be found in a bottle of root beer passed around on a hot August evening. But joys are harder to come by when the footfalls of poverty dog you throughout life, and for the immigrant population of Salem's Irish Catholics of the 1940s that is how life was lived. "We were poor," says a Salem old-timer named Ed Curtin, now pushing seventy, who grew up with Welch on Lovett Street. At the age of thirteen, Ed was a corner candy store regular with Welch after school and on weekends, though he is not mentioned in Welch's memoir. "I mean, really and truly poor," Ed reports. "In my family we had to put a quarter into the meter to get electricity for the apartment. And everyone I knew was in pretty much the same situation, including Jack Welch."[4]

By just about every demographic measure imaginable—from morbidity and infectious disease rates to educational levels, housing conditions, and the unemployment rate—Salem, Massachusetts, in the 1940s and 1950s was hardly an inviting place to live, especially in the town's Irish Catholic North End. In wave after wave, the Irish had poured in, desperate to escape the poverty of their country's collapsed economy under the boot of the English. Entering by way of Boston, many wound up getting no further than Salem before exhaustion and lack of money ended their travels in the permanent underclass of the town's North End ghetto.

Among them was an immigrant laborer named Luke Welch, who made his way north to Salem where he married another recently arrived Irish immigrant named Mary Walsh. In 1895, the couple produced a son whom they named John Francis Welch, who grew up a gangling fellow with taciturn ways and large, almost elephantine, ears. This man became Jack Welch's father.

Meanwhile, yet more Irish immigrants had arrived and made their way to Salem, where two members of the growing Irish American community—William Andrews and Bridget White—were likewise in time married. In 1899, they produced a daughter whom they named Grace. She too was marked by a striking physical aspect, captured in a determined and forceful jawline and thin lips that opened into an occasional and reluctant smile. In her face seemed to be the foreshadowed knowledge of what life held in store for her, and it was something she did not seem to welcome.[5] This woman became Jack's mother.

Although both John and Grace were gainfully employed at the time of their marriage, he as a trainman on the B&M and she as a clerk, it took the twenty years that followed, from their wedding day in November 1924 until nearly the end of World War II, for the couple to save enough money to purchase a home of their own. For at least the first eleven of those years, the couple did not even have enough money to afford a *rented* place of their own and wound up living with Grace's parents on Dunlap Street, also in Salem's North End.

When John and Grace's only child, Jack, was born in November 1935,* the couple was still living with the Andrews family on Dunlap Street. They finally moved into a home of their own when Jack was nine. The move was into a small, stuccoed row house at 15 Lovett Street, a mere two blocks from the Andrews home on Dunlap Street. And it was there that young Jack Welch finished out the years of his youth—the latest in a family of Irish Americans to have become seemingly mired forever in the bog of New England's working poor.

This was the backstairs reality of the world into which Jack Welch was born—a world in which uneducated and resentful parents would typically fight with each other, beat their children, and drink themselves to death from the despair that challenged them at every turn.† Though Welch sought to recall his family life with warmth and compassion in his autobiography, other feelings percolated just below the surface, bubbling up from time to time during interviews in which he described his childhood as being one with his "nose pressed up against the glass"—the proverbial outsider, doomed to a life of coveting what lay just beyond his grasp.

---

* On Jack's birth certificate—issued by the Commonwealth of Massachusetts, Office of the Secretary, Division of Vital Statistics—his name is given as John Francis Welch, without the "Jr." His date of birth is listed as November 19, 1935, in the town of Peabody, Massachusetts.

† In the Irish and Italian ghettos of Greater Boston, a popular bit of doggerel was repeated back and forth among children of the era that recalled the background hum of domestic violence that permeated life for America's immigrant urban poor during much of the early twentieth century. The rhyme referenced a highly publicized murder trial in nearby Fall River, Massachusetts, some years earlier, in which a crazed young woman was tried and acquitted for killing her parents. The rhyme went:

> Lizzie Borden took an ax
> And gave her mother forty whacks
> And when she saw what she had done
> She gave her father forty-one.

Nor do his reminiscences about the warmth of his actual family life come off as very convincing. Instead, they seem grudging, contentious, and against the known facts. Like nearly all Irish Catholic families, the Welches, Walshes, Andrews, and Whites were overflowing with uncles, aunts, and cousins—a the vast and spreading tree of Jack Welch's extended family. But we encounter none of them in Jack's memoir, nor in any of the other recollected moments of his life.

Welch rarely mentions any of these people in his interviews and reminiscences about his early years. One exception came during an interview with a reporter for an obscure Boston newsletter covering Irish affairs.* During the interview, Welch was asked about his extended family of aunts and uncles, and all he could think to say was that they included a couple of uncles "who drank too much"—a comfortably vague acknowledgment that alcoholism, known from the local perspective as simply the "Irish disease," was very much a part of Jack Welch's childhood.†

---

* See *Irish America* (January 31, 2002). The interview is unusual for the manner in which the reporter, Patricia Harty, succeeded in catching Welch off-guard in reflective moments. The two unnamed uncles he refers to in the interview as having been excessive drinkers appear to have been brothers of his mother, Grace, and "were always getting in trouble . . ." so much so that his mother would sometimes sneak money from his father to help get her brothers "out of trouble." On another occasion, Welch muses as to why his mother hadn't made more of her life, saying, "I wonder why my mother didn't do better in school. I wonder why she and her family didn't progress further."

† Six decades later, Welch was living in grand circumstances indeed, in a 10,773 square-foot home, with a squash court and chauffeur's quarters, on 6.5 acres overlooking Long Island Sound, in Fairfield, Connecticut. Yet, he could still be found periodically boozing it up with a group of working-class cronies on weekday evenings in a bar known as Mario's, in the Italian-American community of Saugatuck, Connecticut. A local Fairfield County columnist, Pete McGovern, wrote of a Welch sighting in early 2003, "Jack Welch, GE's genial literary former chairman, author of his red-hot bestseller *Jack*, was reported by regular observers to be present last week at his usual sit-down of his private assembly again at W'port RR Pl, popular Mecca, Mario's Place. Despite any entanglements of legalities, the attendees, composed of his four footloose and friendly long-time comrades, engaged in mostly broad male pleasantries, dominating the session of many hours in his favorite haunt over many years." See the *Westport Minuteman*

For Jack's remoteness from his own family, there is no explanation in his memoir. And odder still, when it comes to confronting the fact that he himself was an only child (a rarity in Irish Catholic families) and, moreover, that he arrived late in the lives of his parents (when John was 41 and Grace was 36), he explains only that his parents had been trying in vain to have a baby "for many years."*

Perhaps Jack arrived late in the lives of his parents because another mouth to feed was hardly viewed as a big new opportunity by Grace's elephant-eared husband John, who had apparently been free-loading for years, along with Grace, as live-in members of her parents' extended family household on Dunlap Street.

John Welch, as tall and gangling in middle-age as he had been as a young man, was still working as a trainman on the B&M when Jack was born. And though Jack's reminiscences of his youth overflow with the "mentoring" presence of Grace, he almost never mentions his trainman dad, John. At best, he is evoked as a hale fellow with a smile and a pinch of blarney for any passenger on his train run in and out of Salem. But, reports Jack without explanation, "His cheerful disposition on the train would often contrast with his quiet and withdrawn behavior at home."[6]

The mood change that would come over him daily as he headed home from the eighty-mile round-trip on the B&M that he traveled for years—through the factory towns and fishing villages of the North Shore—is never explained. We are left to wonder what it was

---

(February 6, 2003). In his autobiography, Welch references another local bar that he and other GE executives frequented, the Hi-Ho, a local watering hole near GE's headquarters. See Welch, *Jack: Straight from the Gut* (New York: Warner Books, 2001), p. xii.

* In a 1998 profile in *BusinessWeek*, writer John Byrne, who eventually wound up collaborating with Welch on *Jack: Straight from the Gut*, extended this proposition mathematically to the realm of what would be, for a Catholic, actual mortal sin, reporting that by the time Welch was born in 1935 his parents had been attempting to conceive a child for 16 years—an awkward revelation to say the least since they'd only been married for 11 years. See Byrne, "I Had a Pal in My Mom," *BusinessWeek* (June 8, 1998). (John F. Welch Sr. and Grace Andrews were married November 19, 1924, in Salem, Massachusetts.)

that would pitch John into such black despair that Grace would complain of it the very instant he walked in the door. What would cause him, at the first hint of bad weather, to rise from his chair and head back to the station, to spend the night sleeping in one of the coaches so as not to miss the run the next morning? Was the old man carrying on? Did Grace sense something was up? The tension in these moments is obvious, but the author does not explore it.

Though Jack Welch has time and again portrayed his mother as the person who taught him everything worthwhile he ever learned in his life, from how to get to Fenway Park to how to "stand up to anybody," John Sr. is presented as having taught him essentially nothing at all. As a father, he just wasn't there, leaving to Grace the task of being not only the mother but the father as well.*

How Grace felt about this isn't known because she left no memoir to mark the passing of her life. But she seemed to think and act in competitive—and often angry and hostile—ways at the oddest moments. In the very first scene of Jack's memoir, the reader encounters Grace in action, bursting into the boys' locker room of Salem High School after Jack's hockey team lost a game and Welch threw his stick across the ice in a rage.

"You punk!" she screams. "If you don't know how to lose, you'll never know how to win!"

Now there are many things one may wish to know about what happened next, beginning with whether the steamy air of the boys' locker room—thick as it must have been with the aromas of naked teenage boys who had just played a losing hockey game—was

---

*According to Dr. Trisha Macnair, a family health expert in Britain, fathers are particularly important as role models for boys ages 6 to 14, when they are still uncertain of their sexual identity and how to deal with conflicts involving peers. Lacking effective fathering role models, such boys often overcompensate and try to act tough and uncaring to provide a shell to hide their insecurity. Macnair, a regular commentator on such matters for the British Broadcasting Corporation, says the surges of testosterone that come with puberty can make the problem worse.

thereupon rent with the sounds of catcalls, whistles, and snapping towels. Alas, what the reader learns instead is that, according to Jack Welch, this is what a mother's love is ultimately all about: calling your son a punk.

Such was the subtext to the day-to-day behavior of the most powerful role model in Jack Welch's life—his mother, Grace. In the merciless world of Salem's Irish American ghetto, with its inbred relationships and Darwinian value structures, what was a young boy to think when love, hate, success, failure, and a dozen other profound life experiences all somehow seemed wrapped up in the person of this woman, his own mother, raging at him one minute for bringing home a "B" on his report card, then clutching him to her breast in the next for bringing home an "A"? From such contradictions can develop deep and profound confusion over how to relate to people in general, and women in particular. How is a boy to know whether love is staring him in the face when, from all past experience, it might mercurially transform into anger and even hate at a moment's notice?

There is a moment that has apparently played itself out over and over again in the mind of Jack Welch, versions of which appear at least twice in Jack's autobiography. When the moment is first encountered, Jack is not yet thirteen years of age, not yet a teenager, not yet into puberty. He is small for his age, with a pronounced stutter and uncertain reflexes. It is late in the day, and he is standing at the doorway to the house on Lovett Street, watching as his mother heads to the station to collect his father after work at the end of his daily run on the B&M line north out of Boston.

But the minutes pass by, and soon a quarter hour has gone, and then even more time passes. And out of nowhere, a desperate panic sweeps through the young boy: His mother has left him. And in an onrush of feelings that he neither understands nor can control, he rushes into the street and down the sidewalk toward the station, consumed by the panic that his mother has left him, never to return.

Over and over, this happened to Jack Welch as a young boy growing up in Salem, Massachusetts. And over and over, he reacted the same way. How would he cope or survive even another day, if he were to be abandoned to fend for himself on the mean streets of Salem? And over and over, the answer was the same, as from around the corner his parents would reappear—the man/woman he knew as Mom, and the other person, known vaguely as Dad. And, one may suppose, the fear of abandonment worked its way into him deeper and deeper as the years unfolded, until the day finally came when his mother really did abandon him to death, and a kind of hardened emotional shell grew around him and, taking his mother's survival lessons to heart, he began abandoning the women in his life, one after the next, before they abandoned him.*

ack Welch was small for his age, and he lacked the muscular strength and agility to be a dominating presence in sports. But his mother had taught him the value of competition and the power of a dominating personality, and with that skill set, he had emerged in no time as a leader among his peers. Many who have known Welch say he is charismatic by nature and was born with the world's eyes upon him.† But it is also possible that he simply moved into the role

---

*In *Sexual Detours* (New York: St. Martin's Press, 2000), author Holly Hein argues that fear of abandonment sometimes causes individuals to stay glued to another, preserving an illusion of intimacy that protects the person from the vulnerability of true intimacy.

†Stratford Sherman, who has written extensively on Welch over the years, observed this about him in a *Fortune* (March 27, 1989) profile, "A charming firebrand with hot Irish blood, Welch seized the General Electric Co.'s vast bureaucracy by the scruff of the neck and shook it till it saw stars." Similarly, Linda Grant of the *Los Angeles Times* (May 9, 1993) wrote of Welch in a story involving his appearance at a University of Southern California leadership videotaping session, "For a man who lacks the gift of eloquence, Welch is an oddly riveting speaker." Or consider Warren Bennis, a visiting

of leader as a kind of natural progression from having grown up the only child in an Irish Catholic household in 1950. In such circumstances, a fellow can develop a taste for the spotlight from a very early age.

It is hardly surprising to learn from Ed Curtin, as memory's veil falls away, that rare was the summer evening for Jack and the boys—as they passed the time in front of the corner variety store at the end of the block—when the conversation did not sooner or later turn to an attractive young lady named Marilyn Walker, who was a year ahead of them in school.

It was the start of the 1950s, and Marilyn Monroe had just burst on the scene as Angela Phinlay, the temptress with a cynical shell and a heart of gold in *The Asphalt Jungle* . . . which meant, of course, when you got right down to it, that in the summer of 1950—and at least in front of the Fairmont Variety Store at the corner of Barstow and School Streets, in Salem, Massachusetts—Marilyn Walker effectively *was* Marilyn Monroe, and thus by implication had precisely the same thing on her mind as the crew in Jack's gang had on theirs. By such speculations could almost any group of fifteen-year-old boys keep themselves occupied all summer.

That is because the male body heralds the onset of adolescence by going pedal-to-the-metal in the production of the hormone testosterone, and the next thing a young fellow knows, it's party time in his pants. As Mae West said to George Hamilton in the

---

scholar at the Harvard University's Center for Public Leadership, who recalled following two separate interviews with Welch not so much for what he said as for his "passion, his intensity, his energy, his need to engage." See Bennis, "The House That Jack Built," *Leadership* (Autumn 2001). Or consider Betsy Morris, *Fortune* (December 11, 1995), who wrote of Welch, "He became known as a fearless negotiator who, through aggressiveness and charisma, could talk the bigger kids into sharing the basketball court. He was a ferocious and judgmental competitor. His teammates 'always knew where they stood,' recalls one."

movie *Sextette*,"Is that a gun in your pocket, or are you just happy to see me?"*

For teenage boys, the sexual drives unleashed by testosterone production become the energizing forces of their lives. Grace Welch may have thought the call to holy orders would enable Jack to avoid all that. But if that was her reason for trying to steer him into the priesthood and thereby keep him forever chaste in the conflicted miseries of Roman Catholicism and its promise of redemption through the pain and guilt that are every Catholic's birthright, she was certainly disappointed.[7]

In response, Jack sought sanctuary in the rituals of rebellion with his boyhood friends—escaping to Old Orchard Beach, an amusement park in Maine . . . combing the beach for returnable pop bottles . . . playing hooky to get "juiced up on some cheap 50-cents-a-bottle muscatel" on the street corners of South Boston on St. Patrick's Day.[8]

In the down-and-out world of Salem's Irish Catholics, it was how a boy found his place in life . . . on the weedy running paths of Salem's sandlot baseball field, which was known as "the pit" . . . in the bleachers of Fenway Park as Ted Williams stepped to the plate . . . at the CYO and Teen Town dances, where the boys all wondered what it would be like to work your leg between the thighs of Marilyn Walker and murmur something so close to her mouth that your lips just barely touched while the record player turned at 78 RPMs and the sounds of Les Paul and Mary Ford singing *Vaya Con Dios* filled the darkened gym.

---

*The hormonal and behavioral changes that take place in a sexually aroused adolescent male are complex and wide-ranging, affecting the entire nervous system of the body, and leading to the elevated secretion of an array of mood and behavior-altering hormones, from oxytocin, dopamine, and norepinephrine to endorphins, estrogen, and testosterone. They are the only such changes a boy can bring about in his own body entirely by himself. See J. Shibley, *Understanding Human Sexuality*, 4th ed. (New York: McGraw-Hill, 1990).

On weekends and summers, the action swung to Salem's Kernwood Country Club, where the boys from the North End made money caddying for the rich—and largely Jewish—members of the club . . . men who arrived at the clubhouse in new postwar Packards and Desotos—cars with automatic windows and power seats and "fluid drive" transmissions in which you didn't have to press down the clutch to shift gears. They were grand, humbling vehicles, promising a life of affluence and ease in postwar America. And here were the lads of Salem's North End, locked out from that future with nothing before them but the chance to stick $1.50 in their pockets for dragging around a rich man's golf clubs for three hours in the summer sun. It was what Welch meant by growing up an outsider, with his "nose pressed up against the glass"—forever on the outside looking in.

An interest in golf, which became something of an obsession with Welch later in life, was one of the few things that his taciturn and distant father, John Sr., seems to have instilled in Jack. In the trainman's experience, golf was what the "big shot" commuters on the B&M discussed on their way to and from work. If Jack had any hope of escaping Salem, it would be by learning how to play golf. At least that's how John Sr. saw things, with the result that by the time Jack Jr. was nine, his father had press-ganged the boy into weekend work as Kernwood's youngest caddy. After all, reasoned his father, golf was certainly a step up from street hockey, which by that age was the socially appropriate sport of choice for many of the North End's young boys. And besides, even if he failed as a golfer, at least he was learning early what it meant to turn in an honest day's work.

Jack's own view of golf seemed similarly conflicted from the start, and as time passed, it grew worse. In his autobiography, he recalls an incident during his senior year of high school, when he was caddying for one of Kenwood's "stingiest" members. The man duffed the ball into a pond off the sixth tee, then ordered Welch to wade into the water and retrieve it. Instead, Welch writes that he told the man to stuff it, and uncorking the pent-up resentment at his life as a packhorse for the rich, he threw the man's clubs into the water and stalked off the fairway.*

Looking back on his teenage years, we see little in Welch's life to mark him for future greatness. His high school grades were okay, but the challenges weren't great so he always looked smarter than he was. This helped for a time to mask his intellectual shortcomings, which he later made up for in street-smart snap judgments and eclectic curiosity. "No one would have accused me of being brilliant," he wrote of his academic accomplishments in high school.[†]

As far as college went, it was a topic he seemed willing to discuss if it made his mother happy, and that was about it. To that end, he applied for a Naval ROTC scholarship in his senior year at Salem High—apparently for no deeper reason than that two of his friends were doing the same—and predictably enough, wound up being turned down.

Thereafter, he basically did nothing, not even bothering to apply for admission to a college. At one point, John Sr. intervened on his behalf and managed to importune a local politician for some help. But the effort led to nothing, which undoubtedly further encouraged Jack in his view that his father was a figure of limited importance in his life and, in that sense at least, not to be taken seriously.

In desperation, and with graduation day approaching, his mother seized the initiative and simply shoved him into the state

---

*Three decades later, Welch's irritation boiled up with his second wife, Jane, because she had never learned to play golf and thus couldn't accompany him on deal-cementing golf outings with business associates and *their* wives. To appease him, she eventually learned to play as well, and he thereupon pronounced her his "perfect partner"—a crown she wore for the following decade until she no longer seemed so perfect and he began edging out the door.

[†] A now-retired colleague of Welch's reports that evidence of Welch's defensiveness about his intellectual abilities followed him right into his office as chairman of GE: A sign on Welch's desk read, "Where Is It Written That To Be Successful In Business You Have To Be Smart?"

university program, where he was accepted as a freshman at the University of Massachusetts in Amherst—an institution that aspired to little beyond preparing its students for careers as cogs in the machinery of western Massachusetts businesses.

What hopes Grace Welch may have had in sending her son down this path are lost forever, but the impact her action had on the young man was quickly evident since Jack had no interest in college, and for all his neighborhood bravado, he was hardly equipped to endure any lasting separation from Grace. We thus find him discovering in his memoir that freed from Grace's apron strings, he wasn't the "macho guy" he had thought he was; his clinging need for her support simply deepened and intensified. At one point in the recollected moments of his college years, we come upon a familiar scene: the young man running hysterically down the street, tears welling in his eyes.

This time, the cause was not the fear that his mother might not return from the train station with his father at the end of the day. This time, the reason was more serious—the news that his mother has just suffered a heart attack back in Salem and might be dying. In the frieze of Welch's career, it is not his many images as the world's most famous businessman that define him; it is this eternal tableau, frozen in time like Jesus on the road to Cavalry: the CEO as a little boy, forever pursuing the woman who might abandon him, down the dark road of life.*

---

*This incident, marking the first of Grace's three heart attacks, occurred when Jack was still in college. Though she recovered, two more heart attacks eventually followed. Grace Andrews Welch died of her third attack, while vacationing in Fort Lauderdale, Florida, January 25, 1965. A short announcement appeared three days later in the *Salem Evening News* (January 28, 1965). Jack's father and an aunt brought the body back to Salem by train. Her wake was held at the Murphy Funeral Home, followed by a requiem mass in St. Thomas the Apostle Church, the same church where Jack had served as an altar boy. See Jack Welch and John Byrne, *Jack: Straight from the Gut* (New York: Warner Books, 2001), p. 38.

2

"I WANT TO PLAY IN THE BAND!"

Even as Jack Welch was adjusting to college, an angry young man from the streets of Hoboken, New Jersey, was preparing to follow almost exactly the same escape route out of his own difficult childhood. He too was beginning an odyssey that would lead over the following four decades to the pinnacles of corporate power. And in his case as with so many others, it would end in a spectacle of shame, with the eyes of the world on him.

It was 1956, at the start of Dwight Eisenhower's second term—the high point of postwar America's celebration of cultural conformity—and the young fellow's name was Albert J. Dunlap Jr. As had been the case with Welch, he came from financially stressed family circumstances. Like Welch, he was the only son of an overbearing mother; and he, too, had a father of limited prospects—in Dunlap's case, a Hoboken shipyard union steward. And like Welch, Dunlap burnished his personal history until it fit his own sense of what he had wanted it to be.

Yet unlike Welch, who looked back with fondness on his childhood years, Dunlap—in interviews decades later—recalled his childhood as having been filled with misery and financial hardship. He emphasized the negative aspects of a life that could only be overcome by the sort of brute struggle of which he was uniquely capable. In an interview with *People* magazine, he claimed that the first place he could remember living was in a basement apartment in Hoboken, under a beauty parlor.[1] In fact, though the Dunlaps may have begun as a financially strapped family, they certainly weren't impoverished, and their financial circumstances improved steadily as the years passed—not least because union wage scales in the shipbuilding industry were good, and Al's father was rising steadily within the rank-and-file.

Though they hardly lived like the Duke of Bedford, the Dunlaps belonged to the ranks of America's rapidly swelling postwar middle class, moving in 1948 from a red brick rowhouse apartment in Hoboken to the seaside town of Hasbrouck Heights. At the start of the 1950s, Hasbrouck Heights was a one-square-mile village with a small downtown shopping strip along Route 17. Several of the town's roads were still unpaved. But the economic boom of the postwar era was beginning to transform the face of Hasbrouck Heights, just as it did the rest of the Jersey Shore, lifting the property values of the town and the living standards of its inhabitants—the Dunlaps included—in the process.[2]

Why Dunlap nonetheless chose to see his life as nothing more than a series of obstacles that he had to confront and overcome, beginning with his parents, may never be known. Yet from Day One, the face that young Al Dunlap showed to the world was as life's angry young man, defiant and raging at all that came his way.

Unlike Welch, who grew up so desperate for love and approval that he turned the whole of GE into a kind of Cathedral of Saint Jack, the man who came in time to be known as "Chainsaw Al" Dunlap grew up angry at his parents, at his friends, at his classmates and teachers until, eventually, he was raging at the whole world. "He was the most unpleasant, personally repulsive businessman I ever met in my life," said a New York image consultant whom Dunlap had wanted to hire. "Every conversation began in a normal tone of voice and ended with the man yelling, red-faced and furious, at whoever was standing in front of him. It was unbelievable."[3]

What deep resentments and insecurities drove Dunlap to behave so vituperatively are not known. Physically, Al Jr. was large, and intimidating, like his father, Al Sr. He played offensive and defensive lineman on his high school football team, and threw the shot put and discus in track-and-field. He seemed to go through his days wearing the game-face scowl of a jock and was still remembered decades later for the hostility and arrogance that enveloped him wherever he went.*

Clinically, the man seems to have had problems, and at their core there could have been physiological issues. In 1849, a Vermont railroad foreman named Phineas Gage suffered an incredibly gruesome accident when a nearly four-foot-long iron crowbar pierced the left side of his skull, destroying the left frontal lobe of his brain. Amazingly, he survived and eventually recovered. But he also underwent a profound change of personality as a result of the accident, turning from a stable, pleasant, and sociable individual into an obstinate, foul-mouthed, capricious person who was shunned by all those around him.

The case of Phineas Gage, regarded as a watershed in scientific research about localized brain functions, has led to further research involving the processes that occur in the type of brain tissue that was destroyed in Gage's accident. This research shows that

---

* A profile of Dunlap by a New Jersey reporter for the *Bergen Record* newspaper in 1996 offered the recollections of local Hasbrouck Heights residents who still vividly remembered Dunlap forty years later as "aggressive," and "very impressed with himself." See L. Lavelle, "Boy Next Door to Rambo in Pinstripes," *Bergen Record* (November 10, 1996), p. 1.

the ventromedial portions of the brain's frontal lobes are where emotional information from the limbic region enters the frontal cortex. Once there, it is processed into a person's self-awareness of feelings in one's self and in others. If this area is incompletely developed or damaged, a person may be unable to match emotional responses to the dictates of reason.[4]

So let us pause to ponder No. 73 on the Hasbrouck Heights High School football team, class of 1956—young Al Dunlap—in his starting position of left guard. We are told that in grade school and junior high, Al was a quiet kid who didn't have many friends, preferring to spend long hours in his room staring at the ceiling, from which he had hung a collection of model planes. But by high school, the complex chemical outpourings of his pituitary and adrenal glands, and his testes, had produced a hulking six-foot, 200-pound adolescent in his stocking feet.

Suited up in the limited protective gear of high school football in the mid-1950s, 200 pounds is a lot of mass to be moving on a football field, only to be brought to a sudden and jarring stop by an equally large mass moving in the opposite direction—not once or twice but maybe twenty or more times per game—for game after game.* The Dunlap retrospective by Lavelle in the Bergen *Record* newspaper quoted a high school teammate of Al's as describing one block that

---

* The Centers for Disease Control and Prevention report that Americans suffer 300,000 sports-related head injuries yearly. Many of the most dangerous, and least understood, involve concussions (Associated Press, October 23, 2003). A study by researchers at Virginia Technical Institute finds that football players are routinely hit 20 to 50 times per game with impact forces equivalent to car crashes. Experts say the resulting repetitive impact can permanently damage brain tissue. Studies involving retired football players and combat veterans from World War II show that concussions can increase the risk of clinical depression later in life. Because the results of concussions often do not manifest themselves immediately, victims of severe concussion-type sports injuries often get up and go right back in the game, bringing on yet more impact damage. See the Associated Press (January 3, 2004).

took Al down so hard he couldn't breathe, leaving him motionless in the dirt with his eyes crossed.[5]

The Bergen *Record* story quoted Al's coach, Andrew Kmetz, as recalling something else as well regarding the way Al played the game: A personality change would overtake him if he got hit good and hard. His face would redden and take on a "mean" look, and Al would change from a plodding, dutiful lineman into the high school equivalent of an out-of-control human tank—the very aggressive and angry personality that Al chose to celebrate in his "life as combat" business memoir in 1996—*Mean Business: How I Save Bad Companies and Make Good Companies Great.**

Whatever the causes of his nasty disposition, they were certainly aggravated by the tortured feelings he clearly felt toward his mother, whose career outside the home extended no further than working as a clerk at a nearby Woolworth's.[†] On the one hand, Dunlap spoke of her in terms that are remarkably similar to those that Jack Welch used to describe his own mother, Grace, who also put food on the family table by working at a low level job (Grace was a bookkeeper).

To Dunlap, his mother, Mildred, was a "strong, disciplined woman"—just as, to Welch, his own mother, Grace, was "clearly the disciplinarian in the family." As recalled by Dunlap, his mother Mildred was the person who set the standards of performance he

---

* If Al had suffered neurological damage on the high school gridiron, it certainly didn't get any better after he entered West Point. There he pursued boxing and was remembered as "aggressive and tough to hit." His roommate, Philip A. Tripician, recalled him as fighting "out of a crouch," and that "When he hit you he stung you." See *Business Week* (January 15, 1996), p. 61.

† Dunlap mentioned his mother's job as a clerk at Woolworth's during a June 1995 interview with a reporter from the *Miami Herald* newspaper. See "Rambo in Pinstripes," by Patty Shillington, the *Miami Herald* (June 5, 1995). But the fact, as presented in the resulting story, simply emphasized his working-class roots, and not how he overcame them, and he does not seem to have ever mentioned it again. His mother's employment history appears nowhere in his book *Mean Business* (New York: Times Books, 1996), which was published the following year.

was expected to meet academically in school, who taught him to "stay out of trouble," who instilled in him the "self-discipline it took to succeed."

They could have been the words of Jack Welch, speaking of Grace, the mother who taught him to be "strong, tough, and independent," who "checked constantly to see if I did my homework . . ." and who taught him "the value of competition" and the "pleasure of winning."[6]

Whereas Welch idolized—and idealized—his mother, suffering enormous personal pain when she died in January 1965, Dunlap seems to have spent much of his life trying to repress and blot out all memories of both his father and his mother, reducing his father, Al Sr., to a single sentence in his business memoir, *Mean Business,** and his mother, Mildred, to a single paragraph.[†]

Regarding Mildred's physical appearance, the woman seems to have made no more of an impression on Dunlap than did his father, Al Sr., whose standout feature seems to have been simply that he was "bigger" than Al Jr. As for Mildred, Al writes that she was "very

---

* "Physically, my father was a bigger man than I grew up to be, but people remarked that we walked and looked alike, . . ." (p. 109).

† At the end of *Mean Business*, Dunlap included an "Acknowledgments" to give credit to various individuals who had helped him in both his career and the writing of his book. The page-and-a-half passage contains the most revealing sentences in the entire book. Included as nothing more than a seeming after-thought on the way to the printer is the following: "Writing *Mean Business* caused me to examine not only the elements of what makes a successful business, but what makes a successful individual. In my book, it comes down to one word: family." What did Dunlap mean by the word "family"? Certainly not his parents or younger sister, Denise, who appears nowhere in the memoir, nor in any of his various magazine interviews over the years. And "family" does not include his first wife, Gwyn, who is also absent from the book. Instead, Dunlap's family, as delineated in the Acknowledgments, consists of his second wife, Judy (who rates one and a half pages in the narrative), his two German shepherd dogs, who are mentioned often, and a curious reference to his son whose name only appears in the book for the first time—and for just half a sentence—in the Acknowledgments. The sentence reads, "My family also includes my son, Troy, and our beloved dogs and constant companions, Brit and Cadet." Troy Dunlap, born in January 1963, was Al's only child, the result of his marriage to his first wife, Gwyn, which Dunlap faded from his memoir as if it were nothing more than an unfortunate incident.

pretty" and that he has her "eyes and nose." When his two parents died, within six months of each other at the end of 1992, Dunlap did not bother to attend the funerals of either one.

For both Dunlap and Welch, their mothers loomed large because of their roles as the authority figures in the two families, filling the voids created by the emotionally absent father figures. This was a task that Mildred Dunlap clearly resented, and blaming her husband for dumping it upon her, she wound up developing a highly neurotic and controlling persona as the family cop. An insecure, distrusting woman, she seemed obsessed with the belief that her husband, Al Sr., was cheating on her—which she dealt with by spying on him relentlessly, often dispatching Al Jr. on snooping missions designed to catch him in the act. It was precisely the sort of misguided task to leave lifelong scars on her son as well as cause her husband sooner or later to begin engaging in the very behavior she suspected of him.[7]

By the time he graduated from high school in 1956, Al Dunlap seemed a warrior without a war, so it was hardly surprising that he wound up heading for West Point, where his martinet's demeanor was honed against the whetstone of Cold War era discipline in the U.S. Military Academy. He was a poor student, he was angry, and he was a brute. Yet, whether they did so out of fear or pity, his class-mates helped him along academically and he managed to graduate, in 1960, near the bottom of his class.

But a volcano of rage had by now built up in the young man, and it wasn't long before he found a target for his fury—a confused and vulnerable eighteen-year-old plumber's daughter named Gwyn Donnelly, whom he met in a bar.* Swept away by his worldly blather

---

*Dunlap's behavior may well have been aggravated by something else—a trait that Welch may have shared as well: An environmentally stimulated high testosterone level. See D. Blum, *Sex on the Brain: The Biological Differences Between Men and Women* (New York: Viking Press, 1997). Blum cites a 1986 study of male testosterone levels in which two re-searchers—Allan Mazur and Alan Booth—found a direct correlation between high testosterone levels and males living in challenging urban environments. Blum quotes

about the military and his grand vision for the future, she fell for him instantly and within a year they were married.

Almost immediately, the new bride discovered that the man she had married was not the man she had thought he was. Perhaps seeing in Gwyn a lightning rod for his conflicted feelings toward his mother, he turned their five-year marriage into what a divorce judge eventually pronounced a saga of "extreme cruelty." As rendered by Gwyn in a 1965 divorce complaint against him that Al did not fight in court, he dropped his pose as an Officer and a Gentleman to assume a whole new role as a beast.*

Mazur as saying, "After a while we began to suspect that what we were seeing was pure response to stress. These men were living in an atmosphere where they were constantly being challenged. It was survival." See as well Mazur and Booth, "Testosterone and Dominance in Men," *Behavioral and Brain Sciences* (1998), pp. 353–397.

Blum cites other research showing that males with elevated levels of testosterone are more likely to mismanage their relationships with females than are males with low testosterone levels. They are also more likely to become abusive emotionally, and sometimes even physically, than are low-testosterone males. Moreover, as relationships begin to collapse amid fighting and abuse, the testosterone levels in high-testosterone males are likely to rise even higher, begetting even more intensified levels of aggression. See J. Dabbs and A. Booth, "Testosterone and Men's Marriages," *Social Forces* (December 1993), pp. 463–477, as referenced in Blum, *Sex on the Brain* (New York: Viking Press, 1997), p. 174.

Blum's engaging book contains a fully developed discussion, in plain English, of the chicken-or-egg argument over whether elevated testosterone begets aggressive behavior, or stressful circumstances beget responses that elevate testosterone production. She concludes that elevated testosterone levels in males do not automatically have to result in violent behavior. Not only are there counterbalancing hormones to buffer the impact of testosterone on male behavior, but human society has developed an elaborate system of socialization restraints to channel testosterone-fueled aggression into socially acceptable activity.

*Gwyn's view of her life with Al, as set forth here and in Chapter 5, is detailed in the unrebutted complaint filed against him in *Gwyn B. Dunlap v. Albert J. Dunlap*, Superior Court of N.J., Union County, New Jersey, April 27, 1965. Al's only public response to her allegations came 30 years later, in 1996, after *BusinessWeek* obtained a copy of the divorce documents, and Dunlap issued a statement saying, "Anyone taking the time to look at the grounds for divorce before no-fault divorce laws were passed in the 1970s knows that lawyers had to be very creative in establishing grounds for divorce. I think the fact that I have been happily married to my loving wife Judy for the past 29 years speaks volumes."

The "other" Al Dunlap began to emerge within weeks of his marriage to Gwyn, as he began to demean and marginalize her as a human being, using increasingly hurtful and cutting comments that eventually escalated to yelling and finally physical abuse. As claimed by Gwyn in her divorce complaint, Al took the $1,500 they had received as wedding gifts and deposited the money in an account under his name, denying her access to any of it for months. He refused to buy furniture for their home, an army-base officer's residence in Maryland. He made her dye her hair blonde because, he said, it reminded him of a former girlfriend. He repeatedly pushed her and shoved her around the house. He regularly came home from work and conducted military-style white-glove inspections for dust. If he found any, he would yell and swear at Gwyn.

When Gwyn told him she was pregnant, he flew into a rage and said he would divorce her so he would not have to support "you and your brat." When she was five months pregnant, he ordered her to get a job. Two weeks before the baby was due, Gwyn fell ill and was rushed to the hospital. Al flew into a rage at having to pay the $25 admission fee and asked the attending physician to induce labor so that he wouldn't have to pay another $25 when it was time to readmit her.

Meanwhile, Al had been going out at night to parties, leaving Gwyn home alone because, being pregnant, she "looked ugly" to Al. He refused to buy her any maternity clothes because he said they were a waste of money. And when the baby was born, he refused to buy the infant any clothes either because, as he put it, he had never wanted the baby in the first place. Eventually, he even stopped buying food for the house, telling Gwyn that $10 per week for food was plenty enough for her and the baby. Result: When the food ran out, the wife and child didn't eat.

When the conversation started to drag, Al would liven things up by telling Gwyn how he liked to torture children. He said one of his favorite tricks was to wait until a two- or three-year-old child approached, then to stomp on its feet and laugh as the infant hobbled away crying. Or he might pick up a Bowie knife and point it at Gwyn menacingly, saying, "I've often wondered what human flesh tastes like." On other occasions, he told her how much he wished she were dead so that he could collect on her life insurance.

He liked to push her around so that she would fall against what few pieces of furniture the house contained. When that happened, he would curse at her and say he was going to kill her.

He liked to go through her closet and pick through her clothes, choosing which ones he thought were the ugliest. Then he'd would take them to a thrift shop and sell them, keeping the money for himself.

He kept a small arsenal of guns in the house, and if he could think of nothing better to do, he would take a few of them out, clean them up, cock them, point them at her, and say, "You'd better shape up!"

He also liked to insult Gwyn's parents and thought it fun to give the middle finger to her mother at church services, to ridicule Gwyn's friends, and to mock his infant son, Troy.

All this and more is set forth in Gwyn's petition for divorce, which she filed in New Jersey Superior Court, April 27, 1965. Al did not contest the divorce, nor rebut Gwyn's astounding accusations, but instead hired a lawyer to appear in the case and work out a settlement. And getting Gwyn to agree doesn't seem to have been very hard. For five years she had been chained in matrimony to New Jersey's own (and less literate) Marquis de Sade. Now it seemed that she wanted so badly to be free of him that she was willing to accept a $4,000 lump-sum payment along with $500 for her attorneys' fees, and $15 per week in child support in return for freedom for herself and Troy. On February 26, 1967, she finally got it.

But Al had already left Gwyn and had taken up with a Wisconsin bank teller named Judy Stringer whom he met on a blind date. In March 1968, they were married.

〰〰〰

Nor were Welch and Dunlap the only young men preparing to turn stressful childhoods into a revolution in American business. Like Al Dunlap before him, and like Jack Welch in Massachusetts, a third star-crossed young man would soon be heading for New York on a mission to reinvent his past—a past that once again involved the painful truths of economic struggle and an immigrant background—in this case, featuring a minimum-wage mom and a father who bounced from one job to the next.

The young fellow's name was Leo D. Kozlowski Jr.* He was a streetwise Polish teenager from the inner-city projects of Newark, New Jersey, and he was maneuvering his way through the city's predominantly black West High School in Newark's Fourth Ward even as young Al Dunlap was sweet-talking Gwyn Donnelly into his bed a short drive to the south.

When Kozlowski was arrested thirty years later and charged with evading more than a million dollars in New York State sales taxes on fine art and other purchases, few business reporters had yet even heard of the company he ran, Tyco International, and fewer still had heard of his name. But the arrest, coming amidst a seeming avalanche of similar type CEO scandals, sent reporters frantically searching for any background material they could find regarding who this Kozlowski person actually was.

Since reporters are naturally drawn to the human interest elements in any story (because human interest attracts readers), it is

---

*He later began using a restyled version of it—L. Dennis Kozlowski—as if parting a comb-over, in an apparent effort to add a kind of Social Register caché to the name.

not surprising that within days of Kozlowski's arrest, newspapers all across the country were reporting—with the appropriate heavy irony that the fact invited—that America's latest chiseling CEO actually grew up with a Newark Police Department detective for a father.

The tidbit came from an interview that a New York City public relations executive had arranged for Kozlowski three years earlier to help promote him on Wall Street as the "next Jack Welch" and his company, Tyco, as the "next GE." In the interview, Kozlowski had been asked what his father had done for a living, and without missing a beat, the aspiring CEO had answered that his father, Leo, had been a Newark police detective.

Whether Kozlowski had given that answer to add some perceived moral heft to his own public image, is hard to say.* Yet

---

* Reinventing one's past is a common trait of leaders everywhere. In A. Ludwig, *King of the Mountain: The Nature of Political Leadership* (Lexington: University of Kentucky Press, 2002), the author observes of national leaders ranging from dictators to monarchs to democratically elected presidents and prime ministers: "Because they act godlike at times and inspire awe, it is sometimes hard to picture rulers as once having suckled at their mothers' breasts and as having been helpless and dependent as children. Yet they obviously had, although you would have trouble proving it. With notable exceptions, that is because so little biographical information is available about their early lives, and what little information exists comes from self-serving memoirs, which never reveal their failings. [T]here are many reasons information about their childhood is so unreliable and sparse, but the biggest one is that the leaders themselves do not want it known." But, concludes Ludwig from his research, "The main reason for the blanket of secrecy many toss over their pasts is their fear that others will discover their very ordinariness" (pp. 127–128). Nor is this fear—and the method of dealing with it—confined simply to political leaders. In R. Bak, *Henry and Edsel: The Creation of the Ford Empire* (New York: Wiley, 2003), the author writes of Henry Ford Sr.: "In later years, Ford, who enjoyed tinkering with his personal history nearly as much as he did with machines, portrayed himself in interviews and ghosted autobiographies as the typical American hero; alone, misunderstood, lacking two nickels to rub together, but prevailing against great odds nonetheless. The public readily bought into the image. But 'Crazy Henry' was a myth." Bak notes that Ford was neither penniless nor scorned and, throughout his career, crowds of supporters and financial backers assisted him (pp. 27–28). Or consider the portrait of movie mogul Steve Ross that appears in R. Clurman, *To the End of Time: The Seduction and Conquest of a Media Empire* (New York: Simon & Schuster, 1992), which reveals that Ross's claimed career as a war hero in World

asserting that his father was a police detective may well have sounded better, to Kozlowski at least, than the truth. In fact, according to the available evidence, his dad seems to have held only one steady job in his life—as an investigator for what is now known as the New Jersey Transit System, and which bore the name Public Service Transport when he joined it in 1946. Unfortunately, how long he actually worked there is unclear since the records of the period have been lost and both Leo and his wife, Agnes (Dennis' mother) have since died.* In October 2003, Dennis went on trial in New York facing an array of securities fraud and larceney charges, and hasn't given interviews in nearly a year.† He has two sisters, Joyce and Joan, but neither could be reached for information regarding their brother.

Most of the people who were the Kozlowskis' Newark neighbors are scattered to the winds themselves by now, their neighborhood having long since been razed as part of a Newark urban redevelopment program. This has left only a few sources who can any longer even be located regarding what Leo Kozlowski was all about as a breadwinner and a father.

A couple of old-timers who say they knew him as a young man in Newark claim Leo talked of having been a prize fighter for a time; one published account asserts that he fought under the name "Kid

---

War II was almost entirely fiction. Three of the four major CEOs examined in this book (Welch, Dunlap, and Kozlowski) all engaged in revisions of their personal histories. Of the four, Perelman stands out as the exception, though only because he has said almost nothing at all publicly regarding his past.

*Leo Kelly Kozlowski died a few weeks short of his 79th birthday on July 7, 1990, and Agnes died at the age of 77 in March 1995.

†Kozlowski is a defendant in other pending litigation as well. They include securities fraud actions by the Securities and Exchange Commission, various shareholder class action suits, litigation against him by his own former company, Tyco, and a New York State criminal tax fraud case in which he is charged with failing to pay roughly $1 million of New York State sales taxes on fine art that was purchased in New York City.

Kelly." But no New Jersey boxing associations have any records of such a fighter—then or ever.* And no remaining promoters from the era who are still alive remember him either. If he was a fighter, he probably fought a few bouts, for cash, in Newark area clubs, and that was it.

Leo was also said to have played minor league baseball with the old Newark Bears—a farm team of the Yankees during the 1930s. But the team that currently has the name "Newark Bears" is unrelated to the original team, whose records have long since disappeared. A search of all available secondary records produced no player by the name of Leo Kozlowski during the era.

There are also those who say Leo worked for a time as an Associated Press reporter. But the AP says it has no record of ever having employed such a person anywhere within its system.

Others say Leo was a wheel in local Republican Party circles in Newark and was close to former Governor Thomas Cahill. But Cahill is now deceased, and further research suggests that Leo may never actually have been more than a part-time Republican Party ward heeler in the Fourth Ward.

Finally, there is Leo's work as a New Jersey transit system investigator. According to one of his friends of that time—a retired Newark lawyer named Peter Pietrucha[8]—Leo even wound up with two bullets in his neck while moonlighting as a detective for the Bergen County prosecutor's office. But officials in that office have been unable to produce records supporting that either.

By contrast, Leo's wife and Dennis' mom, Agnes—like Al Dunlap's mother and Jack Welch's—did seem to have had steady daytime work. What's more, the job involved actual bona fide law enforcement,

---

*The only known professional prize fighter bearing the name Kid Kelly was an Albanian immigrant named Vasil Apostal, who fought in the Worcester, Massachusetts, area before hanging up his gloves to become an employee of the American Optical Corporation. Apostal died in 1999 in Southbridge, Massachusetts, at the age of 92.

though not of a kind that Dennis might have wished. According to records maintained by the Newark Fraternal Order of Police, Agnes worked as a Newark school-crossing guard.

Nor did Leo leave much to mark his passing as a member of the community. One of the few people who still remembers him is a woman named Sylvia Levine. She said the Kozlowskis lived next door to the Levines, in a two-family row house on a cul-de-sac. She said Leo seemed a nice-enough man from a distance, but up close and personal, the only thing she could recall was that he was strongly anti-Semitic.

Be that as it may, Dennis Kozlowski grew up seemingly no different from countless others like him in Newark's Fourth Ward. Social life for the Kozlowskis revolved around the local Newark chapter of a Polish-American support organization known as the Polish Falcons of America. The group was founded in Poland in 1867 to promote what was known then as "physical culture," and it spread to the United States two decades later, where it took on aspects of a family and social support group for Polish American immigrants.

The Newark "nest," which maintained a meeting lodge in the Fourth Ward and a summer sleep-away camp for children in the town of Summerville, New Jersey, had a membership of more than 250 families when the Kozlowskis belonged. For a time, Leo was the club's treasurer. Meetings were held once a month and mostly seemed to involve eating kielbasa, drinking beer, and griping among the men about how the blacks were taking over Newark.

Children ages nine to sixteen were encouraged to participate in the life of the nest, but Dennis was not a regular. One club member of the period, Walter Dupicki, who went on to graduate with Dennis from Newark's West Side High School in the class of 1964, recalls him as a likable enough kid—tall and lanky, with a bright red head of hair. So far as what Dennis later became, well, Walter says it was a big surprise to him because Dennis Kozlowski never seemed to be much more than a face in the crowd. Not only was he rarely seen at the nest, but he never attended the summer camp—at least so far as Walter could recall.

Other kids at West Side High recalled him in similar terms, as an easygoing, average Joe—not much more than a kid with ho-hum grades and a smile when he could make somebody laugh. Many didn't remember him at all.* One such person was Bart Zoni, who drew a blank on the name until he looked in his yearbook, and even then couldn't recall much of anything about him. "I didn't even know this guy," Bart mused aloud as he looked at the picture, next to which Dennis had written an inscription that now spoke to him through the years. It read, "Remember the years at West Side High."†

But something happened during his high school years that, in retrospect, changed everything. The man who reported it was James

---

*Press reports regarding Kozlowski's claimed athletic abilities multiplied after he became famous. But the details often don't tie out. In a *Barron's* (April 12, 1999) profile based on interviews and information supplied by Kozlowski and an outside image consultant, the newspaper reported that the Tyco exec "starred on both the football and basketball teams at West Side High School," but that he gave up athletics when he went to college. Yet, three years later, a *Time* (June 12, 2002) profile limited Kozlowski's athletic achievements to playing basketball in high school and attributed no starring role to him in the effort. Seven months after the *Time* story appeared, came a profile in the *New Yorker*, which said nothing about Kozlowski's high school athletics one way or the other, and reported instead that he played basketball during his first year at Seton Hall University. ("Not very well, but good enough to get a couple of hundred dollars knocked off his tuition.") See the *New Yorker* (February 17, 2003), p. 132. In fact, the best original source document available—West Side High School's class yearbook for the class of 1964—says only that Kozlowski belonged to the high school track team.

†Dennis himself seems to have had little trouble remembering those wonder-filled years at West Side High, even if what he remembered never actually happened. In his interview with the *New Yorker's* James Stewart, he told of being a member of the debating team and of gaining confidence in his abilities by debating in school assemblies in front of the entire student body. He spoke as well of being chosen the school's "principal for a day" during his senior year, saying that this taught him he could be a leader if he just applied himself. Unfortunately, his yearbook lists none of these accomplishments, citing only that he had been a "hallway monitor," and that he had belonged to the track team. See J. B. Stewart, "Spend! Spend! Spend! Where Did Tyco's Money Go?" *New Yorker* (February 17, 2003), p. 132.

Stewart, a writer for the *New Yorker*, who interviewed Kozlowski not long after his arrest on New York State sales tax charges. In the process, Stewart learned that during Dennis' senior year of high school, his history teacher reached out and touched him with the gift of a future. In the magical way that only a teacher can manage, the man somehow made young Dennis Kozlowski feel he could be "a leader," wrote Stewart, and in that moment the seeds were sown, if not for future greatness, then at least for a lot of headlines.

Kozlowski became a college man, living at home while attending classes as a day student at Seton Hall University in nearby South Orange, where he studied accounting. To make ends meet, he waited tables, while doubtless wondering how far down life's road he would have to travel before the spotlight of public acclaim would fall upon him as a leader of men.* In the meantime, he scratched the itch by playing guitar in a band called the Hi-Tones.†

---

* In a flattering October 2000 profile in *Forbes*, Kozlowski is portrayed as a young man who had a head for numbers right from the start. As a waiter, Kozlowski was said to have objected to the policy followed by the restaurant where he worked—namely, that the waiters were all supposed to pool their tips at the end of each evening and then divide the pot equally among themselves so that one or two waiters wouldn't benefit unfairly from having waited on some big tippers during the evening while other waiters had the bad luck to wind up with cheapskates for customers. But Kozlowski argued that he worked harder than the other waiters and deserved to go home with more tip money. When the restaurant wouldn't budge, Kozlowski reportedly quit and went to work for an establishment that let him keep 100 percent of his tips. See S. Chakravarty, "Deal-a-Month Dennis," *Forbes* (October 16, 2000), p. 66.

† Kozlowski was not the only CEO to yearn for the adulation that often comes with rock star fame. Richard Scrushy, the CEO of Alabama-based HealthSouth Corporation, was accused by prosecutors of turning his company into a swindle machine even as he was busy cutting demo CDs and touring clubrooms as lead guitarist in his own rock band. Ronald Perelman, the Revlon head, enjoyed stepping into the spotlight as a rock star wannabe whenever the opportunity presented itself. During weekend house parties thrown by "Margaritaville" balladeer Jimmy Buffett in the Hamptons, Perelman could sometimes be seen settling behind the drums to keep time in impromptu jam sessions for rock legends Rod Stewart and Billy Joel. Even President Bill Clinton, a kind of CEO for the whole of America, enjoyed playing his saxophone on late-night TV during the 1992 presidential campaign.

3

A COURSE FOR NEW PROVIDENCE, OR THE DROWNING POOLS OF NARCISSISM?

They lie only thirty miles from the slums of North Jersey, but the broad lawns and stately mansions of the towns that stretch westward from Philadelphia along Montgomery County's City Line Avenue are an instant reminder to any visitor that the privileged residents of the "Main Line" belong to a different world from the one inhabited by the residents of Newark and Hoboken.

Yet, social class and demographics are hardly the only pressures weighing on a young man at the portals of adulthood. There are also the more intimate matters of family and parents, and what a young man learns from them to make his way in the world—and sometimes these lessons have nothing at all to do with economics.

Unlike Welch, Kozlowski, and Dunlap, who were all born into worlds of scarcity and financial stress, Ronald O. Perelman was born into a world of Main Line abundance—in his particular case in the affluent and predominantly Jewish suburb of Elkins Park, just north of the WASP world of the Main Line.* Yet coping with the demands of a problem parent eventually caused Perelman to flee his past just as determinedly as Welch, Kozlowski, and Dunlap fled theirs. And, like them, he scaled the heights of public acclaim, only to begin making a fool of himself as he approached the summit.

Unlike Welch, Kozlowski, and Dunlap, who each entered adulthood bearing the scars of what amounted to absentee fathers, young Ron Perelman grew up in exactly the opposite circumstance, gasping for air as the eldest son of an overbearing, controlling father from whom no one in the Perelman family could escape. A woman who knew both of Ron's parents well offered this opinion: "Actually, Ruth was a piece of work in her own right. But if I had to pick one or the other, I guess I'd give the nod to Ray. He's the one who warped Ron into the ogre he became."[1]

Ron's father, Raymond, was the son of a Lithuanian émigré named Morris Perelman, who arrived in New York in the floodtide of turn-of-the-century Eastern European immigration. Thereafter, Morris made his way to Philadelphia and started a paper products company. The business was a success, enabling Morris to send Ray to the Wharton School at the University of Pennsylvania, where the young man obtained a degree in business. He then joined his father at the paper company.

In time, Ray married a young woman named Ruth Caplan and fathered three children, of whom Ronald was the eldest. Along the way, Ray became a partner in a company that acquired a metal stamping plant called Belmont Iron Works, which was eventually renamed Belmont Industries.

---

*The most complete portrait of Ronald Perelman's early life is found in R. Hack, *When Money Is King: How Revlon's Ron Perelman Mastered the World of Finance to Create One of America's Greatest Business Empires, and Found Glamour, Beauty and the High Life in the Bargain* (Los Angeles, CA: Dove Books, 1996)—the only book-length and detailed biography of Perelman ever published. The book was not an authorized biography, but according to Hack, Perelman reviewed the manuscript prior to publication.

Ronald was born on January 1, 1943, in Greensboro, North Carolina, where his father was stationed in the Air Force. When Ray and Ruth Perelman moved to Philadelphia, they were still virtual nobodies on the social scene. But Ray had his dreams, and he saw in his son Ronald the route to their fulfillment: He would mold the boy into a kind of mini-me version of all that he imagined himself to be. The result was that before young Ronald had turned thirteen, Ray was bringing him to business meetings, to sit at the table in a blazer and tie, and "listen and learn." Pressured by the expectations of a domineering father in a stern and conservative Jewish household, young Ronald developed into an angry and conflicted adolescent. In later years, his classmates of the period recalled him as silent and distant—"a loner." He seemed devoid of humor, ill at ease with his peers—especially the boys—and in many ways appeared old before his time. When they teased him because he couldn't take a joke, he never laughed it off because he didn't know how. Instead he'd rail back that they weren't being fair, which only made the ribbing worse.

His parents sent Ronald to follow in his father's footsteps at the University of Pennsylvania, where he entered as an undergraduate at the Wharton School of Business in 1960. From there, he proceeded on through to graduation while leaving no apparent marks of his passing—though his philanthropic gifts in later years proved generous.

Ron met the girl who would become his first wife—a young woman named Faith Golding—while he was on a trip to Israel during the summer following his graduation from undergraduate school and before beginning the Wharton MBA program the following year. A photograph of the period shows her to be small and almost frail looking, with large trusting eyes, and cropped blonde hair styled with a curl above the shoulders—sensible in a way that would please a mother to see. How the Goldings felt about Ron is not known, but we may suppose that Ron was quick to embrace his in-laws, who were wealthier and better connected socially than was his family. They had large real estate holdings in Philadelphia and New York, where they also owned a bank.

Ron and Faith were very young when they married. He was barely twenty-one and she was only seventeen. And whatever the experience of marrying so young may have done to Faith, it certainly presented challenges for Ron. Not only was he now in a marriage that would continue for the next eighteen years, but he spent the first decade and a half of them working under the angular gaze of Ray at Belmont Iron Works, which Ray wound up turning into a miniconglomerate of sorts.

It was undeniably a stressful time for Ron Perelman. Here he was, a graduate of one of the nation's most prestigious and entrepreneurial business schools, eager to build his own future (with his wife's sizable purse to help finance him), yet, instead, every morning he found himself face-to-face at the office with Dad.

All around him, his classmates from Wharton were heading for New York—and typically straight to Wall Street—to get in on the action from the booming Vietnam era economy. And here he was, stuck in Philadelphia, with his difficult father.*

~~~~~~

I n all the ways that ultimately turned out to matter the most, these four individuals—John F. Welch Jr., L. Dennis Kozlowski Jr., Albert J. Dunlap Jr., and Ronald O. Perelman—typified both the promise

---

*That view of Raymond Perelman was held by more people than just his eldest son. In 1993 and at the age of seventy-five, the irascible elder Perelman launched an attack on Champion Parts, Inc., where he had been a board member, to lift its sagging stock price. Ousting the CEO, he seized control directly, but the other board members recoiled, and after only a few weeks, they threw him out. Explained another board member, "He's a rough customer. A month of him as CEO was all the board could take." See L. Spiro, *BusinessWeek* (August 1, 1995), p. 54.

and the limitations of an entire generation of their peers. All four were males and were born during an eleven-year span between 1935 and 1946 when economic opportunity still remained largely confined to the less than 18 percent of the population consisting of white males.

The four were also either the eldest, or only, sons of families steeped in cultures that valued sons over daughters, and boys over girls. All grew up in households in which one parent or the other seized on them to work through their own personal conflicts and problems. And all were steered into college to take career-oriented courses of study at a time when the traditional liberal arts programs of the Ivy League were still viewed as a nearly indispensable door opener to the upper reaches of American big business.

In this way, they all entered adulthood thinking of themselves one way or another as people potentially marked for great things—if life would just give them a chance. At almost any other time in the nation's history, they might have lived out their lives in furious anonymity, barroom philosophers railing at the world that never gave them a break. Yet, no group of men ever arrived at the threshold of adulthood at a luckier moment than did this group. As the 1960s unfolded and one after the next they entered the labor force, the world that awaited them was beginning to undergo a series of changes more radical and disruptive—and rich with promise for the nimble and opportunistic—than anything American business had experienced in a century.

Gone was the imperial hegemony of the U.S. dollar around the world, and going fast was the guaranteed predominance of U.S. products that came with it. A single global market was starting to emerge, as U.S. manufacturers of everything from automobiles to tab-collar shirts began to learn that their biggest competitors weren't American companies at all but manufacturers from nearly every country on earth. It would become the challenge of men like

Welch, Dunlap, Kozlowski, and Perelman to preserve America's interests in this world of onrushing economic change, and before anyone knew it, Americans by the millions would be proclaiming them the nation's new heroes.*

In his epic poem, *Ulysses*, Alfred Lord Tennyson wrote:

> . . . . Come, my friends,
> 'Tis not too late to seek a newer world.
> Push off, and sitting well in order smite
> The sounding furrows; for my purpose holds
> to sail beyond the sunset, and the baths
> of all the western stars, until I die.

But by whose compass was the voyage to be guided? And how would one know, when the lines were cast off and the mainsails swelled with hope and expectation, whether the hand on the tiller would steer a course to New Providence—or into the wine-dark drowning pools of narcissism and man's deepest demons?

Never before in American business history had a bigger bet been made on a more limited sense of what was actually being gambled. By the fortune of the Gods, the leadership of many of America's biggest and most treasured businesses was about to be handed over, without so much as a second thought, to a generation of

---

*Businessmen began to emerge as pop culture celebrity heroes in the 1980s and, generally speaking, they tended to be deafened by the applause. See J. Wareham, *Wareham's Way, Escaping the Judas Trap* (New York: Atheneum, 1983). Consider GM's John DeLorean, who captured the imagination of the media as a kind of bad boy version of auto industry superstar Lee Iacocca. With a bio that featured a fashion model wife at his elbow, DeLorean eventually took to posing for publicity photographs draped in disco chains while trying to produce and bring to market a homegrown version of a Ferrari sports car, dubbed appropriately enough the DeLorean. His career went up in smoke when the government brought drug charges against him, and though he was eventually acquitted at trial, he never fully escaped the allegation's taint and thereafter sank into obscurity.

tough-talking young outsiders—men whose very presence in corporate boardrooms was both bracing and even scary.

They were of a type who had not gripped the levers of corporate power since the days of Rockefeller, Morgan, and Vanderbilt. They were brash, outspoken, and intimidating in their conviction. Generally speaking, they came from modest—even Lincolnesque—beginnings, or at least claimed to have done so. And they all soon discovered that in a world of boundless uncertainty, claims of a world-transforming vision of the future could mesmerize any audience.

Yet, none of these men, with their glib turns of phrase and their mesmerizing vision of tomorrow, were in any way prepared for the temptations that success would place before them, and in the end nearly all fell victim to the tug of earthly desires—of mammon and the flesh—that few men can resist.

4

GE LOVES ME!

Not far from the New York State border, in the Berkshire foot-hills of western Massachusetts on the Housatonic River sits the city of Pittsfield. The Berkshires are one of southern New England's most bucolic and charming areas, thick with the fo-liage of maples and birch along country roads where you can spend hours at a time and never see a passing car.

Yet the region's very tranquility also seems to give its only urban center, Pittsfield, a kind of uninvited and out-of-place feel. Why is it even here? With the Hudson River blocking passage to the west, and nothing to the east for fifty miles until you reach Springfield, Pittsfield seems to be a city at the end of the road, quarantined from the rural beauty all around it, with no point or purpose.

The vistas of Pittsfield offer no majestic mountains to behold in the distance. Nor are there navigable waterways closer at hand to facilitate commerce. Pittsfield boasts no spas or mineral baths to beckon the weak of body, nor any grand architecture to lift the ex-hausted spirit. Pittsfield is home to no great museums, nor even to a second-tier college or a high-tech company in microelectronics. It is a city with no stately homes—a place as ordinary and dreary as any other early twentieth-century industrial town that time has passed by. In this town, you will find neither hope nor despair, but simply 45,000 residents, dragging themselves back and forth to work each day in a world where the key to tomorrow opens the door to entry-level jobs in massage parlors and diners.

In Pittsfield, what energy one does encounter seems to come mainly from people who look to be just passing through. Often as not, such people turn out to be on their way to or from Vermont, which beckons the hopeful from New York and points further distant with its make-believe dreams of a land where cheese and skiing are imagined to count for a lot.

Until recently, most of the rest were executives cycling through career-advancing (or ending) assignments at one division or another of Pittsfield's largest employer, GE.

Now not even many of them show up anymore. And for that, the residents of Pittsfield have long since agreed whom they need to thank: GE's Jack Welch. Arriving in 1960 as a junior "process engineer" in the company's Plastics Division, Welch departed seventeen years later to become the most controversial citizen in the city's history—detested by many for destroying Pittsfield's economy to make GE's stock price rise . . . and equally adored by others, if they were fortunate enough to be owners of GE's stock.

Stories of Welch's arrival in Pittsfield have by now become the stuff of GE corporate legend. It is said that Welch learned to hate unions because he had to cross a picket line to get to his office on the morning of his first day at work and an angry striker spat on him. It is said that Welch . . .

In fact, Welch began his career at GE in a haze of incident-free anonymity, as a $10,500-per-year GE process specialist in the company's Plastics Division, a sub-department within GE's Chemicals Development Operation—about as far down the GE food chain as one could get in 1960.

Developing plastic into a commercially viable product had been a GE pursuit for more than thirty years at that point, but the effort had not yet amounted to much, mainly because other companies for which chemical engineering wasn't a sideline but the main business kept beating GE to the punch. Companies like Du Pont, B.F. Goodrich, and Dow Chemical. These were the companies that led the plastics revolution, ushering in products that ranged from Saran Wrap, to Teflon, to vinyl.

GE's own "firsts" tended to develop out of the company's own historical roots in the commercialization of electricity: The first light bulb (1879), the first X-ray machine (1896), the first electric fan (1902), the first toaster (1905), the first television (1927), the first in-sink garbage disposal (1935), or the first two-door refrigerator (1947). At the time Welch joined GE in 1960, the Plastics Division's only important commercial product—Lexan—had been in the market for barely two years.

As a result, when Welch joined GE in 1960, ambitious young employees all wanted to work in operations like the company's Ordnance Department and its Power Transmission Group, which collectively employed more than 10,000 workers in the Greater Pittsfield area already. By contrast, GE Plastics had a total payroll of barely 300 and was widely viewed throughout the company as a corporate backwater that might be shut down or sold off at any moment. Among the operation's employees, a grim joke summed up the prevailing mood. Question: What's a Plastics Division optimist? Answer: Someone who actually brings his lunch to work.[1]

In the literature of deification that enveloped Welch as he entered the final decade of his career, he was often extolled for cannily exploiting the "casual" and "freewheeling" environment he encountered in the Plastics Division. But the truth is just the opposite, for Welch's career-long crusade to eviscerate GE's bureaucracy and purge the company of its middle-management ranks in fact began in Pittsfield, where he clashed angrily and openly with the whole world of GE, from almost his first day on the job.

Discovering soon enough that the title of "process specialist" in the Plastics Division amounted basically to a joke, he began blaming everything—and everyone—around him for the dreary circumstance in which he found himself. He complained about the Plastics Division's "penny-wise" culture, which he took as the culture of GE as a whole. He complained about his miserly salary, which he began padding by nickel-and-diming the company on his junior exec's expense account.*

He complained about his boss, a man named Burt Copeland, whom he quickly sized up as a "bum,"† and whose other big offense seemed to be that he was "thin." He complained about having to

---

* In his autobiography, Welch described the frustration he felt at being paid so little that he wound up actually looking forward to driving in his own car from Pittsfield, MA, to Schenectady, NY, on GE business, and thereby getting to pocket a standard per-mile reimbursement that worked out to $7 more than his actual cash outlay. Writes Welch, speaking of himself and his colleagues in the Plastics Division, "It seems crazy now, but all of us would drive somewhere at the drop of a hat to get a little extra cash." See J. Welch and J. Byrne, *Jack: Straight from the Gut*, p. 23.

† Welch's characterization of Copeland as a "bum" was clearly not meant to describe Copeland's economic status but was simply symptomatic of the blunt way—both positive and negative—that Welch spoke about people in general. The derisive characterization came during an appearance at the University of Chicago Graduate School of Business, December 4, 2002. In it, Copeland was not mentioned by name, but was simply referred to by Welch as his "first boss" during a rumination by Welch regarding his own early years at GE. In a question-and-answer exchange with Chris Matthews of CNBC television's *Hardball* program on December 4, 2002, Matthews asked Welch, whose troubles with his second wife, Jane, were by then making headlines around the world, to comment on the role of "the corporate spouse" in shaping an executive's career. Welch ducked the question awkwardly, saying, "Look, I don't want to offend corporate spouses in any way, shape, or form, and this is a who-when did you beat your mother last or something . . ." after which he veered into a reminiscence of his own early career at GE and of the role his first wife, Carolyn, played in it, saying, "In getting you started in a company, and the first year you come home and you hate your boss and you hate the environment, and your boss is a bum and you're smarter than your boss and all those things you do . . ."

share a cramped office containing one desk and two telephones with three other junior employees.

When he and his wife Carolyn finally found an apartment they could afford, in a two-family home in downtown Pittsfield on First Street, he'd come home from a day of complaining at the office and start complaining all over again—that the apartment was dreary and the landlady was chintzy. And because there was really nothing else she could do, his young wife would just stand there, in understanding silence, at the pity party that had become his life, and hers.*

For Welch, the tipping point came after a year on the job, when he received an automatic $1,000 raise just as did everyone else at his level in the organization. Fuming that he had been working harder than his colleagues and that he thus deserved a bigger bonus, he announced that he was quitting.†

By treating Welch like everyone else, GE had pushed his ultimate hot button. It had told him, loudly and clearly, in a language that no one could have misunderstood, that the General Electric Company wasn't Grace Welch and that Jack Welch wasn't GE's only child and that he wasn't the center of the universe. He wasn't special, he wasn't unique, he was just another brick in the wall.

And by threatening to quit, Welch had given it right back and pushed the company's ultimate hot button in response. After merely a year on the job, he announced, to the astonishment of those all

---

*Welch's resentful and petulant feelings toward his situation at GE are fully detailed in his autobiography. See, in particular, Chapters 1 and 2.

†Welch's complaint that he had been working harder than his colleagues and that he thus deserved a bigger raise echoes the nearly identical complaint of Dennis Kozlowski when he quit the restaurant where he worked as a college student, after objecting that its tip-pooling policy rewarded lazy waiters and penalized those such as himself, who worked harder. In these complaints, both men were expressing, early in their careers, a welcome sensitivity to the arguments in favor of incentive pay to encourage employee performance. Unfortunately, by the end of the 1990s, greed and a booming stock market had turned "incentive" payments into a code word for colossal self-enrichment by CEOs everywhere.

around him, that a career at GE just wasn't worth having. At the start of the 1960s, the 1950s-era consensus values of the Organization Man may have been fraying elsewhere, but not at GE. Junior executives at this company just didn't quit. Doing so would be like rejecting America.

In fact, Welch's "take this job and shove it" gesture appears to have amounted to little more than an opening parry in the art of organizational politics, which Welch would eventually come to master not by finesse but by a combination of bullying, charm, and the steamroller force of his personality. Sizing up his boss, Copeland, as someone who could be outflanked and intimidated from above, he had begun sucking up to Copeland's boss, a fellow named Reuben Gutoff, who lived in Connecticut and oversaw Plastics and several other GE operations.

If Gutoff asked Copeland for a report on the potential market for some particular type of plastic, for example, Welch could be counted on to volunteer to do the work—then to deliver Gutoff a report on the outlook for the entire plastics industry. The obvious goal: To get himself noticed by his boss's boss, thereby to develop a line to Gutoff that would enable him to be "pulled" up and over Copeland instead of having to push his way through.

By threatening to quit, Welch was gambling that Gutoff—aware now of Welch's eagerness to please him, while at the same time fearing a blemish on his own career if the young man were to leave in such a public snit—would reach down from headquarters and intervene. This would eliminate Copeland as an obstacle and free up the scheming young streetfighter beneath him to rise more rapidly within the organization. And when Gutoff did exactly that, promising Welch more money as well as freedom from the suffocating bureaucracy embodied in Copeland, Welch drew the obvious lesson: This was an organization that could be pushed around. Line up the right protection from above, and the more disruptive and risk-taking you became down in the trenches, the more all those around you would back off and let you have your way.*

~~~~~

Over the course of his career, Jack Welch's dominance over GE became so complete, and his seeming need for acclaim so embracing, that by the end of his tenure as chairman and CEO, he seemed—to the outside world at least—to be running GE almost single-handedly.†

Yet many of his accomplishments—whether they were the result of something that Welch actually did, or perhaps something he just managed to take credit for—were hardly unique or even unusual in the grand sweep of GE's history. From its inception as a public corporation, GE has been regarded as an organizational and management model to be admired and emulated. By 1929, *Forbes* had already labeled GE one of the best-managed companies in the United States. In the 1950s, GE's president, chairman, and CEO, Ralph Cordiner,

---

*There seems little doubt that another force was at work here also: Welch's lifelong search for what psychologists sometimes refer to as "stroking"—a particularly powerful need among only-child males with doting mothers. In a 1988 interview with author Ken Auletta, Welch touched the raw nerve of what he had really been seeking in his temper tantrum, and why he had agreed to stay. He told Auletta, "Someone told me they loved me." See K. Auletta, *Three Blind Mice* (New York: Random House, 1991), p. 97. In his own autobiography a decade later, Welch toned down the quote, perhaps to obscure the vulnerability it revealed. Nonetheless, the unwitting insight into the deeper lesson he drew from Reuben Gutoff's offer of money and more freedom if Welch would simply not resign showed through. He quoted himself as follows: "Gutoff showed me he really cared." J. Welch and J. Byrne, *Jack: Straight from the Gut* (New York: Warner Books, 2001), p. 25.

†Welch actively encouraged the perception, insisting that the most successful companies of the future would be those with the "flattest" hierarchies and the least bureaucratic overhead, so that the voice of one leader could directly reach thousands and even tens of thousands of rank-and-file employees without the intervening involvement of a bureaucracy. In a parting thought in his autobiography, Welch limns a future in which "Hierarchy is dead. The organization of the future will be virtually layerless and increasingly boundaryless." He foresaw ". . . a series of information networks in which more electrons and fewer people will manage processes." See J. Welch and J. Byrne, *Jack: Straight from the Gut* (New York: Warner Books, 2001), p. 433.

was widely praised for precisely the sorts of accomplishments that Welch was lionized for nearly four decades later. As of spring 2004, GE is the only original member of the Dow Industrial Average to remain in the Index from its inception in 1896.

As the U.S. economy has changed and evolved, so has the face of GE, which had the distinct advantage of beginning its corporate life in possession of what was, up to that time, arguably the greatest invention since the printing press: the incandescent electricity-powered lamp. In 1890, Thomas Edison, the inventor of the device, assembled his businesses together in a vast, horizontal trust he called the Edison General Electric Company. He then merged it in 1892 with a group of rival companies going by the name Thomson-Houston Company. The merger gave the combined business what amounted to a patent stranglehold on the commercial use of electricity at the very dawn of the Electrical Age.

When the market called for vast, infrastructure development applications based on electrical power, GE was right there with everything from electric locomotives to steam turbine generators to electrically powered communications networks. As living standards rose and the nation developed into a transcontinental consumer market, the focus of GE shifted toward electrically powered appliances for the home.* And when money and credit became more valuable in the United States than either natural resources or the labor to exploit them, the company's focus shifted yet again, to the business of finance.

---

*GE's Pittsfield-based Power Transmission Group manufactured the step-down transformers that carried electricity from distant sources such as hydroelectric plants, to residential communities and into the home. A carcinogenic by-product of the manufacture of these transformers—polychlorinated biphenyls (PCBs)—was dumped into ditches and culverts by GE for more than twenty years before Welch went to work in Pittsfield. But PCBs became a major headache for him and a stain on his public image when he became chairman of the corporation in 1981 and was stuck with having to cope with the consequences of their reckless disposal in the past.

These changes were not the work of visionary individuals or dynamic corporate leaders. Mostly they were pulled from the inherently resistant bureaucracy of the company by the demands of the market and the changing uses of electricity itself. When the company's leaders have attempted to anticipate those changes and position GE for future conditions and marketing opportunities not yet in evidence, the results have generally been no better than those of anyone else attempting to predict the future.*

Finally, and for all its talk about corporate values, integrity, and the "GE Way," the company was, in its most important respect of all, no different from almost any other large and successful U.S. corporation at the start of the 1960s: It was full of people steeped in the consensus values of a period that was already fast disappearing. And once Welch discovered that edgy, unpredictable behavior was something for which these people simply had no frame of reference, he had their number.

It was as if the veil of mystery had suddenly fallen away, and he understood the rules of the game—the same rules he had followed

---

*In 1964, GE's newly appointed CEO, Fred Borch, listened to the advice of a group of the company's strategic planners that the company should go toe-to-toe with IBM in the mainframe computer market. On that advice, GE paid $100 million to acquire a computer business that the Olivetti office equipment company wanted to sell—based on advice from *its* strategic planners that *no* company could go up against IBM and survive.

Six years and more than $400 million in losses later, GE retreated from the field in 1970, selling what it could of the business to a group led by Honeywell Corporation, whose strategic planners figured Honeywell could succeed where GE had failed. Sixteen years later and Honeywell exited the business also, in 1986, taking a $400 million write-down of its own.

By now the cost of this misguided stargazing was approaching $1 billion, but more was to come. That's because, while GE and then Honeywell were struggling to get into the mainframe business, the machines themselves were rapidly becoming dinosaurs, leading eventually to the near-collapse of the one company all thought invincible—IBM—and the ignominious departure of its chairman, John Akers. To complete the circle of wrongheaded futurology, Welch's last—and bitterest—defeat as chairman of GE came in 2001 when, declaring it a "perfect fit for the future," he tried and failed to acquire the very company that GE had saddled with its failed computer gambit 30 years earlier: Honeywell Corporation.

from his earliest days on the streets of North Salem: To get people's attention, do the unexpected; don't hold your temper, *use* it. Be quick, be smart, keep everyone off balance.

Seemingly overnight, Welch exploded in energy. Gone was the complaining about the miserable working conditions in the wretched two-story brick building where the Plastics Division was housed. So what if it had previously been used as a manufacturing site for electrical transformers from the Power Transmission Division. Welch didn't have time to worry about that now. There was so much to be done— and so little time.

With his boss, Burt Copeland, now neutralized and out of the way, Welch had a pipeline straight to Copeland's boss, Reuben Gutoff, who had overnight become his godfather. But the relationship was more complicated than that, for although Welch still needed to suck up to Gutoff and curry favor with him, Gutoff now had his own career-skin showing in Welch's future steps. And that meant Welch could keep pushing and pushing, advancing across more and more of GE's institutional turf, and Gutoff would have to support him.

The results astonished everyone. Welch's job as a process specialist had made him a very small cog in a very large gearing process, working as a member of a team of designers trying to devise production plans—in effect, to sketch out an actual factory—for a plastic known as polyphenylene oxide. This gooey material, jointly developed more than twenty years earlier by GE and a Dutch company, had extraordinarily high resistance to heat, and for that reason was thought to have considerable potential commercial appeal.

These days, PPO, as it is known, gets mixed with other types of plastics and fibers to make everything from roofing panels to car bumpers and the casings on desktop computers. But in 1960, no one had any idea what it was good for. Not only was the material expensive to produce, but it was inherently brittle and would begin to crack in only a few months' time. As a result, polyphenylene oxide sales accounted for only a small portion of revenues for the entire Plastics Division, which was running at barely $25 million annually. All of this meant that Welch's job boiled down to designing production plans for a product no one wanted to buy and that GE had no idea how to sell.

But Welch hardly seemed ready to let that stop him, and because the PPO operation had little real oversight or control, he simply moved into the vacuum and took over. For the first two years of his work in Pittsfield, Welch didn't even have a title, remaining nothing more than a team member of his obscure little group of production designers.*

Yet Welch had something no other team member had: the reflected glow (and presumed authority) of his uber-boss, Gutoff. With it, he turned the PPO operation into the corporate version of a renegade gang, and with Welch himself positioned as its leader he began assigning his colleagues to tasks to turn PPO into something that could be sold commercially.

A more timid man would hardly have dared attempt any of this. But Welch now had the wind at his back, and the more he advanced, the more he saw the forces of resistance simply melt away . . . which only encouraged him to press ahead harder.

In 1962, he got his first merit badge—the somewhat overwrought title of "manager of manufacturing development"—a title

---

*Though Welch was quickly, and almost universally, viewed upon his arrival at GE as an ambitious young executive, his own self-perceptions regarding ambition suggest a different view—or at least one more tailored to the existential requirements of the moment. In a conversation with Robert Joss, dean of the Stanford University Graduate School of Business, before the Commonwealth Club of California, Joss said to Welch, "It took you 20 years to become CEO. Did that seem to you then like a long time? Were you impatient? Did you want it to come faster?" Welch answered: "No. I just did every job I had, and it sort of kept happening. Good things happened. I never thought about being CEO. For the first few years, I didn't even know who the CEO was." Commonwealth Club Interview on November 12, 2001.

that contained nearly as many words as the number of people for whom he was now responsible. The title simply reflected the job he had been doing all along anyway: trying to manage something into a state in which it could actually be manufactured.

In *Jack: Straight from the Gut*, Welch tells an entertaining story of what happened next, as he shepherded polyphenylene oxide through to commercial development as a plastic that GE wound up naming "Noryl." The story is meant to illustrate Welch's willingness to make gutsy, out-on-a-limb decisions when he believed in what he was doing—and how the outcome would typically result in a big payoff for the risk taker. His work heading up the commercialization of Noryl is thus presented as the breakthrough moment of his career, without which his abilities as a leader would never have been recognized by higher-ups.

The story itself is told in generalities that manage to include Welch in what is cast as the gutsiest single decision in the entire affair: To build a $10 million manufacturing plant for a commercially viable form of polyphenylene oxide even before the bugs had been worked out of the product.

To add drama to the decision, Welch and his boss, Gutoff, and an R&D man from a GE lab in Schenectady, New York, are presented as touring the plant's construction site in the town of Selkirk, New York, thirty miles west of Pittsfield, one winter's day in 1965, and gazing down into a thirty-foot hole in the ground that is destined to become the main building's foundation. Staring into the abyss, Welch reports that he saw his career flash before him. After all, here he was, apparently responsible to Gutoff and the company for the outcome of a $10 million investment in a product that in reality did not yet exist and might never be developed at all.

So, writes Welch, during the six months that followed, he "practically lived in the lab," mixing "every compound we could think of into PPO to see if it would stop the cracking." From these efforts, writes Welch, a team of chemists in Pittsfield came up with the solution by mixing PPO with rubber and polystyrene, creating a durable, heat-resistant but flexible plastic.

Unfortunately, the story is missing its real hero, for the star in the development of Noryl wasn't Welch at all but an obscure GE employee named Eric Cizek, who had joined the company's Plastics Division in Pittsfield as a chemical engineer in August 1961, at just about the time Welch was threatening to quit.[2] Assigned to the team that was trying to work the bugs out of PPO, Cizek soon grew disenchanted with the bizarre and frenetic way in which everyone was rushing about in a panic, mixing anything they could think of with the product in hopes that it would stop cracking.

Methodically, Cizek went about his own research, and since he didn't seem to be a "team player," no one paid him much mind—least of all Welch—as week after week, Cizek would laboriously test out his ideas and write down the results in lab notebooks, which he would fill from front to back, then place in his desk, one after the next.

Oblivious to his efforts, Welch raced about faster and faster in search of a solution, leaving skid marks from Indianapolis to Fairfield as he dashed from one GE facility to the next to find the scientist with the magic formula that would stop polyphenylene oxide from cracking.

With Welch setting a tone of energized desperation over the elusive cure to the PPO problem, a kind of quiet panic began to spread throughout the division back in Pittsfield, and it was only a matter of time before Cizek's self-imposed isolation from the PPO research team began to be seen as evidence of a bad attitude. So not even Cizek himself was terribly surprised when he came to work one day in 1964 and was handed a letter from his boss, a fellow named McKellum, suggesting that all things considered it might be a good idea if Cizek started looking for another job.

Cizek soon found one at Ford Motor Company and departed, leaving behind that desk full of lab notebooks of research efforts that the rest of the group viewed as a waste of time. It wasn't until another three years had passed, and after more millions of dollars had been spent in a search for a fix to the PPO problem that someone looked, in desperation, in Cizek's desk and discovered that the previous four years had been a waste of time and money because Cizek had come up with the cure to the PPO dilemma in 1964. Since no one would listen to him, he simply wrote it down in his lab book and put on a longer and grumpier face than ever when he was around the office.

What Cizek had invented—and Welch's team had taken nearly four more years to reinvent—was a whole new plastic. With it, you could make almost anything that you could make out of sheet metal, and a lot of other things besides—and for a lot less money. The company called it Noryl, a name of meaningless content, and thus limitless possibilities.

Meanwhile, Cizek and his family had moved to Ann Arbor, Michigan, and in 1968, while working for Ford, he received a letter from GE informing him of what had been found in his desk in Pittsfield and asking him to sign over the rights to GE. Cizek signed the required papers and thereupon assigned to GE the rights to Noryl, for which GE had already obtained a patent in his name, dated May 14, 1968 (U.S. Patent No. 3,383,435). In return, GE gave Cizek a paperweight and flew him and his wife to New York for a Broadway theater weekend, while Noryl went on to launch Welch on his ride to the top of GE.

The Selkirk plant was completed on schedule, summoned from that thirty-foot hole in the ground by Welch and his team, a group of young men still in their twenties. They had never before attempted anything so complex and challenging as what had now come to completion before their very eyes, and they reacted as one might expect, as the testosterone began to flow.

In a provocative piece of scholarship by Professor Arnold M. Ludwig into the roots of male behavior,[3] you will find a discussion of what happens to Alpha males when they are presented with challenges that they overcome: Put simply, they become more Alpha, and more male. "Throughout history, rulers who attain legendary status often tend to be those who have conquered other nations, won major wars, expanded their country's boundaries, founded new nations, forcibly transformed their societies, and imposed their own beliefs on their subjects," Ludwig writes, and something like that was starting to happen to Jack and his gang now, as the Hudson River town of Selkirk, New York, began to hum with the evidence of his leadership and their presence.

Here they were, young men, not yet into their thirties, and they were sharing in a feat of willpower and accomplishment that none had even imagined was in them.* And almost inevitably, a kind of subtle sense of superiority began to spread among them, and the behavior of teenage boys moved from the locker-room into the office.

They called it just letting off steam, and because he was their leader, Jack set the pace. So they laughed—some a bit awkwardly—at his crude jokes and bullying asides, as when a colleague on the design team, Larry Burkinshaw, who had failed to gain Jack's favor, passed him in the hall and Welch remarked in a loud-enough voice to be unmistakable in its hurtful intent, "Pick up his skirt and kick

---

*In research into male aggression, one study found that testosterone levels in athletes rise shortly before competition, and in the winners (but not the losers), it continues to rise afterward. See P. E. Stepansky, "A History of Aggression in Freud" in *Psychological Issues*, vol. X, no. 3, Monograph 39 (New York: International Universities Press, 1977).

Nor is this type behavior confined only to human males. In a review of the work of Stanford University primatologist Robert Sapolsky, *Fortune* reported, "The Alphas who get to the top and stay there are great at forming coalitions and being psychologically intimidating, as well as using bluffs and suggestions of violence instead of actually getting into fights . . . This is a species, after all, in which males who want to say howdy to friends will often . . . give a nonchalant yank on each other's penis." See D. Grainger, "Alpha Romeos," *Fortune* (August 11, 2003), p. 48.

him in the cunt . . ."[4] at which the young men on either side of him laughed in an approval-seeking way.*

In a similar spirit of encouragement, or at least accommodation, no one said anything when several members of the gang attended a dinner party at the home of a plastics executive, where they beheld yet another example of Jack at his wittiest—this time face-to-face with an actual live woman. Exercising his presumed rights and privileges as the senior GE man at the party, Welch smiled at the host's good-looking wife while he reached out and goosed her in front of her guests.[5]

Meanwhile, a clique of admiring young sales and marketing people had begun to gather around Welch. Mostly they were Irish Catholics. And as was the case with Jack, they liked to drink and let off steam.

By general agreement, Welch's second-in-command soon emerged as a strapping young fellow named Tom Fitzgerald. "Fitzy"[†] Fitzgerald had been in marketing in the Plastics Division back in Pittsfield, where he had caught Jack's eye, and Welch had brought him over to Selkirk right after the plant came online and made him marketing manager for Noryl.[6]

One colleague who knew Fitzgerald well recalled of him years later, "Whatever Jack was up for, Tom was the first to agree. They were two peas in a pod." Indeed they were. Jack was addicted to golf, and as it happened, so was Tom. Jack had worked as a caddy when he

---

*Eventually Burkinshaw did gain Welch's favor and was made a member of his staff in a 1973 promotion. See "Welch Moves His Offices to Commons," Berkshire Eagle (August 24, 1973).

†In Jack: Straight from the Gut (New York: Warner Books, 2001), Welch refers to Fitzgerald as a "wild Irishman" (p. 45) who was his business "soul mate" (p. 45), and "closest business friend" (p. 57). The only other person in the memoir who comes in for similar praise is Suzy Wetlaufer, the woman with whom Jack had an affair that ended his second marriage. Suzy is included in an Afterword that was added to the paperback edition of the memoir in 2003 and is likewise described as Jack's "soul mate" (p. 445).

was a kid growing up in North Salem, Massachusetts, and Tom had done the same thing while growing up in Westbury, Long Island.[7] Both men came from Irish Catholic families, experiencing some of life's rougher edges as children in financially stressed homes. And both men enjoyed a nip of the sauce after work, and maybe more than one—especially if some lovely young lass happened to be eyeing one or the other of them from across the room as the Schlitz beer clock over the bar ticked down the minutes to closing time.

Realizing that Jack's sweet tooth was women, Fitzy developed himself into a clearinghouse of information about the sexual politics of the Selkirk facility, becoming a source of unending tips to his colleagues about which secretaries were the easiest for executives to score with.

Fitzy was also more than accommodating in permitting his second-floor office in the administrative building to be used as a "safe" place for his colleagues to take their prey after-hours or on weekends. Then he'd walk in unexpectedly and feign surprise at the couple engaged in carnal gymnastics on his desk and say something clever like, "Don't mind me, I'll be out of here in a minute . . ." and begin rummaging around pretending to look for something in the desk under them. Thirty years later, the Jack Pack was still laughing over Fitzy's retelling of that one.

A plastics man named Donald Blanchard also had clout with Jack. Known by his middle name "Rex," which served as a nickname of sorts among his friends, Blanchard viewed Welch with unalloyed awe and was ready to follow him on any mission.*

---

* By the start of the 1980s, Blanchard had been promoted by Welch and transferred to the Netherlands. In 1983, he returned to the United States to stand trial for federal income tax evasion, for which he pleaded guilty and was sentenced to six months in prison. See *Business Wire* (May 30, 1985). Thereafter he broke off contact with GE and was said by his one-time colleagues to have dropped out of society entirely and moved to a cabin in the mountains. Blanchard, who is now living in retirement in Willard, Utah, was located and interviewed for this book.

Regina Hacker Paulsen. A good-looking brunette, and secretary for a soul-mate, she went from quiet young woman to wild party animal for the boys of the second floor. Then down the corporate memory hole she fell, and there she stayed for twenty years, while the men of Becker House just went about their lives and looked the other way. From the far side of seduction beckoned the ghost of someone wronged. No flowers for the dead? (*Photo credit:* Forest Hills High Yearbook, 1960, The Comet Press Inc., New York.)

A third young man, named Robert J. Kunze, also worked for Jack. Kunze, a hulking fellow from Bates College, had gone to work in Pittsfield and been assigned to Selkirk after the plant had come on line. But Kunze never quite became part of Jack's inner circle—and never seemed all that eager to do so either. On the other hand, the same could not be said for his secretary, a good-looking brunette named Regina Paulsen.

The workdays in Pittsfield all ended the same way, with Jack rounding up the Jack Pack and heading for town. There was rarely a turndown to his invitations because this was, after all, the manly thing to do, and the macho way to be.

The gang's favorite hangout was a place called the Five Chairs, a kind of mirrors-and-velvet pickup joint on the Pittsfield/Lenox line. Closer to the plant, you might also find them closing down the joint at a place called the Bubble, which had a bowling alley and a year-round swimming pool enclosed in an inflatable dome next door.

One particular evening gained instant fame for how it revealed Jack in action, and wound up being told and retold and embellished on so many times down the years that it eventually became Jack Welch folklore—useful more for what it says about how Welch's one-time colleagues in the Plastics Division now choose to remember him than what may precisely have occurred during the actual incident.

It all began around 10 P.M. when Jack and Fitzy headed into the Bubble. As usual, the place was jumping already with 1960s Motown, and the dance floor was packed. Once inside, Jack scanned the crowd and, zeroing in on his target—an attractive young woman who appeared to be alone—he prepared to hit her with the irresistible Welch charm. Fitzy ordered himself a drink and settled in to watch the master in action.

But the dance floor was so packed that Jack was soon lost from view. Surveying the tables ringed around the outside, Fitzy spotted some familiar faces from the Plastic Division's engineering department and flicked a nod in their direction. They, too, had been watching Welch and had likewise seen him draw a bead on the girl and begin to move in—though once again he was quickly lost among the writhing bodies on the dance floor.

A minute or two passed, as the music and the dancing continued, punctuated by the random voices of people trying to talk to each other in the din. But then suddenly they heard the ominous and telltale sound of several voices rising at once, as a little knot of compacted people began to form. A few seconds more and a fight was in progress, and as frightened guests gave way, the knot began edging toward the exit door amidst a rising volume of animal-like shouting from somewhere within it. Fitzy rose to look. Yet, it was only as the knot approached the doorway to the parking lot that it loosened enough to see what was going on: Two men were locked in a desperate and nearly motionless struggle—one straining to grab the other . . . who was straining to get away.

At the doorway, the knot separated and ejected the two into the parking lot, and in that instant Fitzy caught the flash of his boss's face, as Jack and another man tumbled into the lot. But it was what happened next, as Fitzy rushed to the door along with the group from Engineering, that quickly became part of the Legend of Jack

Welch. As the young GE men watched in disbelief, they beheld their leader racing frantically around the lot, screaming for someone to call the police, as the husband of the young woman he had tried to pick up chased him, waving a beer bottle and shouting, "I'll get you, you little prick."

Next day at the plant, the word spread like wildfire: "Did you hear what happened at the Bubble last night? Jack Welch set the world record for the 220 dash in a parking lot (bwahahaha) . . . !"

But the hardest partying of all took place in Selkirk, where the Jack Pack besieged bars almost nightly. When the action died away in Selkirk, they would head off to more distant opportunities, some-times as far away as Greenville, thirty miles outside of town.

On Fridays, the Selkirk plant's weekly newsletter, called the *Insight*, would be delivered to in-boxes, and in the spirit of college boys on spring break, someone could be counted on to shout down the hall, "Anything new in *Incest* (Bwahahaha!)" and the ruckus would begin.

More than once, you could have found Jack and a few of his trusted pals gathered around the jukebox long after midnight at a Selkirk watering hole called the Feura Bush Tavern, named after a neighborhood not far from the Noryl plant.* Then six hours later, they'd be back on the job in the Selkirk plant's administrative headquarters, called Becker House—all serious, crisp, and efficient looking.

Pumped up by everything that was erupting all around him, Welch began to pack on the promotions, and with each step up the man-agerial ladder he grew more pumped to take the next step quicker

---

*The tavern was known to the Jack Pack simply as "the Bush"—as in "Anybody up for some bush . . . ?"

and try to step higher. In fact, scarcely was the Selkirk plant open and running, than he came up with his most ambitious idea of all: to expand into Europe. In no time the obliging Gutoff had paved the way for a Noryl production deal in the Netherlands, and after that in Japan as well. What's more, Gutoff arranged things so that the plants would bypass the existing organizational structure of GE and report directly to him—and through him, to Welch.

By the summer of 1968, Welch had already been promoted to manager of the plastics operation, and now moved his office back to Pittsfield. In 1971, he was promoted yet again, to the job of heading up GE's worldwide chemicals businesses, as well as its man-made diamond business, and GE metallurgical operations that stretched from Houston, Texas, to Milan, Italy.

The energy that radiated from him was like nothing the employees at GE had ever seen before. Here he was, barely half way into his thirties, and he was opening production plants wherever one looked, creating what amounted to an entire shadow-GE on what seemed to be little more than his own say-so.

Not everyone who worked for Jack looked back on the experience fondly. A process engineer in the Plastics Division, John Theberge, recalled organizing a pickup game of basketball one Saturday morning at the Pittsfield YMCA. Welch had a reputation as a bad loser in office sports and no one wanted him to participate, so Theberge hadn't invited him.

But Welch's radar had picked up plans for the game anyway. On the fated Saturday morning, just as the teams were going through their warm-ups on the court, Welch stormed into the YMCA gym. His face was purple with fury, and he began cursing at Theberge in an out-of-control stammer: "Why the f f f f fuck wasn't I invited to this f f f f f fucking game! This is going to be very b b b b b bad for your career here you p p p p prick . . . .!" Then he turned on his heel and stormed from the gym.

But for every John Theberge, there were ten Kevin Murrays. Kevin had been born and raised in Pittsfield, the youngest of nine in a working-class Irish Catholic family, which instantly endeared him to Welch. Jack hired him in 1963, when Kevin was twenty-three, to work in the grandly labeled "Chemical Development" operation, which really meant that Kevin pretty much *was* the department. As such, he was one of the first four or five who started out under Jack, which gave him ground-floor credentials that he wore on his sleeve.

Forty years later, Kevin seemed ready as ever to pick a fight with anyone in the bar who even glanced sideways at the memory of his first boss. "He was a follow-me guy," recalled Kevin. "He could turn you on, get you excited. He was great! And could he be a prick? Was he confrontational? Well yes, and so what!"

No one could recall a GE executive who had ever generated such fierce loyalty among his subordinates. So what was it in the man that had begun turning the entire workforce of GE into putty in his hands? Why did so many of them feel, in the words of a plastics engineer who worked for GE in Europe at the start of the 1970s, that, from the first time he met him, "Welch was God"? Why were they so willing to put up with hours and days of his abusive tongue and haranguing put-downs, simply to be treated to a brief moment of endearment and emotional embrace at the end?

One clue may have to do with what are by now certain well-understood principles of group psychology in hostage situations. On August 23, 1973, a group of Swedish bank robbers were interrupted while looting a bank vault and they responded by taking four of the bank's employees hostage as pawns to negotiate their release. During the six days that followed, the captives wound up bonding emotionally and psychologically to their captors while growing progressively more frightened at the prospect of being rescued—a phenomenon now understood as the "Stockholm Syndrome."[8]

Similarly, in the psychological dynamics of spousal abuse, battered wives often develop a view of their husbands as good and decent human beings whose violent and abusive behavior stems from deep-seated problems that the wife can help him understand and shed. In so doing, the victimized spouse focuses on, anticipates, and seeks out not the abuser's predominant acts of brutality, but his occasional acts of kindness.

Was this what Jack Welch was all about—a rogue industrial psychologist in the process of hijacking the nation's fourth largest corporation? Or were there perhaps forces bearing down on the brilliant young executive that even he didn't grasp or understand? Perhaps Welch was simply applying to his colleagues the very same treatment he had received from his mother while he was growing up in the streets of North Salem: "Hugs and kicks," he eventually called it in his memoir,[9] as his mother stood before him, the cat-o'-nine-tails in one hand and the bandages and balm in the other, to lash his bleeding soul with her bizarre words of love ["*You punk!*"] then clutch him to her bosom in the shame of her abuse.*

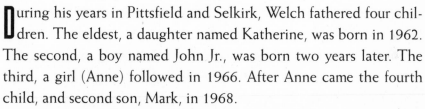

During his years in Pittsfield and Selkirk, Welch fathered four children. The eldest, a daughter named Katherine, was born in 1962. The second, a boy named John Jr., was born two years later. The third, a girl (Anne) followed in 1966. After Anne came the fourth child, and second son, Mark, in 1968.

Yet for all the interest Welch showed in them, his children might as well have been livestock he kept in a barn. And the same can be said for his treatment of their mother, Jack's wife, Carolyn. One encounters the occasional moment in his autobiography when Carolyn makes a brief, walk-on appearance. But the occasions are leaden, forced, and distinguished by their insincerity and almost unbelievable

---

*John Wareham offers the following thought, "In the unresolved debate as to whether human behavior springs from genetic inheritance or environmental conditioning, one vital fact is often overlooked: *parents provide both.*" See J. Wareham, *Wareham's Way: Escaping the Judas Trap* (New York: Atheneum, 1983), pp. 18–19.

self-centeredness, as when he reports that with each of his promotions "she and the kids" would "celebrate by decorating the house and driveway with colorful streamers." Welch could as easily have been describing the activities of the hired help as those of his own family.

Yet there is more missing from these scenes than we might imagine, for beneath the portrait of Jack Welch as *Father Knows Best* swirled the rumors. Nearly forty years later and he was still rubbing at them—the stain that wouldn't leave—writing cryptically in his memoir, in artfully chosen words that reveal the darker truth they are intended instead to camouflage, of his "behavior that wasn't the norm . . ." at "frequent parties at local bars . . ." whenever some new victory on the battlefields of plastics gave the gang something to celebrate.[10]

Mary Jane Tichenor, the society editor of Pittsfield's local newspaper, the *Berkshire Eagle*, had heard plenty of rumors about Jack, and four decades later she could still recall them. Mostly, they seemed to concern "the girlfriends." He had plenty of them, Mary Jane ruminated, "Everyone knew that, it was common knowledge." Not for nothing was he known as Jack the Zipper from almost the day he hit town.

There were rumors about Jack and a secretary named Louise, who worked in the Pittsfield office. And there were other rumors, too. Over and over again, one heard them—the stories about "the behavior." The night after night of "turn out the lights" drinking bouts, and about that poor pathetic creature from across the way in Coeymans, New York, who had worked as a secretary at the plant in Selkirk. Those sorts of rumors.

5

AL AND DENNIS IN THE PASSING LANE

After his tour in the U.S. Army, Al Dunlap landed his first job in civilian life as an executive trainee at the Kimberly Clark paper mill in New Milford, Connecticut. The start of his career in business also coincided with the final death rattles of his disintegrating marriage with Gwyn.

The three of them—Al, Gwyn, and their son Troy, barely six months old—had jammed themselves into a two-bedroom garden apartment north of Danbury, Connecticut, a quick thirty-minute drive south down Route 7 from Pittsfield, where Jack Welch was already making a name for himself as an "out-of-the-box thinker" in GE's Plastics Division.

But Al's personal life was now in such chaos that it is a wonder he was able to turn up for work at all.[1] At odd and unpredictable moments, he would erupt in tantrums and storm about the apartment inspecting the furniture for fingerprints. One such bout lasted for nearly three weeks.

For the Christmas holidays of 1963, the young family went to visit Gwyn's parents in New Jersey. The first day or two passed uneventfully. But predictably enough, a fight eventually broke out—this time while Gwyn's parents were out and she was alone in the house with Al and Troy. They had agreed to spend the day visiting their grandparents, who all lived within driving distance. But the question next became whose grandparents would they visit first, Gwyn's or Al's? As the yelling escalated, Al suddenly pushed his wife into a nearby coffee table and onto the floor. Then standing over her, he raged, "You son of a bitch, I'll kill you."

At that precise moment, the telephone rang. It was Gwyn's mother, phoning home while on some shopping errands. As Gwyn reached for the receiver, Al roared, "Gimme that phone or I'll smash you with it." Hearing this, Gwyn's mother began to shriek, "Call the police! Call the police!"

In a flash, Al was out the door and heading for his car. At the end of the day, he returned, scooped up his clothes, and left again. Where he went isn't known. But three days later, when Gwyn at last decided to venture out of the house and got in her parents' car with Troy in a baby's seat and began backing into the street, Al abruptly appeared out of nowhere and began following her, blowing his horn and attempting to force her to the side of the road. At her wit's end and fearing an accident, she finally pulled over.

Somehow, Gwyn managed to calm Al down, and they agreed to meet in a nearby diner in the town of Westfield and talk through their issues. But once they settled themselves into a booth, Al's voice began to rise, and suddenly he was cursing and yelling at her all over again—and Gwyn scooped up Troy and fled. Al caught up with her in the parking lot and began trying to push her into his car. The baby began to cry and so did Gwyn. A crowd gathered and several people stepped to her defense and drove her to the Westfield Police Station. There she told her story, and a policeman escorted her back to the diner in a patrol car. Al was now no longer anywhere to be seen. So Gwyn got out, put Troy in his seat in her car, and headed back to her parents, escorted by the police cruiser as far as the West-field town line.

A family priest, Father Flanigan, was asked to provide counseling, and on Al's assurances, which all agreed were genuine, that he was sorry for his past behavior and would mend his ways, the couple returned to Connecticut and Al went back to work. But it wasn't long before the violence and vituperation began all over again, now with the menacing additional element of Al standing before her, brandishing one of his guns, and musing about cannibalizing her body.

In November 1964, after less than eighteen months in the New Milford garden apartment, Gwyn could take it no longer. And following a particularly brutal shoving incident that ended with Al waving a kitchen knife in her face, she grabbed up Troy and fled one final time—for good.

Soon thereafter, Al was transferred by Kimberly Clark from its New Milford plant to the job of shift superintendent at a company plant in Neenah, Wisconsin. The plant's general superintendent was a man named Ben Nobbe, who enjoyed snarling at his subordinates. Al seemed to regard Nobbe as a nasty-tempered old coot—except that he also seemed to view the man's behavior as somehow endearing—or at least as worthy of emulation. "He wore his bastardness like a well-worn badge of honor," Al said of Nobbe in his memoir, *Mean Business.* He was a "stern disciplinarian and a tough guy who didn't take crap from anyone."*

Mimicking Nobbe's management style, Al quickly became his most trusted aide and was soon accompanying him on trips to meet with suppliers and contractors. One of those trips brought him into contact with a man who owned a plant that supplied toilet paper to

_____
*The admiring characterization of Nobbe as a "stern disciplinarian," echoes Dunlap's equally admiring characterization of his mother, Mildred, as a "strong, disciplined woman." See A. Dunlap, *Mean Business* (New York: Times Books, 1996), p. 112.

Kimberly Clark as a subcontractor when the company's own plants could not meet demand. The subcontractor, Sterling Pulp & Paper, in Eau Claire, Wisconsin, was heavily in debt, and burdened with an obstinate workforce. Whether Nobbe was beginning to feel threatened by Al at Kimberly Clark isn't known. But whatever his reasons may have been, Nobbe suggested that Sterling hire Al to shape the place up.

This lifted Al, in less than four years, from trainee in charge of no one, to plant manager of a 1,000-employee factory—and he was still not yet thirty years old. It was a career trajectory that seemed, in the very suddenness of the takeoff and the overnight explosion of the resulting responsibilities, no different from what Jack Welch was undergoing at that very moment back in Pittsfield, Massachusetts, where GE was soon to anoint him general manager of the Plastics Division—at the age of thirty-two, the youngest general manager in the company's history.

Yet, there is a point at which youth becomes a liability for someone in a leadership position; the energy of youth can overwhelm the limited experience such a person possesses, impairing the ability to make judgments based on those experiences. Leadership is more than simply being the person who can yell the loudest or bully the weak most aggressively. Often leadership involves finding a consensus "sweet spot" among a variety of individuals, all with competing and differing opinions about how to handle a situation.

Dunlap had never learned the subtleties and finesse of leadership since his only prior exposure to the challenges of leadership had involved the command-and-control structures of the military. In that environment, barked orders from junior officers are most effective when the thought of disobeying them looms as even more frightening to a subordinate than following them—possibly into the teeth of opposing enemy fire.

Al went to work as general manager of the Sterling Pulp & Paper factory in June 1967 and found himself trying to ram layoffs down the throats of the company's volatile and unionized workforce. But his tactics of yelling and bullying only succeeded in making the situation worse. Soon he was receiving death threats from anonymous callers to his house.*

Meanwhile, the owner of the company, a fellow named Ely Meyer, had introduced Al to a bank teller named Judy Stringer. Quickly picking up on Meyer's suggestion that he'd go a lot further in business if he had a wife, Al married Judy a few months later.

Al's idea of courtship seems to have featured all the tenderness of a rotary lawn mower running full throttle. At one point, he began pressuring Judy to marry him before December 31 so he could save $600 on his federal income taxes that year. The actual marriage, which in fact has wound up lasting for more than 30 years, does not rate a single line of detail in Dunlap's memoir, and Judy herself rates only two more brief mentions over the course of his career-long narrative.

Soon enough, Judy began what amounted—at least so far as the world at large could see—to a slow but relentless retreat from involvement in his career. Wise to his uncontainable ego, she stopped playing golf with him because she could consistently beat him at it, and took up tennis, which proved to be a game in which he could beat her.†

She also discovered a disarmingly sneaky side to the man that she had not expected. During their first Christmas together, Judy

---

*The details are set forth in Dunlap's 1996 business memoir, *Mean Business: How I Save Bad Companies and Make Good Companies Great* (New York: Times Books, 1996). In Al's recollected version of events, his relations with the plant's union is characterized as "pretty good," but it is never clearly explained why his tenure at the plant would lead to "threats of violence" and "anonymous calls and letters from nuts who said they were going to blow up my car or shoot me in the parking lot."

†See P. Shillington, "Rambo in Pinstripes," the *Miami Herald* (June 5, 1995), in which Shillington reports, "Dunlap is a better tennis player than golfer. He shoots in the 'high 90s.' His wife can beat him; Dunlap, as you might predict, doesn't like to lose. 'I think that's probably why we got into tennis,' Judy is quoted as saying, 'because he can beat me at that.' Dunlap laughs heartily at his wife's insight, nodding in agreement."

went out for the afternoon to visit with some friends. Returning home earlier than expected, she discovered Al on his hands and knees in the living room carefully rewrapping various presents he had unwrapped to peek at while she was out.[2]

Eventually Judy retreated into the escapist world of novels, which she devoured avidly. When the subject of "Life with Al" came up in an interview with a reporter, Judy acknowledged that her husband would needle her for wasting her time by reading novels, but she just laughed it off . . . as she did the evident fact that living with Al was like living with a platoon sergeant on field maneuvers. Among his quirks: Every trip had to be planned with military precision—right to the point of insisting that all suitcases and luggage had to be unpacked on arrival at any destination, even if it was 3 o'clock in the morning. But Judy had long since figured out how to deal with such demands: Just follow orders (and keep on reading those novels).[3]

Al lasted at Sterling Pulp & Paper for roughly six years, from June 1967 to June 1973, leaving when the company's aging owner, Meyer, died. Realizing no doubt that he'd never be able to survive at the company without Meyer around as his protector, he left for a new job at a rival's plant, also in Eau Claire. The company, Max Phillips & Sons, offered him a three-year contract, but this time around there was no Nobbe-type fellow—the cantankerous older superintendent he had worked under at Kimberly Clark—to protect him from the colleagues he abused with his snarling temper. Quickly realizing it had made a terrible mistake, the company fired him after less than two months on the job.[4] The apparent reason: He arrived with a chip on his shoulder and began bad-mouthing his boss so viciously that it had started to hurt the business.*

---

*The same type complaints were echoed about Dunlap two decades later. Listen to an executive named Jerry Ballas, who worked with Dunlap at Scott Paper Company in the mid-1990s. Characterizing his management style as "terrorizing," Ballas told an interviewer for Public Broadcasting, "I mean it literally, it's terrorizing working for

After being dumped by Max Phillips & Sons, it took Al almost six full months to find another job, which he finally did in May 1974 at yet another paper mill—though accepting it meant that he and Judy had to move from Eau Claire, Wisconsin, to Niagara Falls, New York.

The company, Nitec Paper Corporation, had originally been a Kimberly Clark facility; and back in the 1950s it had enjoyed a booming business with three shifts running twenty-four hours a day, six days a week. But business had deteriorated, and the plant had eventually been sold to Nitec, which had let it deteriorate even more. Al was given the title of Chief Operating Officer and the job of shaping the place up.[5]

The man who hired him, Nitec's chairman of the board, George Petty, apparently liked Dunlap—so much so that if the sworn testimony Al eventually gave in a subsequent lawsuit is to be believed, Petty soon invited him to join in on a little side action he had going. The action involved a paper company in Canada that Petty controlled . . . and various secret offshore bank accounts in places like Switzerland and Bermuda.*

---

the man. What you do is you avoid, at all costs, getting near him . . . avoid contact with him." From the transcript of "Running with the Bulls" (Hedrick Smith Productions, 1997/1998) for PBS.

*The details of Dunlap's secret Swiss bank account, as well as those involving his eventual falling out with George Petty and others at Nitec, are set forth in the case of *Albert J. Dunlap v. Nitec Paper Corporation et al.*, U.S. District Court for the Southern District of New York, 77 Civ. 3056, 1977, the background to which litigation is discussed elsewhere in this chapter. At one point in a July 9, 1979, affidavit in the case, Dunlap stated: "I was privy to a variety of conversations to which Mr. Petty and one of his lieutenants, Joseph Mason ('Mason') were parties. During these conversations, Petty described the wide use by him and Mason of secret numbered Swiss accounts (and for that matter similar Bermuda bank accounts) maintained either by them or by shell companies in connection with various questionable transactions. Among the transactions thus described by Petty included a type of transaction in which in substance Petty, through the use of a corporate shell, bought pulp from one company he controlled and sold it at a substantially higher price to another company he controlled, depositing the profit in his own Swiss or Bermuda bank account. Accordingly, in reality it is Petty and Mason and not I who have the most about which to be embarrassed."

To listen to Petty explain what he and a colleague had been doing with those accounts made Dunlap "extraordinarily uneasy," he later claimed—since, presumably, his instincts told him that maintaining a secret Swiss bank account was a dangerous thing to do. But knowing something is wrong is one thing, and refusing to participate in it is quite another. So it was against all his better judgment, and in seeming disregard of the questionable legality of what he was becoming involved in, that he opened a secret numbered account at a Zurich-based private Swiss bank called Hottinger & Co.—following which, according to Dunlap, some $40,000 in "consulting fees" was deposited in it by Petty. This of course dragged in Dunlap even more deeply, presumably making him even more nervous about the matter. Yet, still he said nothing, as if it were all a bad dream that would go away once he woke up.

Meanwhile, Al had already begun earning a reputation for himself—not just at Nitec but throughout the whole of Niagara Falls—as an insufferable and self-possessed boor. Seemingly oblivious to how he was viewed by those all around him, he befriended the mayor and the two became frick and frack, turning up at public functions together as a sign of Niagara Falls' "partnership of business and government."

Among Nitec's many problems was its outdated pollution control equipment. To get the company to upgrade it, the city of Niagara Falls had to give Nitec a variety of tax breaks. But this meant that the Niagara Falls City Council had to ask for periodic briefings from Dunlap about the company's progress in installing its new equipment. The briefings themselves were always the same: Dunlap would strut into the Council chambers, decked out in one of the hand-tailored suits that he had now begun to wear as the plant's top manager. Comfortably positioned as the center of attention, Al would thereupon begin to spew forth an unending stream of bombastic self-celebration about how much he was doing and how hard he was working, to "save" Nitec Paper.[6]

Not surprisingly, the city's more seasoned businessmen spotted Dunlap's Achilles' heel right away—his preening sartorial vanity—and were soon using it to maximum effect. One local insurance agent signed him up for some Nitec key man insurance by complimenting him on his wardrobe at every opportunity. He would spot Al in the crowd at a benefit perhaps, and walk up and say something like, "Jesus Al, that's the most spectacular suit I've ever seen! I'd just say it's lucky there's only one of them because no one could possibly wear it as well as you . . ."—at which Al's chest would puff out and his head would tilt back to display the full and glorious profile of this one-of-a-kind businessman in his one-of-a-kind suit.

The only problem that Al's flatterers faced was getting paid. Former Vice President Dan Quayle's uncle, Robert Quayle, was a marketing vice president for the Carborundum Corporation, which supplied components for Nitec's pollution control upgrade equipment. Quayle complained often that Dunlap would demand instant delivery of the equipment but would dally endlessly when it came to paying for it after it arrived. Said one of Quayle's colleagues of Dunlap, "Frankly, he was a world-class asshole. He'd stiff you for months on bills then get abusive the second you asked for payment. He was just the worst. There must have been something wrong with him."[7]

Al's turnaround talents brought about a small profit in 1974 and a slightly bigger one in 1975, and apparently believing himself to be the greatest business leader the city had ever seen, Al joined the Niagara Falls Country Club and began challenging members to meet him on the tennis courts.* But it took no time at all before he found

---

*Tennis players experience an elevation in testosterone levels following a successful tennis match, whereas the losers experience a decline in testosterone during the same period. Actual percentages of testosterone change have been measured in monkeys following fights. Victorious monkeys show a 20 percent increase in testosterone levels for roughly 24 hours following a fight whereas the level may fall by as much as 90 percent—and stay lower longer—for monkeys that lose. See D. Blum, *Sex on the Brain* (New York: Viking Press, 1997), pp. 167–171.

it almost impossible to find anyone willing to play him.[8] The problem wasn't that he was better than anyone else, but that he cheated
so outrageously—and got so abusive of opponents who questioned
him—that the members quickly stopped playing with him.*

Not realizing how the other members felt about him, Al threw a
birthday party for himself at the Club and invited 200 of his presumed admirers to attend. The event was scripted down to the second and was designed to make maximum theatrical use of the club's
location overlooking Lake Ontario. A dress rehearsal was held, cued
to the precise moment of sunset. At that exact moment, with the city
lights of Toronto flickering to life beyond the horizon, a four-layer
birthday cake would be wheeled into the Club's grand salon, and the
assembled revelers would burst into a spontaneous chorus of *Happy
Birthday, Al Dunlap, happy birthday to you.*

The rehearsal went off flawlessly. Yet when the big night came,
the two busboys who began wheeling in the cake managed to snag
one of the trolley cart's casters in a seam of the carpet. As the assembled guests watched transfixed, the entire four-layer cake began
to move forward with the slow but irresistible force of a tectonic
plate until it eased over the edge of the trolley and arced downward
in a slow-motion forward flip, landing upside down with a vulgar-
sounding SPLAT on the floor.

For what seemed an eternity, no one said anything as all just
stood and gawked at what had happened, savoring all that the moment seemed to convey about the man they had been summoned
to applaud. Finally, from out of the crowd came a tentative and

---

*Dunlap's experience on the tennis courts is similar to what Jack Welch encountered
throughout his life in sports. In *At Any Cost: Jack Welch, General Electric, and the Pursuit of
Profit* (New York: Knopf, 1998), author Thomas O'Boyle reports that Welch, although
not accused of cheating, was driven by a competitive zeal so strong he eventually was
unable to find anyone willing to let him play on GE's weekend softball team. On another occasion, O'Boyle reports that Welch, an avid golfer, was given the cold shoulder
by other golfers at the Berkshire Hills Country Club (p. 48).

exploratory snicker. Then came another . . . and another . . . and after that several at once, until suddenly the entire room was awash in gales of laughter at this perfect moment of deflation for the city's biggest and most self-possessed jerk.[9]

Meanwhile, the whole hidden matter of Al's secret Swiss bank account had apparently continued to nag him, and he finally decided to take action and shut the thing down. So, flying to France on what was ostensibly a vacation, Al checked into a hotel in Monaco, then went into the street to look for a public pay phone kiosk. Finding one, he called Switzerland, got the bank on the phone, and told the manager to wire him what was in the account and close it out. He then collected the wire transfer, returned to the United States, and gave the check to Nitec's attorney and told him to deposit it in the United States in a proper and above-board account, where it had belonged all along.

Whether or not Dunlap thought he had finally gotten the problem behind him, it eventually blew up in his face. This happened when Petty abruptly dismissed him, claiming that Dunlap had so completely alienated those around him that Nitec faced a mass resignation of all the company's vice presidents if he weren't let go. This stunned Dunlap, who as always, had been seemingly oblivious to the effect he was having on those around him. So, raging that Petty was simply trying to get him out of the way—and mindful no doubt that he, Dunlap, held some leverage over the man because of what he suspected about Petty's own offshore activities—he negotiated a $1.2 million payout to leave.

But scarcely had Dunlap emptied out his desk and left (the date was August 30, 1976) than Nitec's auditors at the accounting firm of Arthur Young & Company reported that the anticipated profits Dunlap had been promising were apparently the result of massive falsifications and fraudulent accounting entries on the company's books.

On learning this, Petty realized that he now held the upper hand and announced that Nitec was rescinding its promise to pay Dunlap the payout it had promised. Furious at this turn of events, Dunlap sued for breach of contract, and Nitec countersued. Yet whether or not Al was responsible for Nitec's suddenly worsening circumstances, the company was undeniably in a financial mess, and it finally collapsed and the case was dropped, with Al settling for a $50,000 payment to end the litigation.

By then, it was the summer of 1983, and Al had long since gone on to other things anyway, conveniently deleting the disastrous two years in Niagara Falls, New York, from his resume—just as he would eventually delete it from his *Mean Business* memoir.

Even the case file of the lawsuit seemed to disappear. Box after box of pleadings and deposition testimony—thirty-eight days' worth from Al alone—was crated up by clerks in New York's Federal District Court in Lower Manhattan and shipped to a vast National Archives storage facility in Lee's Summit, Missouri. There it came to rest, logged onto a shelf in a cavernous space suggestive of the last scene of *Raiders of the Lost Ark*. And there it remained for the next twenty years, forgotten by everyone . . . everyone, that is, but Al Dunlap.[10]

Even as Al Dunlap was fleeing from the wreckage of his career in Niagara Falls, New York, business prospects were brightening for New Jersey's other up-from-the-streets CEO in the making: Dennis Kozlowski. Having graduated from Seton Hall in 1968 with a degree in accounting, he landed a job as an auditor at the old Smith-Corona typewriter company. The company had in fact changed its name six years earlier, to the nondescript SCM Corporation in hopes that removing the word "typewriter" from the name might open up broader opportunities for a one-product company when the highest stock prices on Wall Street were being bestowed on the trendy new business concept of the era, the so-called corporate conglomerate.*

By the time Kozlowski arrived on the scene—becoming, as had Welch and Dunlap before him, nothing more than a nameless cog in a large corporate machine—SCM Corporation was basically just a collection of what its own CEO would soon be dismissing disparagingly as "bits of this and that." The company was still making a line of typewriters, both electric and manual. But IBM had by then devoured the office products market almost totally, and SCM was losing money on every typewriter it sold. Meanwhile, the company had gotten into everything from the paint business to the mustard business, by playing "white knight" (another corporate fashion of the time) to defend a Cleveland conglomerate, the Glidden-Durkee Company, in a takeover fight. The result was that SCM wound up with Glidden-Durkee as its own, increasing its visibility on Wall Street as a conglomerate.[11]

Around this time, with Kozlowski just beginning his new job at the company's New York headquarters, his eye fell on an attractive young woman from the Bronx who was working at the office as a secretary. Her name was Angeles Suarez, but she was known around the office as Angie. Dennis quickly zeroed in on her good looks, and they became an item and were married in her home borough of the Bronx on March 13, 1971.[12]

---

*Wall Street's merger mania of the 1960s created the conglomerate movement's golden age, lifting such industry leaders as Royal Little of Textron Corporation, James Ling of LTV, Charles Bluhdorn of Gulf & Western, and Harold Geneen of ITT to a level of fame in the popular press that businessmen did not enjoy again until the boom of the 1990s. Thirty years later, LTV is bankrupt, Gulf & Western is now a part of Viacom International, Inc., and ITT has been broken into several separate and independent companies. Of all these conglomerate hero-stocks of the golden age of conglomerates, only Textron continues as a publicly traded company, with its shares still listed on the New York Stock Exchange.

Between his graduation from Seton Hall University in 1968 and the start of his employment at Tyco Labs in 1976, Kozlowski held at least two jobs—SCM Corporation in New York and Nashua Corporation in Nashua, New Hampshire. In subsequent years, he also claimed to have lived in Arizona while looking for a job as a commercial pilot, and even to have flown helicopters for the Central Intelligence Agency in Cambodia during the first two years of the Nixon administration.*

Dennis's past grew even murkier once his career at Tyco began to gain lift, and the company began to issue press releases that further embellished his history. One such press release moved the place of his birth from the crime-ridden city of Newark to the more bucolic and friendly sounding community of Maplewood, New Jersey.[13] Another awarded him an MBA degree from an obscure New England institution called Rivier College, though he only

---

*Kozlowski's early postcollege career is full of holes and contradictions, and inconsistent press reporting has made it worse. The *New York Times* has reported that Kozlowski began his employment at Tyco in 1973, *New York Times* (December 11, 1989), Sec. D, p. 4; the *Boston Globe* has stated that he began at Tyco in 1975, *Boston Globe* (December 1, 2002), Sec. D1; *Barron's* has given his starting date as 1976, *Barron's* (April 12, 1999), p. 27; and *Investor's Business Daily* has given the date as 1977, *Investor's Business Daily* (May 23, 2000), Sec. A, p. 4. The *New Yorker* (February 17, 2003), p. 132, has reported that Kozlowski began working at SCM Corporation at some unspecified date on or before 1969, and that he joined Tyco in 1975 when his wife was pregnant—an apparent impossibility since the couple's first child, Cheryl Marie, was born on July 19,1974, and the second, Sandra Lisa, in September 26, 1977. *Business Week* (December 23, 2002) reports that Kozlowski moved to Arizona following graduation from Seton Hall, looking for a job as a commercial pilot, and then subsequently joined SCM in New York as an accountant in 1970—leaving an unaccounted-for period that could have included service in the military or CIA. The *Boston Globe* (December 1, 2002), Sec. D1, which cites Kozlowski's interior decorator as the source of his claim to have served with the CIA, also quotes sources as asserting that Kozlowski claimed to have served in Vietnam. But a search of the National Personnel Records Center as well as the Air America archives at the newspaper's request produced no support for the claim that he served in either the CIA or the Armed Forces. During research for this book, the author heard both these apparently apocryphal claims of CIA and/or military involvement repeated, citing Kozlowski as the source, by a business leader who had extensive dealings with him during the 1990s. The claims have proven impossible to verify.

took a couple of evening classes at the school, which didn't grant MBA degrees anyway.[14]

At Tyco, Dennis found himself on the fast track thanks to the man who had hired him: the company's gorillia-like chairman, Joseph Gaziano, who became his mentor. Jack Welch had such a man in Reuben Gutoff at GE; and Al Dunlap had Kimberly Clark's curmudgeonly plant superintendent, Ben Nobbe, in Neenah, Wisconsin. Even Ron Perelman had a role model of sorts in the warped "people skills" exhibited by his father, Ray. In Gaziano, Dennis now had one as well.

In later years, Gaziano was described in press accounts as a "legendary" figure on the mergers-and-acquisitions scene. But he was no Harry Figgie or Jimmy Ling, two of the 1960s-era conglomerateurs whom Gaziano sought to emulate. And he was certainly no Harold Geneen of ITT, whom he had once worked for and now regarded as his own ultimate role model. In reality, Tyco Labs was little more than a small-beer version of SCM itself, with barely $50 million in revenues when he took over as chairman and CEO in 1973.

As had been the fashion of the 1960s, Tyco had put together its own bizarre little collection of random industrial companies, and like the other conglomerates of the era, it was now struggling to avoid collapse in the stock market downturn of the first Nixon term. It was the era of the so-called Nifty Fifty, when the seers of Wall Street were all advising their clients to make their investment choices from a list of just fifty "one decision" (buy-and-hold) stocks. On that list were companies like Avon, Polaroid, and Coca-Cola. Tyco was not among them.

Reviewing its list of portfolio holdings from the perspective of thirty years, we marvel at the utter incoherence of it all, as if the contents of a ten-year-old boy's dungaree pockets were somehow turned into the portfolio assets of a public company. In the dungaree pockets of Tyco could be found some wire, some solar panels, some electrical switches, some land, some silicon, some hi-fi gear . . . and so on and so forth.

But the purpose of acquiring such businesses wasn't to sell more of the products, it was to cause Wall Street to mark up the price of the acquiring company's stock.* And for Gaziano, a one-time New Hampshire lobsterman with a social pedigree to match Kozlowski's, the ultimate goal of the entire exercise was to make a lot of money and then spend it on himself. Scarcely had he joined Tyco than he began filling up his CEO's toy box with the trappings of power— not simply one home but three—and, of course, the toy that was already becoming the *sine qua non* of the power-CEO, a private plane.

This was the world in which Kozlowski now went to work. And it was certainly a confidence-builder for the young accountant—already turning into a balding and increasingly beefy six-footer. He showed up for work each day knowing that the man who had hired him was not only the company chairman, but actually looked like an older version of Dennis, and came from the same coarse background.

In no time at all, Dennis also began to accumulate the trappings of wealth and place them in his own modest toy box of parvenu privilege. First acquisition: an appropriately impressive collection of wines, which he described to friends not by the vintages of the various selections of Bordeaux in the collection, but instead by the number of bottles he possessed, as if the sheer heft of the collection was what ultimately mattered.

---

*For an illuminating discussion of the alchemy by which these markups were achieved, see B. G. Malkiel, *A Random Walk down Wall Street* (New York: W.W. Norton, 1999), particularly pages 62–69. The passage sets forth the arithmetic by which the acquisition of a company with a low price-earnings multiple by one with a higher multiple automatically resulted in Wall Street marking up the low price-earnings of the acquired company to the high multiple of the company that now owned them. In this way, the bull market enthusiasms of the 1960s fueled the entire conglomerate boom, which was built on the acquisition of progressively less valuable companies in order to have their earnings revalued upward.

By the time the tonnage had reached 1,000 bottles, Dennis had already flown to London to take a course that would teach him everything he needed to know about the mushroom-like growth of the wine collection that was filling up his basement. At the end of the course, he returned to the United States, the proud possessor of a document certifying him to be a "master mixologist"—a title that is actually bestowed on the graduates of various bartending schools, and sounds eerily like what the Professor bestowed on the brainless Scarecrow at the end of the *Wizard of Oz*: "By the powers invested in me, I pronounce you a Doctor of Thinkology." It was but the first of many such cultural trophies that Kozlowski would go in search of as his career at Tyco Labs began to hit its stride.

6

FOOLISH FAITH AND THE CASE OF SUZIE CREAM CHEESE

On a day in 1978, Ronald Perelman, along with his wife Faith and their four children, stepped from a limousine and entered the elegant Sherry Netherlands Hotel at the corner of Fifth Avenue and 59th Street on Manhattan's Upper East Side. Ron's mission: To begin a new life.

It had taken him eleven long years to make the break with his father, Ray, and with the Perelman family business—and now he had finally done it. He and his own family had packed up and moved to New York, where the most glamorous race, on the fastest track, is always under way. It was where Ray Perelman's son intended to make his way in the world—beyond the reach of his old man's withering stare.

Ray himself hardly seemed overjoyed and wasted no time in making his feelings known about his son's disloyalty, covering a baby grand piano in the reception room with photographs of Faith, including one of her in her bridal gown, which remained on display even after the couple's divorce in 1983. To guests whom he might spot sneaking a second sideways glance at this altar of a failed romance and a wayward son, Ray would say, *"He's* divorced, we're not!"[1]

In New York, the Perelmans took an apartment that seemed to embody Ron's expectations for what the future now held: Apartment 6B of an elegant residential apartment building at 740 Park Avenue. The building, constructed in 1930 in the depths of the Depression by the architect Rosario Candela, was meant to convey a kind of baronial splendor in a time of need. It was topped by a 34-room,

Ron Perelman *(left)* listens to Saul Steinberg explain why he doesn't like to stick his neck out in junk bond deals. Meshulam Riklis? Fuhgedabouddit. *(Photo credit:* Marina Garnier.)

20,000-square-foot triplex penthouse that was widely regarded as one of the most lavish residences in the city. When Ron and Faith moved into Apartment 6B, the penthouse was already occupied by another Wharton alumnus, financier Saul Steinberg, who had paid $285,000 for it in 1971 and was by now enjoying an unrealized capital appreciation extending into the millions in the booming New York real estate market. It was evidence enough of the sorts of investments that Wharton grads were believed capable of pulling off, and certainly a sign of what Ron expected of himself from the launching pad of the same swanky address.

Thusly perched above midtown, Ron borrowed $1.7 million from Faith and bought a 34 percent stake in a company called Cohen-Hatfield Industries, Inc., which was going for cheap. Two years later, the company borrowed $45 million to buy a candy and flavors company called MacAndrews and Forbes, and Ron, as Cohen-Hatfield's largest and controlling shareholder, turned to a novel way to pay the money back: a new financing technique called the "junk bond." It was the single most important decision of his career, and it launched him on a borrowing-and-buying binge that was eventually to make him, according to *Institutional Investor,* the richest man in America.[2]

The young man behind the junk bond gimmick—yet another Wharton grad, named Michael Milken—had been a few years behind Perelman in the MBA program. After graduation in 1970, Milken had gone to work as a bond salesman in the New York office of an old-line Philadelphia firm called Drexel Firestone and Company. From that perch, he had begun to make a name for himself by investing the money of a growing number of investment world notables in the corporate bonds of distressed companies. Milken's theory, based on a 1950s-era study by an academician named W. Braddock Hickman, was that an investor would always come out ahead by buying a diversified portfolio of distressed bonds as opposed to investment-grade bonds because the higher yields on the junk bonds would more than make up for their greater default rate.

Milken's client list already included New York moneyman Laurence Tisch as well as conglomerateur Meshulam Riklis, who had come to the United States from Israel in the 1950s with barely pocket change to his name. By now, Riklis headed a highly leveraged $2 billion conglomerate called Rapid-American Corporation, which held interests in everything from movie theaters to women's underwear. Finally, there was one of Milken's most valued clients of all—none other than the man in the penthouse triplex at 740 Park Avenue, Saul Steinberg, who now headed his own business empire, Reliance Insurance.

Now Perelman became a client of Milken's as well. With Cohen-Hatfield having shed its Levantine-sounding moniker in favor of the ethnically neutral aroma of the candy company it had just acquired (MacAndrews and Forbes), Perelman had the company issue a bit more than $30 million of junk bonds to roll over the existing debt—bonds that Milken thereupon sold to his other investors.

Thereafter came more deals, and more after that, until Perelman was sitting atop his own smaller version of Riklis's Rapid-American Corporation, with interests that ranged from a film-processing business to a cigar business to a supermarket business—all of it sprouting from his wife Faith's initial get-going money along with the subsequent backing of bank debt and Milken's junk bond merry-go-round.

By 1984, Perelman looked to be rich indeed. But below the balance sheet's top-line number, which showed a business with assets of more than $350 million, were debts of nearly as much. At the bottom line, Perelman was in fact worth not much more than he had been on the day that he and Faith had first moved to town. Like everyone else on the Milken merry-go-round, Perelman depended on a combination of rising prosperity and falling interest rates to keep his business above water so that the game of growth-by-borrowing could continue.

Meanwhile, another force had begun to make itself felt in Perelman's life. Freed from the hovering presence of his father, Ron began to focus increasingly on the frustrations he felt regarding his petite and soft-spoken wife, Faith. Having supplied the money with which Ron set himself up in business in New York, Faith now seemed to have become Ron's new Ray, stepping into the controlling and limiting "parent" role from which Ron had finally succeeded in ousting Ray himself.

Here he was, burdened with a woman who could not have helped but remind him day and night of the life he'd left behind in Philadelphia. What did he need a situation like that for anyway? The problem was, how to deal with it—and as is often the case for those who can afford it, the answer was fairly simple.

Along the way, Perelman had begun leading a secret, second life with a woman named Susan Kasen, who was running a florist shop out of a basement in New Jersey around the time he and Faith had met her in 1974.[3] In 1978, at just about the time the Perelmans were moving to New York, Suzie was opening a midtown Manhattan florist shop called the "Green Thumb." It was located between Madison and Fifth Avenues on 65th Street, around the corner from what was destined to become Ron's offices for MacAndrews and Forbes on East 62nd Street.

By the summer of 1982, the Green Thumb had become a huge hit with the residents of Manhattan's East Side, one of the highest-income neighborhoods in the world, and Suzie was raking in the dough. Mindful that the wealthy are as susceptible as anyone else to the need to feel "in the know," she had cleverly positioned her shop as a place where only the ultra-rich were her customers. When a local reporter called around to do a story on her success, she dropped the names of her clients as delicately into his notebook as if they were pearls being dropped into a goblet of Moët Five Star: the Rockefellers [plop], Princess Grace [plop], and of course, the White House [plop, plop].

For Ron, she offered everything. She was blonde, good looking, devoted, and discreet. And what seemed best of all, she was not demanding, never insisting on the attention and interest in her that was not in him to give. When he was done with her, he could just get up and leave. Does it get any better than that?*

Neighbors of the period would often see them dining together, typically for a one-ish luncheon at a favorite neighborhood haunt such as Marigolds on 65th, a few doors down from the Green Thumb. Ron would enter late, in his *de rigueur* dark business suit, to find Suzie already inside waiting, fashionably attired in her own dark suit, made all the more striking when set against her flaxen hair. They would dine quietly at their table for roughly an hour and a half, then rise and kiss goodbye on the sidewalk (Ron was getting bolder now), and return to their Other Lives—she to her flower shop and her champagne goblets of Rockefellers and Raniers, and he to his . . . well, what the hell, in a few more hours he'd be seeing her again and his life could resume . . . for dinner perhaps at Il Cortile down on Mulberry Street, followed by (or perhaps preceded by) some quality time at her East 40th Street apartment in Murray Hill.

Ron charged off a lot of this to the company, which meant of course that since Faith had given him the money to get started in the first place and thus claimed an interest in his stock in the company, she was in effect unknowingly picking up some of the tab for her husband's skulking about with the woman at the end of the block.

As always happens sooner or later in such situations, Faith began to sense what was up. And after the secrets of Ron's hidden world finally lurched into view, she ruminated on the telltale clues that she

---

*At mid-decade in the 1980s, the trend-watching weekly, *W*, estimated the cost of a kept woman in New York to be roughly $60,000 per year, including a pied-à-terre, food, suitable daytime clothing, and a personal trainer, meaning that, as records developed in the first Perelman divorce action now show, his maintenance overhead for Suzie Kasen actually proved to be a bargain.

hadn't been savvy enough to spot at the time, even though they'd been staring her in the face.

"He sure seemed to be hanging around that flower shop a lot," she reflected at one point. Another time, some of his pressed shirts got delivered to the apartment at 740 Park—apparently after the first address on the delivery ticket had been crossed out. It read, No. 30, East 40th Street. What was that all about?

The tipping point came when Faith riffled through the family mail one morning toward the end of 1982 and discovered a bill from Bulgari, the ultra-expensive jewelry shop. Faith had not bought anything lately from Bulgari, and Ron had certainly not given her anything, so she opened the bill. What could it be for? It was for a bracelet, purchased by her husband. The bill contained an instruction to remit to Ron's office, but the letter had been delivered to his home instead. It was another address mix up, only this one was fatal. There were plenty of possible explanations for a Murray Hill delivery address on some shirts from the laundry. But there was no ducking this one: The bracelet had been for his little flower girl tramp—Faith just knew it. And the bill for it had been delivered instead into the open arms of [roll of drums, please] *the wife*.[4]

For Ron, that evening and the next day must have been something else, at least if one is to judge from his behavior during the period that followed. Though Faith seems to have said nothing to him of what had happened that afternoon, he surely detected her cool resolve and her distance.

That Friday, a winter's chill swept in from Central Park—just ten shopping days left before Christmas, they were saying on the radio—and passersby along Fifth Avenue would have had their collars turned against the wind. With their eyes fixed on the pavement ahead the way New Yorkers tend to do, they would not have noticed the two men who came striding abruptly from the front door of 36 East 62nd Street, then swung north at the corner and began heading up the block. They were two men on a mission—Perelman and an aide—and they were headed for the flower shop on East 65th. The goal: Well, that was just it . . . there seemed to be no obvious goal. Anger? Rage? A Ron Perelman International Coffee Moment? Whatever it was, Ron now seemed to know what Faith already knew: Namely, his little secret with Snuggles, the neighborhood Galatea.

She was waiting for him, in her car, and she seemed ready to flee. The windows were up, the lights were on in the gathering dusk, and the motor was idling. She saw him approach and she dropped the car into drive, but he stepped in front and she slammed on the brakes. Watching all this, Ron's aide knew better than to stick around any longer, and turned on his heel and quickly strode down the block and around the corner.

Meanwhile, Ron had begun to yell at his lover through the rolled-up car window: *Get out! Get out!* A crowd began to gather. Suzie dropped the car into drive again but Ron leaped in front and halted its progress. She took a breath and opened the window a crack to talk to him. But quick as a flash he was at the driver's door, and jamming his fingers into the opened window, he began to shake the car violently. *Get out! Get out!* The car began to rock back and forth, back and forth, until in an instant the entire window snapped off, and he went rolling into the street. Seeing this, a bystander leaped from the curb to restrain him in the gutter, at which point the car door flew open and Suzie came bounding out to rescue him. Slumping as well to the ground, she cuddled his head in her lap and began kissing his face.

Ron composed himself and began to stand upright as Suzie wiped the glass shards and tears from his eyes and helped him into the car. The storm had passed, the bystanders dispersed, and Perelman knew it surely was all over now. He had crossed the Rubicon of disgrace with his lover. Could he not see the photographers racing to the scene that very instant, their cameras at the ready? He climbed into the back seat and slumped low, as Suzie slid behind the wheel and eased from the curb, destination: Lenox Hill Hospital.

Yet incredibly enough, when he finally returned to the apartment, Faith said nothing, as if this wildest of street scenes had completely escaped her attention. Was she *that* clueless as to what was unfolding all around her? Maybe Ron had simply imagined her suspicions. Could he really be *this* lucky . . . to have married a woman as stupid as she was rich?

By morning he was feeling better, and as the days passed, his thoughts seemed to turn more and more to what he now planned to be doing the following week: Some business as usual. He planned to be away. On business. A week-long business trip. Abroad, in fact . . . to Paris. Yes, that was it, a week-long business trip to Paris . . . all expenses paid by the company. Did the Hotel Plaza-Athenee sound about right? Champagne and caviar at midnight, perhaps? Two minutes down the street and it's the Champs Élysées. Two minutes in the other direction and it's the Crazy Horse Saloon. And of course, his executive assistant, Ms. Kasen, would be handling the details. *Do we really want to go out? I don't want to get dressed, do you? Maybe later. Hmmm.*

It was Sunday morning, the start of Christmas week, when Ron's driver and limo swung to curbside on East 40th Street, and from the front door of No. 30, and into the sunshine, stepped Suzie Cream Cheese, looking as if she were ready for some St. Moritz après-ski and a cover shoot for *Vogue.* She wore a white cashmere sweater and white slacks, and to accent this dream of alabaster perfection, a long brown scarf that fluttered in the breeze. Draped across her arm, she carried the ebony counterpoint of a Blackglama mink coat—all underwritten by Foolish Faith, the out-to-lunch wife.

At Kennedy Airport, the limo eased to a halt in front of the entrance for Air France's departing Concorde flights, and the couple checked aboard and proceeded to the First Class lounge and bar. At the bar, Ron and Suzie chatted quietly, though wrapped within the studied ease of his blue blazer and gray slacks, Ron betrayed the coiled nerves of a man gripped with guilt. The eyes gave it away, panning back and forth across the room for the recognized face, the lingering expression of *Don't I know you . . .?* of the voice that booms out, *"Hey honey, look, it's Ron Perelman and Fai . . . th?"*

And suddenly, there it was, the dreaded moment was upon him, as Ron's face clouded over at an approaching gentleman and his own female companion. Ron turned quickly to Suzie and whispered some instructions, then stepped forward to greet the approaching couple while Suzie remained behind and turned away. The gentleman introduced Ron to his companion, then glanced awkwardly toward Suzie but Ron did not reciprocate. Several minutes passed—an eternity for each of the four—then the man excused himself and with his companion backed away. Suzie had meanwhile retreated to the far end of the waiting room, where she and Ron now huddled in animated whispering until the Concorde flight to Paris was called a few minutes later.

Eight hours later, local time, the Concorde touched down at Charles de Gaulle Airport in Paris and the two cleared Customs. They then entered a waiting limousine and headed for the hotel—a ride punctuated by long soulful kisses as the happy couple celebrated having made it to Paris for Christmas week, undiscovered by a soul.

At approximately a quarter to midnight, the limo pulled to curbside at No. 25, Avenue Montaigne, and they headed into the hotel. It was working so smoothly; Ron had stolen a week from his wife and his family, and it was all gearing forward with the precision of a Patek Phillipe watch.

The connecting rooms on the fourth floor—404/405—had been opened into a suite, just as Ron had requested, and at about 1:20 A.M., having made themselves suitably comfortable in their lovers' hideaway, Ron cracked open the door to the hallway, and glancing up and down the corridor to assure he was not being observed, placed a pair of shoes outside the door to be shined by morning—a service customarily performed by all of Europe's finer hotels.

Momentarily, a guest on the floor emerged from his own room next door to the suite and headed for the elevator for a late-night errand to the lobby.

Anyone observing what happened next would surely have thought it odd.

But the whole point was that no one witnessed anything—which is what the man was being paid to assure would be the case. He paused momentarily before each of the suite's two doorways and delicately balanced the stem of a match between the top of the door and the door jam above it, then proceeded on his way.

He was a private investigator—one of a team of more than six—who had been keeping Ron under surveillance twenty-four hours a day for his enraged wife, Faith. She had hired them the moment she discovered that infuriating Bulgari bill for her husband's mistress, the flower girl floozie from the end of the block.

The team had tracked his every move, from his afternoon trysts in Murray Hill, to his street gutter spectacle on East 65th Street, to his awkward near-discovery at the Air France First Class lounge, to his flight in the Concorde, where a member of the team had been booked in the seat right behind him, to the ride into Paris, and finally into the fourth floor suite of the Plaza Athenee Hotel, where they had booked the very next room on the floor.[5] It seemed Faith Golding Perelman was gearing up to play some hardball of her own.

7

QUESTION FROM THE CHAIRMAN: HOW MUCH DO I WEIGH?

The U.S. economy was undergoing its deepest and most destabilizing downturn since the 1930s when Jack Welch finally became more than a just a name to GE's chairman, Reginald Jones.[1] Under other circumstances, Jones might never have become aware of Welch at all. But the 1970s were already developing into an extraordinary and, in many ways, desperate time for American business, and Jones could feel the pressures as well as anyone. So a routine planning and budget session that Jones presided over not long after becoming chairman at the start of 1973 carried more importance, as far as he was concerned, than might otherwise have been the case. And as luck would have it, at this meeting he encountered Jack Welch for the first time—at his toughest, smartest, and all-around best.

Jones had officially taken over as GE's chairman from his predecessor—a man named Fred Borch—on December 15, 1972, and the passing of the baton proved awkwardly timed to say the least, for scarcely had the new man settled into his new job than the Egyptian Army crossed the Suez Canal, unleashing the Yom Kippur War. The invasion caused the United States to rush military aid to Israel, and this provoked the oil-exporting nations of the Arab world to announce an embargo of oil exports to the United States. Almost immediately, the stock market collapsed, knocking two-thirds of the value off GE's stock price in a slide that eventually bottomed out but could not be reversed for years to come.

A tall, gaunt, chain-smoking Briton, Jones greeted the world with a reserved demeanor and a furrowed brow even in the best of times. And the start of his career as GE's tenth leader since the company's founding in 1892 was hardly a time to be looked back on fondly by anyone in business, let alone this business leader with the sensibilities of an Old Etonian Tory and the looks of the Duke of Windsor; he was simply overwhelmed by events.

Beset with a collapsed stock market, soaring oil prices, and Spenglerian editorials about the decline of the West, Jones seemed to move through his days enveloped in perpetual gloom about GE's future if radical action weren't taken, and quickly. "The place had become so ossified and hierarchal that it was impossible to get anything done," says an executive who worked at corporate headquarters during the period. "Arguing over inertia had become everyone's job."

The company needed to be streamlined and reorganized so that it could compete in a world in which the only constant seemed overnight to have become relentless, accelerating, and threatening change. But what exactly should he do? Everywhere he looked business leaders were as uncertain as he was.

After a quarter century of global hegemony, an entire generation of American "corporate statesmen" suddenly found themselves with their backs to the wall: Irving Shapiro of E.I. Du Pont de Nemours, Richard Gerstenberg of General Motors, Edgar Speer of U.S. Steel, Walter Wriston of First National City Corporation, John

DeButts of AT&T. For more than twenty years, men such as these—and their colleagues, predecessors, and business leader rivals—had been the voices of unchallenged authority regarding how best to organize economic activity and deploy it globally for maximum return.

Now they seemed to be wondering whether they even knew what they'd been talking about. Whichever way one turned, the American economy looked to be at war with business itself. In the wake of the oil crisis, consumer price inflation, already moving up steadily as a result of the Vietnam War (which by this time was actually winding down), now shot into orbit. Meanwhile, productivity growth began to slow and eventually to peter out entirely, even as unemployment rose steadily. A whole new concept in political economics turned up: the Misery Index. You added the unemployment and inflation rates together and you got an index number of just how economically miserable the American people were thought to be.

Big and presumably rock-solid companies began to teeter, while second- and third-tier companies started dropping like flies. Meanwhile, industries like automaking, shipbuilding, and steel manufacturing—weakened by unions that had been demanding, and getting, some of the highest wages on earth—suddenly found themselves in frantic retreat from rival industries in countries like Japan and West Germany, which many Americans had smugly assumed were still recovering from World War II.

Business leaders everywhere knew something was wrong, but few seemed to have a clear idea what to do about it, and those who did lacked business structures flexible enough to get anything done anyway.

Like many large manufacturing and industrial businesses that traced their roots to the turn of the century, GE had operated from the start as basically a holding company with a small and centralized corporate management ruling over what eventually developed into nearly a dozen separate operating fiefdoms, which the company called "Works." They were scattered across most of the Northeast quadrant of the United States, in the cities where GE either started— or more commonly, acquired—businesses of one sort or another.

During the World War II years, GE and the country's other leading manufacturing enterprises adapted easily to the evolving bureaucracy of the Pentagon and the War Department, and a lot of the resulting heft at the corporate level carried over into the 1950s. But efforts to reform and streamline the structure for the demands of civilian life simply resulted in whole new layers of bureaucracy being piled on top of what was already there.

Ralph Cordiner, the company's president at the start of the 1950s, led the most notable of these efforts.* Standing barely five feet tall in his stocking feet, Cordiner seemed determined to wrestle the GE bureaucracy into submission one way or another—to which end he proceeded to break up the Works operations (by then totaling eleven) into 190 separate "departments," some with yearly revenues of barely $2 million. Cordiner asserted control over this fragmented system through nearly fifty separate and specially created "Divisions"—in effect, a vast new layer of management bureaucracy inserted where none had existed before. These divisions reported to just under a dozen "Groups," and the Groups reported to Cordiner.

To make sure that everyone in these new levels of management was on the same page, Cordiner next set up a management training center in the Westchester County village of Crotonville, north of New York City. He then had his aides codify the collective managerial wisdom of GE (as interpreted by Cordiner) into a five-volume encyclopedia of organizational bafflegab called the "Blue Books,"

---

* Among other things for which he is remembered, Cordiner hired Ronald Reagan ("Tall, handsome, and well spoken . . .") to be GE's pitchman. The company furnished the Reagans with an "all-electric home" that was featured in GE advertisements. Reagan is best known as the host of *GE Theater*, which ran weekly on CBS from 1954 to 1962.

which soon enough generated a whole new bureaucracy of Blue Book "enforcers."[2]

After Cordiner came another GE chairman, Fred Borch, who tried to make GE's superstructure more manageable, only to wind up making it even bigger and more unwieldy. Borch's unique contribution: To increase the number of departments by a third, to 350, and to create an "Executive Office of the CEO" with three vice chairmen sandwiched between Borch and the Groups.*

Somehow, this entire apparatus needed to be disassembled and discarded in favor of something leaner and more nimble, so that it didn't take forever to get the company to act on an idea, or even make a decision. But although Jones knew what needed to be done, his retiring temperament seemed to hold him back, and after three years as chairman and CEO, GE was still weighed down with the same unwieldy management hierarchy it had inherited from Borch. To Jones, reforming GE was turning out to be like trying to alter the course of a supertanker underway; you needed five miles of forward motion to shift the ship's heading by just one degree.[3]

So it was Jones' good fortune—and Welch's as well—that the two men were to meet at a moment when everything Jones felt he needed to begin turning GE in a new direction would wind up standing before him—at this otherwise forgettable budget and planning meeting—in the person of Jack Welch.

At this point, Jones himself had been in his job for less than a year and he was already coming to dislike these sessions—especially the little presentation kits that the various Group heads prepared and used like show-and-tell props. As far as Jones was concerned, they all suffered from the same fundamental dishonesty—what Jones liked to

---

* In one of his last missions before turning over the chairmanship of GE to Jones, Borch led a group of a dozen like-minded CEOs in a pro-business lobbying effort in Washington. The group developed into the Business Roundtable the following year and is today regarded as the leading such organization of its type.

think of as "the hockey stick forecast." Each could be counted on to show basically the same thing: Group earnings declining steadily for several quarters as capital investment in some grand new project ramped up . . . followed by earnings shooting through the ceiling year-after-year for the next half decade as the company harvested the rewards of the Group leader's brilliance. Jones had become fed up with the very idea of these useless forecasts.

But Welch's presentation proved entirely different, and reviewing it in advance of the meeting, Jones could see that a great deal of thought and effort had gone into it. Performance forecasts were set forth in detail, quarter-by-quarter, for every specific product line in Welch's Group. Customer demand forecasts were also set forth, once again in detail, and once again for each specific product in the Group. There were forecasts for penetration into new markets, and flowcharts to show the planned development of new products, indicating when they would become marketable to customers, and when return revenue flows would begin.

It was a completely different presentation from anything Jones had seen before—maybe different from anything that anyone at GE had ever produced before—for *any* chairman or CEO. It was unique—a forecast that fully and carefully brought together the outlook for products and cash flows at the Group level over the next five years.

Reviewing it, Jones thought to himself, "Say, this is really something. This is really well thought through. It's well considered."

By the time the meeting began, Jones had read the presentation several times over and had prepared plenty of questions to ask the young Group head. He was going to put him through his paces, make the man defend his work as if he were facing off against the senior faculty in his PhD orals.

Yet, by the end of the session it was Jones—and not Welch—who'd been rendered speechless. Granted, Welch was a short, pugnacious fellow, with an adenoidal voice and a working-class Boston accent. And he had some annoying nervous habits and twitches that Jones didn't much care for—especially when it came to biting his nails and punctuating his speech with staccato-like stammering at odd moments.

In fact, in every way one might have imagined, the two men were polar opposites. Welch stood five feet eight inches and sometimes looked even shorter, thanks in part to his habit of wearing blue blazers and gray slacks to every function—a two-toned color ensemble that emphasized the very stubbiness of his fire hydrant frame. What's more, he liked to boast of maintaining an "open door" policy to his office—though the boast was meaningless because few executives seemed to welcome the experience of barging in on him unannounced.

By contrast, Jones stood six feet four inches and looked even taller—thanks largely to his office uniform of a dark blue suit, white shirt, and muted tie. Taken together, the ensemble created the appearance of an individual who somehow seemed larger than life. Other GE executives spoke of the hushed stillness of his office, and the sense that would overtake them upon entering it, of being in a mighty place, ruled by a powerful but benevolent leader. One did not raise one's voice in this place, for the simple reason that one did not need to: When the leader spoke, the mere speaking of the words was enough to command attention.*

Yet so far as Jones was concerned, all that was nothing when weighed against the substance of Welch's answers: He had a ready, well-reasoned response for every single question Jones put to him.

---

*Said a GE executive not long after the Welch appointment as chairman and CEO was announced, "When I used to go to see Reg Jones, I thought I was entering the Oval Office. But when I go to see Jack, it's just like visiting one of the guys." *Business Week* (March 18, 1981), p. 110.

In fact, when Jones later reflected on the performance, it seemed almost as if Welch had actually anticipated Jones' questions—and rehearsed his answers—before he ever left Pittsfield.*

After the meeting, Jones asked Welch's immediate boss, a vice chairman named Herman Weiss, to chat for minute. He said, "Herm, this Welch fellow is someone we've got to be bringing along. I think we should get him down here to Fairfield, show him some more of GE than what's up there in Pittsfield."

Not long after, Weiss reported back that he had put the idea to Welch, but that the young man had declined; and Jones thought, "He's a big fish in a small pond up there, but he's going to have to make up his mind."

〰〰〰

As the economic crisis of the 1970s continued to spread, Jones came to see Welch more and more as a potential savior for the corporation. And it thus became easier and easier to accept the very unpredictability of the man—charming one minute, abrasive the next—as the price one had to pay to purchase his strengths. And those strengths were, frankly, obvious. First of all he was smart, with a knack for taking complex ideas and reducing them to core concepts that helped him make his point. And who knew, when people spoke of his street fighter's charisma, maybe they were referring to that adder-like wit and the mercurial tongue.

Of course, dogged as Jones was with the problems besetting his company, he had little time to inform himself of the downside to Welch's odd and idiosyncratic approach to employee relations—especially when their greatest impact might lie buried in bureaucratic

---

*In that, Jones was certainly right. All sources who were interviewed for this book regarding Welch's management style agreed that he was almost fanatical in his attention to detail concerning both the substance of his presentations and the theatrics with which he liked to embellish them.

effluvium twenty-five levels down in the organization. As Jones himself was willing enough to admit, the bureaucracy of GE had grown
so suffocating over the years that it was hard to stay abreast of the
day-to-day activities of executives even three levels below him.*

So given all that, it is highly unlikely that Jones knew anything
at all of the bizarre world of Becker House that had been Welch's
springboard to higher office, let alone of the person who became its
first casualty. Yet, plenty of people in Selkirk itself knew, and one of
them was Bob Kunze.

Not terribly comfortable with the situation in Selkirk to begin
with, nor seemingly very eager to ingratiate himself with Welch and
the Jack Pack, Kunze eventually landed a job in GE Plastics, Europe,
and by 1968 he was gone even as Welch himself had by now returned to Pittsfield to take on broader responsibilities than just the
Noryl project in Selkirk.

But it was Welch who had set the tone of the place in Selkirk as its
first leader. And after his departure, nothing changed. In fact, things
seemed to grow worse. As a result, stories from Selkirk kept reaching
Kunze—in particular about his former secretary, Regina—who had
apparently morphed during her brief GE career from a quiet young
woman who minded her own business into a kind of wild party animal who was getting passed around among the men of Becker House
as if she were nothing more than a slab of meat with tits.

The gossip about Regina's behavior was relentless, and so was
the seeming enthusiasm of her new boss, Tom ("Fitzy") Fitzgerald,
to keep everyone up to speed on the latest developments. Did you
know, for example, that Regina had been seen in town the other day
with one of the hardhats from outside in the yard? Or did you know

---

*In N. Tichy and S. Sherman, *Control Your Destiny or Someone Else Will* (New York: Harper
Business Books, 2001), the authors note that by the time Jones retired in 1981, nine entire layers of management separated department level executives from the CEO (p. 58).

about the other night at the Bush? You didn't hear what happened? How she was over there by the jukebox, smoking and flirting with half the second floor, when her husband came storming in and dragged her out, and there was a big row in the street? You missed all that?

It is unclear when Bob Kunze actually learned of the suicide of Regina Paulsen. By the time she took her life, in August 1974, Kunze was gone not only from Selkirk but from GE entirely, and was about to begin work in a management position at W.R. Grace & Company, the chemicals firm, which he thereafter left as well. Nonetheless, the news of what had happened to Regina eventually caught up with him anyway.

Leaving the chemicals and plastics industry, Kunze moved next into investment banking, becoming a partner in the West Coast venture capital firm of Hambrecht & Quist, where his career flourished in the biotech and high-technology booms of the 1980s and 1990s. He became a wealthy man and an outside director on the boards of various companies. But neither the passage of time nor the accumulation of wealth could bury for long his festering thoughts about his secretary back in Selkirk.

Carbon monoxide poisoning is the most common form of toxin-induced death in the United States. The gas, which is both colorless and odorless, kills its victims by starving them of oxygen. This is because red blood cells, which transport oxygen to the cells of the body, are 200 times more likely to bind to carbon monoxide than to blood, so that a relative small quantity of carbon monoxide can block the blood from transporting *any* oxygen to the cells. Starvation occurs first in the brain and heart—the two internal organs of the body that have the highest metabolic rates and thus need the most oxygen to function.

Because the amount of gas that is inhaled determines the effects of carbon monoxide poisoning, it is possible to become incompletely poisoned from carbon monoxide inhalation and begin to display symptoms of a variety of common illnesses and infections, including influenza and Parkinson's disease. A person suffering from carbon monoxide poisoning as a result of low-level leakage of the gas into his residence over many years can be misdiagnosed as suffering from chronic diarrhea, hearing loss, vertigo, kidney failure, edema, angina, memory impairment, Tourette's syndrome, fecal and urinary incontinence, and schizophrenia. All these can be caused by an incompletely burning flame on a gas-fired water heater with a partially blocked chimney flue.

But the intentional breathing of carbon monoxide fumes in a confined space can also bring about certain death in a matter of five to eight minutes. The progression of the poisoning begins with the acceleration of the heartbeat, as the heart struggles to increase the flow of blood containing its diminished supply of oxygen. Next, the room begins to grow progressively darker. The victim soon senses a constricting feeling of tightness across the forehead, followed by chest palpitations. Next the skeletal muscles collapse and lose the ability to function. After that, the brain enters a coma and the heart's beating grows weaker and fainter.

Even at this point, it is still possible to revive a person from carbon monoxide poisoning, and the victim will usually show no lasting effects. The simple and most effective method is to administer pure oxygen for twenty to forty minutes. Failure to do this before the breathing grows too weak to transmit the lifesaving gas to the lungs will bring on death, which is how the life of Regina Paulsen ended at some point during the daylight hours of Monday, August 26, 1974.

There were plenty of reasons for a person to have felt depressed in the United States during the month of August 1974—at least politically. On August 2, the two top aides of President Richard Nixon were jailed for their cover-up roles in the Watergate scandal. Six days later, Richard Nixon became the first president in American history to resign from office, quitting as the climax to the two-year-long scandal, the worst of its kind in U.S. history. The economy was equally troubled, with short-term interest rates climbing to their highest levels since the end of World War II, while the stock market fell to its lowest levels since the Great Depression.

It is doubtful whether any of these developments contributed to Regina Paulsen's decision to kill herself, but it is impossible to be sure because she left no suicide note. Neighbors later told New York State Police investigators that she had been despondent in recent months, yet no one seemed to know why.

Her husband, John, discovered the body when he returned home from work late that afternoon, opened the garage door, and found his lifeless wife slumped on the floor in a doorway into the house, her skin bright red.

An autopsy was performed by the Albany County Medical Examiner, DeForest Deitz, and the obvious ruling was rendered: Death by suicide, carbon monoxide poisoning. Several months later, John Paulsen put their home up for sale and moved from the area, dying theafter of heart failure. After that, the New York State Police barracks that had investigated the case was shut down in a budget cutback and its records were destroyed. This was followed by the death of the Albany County Medical Examiner, DeForest Deitz, and the shredding of his files as well.

In time, all that remained of Regina Paulsen's life was a seven-sentence story in the Albany *Times Union* newspaper that bore the headline, "Coeymans Death Ruled Gas Suicide," and was judged so small and inconsequential that it was never entered into any electronic news database. In the process, almost all traces of the life of Regina Paulsen were effectively erased from the earth.

Yet, there is nothing more haunting than the ghost of someone wronged, and for the following twenty years the dead hand of Regina Paulsen beckoned from her grave, as the men of Becker

House turned away and went about their lives, until, it would seem, Bob Kunze could stand it no longer and turned back to look.

∼∼∼

Meanwhile, the situation for both GE and Jones continued to worsen. The left-leaning Club of Rome* had already set the tone of the decade in 1972 by calling for "zero growth" in the developed nations of the West—this allegedly being the only way that mankind could save itself from the profit-driven scourge of capitalist organizations like GE. Amidst all this, the president of the United States was driven from office by the Watergate scandal. His successor, Speaker of the House Gerald Ford, had held the office for all of seven weeks before giving a speech in Detroit in which he warned of an approaching "breakdown in world order and safety."

As if on cue, Palestinian terrorist leader Yasir Arafat turned up at the United Nations and addressed the General Assembly . . . with a gun strapped to his waist. Four months later, the U.S.-backed leader of Saudi Arabia, King Faisal, was murdered. Weeks after that, Saigon fell to the Communists; and days later still, a group of Cambodians in patrol boats captured a U.S. merchant ship, the *Mayaguez,* and a U.S. rescue party of Marines trying to recapture it was repulsed with a loss of thirty-eight lives.

It was in that context that Jones seemed, in a way, to put GE on automatic pilot as he began to add what he hoped would be a clarifying voice of reason to the panicky babble that had engulfed Washington. He began to testify before Congress on the need for stimulative tax credits for business. He joined presidential committees and

---

* This global think tank enjoyed a considerable following during the stagflation 1970s, in large part because of a book of dire economic forecasts entitled *The Limits to Growth* that was published in 1972 under the organization's aegis. The global economic boom of the 1980s and 1990s seemed to undermine the book's grim vision of the future, with the result that the organization lost much of its clout as a voice in world economic affairs.

panels, spoke before trade groups, and soon was making almost weekly appearances of one sort or another in Washington. Meanwhile, he turned his co-chairmanship position at the Business Roundtable and his chairmanship of the Export Council into pulpits to encourage other business leaders to join him. And all the while, the problems at GE continued to worsen.

By 1977, it was clear that something simply had to be done, and in what amounted almost to a desperation move, Jones picked up the phone and called Welch in Pittsfield and summoned him to Fairfield to lay it on the line. He said, "You're obviously very ambitious, Jack, and you want to move up in the company. You've done very well, but with a small slice of this business, and as you know we are diverse way beyond just the Plastics and Materials part with which you've been associated. If you aspire to a higher level, you've got to come to Fairfield to work at some other businesses of this company. You have to understand the breadth and diversification of General Electric."

Two days later, Welch telephoned him back. He said, "I've made the decision, I'll do it."

What happened next is something that no one who lived through it will ever forget. Promoted to the job of "Sector Executive" and given responsibility for managing GE's consumer products and finance operations, Welch found himself teed up against several rivals in competing "Sector Executive" posts. It amounted to a three-year-long beauty contest to be crowned Jones' successor as GE chairman.

With the eyes of both the chairman and the board of directors thus on him, Welch thereupon erupted in a brutal, attention-getting campaign of cost cutting throughout his sector's far-flung operations. It was Welch's way of saying, "Make me chairman and this is what I'll do to the whole corporation." And though his sector's abruptly surging earnings impressed Jones, his performance became the talk of terrorized rank-and-file employees and their managers throughout the corporation, as Welch drilled home the message at every plant he visited: Things were going to be different now.[4]

On a visit to the Cleveland headquarters for GE's light bulb manufacturing operation, Welch waved a bulb in the face of the department head, and snarled, "They can make these things in Hungary for half what we charge! Any idea why?" Next, Welch sent the bulb to a GE lab for an analysis of its similarities and differences versus a Hungarian bulb. The answer that Welch had expected came back from the lab: There were no differences between the two. Welch's anger reached the boiling point when he learned that the Cleveland headquarters had a full-time barber and dentist on the payroll, and that the company was maintaining an onsite swimming pool for executives. It was all the ammo Welch needed: Bye-bye, department head.

GE employees fretted that they might fall victim to one or another of various and random prejudices that Welch was believed to nurse—such as his rumored dislike of fat people, and of people who wore white socks.

During a visit to the company's small appliances operation in Bridgeport, a twenty-minute drive from the corporate headquarters in Fairfield, the trembling became almost palpable when Welch asked the plant manager, "How much do I weigh?" An assistant scurried off, then returned with one of GE's new line of digital bathroom scales, and placed it on the floor before the new chairman.

Welch stepped on the scale, looked down, then stepped off. Then he stepped back on. Then he stepped off. Then he roared, "What the fuck is this! Every time I step on this thing I get a different weight! I still don't know how much I weigh!" Thereafter, he began talks to sell the entire small appliances operation to Black and Decker.

Everywhere he went, news of his favorite expression preceded him: "What the fuck do I pay you for!" He was diabolically clever at reading the psychology of anyone who seemed intimidated by that question. During a visit to a housewares trade show in Louisville, Welch watched as a group of nervous GE execs wheeled out a GE dishwasher. Then he exploded: "What the fuck are you showing me this for? I haven't been in a kitchen in ten years!" Then he answered his own question. "I know what you're doing, you brought that thing out here so you can say, 'See this new machine? Isn't purple a great color?' Then if the machine doesn't sell, you can say that I agreed purple was a great color, so you're off the hook. Well, fuck that, I'm not going to say it."

Meanwhile, though Jones played along with the process he had initiated, and wound up eventually dragging it out until nearly everyone in the beauty contest except Welch was ready to quit the company, he seemed on some personal level to have made up his mind from the start: This company had to be shaken to its roots, and of all the available candidates for the job, only Welch seemed up to the task.

As a result, on December 15, 1980—the same day that the New York Yankees signed slugger Dave Winfield to a $25 million contract that would make him the highest paid and most talked about player in baseball—Jones told Welch that GE's board had voted unanimously, on Jones' recommendation, to offer the job of chairman and CEO to Welch.

For the company, its employees, and its shareholders, a new day had begun, as the human tornado known as Neutron Jack Welch prepared to rip through their lives. And he began immediately.

With the whole of the corporation now in his grasp, Welch did exactly what his performance as Sector Executive had anticipated, initiating a corporate Reign of Terror that wiped out nearly 40,000 jobs in the first nine months and slashed another 60,000 from the payroll in the following two years. He fired every strategic planning specialist GE had on its payroll and transferred their functions to line managers. He eliminated the sector management level created by Jones for the beauty contest, along with all its staff support—and that was only the beginning.[5]

When news reached a plant or factory that the new CEO would be arriving for a visit, local managers would panic. All fat people were told to stay out of sight. In Cincinnati, the local plant manager grew so desperate to show progress in a head-count reduction that he had a list prepared of every deceased GE employee who had worked in Cincinnati, to have at the ready if Welch should ask for a head-count reduction total.

At Becker House in Selkirk, New York, local executives had recently hired the plant's first black scientist, a young chemical engineer from MIT. Not knowing whether Welch felt the same about blacks as he was said to feel about fat people, and not wanting to take any chances, the man's boss took him aside with an urgently whispered instruction: Neutron Jack was on the way, so Joe was to stay out of sight until he got the all clear.*

Through it all, few areas of the country suffered more than the mid-Hudson River Valley of New York State and western Massachusetts. In this region—bounded by Pittsfield and the Berkshire foothills of Massachusetts to the east, and the aging industrial communities of New York State's mid-Hudson River Valley to the west—sat the manufacturing heartland of the "old" GE.

Here could be found century-old industrial cities like Schenectady, New York, where Thomas Edison had located GE's first machine

---

*The newly hired engineer, Joseph Jett, remained with GE for three years before leaving to pursue an MBA at Harvard. But GE, and Welch, soon looped back into his life when Jett landed a job as a trader at the Wall Street investment firm of Kidder Peabody & Company, where he quickly developed into one of its most important producers. Almost immediately thereafter, GE bought Kidder Peabody, which collapsed after evidence surfaced of widespread fraud in the organization. This time, instead of telling Jett to stay out of sight, his trembling bosses put the spotlight of blame on Jett himself. See J. Jett, *Black and White on Wall Street* (New York: Morrow, 1999), p. 196.

shop in 1886, in an abandoned broom factory. By the 1920s, Schenectady had grown into the corporate headquarters of the entire company, and was still officially listed that way in government filings
when Welch became chairman and CEO in 1981. Out of GE's
Schenectady factories had poured the turbines and generators that
powered America's electrical revolution in the twentieth century,
giving jobs to nearly 15 percent of GE's entire workforce of
315,000 on the day Welch became chairman.

Ten miles to the east of Schenectady sat the Hudson River town
of Waterford, home to GE's silicone products division, one of the
many GE operations in the region that came under Welch's control
as he moved up the corporate ladder. Twenty miles to the south lay
the town of Selkirk, where GE had constructed the plastics plant in
the 1960s that first brought Welch to the attention of corporate
higher-ups. And across the river from Selkirk to the east lay Pittsfield, where Welch had begun his career.

Like Schenectady, Pittsfield was devastated in the Reign of Terror unleashed by the man who had once called the place home. In
round after round, the layoffs came, beginning with the closing of
the city's transformer factory,[6] and the decimation of the ordnance
operation,[7] until 80 percent of the GE's entire workforce in the city
had disappeared.

As the regional economy began to implode, "out of business"
signs began appearing in store windows of one town after the next.
After that came the drug trafficking and gang violence, and the
spread of burglaries, prostitution, and gay sex for hire. Trafficking in
the latter two vices soon spread from the region's downtown areas
to the rest stops along Interstate 87, the main arterial right-of-way
through the region, threatening the tourist industry of Saratoga
County and Upper New York State. In towns like Clifton Park, the
local police began surveillance and cleanup drives, but the problem
just kept growing.

Local politicians appealed to Albany, Boston, and even Washington for economic assistance—whatever could be done to bring in new industries and to retrain workers. But GE had been the linchpin of the region's economy for generations, and its departure had come so abruptly and convulsively that people were simply overwhelmed by the resulting devastation.

Searching for a way to strike back, local leaders began focusing on the environmental despoliation GE had left in its wake—most specifically in the form of what are known as polychlorinated biphenyls (PCBs). These chemicals had been used by electrical equipment manufacturers since the early 1930s—in GE's case at two plants that dumped wastewater contaminated with PCBs directly into the upper Hudson River, and at a third plant in Pittsfield that poured the waste into streams feeding the Housatonic River eighty miles upstream from Long Island Sound.

In 1976, the federal government had banned the further manufacture or use of PCBs after a series of studies appeared to show them to be carcinogenic to humans. But by then it was too late—at least for GE—and the company soon found itself entangled in fights with New York State regulators and Washington's environmental lobby over whether the chemicals were in fact carcinogenic at all, and whether GE should have to pay for removing them from the environment.

The dispute had simmered for years and might have died away altogether had it not been for the massive region-wide economic upheaval for which Welch was being personally blamed. Almost overnight, the PCB issue became front-page news all over again as furious citizens of the Hudson Valley renewed their campaigns to get the government to force GE to clean up the environment.

The scapegoating of Welch was unfair because the new GE leader was simply doing what CEOs all over the country were doing as they struggled to lead their companies out of the trough of the

Reagan recession. Yet Welch made himself an irresistible target by his defiant public stance, which seemed to say that he actually enjoyed the attacks—many of them highly personalized in nature—as he went about the unpleasant work of saving his company from ruin. And for that he was destined to pay a price, as GE workers grew increasingly eager to believe the worst about their leader.

8

STRETCH ROLE TIME FOR GARY AND THE PREACHER'S DAUGHTER

Though Jack Welch has been praised for transforming GE from a creaking conglomerate into a grand and lean growth stock, most of what fell to the bottom line as earnings came either from the mass firing of employees or from the efforts of an oddly mannered GE executive named Gary Carl Wendt, who was eventually fired by Welch when he became a contender for Welch's job. When people speak of GE's "transformation" under Welch, what they are really referring to is the redeployment of the company's capital away from manufacturing and toward the GE business that Wendt headed: Financial Services.*

On the day Welch took over as chairman and CEO in April 1981, GE's Consumer Products and Appliance divisions dominated the corporation, accounting for 25 percent of all the company's revenue and

---

*The group, known as GE Credit Corporation when Wendt took it over in 1986, changed its name to GE Capital Corporation in March 1998 and has since been separated into four separate businesses under the overall name of GE Financial Services Corporation.

19 percent of its net income. The contributions eclipsed any other operation of the company in either category. When it came to the conveniences of modern life, GE ruled the American home, from room air conditioners to refrigerators, from kitchen ranges to toaster ovens to light bulbs.

Yet by the start of the 1980s, the markets for these products had matured to the point that sales were growing no faster than the economy as a whole. As a result, the heart of GE had become, in the phrase of the day, a "GNP company," captive to forces over which GE had no control and little influence, such as the federal budget and the nation's money supply.

So Welch embarked on a plan to direct the company's capital into sectors where growth was faster—financial services—while forcing round after round of cost cutting, layoffs, and plant closings on operations such as Consumer Products and Appliances.[1] Years later, Wendt looked back on the period and summed up Welch's leadership this way: "Every planning meeting Jack ran was always the same. He'd tell everyone else to cut costs, and he'd tell me to grow the business."

In the two decades of Welch's chairmanship, the company never wavered from this course, and by the year 2000, revenues from the sale of GE products for the consumer had fallen by 20 percent from their 1981 level, and capital investment in the sector had been cut by nearly 30 percent. At the same time, financial services wound up accounting for more than half the company's revenues and profits.*

---

*GE's Depression-era president, Gerald Swope, had set up GE Credit Corporation in 1932 as a way to help cash-strapped customers purchase GE home appliances such as refrigerators via time payments. In effect, GE was simply substituting its own balance sheet and credit rating for that of its customers.

By avoiding the use of deposits raised from the public and instead obtaining the cash it needed by borrowing the money from rapidly growing—and almost totally unregulated—pools of capital like the Eurodollar market and the so-called commercial

To many at GE, Wendt's squat appearance and short fuse suggested almost a doppelganger of Welch, and when Wendt's name began appearing in print toward the end of the 1990s as a possible successor to Welch, few in the company seemed surprised that Welch fired him—though no one believed the parting was as amicable as Welch wound up claiming in his business memoir, *Jack: Straight from the Gut*.[2] The more likely reason, as everyone knew, was the increasing power that Wendt had been accumulating within the corporation—and the recognition he was beginning to receive from the world at large as GE's secret weapon. And there was plenty of water cooler speculation as well that Wendt's domestic situation may have also played a role in his ouster by Welch.

Gary Wendt was born and raised in the Midwest farm town of Rio, Wisconsin, in March 1942, which was the absolute low point for the United States in World War II. From the date of his birth onward, pretty much everything seemed to go right for America and for Gary Wendt as well. He was smart, he was lucky, and he was also growing up in the Wisconsin dairyland twenty-fives miles from Madison, where the high school class of 1961 was full of young people who still did what they were told by parents who expected no less of them.

---

paper market, GE Credit became in effect the first of the United States' "nonbank banks." At the start of the 1970s, bottom-line earnings of GE Credit stood at less than $43 million annually, or barely 4 percent of GE's overall pretax income. Yet during the following decade, the share more than doubled, and by the end of the 1990s, it stood at nearly 40 percent of total GE corporate earnings. By autumn 2003, the company's credit businesses were contributing more than half of GE's total net income.

Had that growth in earnings contributions from GE Credit not occurred, GE would have wound up no better an investment during the bull market of the 1980s and 1990s than many other stocks in the Standard & Poor's 500 Index. Welch would have been viewed as a good manager, to be sure, but he hardly would have qualified for accolades such as the one *Fortune* bestowed on him in 2000 as "Manager of the Century" (November 22, 1999)—specifically citing the return to investors in GE's stock during Welch's years at the helm.

In this world of received values, where no one yet challenged authority, it seemed only natural—like the passing of the seasons in the rhythms of life—that the class valedictorian, who happened to be Gary, would sooner or later wind up marrying his high school sweetheart. And that is exactly what he did.

Her name was Lorna Jorgenson, and in marrying her he was definitely marrying up.[3] Gary's parents were German-Americans who ran a small limestone grinding business in town. They had never been to college and had worked hard all their lives.

Like many other such couples in this conservative community of 760 residents, the Wendts attended Sunday services at Rio's Redeemer Lutheran Church, where the church's benevolent but stern pastor, Rev. Jorgenson, kept his flock ever mindful of God's Word, that the wages of sin is death (Romans 6:23). Rev. Jorgenson was educated and wise, and when he spoke, the farm folk of Rio listened—especially Gary, who'd been trying to get his hands on the reverend's nubile young daughter, Lorna, from the moment she'd turned up a year behind him in high school as a freshman when he was already a worldly tenth grader.

By Gary's senior year, he and Lorna reigned unchallenged as the school's couple to die for. As befitting a young man of such evident promise, Gary competed in every organized sport the school had going, and Lorna cheered from the sidelines as Gary won letters in all of them. Both Lorna and Gary played in the school band; he played the trombone, she played the oboe. Both were members of the school glee club, and naturally enough, both attended church services each Sunday before the distant but approving gaze of Rev. Jorgenson, who continued to remind one and all that, as it is written in Ephesians 2:3, "Man is born unto the world a sinner, and only through God's Son may the weary find rest" (Matthew 11:28).

In his senior year of high school, Gary was accepted at the University of Wisconsin, where his plan was to obtain a degree in civil engineering and then return to Rio to work for the state highway department. And every weekend of his freshman year, Lorna came to visit him from high school, where she was still a senior.

The trips cannot have caused much joy to flutter in the bosom of the good reverend, though his opinions on the matter do not seem to have affected her weekly round-trips one way or the other. Her father may actually have encouraged her to follow Gary to the university and begin a program of study in the teaching of music upon her own high school graduation.

At some point during these adventures, Gary encountered the same sort of wise and worldly faculty figure that Dennis Kozlowski was encountering 1,500 miles away in Newark, New Jersey: a teacher capable of inspiring a bright young fellow to try a stretch role—in Gary's case, to limn a more distant shore than a life spent as a civil engineer for the Wisconsin state highway department.

Following the man's sage counsel, Gary applied to the Harvard Business School and was accepted. Then he married Lorna, and with tuition money from his parents, and $2,500 in the bank, the two headed for Cambridge, where Lorna began work as a music teacher to pay the rent while Gary acquired the credentials that would eventually lead him to, and through, the portals of GE.

The young couple arrived at GE by way of a series of false starts that did not augur well for Gary's career, Harvard MBA or not. His first job, selling real estate in Houston, didn't pan out. This led to a job selling condominiums in Florida, which cratered when oil prices exploded in the 1973/1974 energy crisis. Finally, in the summer of 1975, he landed a job as a workout specialist in the real estate division of GE Credit Corporation in Stamford, Connecticut. At thirty-two years of age, with two children, and trailing behind him a resume of two false starts that had devoured nearly a decade of his post-Harvard life, Wendt seemed destined for a career of, at best, middle-management mediocrity.

The impression was bolstered by his nondescript stature; this was a man who was neither large and regal enough looking to be imposing, nor small and intense enough to be scary. He was simply the nebbish down the hall, with the sallow complexion and a pair of perpetually wet lips. Who could imagine such a person as CEO of anything? On a hot summer day, one could more easily imagine that Gary Wendt's shoes squished when he walked.

But looks can be deceiving in an aspiring leader, and though a sixty-year-old advertising executive may think he's still "got game" for another half decade with a bit of cosmetic touching up around the eyes, a nobody who is thirty-two and arrives unannounced can move up the corporate ladder rapidly in his camouflage of "You know, that guy down the hall . . . Gary."

What's more, the GE operation that Wendt had gone to work for was, in 1975, no different from the creaking, frightened bureaucracy that GE as a whole had become. And when, in 1977, Reg Jones reassigned Welch from Pittsfield and brought him down to GE's corporate headquarters in Fairfield, Connecticut, where he took on the job of sector executive, Wendt got a close-up opportunity to observe the much-talked-about plastics man in action. Reason: Not only was GE's headquarters a mere twenty-minute drive up the Merritt Parkway from GE Credit in Stamford, but Jones had included GE Credit in the group of businesses, along with Consumer Products and Appliances, for which Welch would now be responsible.

In this way, Wendt saw firsthand how Welch was bringing one GE department after the next to heel. Not only did Welch come to meetings fully prepared on the details of everything that would be discussed, but he seemed to be *always* prepared, whether a meeting was coming up or not. Like Harold Geneen of ITT, who had stepped down as head of the world's best known (and in recent years, most notorious) conglomerate earlier that same year (1977), Welch seemed to know more about the business minutiae of his departments and divisions than did even the executives directly responsible for them.*

What's more, Welch actually seemed to enjoy picking fights with his executives, probing around the table at meetings, looking for whoever had come to the meeting unprepared. Then he would pounce, like some beast lurking in the tall grass of the Serengeti, and rip the man to shreds. Then he would eye everyone else around the table. Anyone want to be next?[†] It was Welch's way of asserting control—the street-corner tough kid and bully from North Salem, keeping his gang members in line.[‡]

Wendt took the performances to heart. He needed to praise people when they did their jobs well, because Welch did that, too. But he also needed to be cold and analytical. He needed to be up to speed on every imaginable detail of the business, and even be

---

* Geneen was said by colleagues to have a computer-like ability to process financial details in his brain and was accustomed to digesting stacks of divisional reports eight feet high in preparation for meetings. When he traveled, aides schlepped along his reading matter for the trip, typically contained in as many as 14 briefcases. Annual meetings, held at the company's European headquarters in Brussels, were said to run for 14 hours at a stretch for nearly a full week, during which Geneen would viciously grill each of the more than 120 executives seated around a massive, horseshoe-shaped conference desk. For more, see *Geneen*, by Robert A. Schoenberg (New York: W.W. Norton, 1985).

[†] Welch's performances were calculated, but some CEOs have behaved like out-and-out nuts. John Patterson, the founder of the old National Cash Register Company, once fired an employee by having his desk taken outside and set on fire. He decreed that employees could not eat bread and butter, drink tea or coffee, or use salt and pepper on company premises, but said it was okay to drink malted milk shakes nonstop. He ordered that each bite of any food had to be chewed precisely 32 times. See J. Useem, "Tyrants, Statesmen and Destroyers," in *Fortune* (November 18, 2002), p. 82.

[‡] Richard Wrangham and Dale Peterson argue that the social structures of chimpanzees are built around ranking systems for male chimps. The ranking systems are totally consuming, involving every aspect of male chimpanzee behavior, from grooming to companionship, from intimidation to guile—all of which is designed to enable a male chimp in his prime to find his ranking as an Alpha male among all other chimps in the group. See R. Wrangham and D. Peterson, *Demonic Males: Apes and the Origins of Human Violence* (Boston: Houghton Mifflin, 1996).

capable of ripping some underling's head off in public, just to make a point.

And Wendt noticed something else: the manner in which Welch seemed ever so subtly to back off from confrontations with the GE Credit executive who was running the operation day-to-day as Welch's deputy—an enormous meat slab of a man named Larry Bossidy. With his huge hands, massive frame, and tent-sized ears, Bossidy did not need to yell at Welch or anyone else to dominate a meeting—he needed only to enter the room. When he did, all voices would instantly drop to a whisper and all heads would swivel toward the door, as the ceaselessly scanning power-radars of everyone present locked in on the high-intensity waves of authority that emanated from Larry Bossidy wherever he went.

Bossidy had a background remarkably similar to Welch's—so similar in fact that the two men seemed in many ways to mirror each other. Both were born in the depths of the Depression, within months of each other in 1935. Both came from financially challenged families of Irish Catholic immigrants who had come to rest in Massachusetts—in the case of the Bossidy family, in Pittsfield, where Larry's father ran a shoe store.

Yet, whereas Welch seemed to use his upbringing as part of what amounted to a schtick to intimidate and control people, Bossidy lived more comfortably with his heritage. Whatever Welch had done with his life thus far, Bossidy possessed credentials that seemed to say "been there, done that"—and in a quiet and more convincing way. Both men had an interest in sports, but Bossidy was a true athlete whereas Welch sometimes seemed little more than a dilettante— especially when it came to his abilities in golf, about which he bragged incessantly. Bossidy didn't need to brag about his own background in sports because anyone who had read the sports pages in the mid-1950s already knew who he was and what he had done. Unlike Welch, who talked constantly about baseball, and his favorite team, the Boston Red Socks, Bossidy actually played the game, so well in fact that he had been offered a $40,000 a year contract to sign as a pitcher with the Detroit Tigers right out of high school. When his father steered him into college instead, he became the star of the Colgate University varsity baseball team, as well as starting pitcher in the college world series.

Bossidy could be as blunt and tough-spoken as anyone, but it wasn't part of some act; it was simply his way of communicating with people, and his colleagues could sense it. He didn't need to yell and put them down in one instant, then embrace them with some emotional reward in the next—for his goal wasn't manipulation and control, it was simply to communicate, and from his communication flowed the ability to lead.*

Observing all this, Wendt realized soon enough the opportunity it presented. Bossidy had Welch's number, and Welch seemed to know it. This meant that the real route upward within GE Credit lay in slipping in behind Bossidy and grabbing hold of his coattails. Safely protected behind the man's massive frame, Wendt could rise as rapidly as Bossidy himself, while remaining out of the line of fire from the *uber*-boss above him.

Positioning himself thusly, Gary began his campaign, advancing from workout specialist to manager of GE Credit's leasing and industrial loans department in less than a year. After that came more promotions until, in the wake of Welch's elevation to the chairmanship

---

*In "The Best CEO You've Never Heard Of," *USA Today* (June 23, 1994), p. 24. Micheline Maynard observes that Bossidy ". . . doesn't just hang out with big shots. You can find him buying chocolate chip cookies—one for himself, two for his assistants—in the company cafeteria. There's no indoor executive garage where cars are washed and gassed; Bossidy parks his black Lincoln Continental with other employees' cars outside. Although his typical workday is 12 hours, Bossidy, the father of nine children . . . pushes his employees to have a life outside the office. In the summer, AlliedSignal employees can go home at noon Friday if they put in nine hours a day Monday through Thursday. Bossidy also goes home early Fridays—around 4."

of the company in 1981, Gary stood right behind Bossidy as the head of consumer and industrial finance, the largest operation in all of GE Credit. In no time at all, he had gone from "Gary . . . that guy down the hall," to Gary Wendt, GE's *other* executive on the rise. With Bossidy as his blocking tackle, Gary could begin to see the goal line beckoning in the distance.

M eanwhile, Welch's elevation to the chairmanship of the company brought him much broader responsibilities than those of the sector he had previously run. And it wasn't long before they began to take him over, curtailing his ability to dig into the obscure details of GE's vast operations. When the chairman now spoke, the words became shorter and more crisply delivered. When he said, "We've got to get the costs out of this business," it was as if he no longer wanted to argue about it, because he no longer had time. He just wanted it done.

Welch certainly knew the sort of corporation he did *not* want GE to be (one with six layers of executive management and forms to be filled out in quadruplicate for everything). Yet, he didn't seem entirely sure what could or should replace it, except perhaps that with most of the growth coming from GE's credit operations, he wanted to see more of the company's resources feeding that business. And as time passed, another opportunity began to beckon: the media game.

It was the 1980s, and after a decade of gloom, deal fever had returned to Wall Street, powered by the vivid imagery of the new president and his vision of Morning in America—"this last, best hope of mankind on earth." It was talk that inspired optimism in tomorrow and in the United States, and it caused listeners to want to take a chance, to embrace a risk. And the stock market showed it, bottoming out in August 1982 at an eight-year low of 769 for the Dow Industrials, then rocketing straight back up again.

As the rise continued, deals began to percolate everywhere—especially in the media, where new words like "informazines" and new businesses like cable TV programming networks had begun to emerge. They promised new opportunities, the blending of the old with the new, as nearly every major investment firm on Wall Street began promoting business deals involving them.

Welch wanted GE to be in the game, too. It would help take the curse off the three years of almost nonstop firings and plant closings over which he had presided. They had earned him an unending string of epithets in the press. By autumn 1982, the *Financial Times* of London had hung the label "Neutron Jack" on him ("He takes out the people but leaves the buildings standing"). To *Fortune*, he was "the toughest boss in America," conducting meetings "so aggressively that people tremble."*

In July 1984, Welch approved his first major acquisition since becoming chairman—a $1.1 billion deal to acquire a company called Employers Reinsurance Corporation that Texaco was selling in the wake of its own takeover of Getty Oil. Everyone knew about the Texaco-Getty situation, which had been making headlines all winter. But almost no newspapers reported anything about the Employers Reinsurance deal, which so far as the media was concerned seemed both confusing and boring all at once.

Nor did anyone seem to care that following the deal, Welch reorganized GE's financial arm by making GE Credit and Employers Reinsurance separate and parallel subsidiaries of a new entity, GE Financial Services, Inc. He assigned to it one of his top aides, Robert

---

*In its August 6, 1984 issue, *Fortune* placed Welch above such well-known martinets of the era as Simon & Schuster president Richard Snyder (distinguished by his "quick, flaring temper"), and the colossally self-impressed Richard Rosenthal of Citizens Utilities Company, who had been known, while flying on commercial airlines, "to give a letter to the pilot instructing him how to take off and land the plane." See S. Flax, "The Toughest Bosses in America," *Fortune* (August 6, 1984), p. 18.

Wright, who had worked as general counsel for Welch when he ran the company's plastics operation. Yet from a public relations perspective, the whole transaction had, frustratingly enough, gone almost entirely unnoticed.

GE got a different—yet equally unwelcome—reaction a few months later when, in March 1985, the company was indicted on criminal fraud charges for bilking the U.S. government out of $800,000 on a Minuteman missile contract. The fraud was not something that Welch had had anything to do with, but the charges were an embarrassing reminder that GE had been periodically embroiled in such activities for the past thirty years.*

In the midst of all this, an obscure midwest company called Capital Cities Corporation made front-page news around the country by announcing that it had paid $3.5 billion to acquire ABC Television, one of the nation's three broadcast networks. This was followed by news, less than a month later, that cable programming impresario Ted Turner, then still a relatively unknown name to the

---

* White-collar and corporate crime have been sensitive subjects at GE for most of the last half century. One reason is that GE holds the unwanted distinction of being the central conspirator in what was reported at the time to be the largest antitrust case ever brought under the Sherman Antitrust Act. The case, which led to prison sentences in 1961 for seven executives at GE and elsewhere in the conspiracy, along with suspended sentences for twenty-four others, involved charges of widespread price-fixing on a broad array of electrical products. Commentators on the case have argued that while GE by no means operated in a climate of corporate lawlessness, the company's emphasis on earnings growth under its then-chairman, Ralph Cordiner, put pressure on executives to the point that ethical business practices began to suffer. See R. A. Smith, "The Incredible Electrical Conspiracy," Fortune (February 11, 1980), p. 174. Thereafter, the company's corporate crime problems continued. The company has been convicted for falsifying claims on a second missile contract; for obtaining classified Pentagon planning documents illegally; and has pleaded guilty to charges of conspiracy, money laundering, and failure to keep accurate books. The company has also paid fines for violations of the False Claims Act, and for various forms of industrial espionage.

general public, was making a hostile bid to acquire CBS.* This left only one network—NBC—and Welch wanted it.

By autumn, Welch and a small group of his most trusted aides and confidantes, including Wright, had decided to see if NBC might actually be for sale. To that end, Welch appears to have approached Felix Rohatyn, a senior partner in the investment firm of Lazard Freres & Company, which numbered RCA among its clients, to see if Rohatyn might be willing to set up a meeting with RCA's chairman, Thornton F. Bradshaw.

Rohatyn agreed, and a get-together was arranged for November 6 at the investment banker's sumptuous Park Avenue apartment so that Welch and Bradshaw could meet each other.[†] Bradshaw, the

---

*Ted Turner. It Ain't as Easy as It Looks. The Amazing Story of CNN (New York: Crown Publishers Inc., 1997), pp. 268–269, author Porter Bibb writes, "What Turner couldn't have known was the panic that struck CBS once news of the Cap Cities takeover of ABC became public. CBS founder Bill Paley, together with fellow CBS director and financier James Wolfensohn, had appealed to James Robinson, chairman of Shearson Lehman's parent, American Express. You don't want this redneck Turner taking over CBS do you? Paley complained. Find some conflict and tell him Shearson can't represent him. Wolfensohn, who had close business ties with both Jim Robinson and American Express echoed Paley's directive, pointing out the danger a man like Turner could represent to the entire broadcast industry. Wolfensohn also reminded his friend that this was the same Ted Turner who had once been blackballed by the New York Yacht Club."

†Like much of what appears in Welch's business memoir, Jack: Straight from the Gut (New York: Warner Books, 2001) the account of how the meeting with Bradshaw came about is rendered in a way that not only flatters Welch but is at odds with the accounts of others. In the memoir's version of events, the get-together had been promoted "out of the blue" by Rohatyn, who had learned of Welch's interest in acquiring a broadcast net after Welch had met with CBS chairman Thomas Wyman with an offer to play "white knight" to help Wyman fend off a hostile bid from Ted Turner. This makes it appear as if GE hadn't been in the market to acquire RCA at all and had been drawn into the deal by Rohatyn, who is portrayed in the passage as a Wall Street deal promoter. (See pp. 140–143 of the hardcover edition.) But other accounts dispute Welch's version, which was published 15 years after the events in question. A better, and more contemporaneous account of how the meeting occurred can be found in the Wall Street Journal only a few weeks after the meeting itself actually took place. In light of an announced SEC investigation into apparent insider trading in RCA's shares, the Journal had been anxious to establish, as precisely as possible, the sequence of events by which nonpublic information about the possibility of a merger between GE and RCA had developed in the first place.

patrician one-time chairman of the Atlantic Richfield oil company, knew plenty about how to conduct negotiations. But since no one at GE had been very specific with Rohatyn as to why Welch wanted the meeting, Bradshaw had no clear idea what to expect when the big day finally came and Welch began offering vague observations about how GE and RCA might fit together. As the musings continued, Bradshaw grew concerned that he'd be late for a speaking engagement, and an ill-concealed glance or two at his watch brought the get-together to an end. But Welch came away thinking a deal could be worked out, and once back in Fairfield, he set up a team to come up with a detailed proposal.

By the start of December, the basic elements of an offer were in hand. On Thursday, December 5—the same day that the Dow Industrial Average broke through 1500 to set yet another record high—Welch put his offer of $66.50 per share, or roughly $6.4 billion, before Bradshaw. The meeting took place in the RCA leader's midtown Manhattan hotel suite in the Dorset Hotel, a few steps west of Fifth Avenue on 54th Street.

Unfortunately, news of the meeting leaked to employees of both GE and Lazard Freres, who quickly—and illegally—began buying options in RCA's shares. By the following Monday, the price of RCA's underlying stock began abruptly to climb—and for no reason so far

---

To that end, the reporters on the story had interviewed all three participants in the November 6 meeting and reported flat-out and unequivocally that the "meeting had been arranged, at Mr. Welch's suggestion, by Felix G. Rohatyn." No corrections regarding any aspect of the story were ever published. See J. Roberts and B. K. Abrams, "Talks That Led to GE-RCA Pact Started Casually," in the *Wall Street Journal* (December 13, 1985). What's more, in September 1987, writer L. J. Davis of *Harpers* published an extensive and detailed article on the sale of RCA for the *New York Times*, and once again the article states flat out that "Welch had asked Rohatyn, a long-time advisor, to set up a meeting with Thornton Bradshaw." The article, which included an interview with Rohatyn, even set forth the conditions that Rohatyn specified before he arranged the get-together. See L. J. Davis, "Did RCA Have to Be Sold?" *New York Times* (September 20, 1987), Sec. 6, P. 2, p. 23.

as the general public was concerned since the offer was still suppos-
edly secret. But the rise was enough to stir speculation that a deal of
some sort was in the works, presenting Welch and GE with yet another public relations setback. The rumors of insider trading had become almost deafening by the time the deal was finally accepted by
RCA's board and publicly announced at the end of the week. Almost
immediately, the Securities and Exchange Commission announced
that it was opening an investigation into unexplained trading in the
shares, further eclipsing the transaction in the shadow of scandal.*

For Welch, it was just the latest in a string of public relations dis-
appointments—another shrewd deal either ignored by the media or
tainted by bad luck. Meanwhile, what about some satisfaction for
Jack Welch himself in all this? His career at GE had certainly made
him a wealthy man. But he was now fifty years old, and except for his
youngest son, Mark, his children—for whom he never seemed to
care much anyway—were now grown. And nobody had to spell out
for Jack Welch what that meant—thirty more years, up close and
personal, with his familiar wife, Carolyn . . . just the two of them, as
the days turned into years and his life slipped away . . . and for what?

Here he was, Jack Welch, the golden boy of North Salem,
Massachusetts. He had money in the bank—a lot of it by now, a net
worth in excess of $11 million if you added everything up.[4] But
what was the point of having $11 million if you had to share it with
Ms. Excitement herself, *the wife?* As he made clear enough in his
autobiography, he had little in common with Carolyn anymore, and
frankly, he wanted action—the action that comes from being the

---

* Seven months later in August 1986, the SEC charged a Houston businessman, Harvey
Katz, and his son, Marcel, a former Lazard junior analyst, and two others, with reaping
$2 million of illegal profits by trading RCA stocks and options on insider information
supplied by Marcel. All four entered consent decrees on the case. A month later, the
SEC charged a GE executive, Thomas M. Harnett, with similar illegal trading. He too
entered a consent decree in the matter.

head of a TV network, with secretaries who walk around in short skirts and heels and no underpants. He wanted to be a babe magnet, okay? And what was so wrong with that? He wanted to feel like he had a full head of hair again and stood six feet four instead of five feet eight—and Carolyn just wasn't doing the job.[5]

After the RCA deal was completed, Welch flew to NBC Television's production studios in Burbank, California, to see exactly what he had bought. Those who witnessed his processional through the facility later remarked at how awestruck Welch seemed throughout the whole tour. But it wasn't the technology of the soundstages that dazzled him, it was the endless comings and goings of beautiful young women.

Finally, unable to restrain himself any longer, he grabbed the arm of a tour guide and, gesturing in the direction of a voluptuous young woman nearby, enthused, "Look at the tits on that one!" a remark that instantly spread throughout the building as NBC staffers took the measure of their new corporate overlord.[6]

9

FITZY COMES OUT OF THE CLOSET

Scarcely was the ink dry on the RCA deal than Jack Welch grabbed for yet another big and complex deal that seemed in tune with the times: the opportunity to become a player on Wall Street by acquiring the Kidder Peabody & Company investment firm.

Like much of American business, Wall Street had gone through periodic bouts of consolidation over the years, and by the spring of 1985, Kidder Peabody & Company remained one of the few major Wall Street firms that had neither sold shares to the public nor been acquired by a bank, an insurance company, or some other well-capitalized financial business. As a result, the firm needed money; its capital base of $100 million was simply too small to compete with bigger and better financed rivals like Goldman Sachs & Company or Morgan Stanley.

What's more, the firm had suffered a devastating loss only three months earlier when Kidder's most valued executive, Martin Siegel, had left for greener pastures. Siegel had come to work for Kidder following his graduation from the Harvard Business School in June

1970. In the decade that followed, he had used his winning personality and drop-dead good looks to build the firm into a force to be reckoned with in the emerging new Wall Street game of mergers and acquisitions.

In 1974, Siegel wrote a textbook on the subject of mergers and acquisitions, and in 1977 he was made a Kidder director. As befitting his enhanced new stature, he bought a weekend place in Westport, Connecticut, on the banks of the Aspetuck River a mile upstream from the home of movie star Paul Newman, and barely a ten-minute drive from the New Canaan home of Jack and Carolyn Welch, who had just moved to the area after Reg Jones had transferred Welch down from Pittsfield to become a sector head in GE's home office.

To add a further name to the gathering cast of characters, the neighborhood even included Chainsaw Al Dunlap. Having escaped from the rubble of his disastrous tour as head of Nitec Paper Corporation, Dunlap had spent months searching for a job before finally landing one in middle management at the American Can Company in Greenwich, thereafter moving to a home in Ridgefield, Connecticut, a few minutes by car from the Welches.

Though Siegel was already a wealthy man by the start of the 1980s, his wealth was dwarfed by that of a mysterious Wall Street financier named Ivan Boesky, who also lived in the area and whose silver hair, gaunt face, and piercing blue eyes had become the talk of Wall Street. More than anyone else in the game, Boesky seemed to know all and see everywhere; the very mention of his name could lower the temperature of any room.

One day in 1981, Boesky invited Siegel to lunch at the arbitrageur's palatial home in Westchester. It was a short drive from Siegel's weekend place in Westport, but it belonged in another world entirely. The gated mansion, complete with formal gardens and artfully positioned Greek statuary, had been built by the late Charles

Revson, founder of the Revlon cosmetics chain that was soon to pass into the hands of Ronald Perelman through a hostile takeover financed with junk bonds.

The grandeur of Boesky's mansion was staggering, and thereafter Siegel seemed to behave ever more humbly each time he encountered Boesky.* By the summer of 1982, Siegel could take it no longer, and during a chat with Boesky at a back table in midtown Manhattan's Harvard Club, he hung what amounted to a For Sale sign on his career, offering to tip Boesky to upcoming Kidder Peabody deals in return for "consultation fees."

In the three years that followed, Siegel became a conduit to Boesky for illegal insider information on virtually every merger or acquisition involving Kidder Peabody. The deals ranged from Bendix Corporation's $1.5 billion hostile takeover bid for Martin Marietta, to various strategies for the sale of Getty Oil, to Henry Kravis' hostile buyout of Beatrice Foods and countless other raids, mergers, and takeovers.

But even this was not bringing Siegel the wealth he desired, and he knew that as head of mergers and acquisitions for Kidder Peabody he would never obtain it. He needed to move onto a faster track at a firm that was doing bigger deals.

The vista of mega-wealth at last opened before Siegel in the summer of 1985. He was approached by Fred Joseph, the head of Drexel Burnham & Company, whose Beverly Hills sales chief, Michael Milken, was marketing junk bonds to finance most of the biggest M&A deals of all. Joseph began courting Siegel with a $6 million

---

* Siegel soon put his Aspetuck River retreat on the market and moved to a grander neighborhood in nearby Southport, Connecticut, on the coastline of Long Island Sound. The new Siegel residence proved to be almost literally within sight of the 6.5-acre parcel of real estate where Jack Welch and his second wife, Jane Beasley Welch, would eventually take up residence in an enormous Georgian-style mansion a decade later.

package of stock and cash—a staggering offer for the period—and in no time at all, Siegel agreed to jump ship.

On February 1, 1986, Siegel dropped the news on his boss, Kidder's portly CEO, Ralph DeNunzio, who knew nothing of Siegel's secret world of crime. But DeNunzio knew it was bad enough simply to be hearing that his firm was suddenly losing its M&A superstar, who seemed to be clued into every deal on the Street. It meant that Kidder's very survival was now up for grabs.*

DeNunzio knew he had to act fast, and in the weeks that followed, he and his top aides tried to figure out what to do. The firm's capital was stretched thin already, and Kidder either had to sell a lot of stock to the public quickly, or find a source of private investment capital in a hurry.

Of the two, a stock sale seemed the least desirable. The paperwork alone would have been time consuming and costly and would have meant having to show the firm's disturbingly weak financial underpinnings to the world. By contrast, a private placement from a deep-pockets financial angel could be arranged relatively quickly, with a minimum of fuss and almost no public disclosure. But who could be talked into ponying up the sort of money that would keep Kidder afloat—and to write out a check quickly?

By the first week of April, DeNunzio had settled on the most likely choice, and on April 9 he placed a call to the one man who had pockets deep enough to buy anything—and the apparent desire to plant his flag in the world of finance: Jack Welch of GE.

At the moment, Welch had plenty on his plate already. GE had just wrapped up its deal with RCA, the largest such non-oil merger

---

*Siegel eventually pleaded guilty to his role as a criminal tipster for Ivan Boesky in the Drexel junk bond affair and became an informant for New York federal prosecutors led by U.S. Attorney Rudolph Giuliani. Boesky also pleaded guilty in the affair and likewise became an informant for the government. For more on the activities of both men in the scandal, see J. Stewart, *Den of Thieves* (New York: Simon & Schuster, 1991).

ever, and Welch hadn't yet even disclosed who would be in charge of running what. But no sooner did he hear from DeNunzio that Kidder Peabody was suddenly on the block than he cleared the decks for GE's second high-profile acquisition in less than four months. To get the two sides together, a dinner meeting was set up in a private corporate dining room at GE's headquarters in Fairfield.

This gave the GE side exactly one weekend to get up to speed on Kidder, and it left them at a distinct disadvantage since nearly everything they would have wanted to know about the financial health of the firm was nonpublic and closely guarded information by Kidder, the seller.

Obviously, nothing would have been lost by asking for more time and some further discussions to explore the matter more fully. But Welch had long since set a tone of "do it now" action at GE that his subordinates now emulated. As a result, by April 24—just two weeks' time—a deal was hammered out and signed. Under its terms, 80 percent of Kidder was handed over to GE in return for $600 million in cash money up front, plus a promise from GE to provide an additional $150 million capital infusion down the road.

The high price for the purchase seemed curious, and reporters began digging into the back-story in hopes of learning why GE had been willing to pay so much for an investment firm that was widely believed to be in trouble. Yet on the very day that the *New York Times* was hitting newsstands with the first fully developed backgrounder to the deal,[1] a far more intriguing situation was unfolding two hours to the north in the Hudson Valley town of Clifton Park.

Like other upstate towns served by the New York State Thruway, Clifton Park was now increasingly besieged by the drug trade and other forms of vice that thrived on the traffic rolling through town on the six-lane Interstate twenty-four hours a day.

If the cars and trucks just kept right on rolling, no one in Clifton
Park would have cared—or indeed even known—what many of the
drivers and passengers inside had on their minds. But the vehicles
were stopping, and the word was getting around: The rest stop at the
northbound exit for Clifton Park had become the hottest spot in the
Hudson Valley for some late night action—at least if you were gay
and wanted to have sex in the dark with a stranger. And month after
month, a steady procession of drivers had been turning off the Interstate and easing to a halt in the darkened rest stop to get exactly that.

Finally, the town had had enough. It was the start of May, and
the vacation travel season was beginning. The chairman of the
Clifton Park Board of Supervisors, Roy McDonald, spoke for all
when he issued a call for action. "They're affecting our pocket-
books," he wailed, "They're affecting people from stopping there,
and that's affecting our tourist trade. We will not allow a piece of
42nd Street to slip upstate."

Surveillance duty for the cleanup went to two New York State
Police Troopers: Edward Morrissey and his partner, R. O. Bennett.
Their instructions were simple and clear-cut: To make routine and
periodic sweeps through the rest area, which contained an unat-
tended small building with washrooms and lavatory facilities, along
with a winding, unlighted road that led to a darkened parking area in
some adjoining woods.

Who wound up telling the truth about the events that were soon
to unfold is unknown even to this day. The man who insisted to the
end to be innocent wound up pleading guilty. But his reasons for
changing his story are lost forever because he is now dead, and he
left nothing but a confusing and not particularly convincing explanation for doing what he did.

As for Troopers Morrissey and Bennett of the New York State
Police, the barracks where they were based was subsequently disbanded in a budget cutback. And the Arresting Officer's Complaint,

with all the subsequent paperwork, was destroyed, as a Freedom of Information Act request eventually revealed.

So all that can really be known (which for present purposes may be entirely enough) is what newspapers reported from the arresting officers' complaint when Troopers Morrissey and Bennett swung off the Interstate at about 10:45 P.M. on the evening of May 5 and eased into the rest area. Dousing the lights on their cruiser, they rolled the black-and-white to a stop in front of the washroom and lavatory building, then picked up a flashlight and stepped into the cool night air.

Much media coverage flowed from what happened next, including television reports and nineteen separate stories in the *Albany Times Union* newspaper and a dozen more in the *Troy Record*.

The coverage was exhaustive, and often featured on the front page, because the whole of the Hudson River Valley simply could not believe what Troopers Morrissey and Bennett had come upon as they stepped behind the washroom building and into the woods. First came the sounds, faint and distant, like tree frogs and crickets. But the sounds quickly grew louder, sharpening into whispers and the scuffling of feet.

Switching on their flashlight the troopers were now able to see what their ears told them was happening already, as half a dozen men scattered into the woods in all directions, while directly in front of the officers just two of the group remained—not yet completely done with what they were doing, but almost. As the troopers moved toward them, one of the men darted off into the dark. A second or two more and the second man would have fled, too, so they reached out, quickly grabbed him, and took him back around the washroom building to the patrol car.

The man was fifty-nine, according to his ID, and when his name broke into print forty-eight hours later, it sent shock waves rolling up and down the Hudson Valley. Whether they spread from there to the elegant estates of Fairfield County, and from there to command the attention of the new chairman and chief executive of GE is not known.

Yet it is difficult to imagine otherwise, for even as Jack Welch pondered the implications of his impulsive rush to acquire Kidder Peabody—a deal that was not yet even two weeks old—the executive ranks of the corporation he headed were seething with gossip at the latest news. The chairman and CEO's best drinking buddy and most intimate business soul mate, who had traveled with him on business junkets from Japan to Holland—Tom "Fitzy" Fitzgerald—had apparently been an after-hours, action-in-the-dark faggot from the start.*

〜〜〜

Beyond the complications developing in his personal life, Welch also faced difficult business challenges as the summer of 1986 began. Key among them: Which of his people should run Kidder Peabody—a matter that had remained unsettled during the scramble to bag the investment bank. Despite the vaunted "strength in depth" of its management ranks, GE simply didn't have enough people to fill the new slots, particularly at the top.

Larry Bossidy was Welch's number one guy—the only executive at GE that he could not intimidate—and in the wake of becoming chairman in 1981, Welch turned to him constantly for guidance in how to handle situations. And Bossidy, in his role as the chairman's unofficial consigliore, almost never disappointed.

When Welch needed to be brought up short, Bossidy wouldn't hesitate. At one point, he and Bossidy were discussing the performance of an executive whom Welch did not like. As the conversation

---

*Thomas "Fitzy" Fitzgerald appears several times in Welch's autobiography, adorned with encomiums such as "great friend," "business soul-mate," and "closest business friend." When he passed over Fitzy for a promotion, Welch described it as the biggest such mistake of his career. See J. Welch and J. Byrne, *Jack: Straight from the Gut* (New York: Warner Books, 2001), pp. 45, 57–58, 301–302.

progressed, Welch grew more and more animated and personal in his criticisms. Finally, he zeroed in on a set of attributes about which he seemed to harbor ill-disguised jealousy and which were irrelevant to the man's job performance in any case: his movie star good looks, his gorgeous wife, and his wealthy in-laws. At last Welch roared his judgment: "The guy's an asshole!"[2]

Bossidy looked at him, and as silence filled the room he said: "You through?"

Welch nodded, and then Bossidy spoke: "If I was as handsome as that guy, and I had a wife as good looking as he does, then I wouldn't give a fuck what you think!"

It took someone like Larry Bossidy to deliver a conversation stopper like that to Jack Welch, and—credit to Welch—it took a man like Welch to accept that he needed him at his side. In the aftermath of the Employers Reinsurance acquisition in 1984, he had promoted Bossidy up and out of GE Credit and made him vice chairman of the whole corporation. Simultaneously, however, Welch left him in charge of overseeing the credit operation while moving Bob Wright in to fill the seat Bossidy had vacated.

The shuffle meant that Wright would have been the logical choice to run Kidder, especially since he had handled the Kidder talks as Welch's top deputy. But Welch had already begun to think about moving Wright out of GE Finance entirely and making him the head of NBC.

All summer Welch wrestled with the problem: If he gave the NBC job to Wright, who then could be found to succeed him as head of GE Credit? In reality, Welch knew there was but one answer. As a person, he didn't much care for the man, it was true. But he also knew that no one could do the job better: The job would have to go to Gary Wendt, the nebbish from down the hall.

On August 26, 1986, Welch announced the Wright assignment to NBC, and the following Tuesday the promotion of Wendt. This certainly pleased Gary, who still had Bossidy running interference for him with Welch. Only now, Bossidy was perched at Welch's elbow as vice chairman of the whole company—with Wendt hiding behind him so close to the top job that he could almost reach out from behind Bossidy and touch it.

As for NBC, the management situation at the network presented problems of a different sort, and mostly they boiled down to the man who had been heading NBC's news division at the time of the deal— a disheveled, professorial executive named Lawrence Grossman. Welch didn't like him. And the feeling was mutual because Grossman didn't much care for Welch either.[3]

To complicate matters still more, Welch realized that Grossman was the man with the most support among his NBC colleagues for the job of running the network. This meant that although Welch had made a point of putting Wright in the job that Grossman seemed to want, he couldn't now fire the man even from his position as head of the News Division without appearing almost spiteful in his dislike. Yet, the news division was one of the first places where Welch intended to clean house—and it seemed he was now going to have to do it with Grossman fighting him every step of the way.

He was right. Not everyone at NBC news liked Grossman, but they certainly trusted him more than they trusted the newcomer Welch—and trust was a quality that counted for a lot in the television news business at the moment, since it was hard for television news people to escape the feeling that they were in an industry under siege. In one bombshell announcement after the next, the pillars of television broadcasting were coming under attack from the Wall Street financed takeover machine, and no one could be sure they'd have their jobs next week. ABC was gone already, CBS was going fast, and now RCA had been swallowed up as well.

In this feeding frenzy, the employees of the news divisions felt themselves especially vulnerable, for "news" was an expensive and time-consuming commodity to produce, and the networks could not easily recoup the expense through the sale of advertising time on the shows. For all their prestige as the "crown jewels" of the networks, the news divisions remained constantly at the mercy of the corporate executives who controlled their purse strings.

To protect themselves in this situation, the news divisions had long since learned, when budget quarrels arose, to retreat behind an exhaustively elaborated (though imperfectly grounded) theory of broadcast news as a "public trust." In this presumed compact, the news was judged the supreme value. From this premise flowed the idea that journalists were professionals embarked on what amounted to a religious mission to roam the earth in pursuit of "the news," then deliver it to the public, whose right to have it was likewise judged to be absolute and unconditional.

Most importantly, the theory of the public trust placed a moral duty on the corporations employing the journalists—likewise absolute and unconditional—to spend whatever was needed, without limitation or even challenge, so that the journalists could do their jobs. Thus, when arguments over budgets arose, news chiefs could denounce any proposed cutbacks as immoral and a breach of the public trust.

Grossman believed that such a trust was real and that it was important, and because he spoke the language of the news business, he was able to calm the nerves of frightened staffers. He had spent his entire career in broadcast journalism, beginning at NBC in the 1950s when legendary broadcast figures like Robert Kintner and Pat Weaver still roamed the halls. He had grown up with television broadcasting and was heading the country's taxpayer-supported public television network, as president of PBS, when he was invited back to NBC in 1984 to become president of the network's News Division.

By contrast, Welch regarded News Division talk of a public trust as nonsense and would start yelling at Grossman in meetings whenever the words were mentioned. With an army of frightened, curious news people usually hovering right outside the door, it wasn't long before almost anything that Welch said or did began turning up on page 6 of the *New York Post*. Welch took this as evidence of Grossman's disloyalty, and proof that the NBC man was embarked on a campaign to sabotage his efforts as chairman of GE.

"But his ideas *were* crazy," Grossman said later. "He wanted NBC to license out the name NBC News to independent producers and TV stations so that we could create a new revenue stream. He wanted us to get rid of all the News Division 'stars' because CNN didn't have any, so that meant we didn't need any either."

By October, the situation had deteriorated to the point that Grossman figured he'd have to break the ice somehow, and he arranged for a dinner party at his home in Connecticut for Welch and his wife, Carolyn, as well as Bob and Suzanne Wright, and several of NBC News' top personalities, including Bryant Gumbel, Jane Pauley, and Tom Brokaw.[4]

But "dinner at the Grossmans" was the last thing on earth Welch wanted. For one thing, his relationship with Carolyn was by now on the rocks. Though it would be another several weeks before he actually filed the papers in court to get rid of her, he could well imagine how difficult and tense an evening with the two of them together would be—especially when the setting would be the home of the appalling Grossman. Worst of all, the night of the party—October 26—was the sixth game of the World Series, with his beloved Red Socks on the verge of taking home their first championship in his lifetime—which simply added to his discomfort at the thought of having to spend the evening with Grossman instead.

10

CHAMPAGNE KISSES AND CAVIAR DREAMS

s the 1980s headed toward mid-decade and stock prices rose, even the best known of America's business leaders were not yet viewed as media celebrities. The most famous CEO of the decade, Lee Iacocca, had yet to publish his autobiography (it appeared in 1984) and had only lately begun to show up in the television commercials that were destined to make him a household name as head of Chrysler Corporation. He had not yet become a regular on TV programs like the *Today Show*, and had not yet publicly flirted with the idea of running for the U.S. Senate or even the White House.*

---

*Iacocca was a trailblazer in this regard. Celebrity endorsers have been a staple of Madison Avenue since the late 1940s when Ronald Reagan began appearing in magazine advertisements for Chesterfield cigarettes. The use of celebrity endorsers nearly doubled during the 1970s, as the impact of mass-market advertising began to saturate every corner of the American consumer market. In the process, film and TV stars ranging from Gregory Peck, Karl Malden, and Laurence Olivier, to James Garner, Dick Cavett, and Candice Bergen all developed second lives in the public eye as corporate spokespersons of one sort or another. But it was much rarer to find business leaders engaged in the same activity—mainly because they did not have preexisting brand-name recognition with

Business world heroes-in-the-making like Jack Welch, Dennis Kozlowski, and Al Dunlap were, if anything, even more obscure. Of the three, Welch had advanced furthest the fastest and was already chairman and CEO of GE by the time GE's one-time TV pitchman, Ronald Reagan, reached the midpoint of his first term as president of the United States (January 1, 1983). Yet Dunlap and Kozlowski were still so obscure that many businessmen in their own industries had not even heard of them.

The business world anonymity of Kozlowski remained for the moment almost total. Having moved to New Hampshire, he had as yet advanced no further than head of a division within Tyco Laboratories—a company that was itself so obscure that it rarely made news of any sort.

For his part, Dunlap was by now a bit more visible. Having escaped the wreckage of the Nitec fiasco, he had finally landed a job in middle management at American Can, where he once again began charging up the corporate ladder, topping out as head of the company's plastics division. Dunlap moved next to the Manville Corporation, where he lasted about eight months as head of the company's forest products operation. That job ended when the company filed for bankruptcy in connection with asbestos-related health litigation. After that, Dunlap resurfaced as head of Lilly-Tulip, Inc., a debt-burdened and struggling manufacturer of paper plates and cups. Dunlap's assignment from the Kohlberg Kravis

---

the public. Along with Iacocca, CEOs such as Frank Borman of Eastern Airlines began appearing in TV commercials as the 1980s progressed, but only occasionally—and only because they were already well known to the public for other reasons. (Borman had been an astronaut, and Iacocca was well known for his role as the creator of the Ford Motor Company's best-selling Mustang sports convertible more than a decade earlier.) CEOs, such as popcorn marketer Orville Redenbacher and food processor Frank Perdue, who both became famous entirely through their roles as corporate spokesmen in TV commercials, were still almost nonexistent. See A. Feinberg, "Madison Avenue's Cast of Famous Faces," New York Times (November 16, 1980), Sec. 3, p. 7; and "Putting the Boss in TV Commercials," New York Times (August 8, 1982), Sec. 3, p. 21.

Roberts & Company leveraged buyout shop that owned the business: Cut costs until the company shows a profit—an assignment that he undertook with the same characteristic vigor he had displayed whenever given the chance previously.

By the start of 1984, *Business Week* had taken notice of the emerging corporate tough guy at Lilly-Tulip, quoting a source at the company as saying of Dunlap, "His people are living in fear of him—absolute fear."[1] And by year's end, *Forbes* had joined in, labeling Dunlap an out-and-out "operations fanatic."[2]

Of the four, only Ronald Perelman had begun to emerge as both a famous financier and a media celebrity. In part, this was because he had begun to lead an increasingly visible private life that was titillating already and promised to become more so as time passed.* It was also because the public's attitude toward wealth was changing†

---

*Businessmen playboys have been a feature of newspaper gossip columns since the days of John Jacob Astor IV. The great grandson of the legendary colonial era fur trader John Jacob Astor, Astor IV was born in Rhinebeck, New York, on July 13, 1864. He fought in the Spanish-American War, wrote a novel about life in outer space, acted in silent movies, and built the Waldorf-Astoria, St. Regis, and Knickerbocker hotels in New York. He is best known for divorcing his wife and marrying his 18-year-old mistress. He drowned in the sinking of the ocean liner *Titanic* in 1912, but his mistress-wife, Madeleine, who was pregnant, survived and gave birth to a son who grew up to become a millionaire playboy as well. For more on the children of history's privileged few, see M. Forbes, *What Happened to Their Kids: Children of the Rich and Famous* (New York: Simon & Schuster, 1990).

† After the long bleak decade of the 1970s, it was once again becoming okay to be rich in the United States. Following a decade of stagnating readership *Money* magazine stopped publishing stories about how to save money by installing woodstoves and riding bicycles, and switched to advice articles with headlines like "What It Takes to Be (Truly) Rich Today," *Money* (March, 1984) and circulation surged. In the nation's capital, *Washington Post* gossip columnists began reporting the $12,000-and-up prices of the designer gowns by Ungaro, Valentino, and Galanos worn by the new First Lady, Nancy Reagan, at White House galas. And on TV, 1970s-era "life is hell" programming like *Welcome Back, Kotter* and *Chico and the Man* gave way to shows like *Dynasty, Falcon Crest,* and *Dallas,* which dominated prime time throughout the 1980s with themes devoted to the "secret lives of the rich." In 1986, came the debut of a program devoted entirely to fawning before the wealthy: *Lifestyles of the Rich and Famous.*

and pop culture views toward marriage and relations between the sexes were shifting as well.* And so far as the media was concerned, Perelman seemed to be doing nothing to hide his pursuit of either money *or* women.

Faith Perelman's discovery that Ron had been having an affair with Suzie Kasen, the owner of Manhattan's trendy Green Thumb flower shop, had sent Faith into orbit and she immediately began divorce proceedings. What's more, she proved to be a surprisingly resourceful adversary, hiring one of New York's most tenacious and feared lawyers, Stanley Arkin, to represent her, even as Ron hired an attorney with an even more menacing reputation—Roy Cohn—as his own legal counsel.[†] Seeing the two sides line up, reporters began to take notice. Just who was this Perelman couple anyway?

Arkin moved quickly into attack mode, filing papers with the U.S. Securities and Exchange Commission to assert Faith's claim to all the stock Perelman held in MacAndrews & Forbes. Yet, as is usually the case in such situations, neither Ron nor Faith really wanted to wind up arguing with each other in an open courtroom, and by September 1983 the two sides had arranged an out-of-court settlement. In it, Ron agreed to give Faith the divorce she wanted, along with the title to their apartment at 740 Park Avenue. He also agreed to surrender all

---

*Stagnating living standards during the decade of the 1970s forced twelve million American homemakers into the labor force to supplement the incomes of their head-of-household spouses. The resulting marriage strains caused the divorce rate in the United States to leap by 53 percent during the period, the largest such rise on record. See National Center for Health Statistics and the Centers for Disease Control and Prevention (rate per 1,000 married females).

[†]The controversial Cohn had gained fame thirty years earlier as counsel to U.S. Senator Joseph McCarthy during the anti-Communist witch hunts of the early 1950s. Subsequently, he established a politically and socially well-connected legal practice in New York. He died of AIDS in August 1986.

claims to any of her real estate holdings, as well as to pay off the bank loan she had cosigned so that he could acquire his shares in MacAndrews & Forbes in the first place. In return, Faith agreed not to press her claim to the shares themselves.*

Faith got the freedom she sought, and so for that matter did Ron. But Ron got something else that he probably didn't realize at the time: the beginnings of an image as a man whose public life as a Wall Street financier was somehow the outgrowth of his private life and entanglements with women. In no time at all, he began to burnish that image by acquiring a wife who allowed him to improve his access to the media while simultaneously parading himself through the gossip columns with a good-looking woman on his arm.

〰〰〰

At the beginning of the 1980s, divorce at the top levels of American business was still widely regarded as a sign of poor judgment and questionable management skills on the part of a corporate leader. If a man couldn't keep his own house in order, how could he be expected to look after the affairs of an entire company and its shareholders?

In 1980, mere rumors of a romantic involvement between the forty-two-year-old divorced head of Bendix Corporation, William Agee, and an attractive young Harvard-trained MBA named Mary Cunningham, who worked in Bendix's strategic planning department, were all it took to drive both individuals from the company when stories about their relationship began making headlines during a takeover fight with the Martin Marietta Corporation.

---

* One reason for Faith's willingness to settle may simply have been the tenaciousness with which Ron fought her. See G. Grig, "Lipstick on His Dollars," *Sunday Times* (September 26, 1993): "After a particularly bitter divorce, Perelman's first wife, Faith Golding, broke down during settlement negotiations when he disputed one-eighth of a percentage point in the interest paid to her."

In the wake of the scandal, an executive recruiter for Ward Howell International simply echoed the prevailing, and traditional, sentiment of corporate boards everywhere: Only a *married* CEO could be expected to keep his mind on the driving and his hands on the wheel. He told *Forbes,* "A freshly divorced guy being considered for a top post might give any board a little pause now."[3] Added a second executive recruiter on the same subject, "A divorce of less than two years is a complete red flag." After all, what corporate board would want to risk the consequences of handing over control of the company to a CEO who had shown himself unstable in one of life's most important arenas already?

Yet by mid-decade, divorce had begun to lose much of the stigma it once had for men holding down the top spots in business. As the melting pot theories of politics in the 1950s and 1960s gave way to a new politics of diversity in the 1970s, men as well as women began to think of themselves in political terms, as individual members of a political community and, more even than that, as belonging to a whole new social action group, with rights acquired solely by virtue of their sex.

If women could color their hair and have face-lifts, then why couldn't men? In 1981, a New York plastic surgeon named James Reardon published a book entitled *Plastic Surgery for Men.* In it he reported that the percentage of males coming to him for cosmetic surgery had tripled, to more than 30 percent of his patients, since the mid-1970s. Plastic surgeons from elsewhere around the country had begun reporting similar gains.[4]

Some of the most startling changes of all began appearing in the upper echelons of business, where male ego gratification found a new form of expression in the legitimization of the girlfriend as "trophy wife." In the 1960s and early 1970s, two jet-setting Greek shipping magnates, Stavros Niarchos and Aristotle Onassis, waged a relentless and public war of one-upmanship over which man could marry the most glamorous and desirable wife—a struggle that the press chronicled closely while simultaneously managing to sneer at the gauche pastime of two tasteless Greek businessmen.*

Yet by the start of the 1980s, it no longer seemed startling to observe a top business leader in his late fifties or sixties being accompanied to some social function by a perfectly proportioned—and achingly thin—wife half his age.† By mid-decade, the rarity had become encountering such a man in public *without* that particular accessory at his side.

Edgar Bronfman, the fifty-six-year-old chairman and CEO of the Seagram Company liquor dynasty, had one—a barmaid named Georgiana Webb Bronfman, thirty-five, whom he met while pub-crawling in Britain in 1975. Junk-bond raider Saul Steinberg had one, too: a socialite named Gayfryd Steinberg. Henry Kravis, the head of the Kohlberg, Kravis & Roberts leverage buyout firm, had one as well in the person of socialite Carolyne Roehm. The head of the Salomon Brothers investment firm, John Gutfreund, had one: a former stewardess named Susan.

Now Ron Perelman was to get one as well. Her name was Claudia Cohen, and she was a former gossip columnist for the *New York Post* who had lately moved from print journalism onto the faster media track of television as a gossip "correspondent" for ABC television's

---

*The press seemed to pronounce Niarchos the winner when he married Charlotte Ford, the daughter of Henry Ford II and heiress to the Ford family riches, in 1965. But the ultimate winner turned out to be Onassis, who ended his relationship with the greatest international opera diva of her time, Maria Callas, to marry Jacqueline Bouvier Kennedy, the widow of the assassinated U.S. president, in 1968.

†In *Bonfire of the Vanities* (New York: Farrar, Straus, and Giroux, 1987), novelist and social critic Tom Wolfe coined the term "X-rays" to describe such women, implying that they were so thin that a bright light could shine right through them.

Gossip Columnist Claudia Cohen. Ron's ticket to the media, she snagged him on the short hop after a luncheon at Le Cirque. In the changing climate of the bull market Eighties, a gal in a Galanos beat a woodstove any day. Yet woe to he who answers the call of the ultimate big game hunt of them all. Add up the assets, deduct the debt, and it's $80 million in get-lost money for a shot at the one trophy every man wants. Anyone for some shiksa goddess? (*Photo credit*: Marina Garnier.)

Morning Show. Claudia was attractive, she was from a wealthy Jewish family, and she was on the prowl for a man,* which meant that, all things considered, she was set to snag Ron on the short hop.

The man who hit her the grounder was a New York press agent and man-about-town named Dennis Stein, who had been hired by

---

*See New York's *Village Voice*, which reported on January 4, 1983, that Claudia was "hunting for a kind, middle-aged tycoon as a 'very special friend.'" Almost two years to the day later (January 11, 1985), she married Perelman.

Ron following the Faith Golding divorce, to get him known in the right circles.*

In business terms, things had been going well enough for Ron in the aftermath of the divorce. He had acquired the remaining public stock in MacAndrews & Forbes and turned it into a holding company for everything else he had begun to acquire—a lot of which came by way of junk bond financings underwritten by Drexel Burnham & Company. But with Faith now out of the way and Suzie Kasen no longer involved in his life either, Ron was looking for some action.† In Claudia Cohen, whom Ron noticed while lunching with Stein at the swanky Le Cirque restaurant in January 1984, he got all the action—and all the resulting publicity—he could have asked for.

After introductions by Stein, Ron and Claudia quickly became an item around town. But the real excitement began later that year when Stein, attending the Breeder's Cup in Los Angeles, bumped into a Broadway producer he knew named James Nederlander. That individual in turn introduced Stein to screen legend Elizabeth Taylor, who also happened to be at the Breeder's Cup. Stein began courting her, and within a month, the two were engaged. The press instantly erupted in a swirl of speculation over what looked to be developing

---

*Brooklyn-born Stein parlayed his charm and distinguished looks into a bicoastal role on the celebrity circuit, and it was the ease with which he moved in those circles that made him attractive to Perelman as a door opener.

†With her attractive looks and knack for self-promotion, Kasen buried her unfortunate involvement with Perelman and went on to enjoy a brief moment in the sun as a role model for women seeking to establish themselves in business. But the tug of the celebrity world soon overcame her wish to be seen as an example of female entrepreneurial success, and she began turning up in the press for things like signing a lease for rock star Billy Joel's Manhattan townhouse, and for throwing a party for a trendy new psychic named Yolana, who had lately become popular among the socially well-connected. By the late 1980s, she had married the then-president of CBS Records International, Robert Summer, and moved to Westchester, where she became a collector of British fine art, sinking eventually into comfortable obscurity.

into Ms. Taylor's eighth marriage—in this case to a man known personally to many working journalists already.

To judge from how he began behaving almost immediately, this was exactly the sort of thing Perelman had been hoping for, since he promptly sent Elizabeth an engagement gift of diamond earrings while making it a point to be constantly seen with the happy couple during the weeks that followed, typically in the company of Claudia as well. Later in December, Ron and Claudia likewise announced wedding plans, with a date set for early in January.

By that time, however, Taylor had cooled to the prospects of wedded bliss with Stein and broke off the engagement. That in turn put Perelman in enough of a snit to ask Elizabeth to give him back the earrings.[5] His own wedding plans continued on track, and he and Claudia were married in January 1985, ushering in the next phase in his increasingly public pursuit of money and the women to spend it on.*

The marriage to Claudia turned out to last barely a third as long as the marriage to Faith—and to escape from wife number two, Ron wound up having to pay almost ten times as much as he had handed over to Faith in divorce number one. But did it really mean much in the end? Not hardly. By the time it was necessary to begin writing out checks, the junk bond riches that Drexel Burnham was poised to shower on Ron and the firm's other clients had altered the entire world's perception of true wealth—so much so that $80 million in alimony amounted to little more than chump change in the grand scheme of his riches.

---

*Though Perelman continued to employ Stein as his press agent and personal promoter for the following decade and a half, Stein's influence with Perelman began to ebb until his role had been reduced to little more than that of a go-fer who arranged for theater tickets and restaurant reservations. Toward the end of his life, Stein complained bitterly of his treatment by Perelman, describing him to the author as a "spoiled brat" and "paranoid." He died in a Calabasas, California, nursing home, at the age of 70, in October 2003.

Ron Perelman had arrived in New York at the start of the 1980s with his first wife and four children in tow, and with what seemed for all the world to be almost no ready cash to call entirely his own. But by the time he married Claudia Cohen in January 1985, the prodigious leveraging power of Drexel Burnham junk bonds had long since enabled him to use the $1.7 million he'd gotten from Faith to float nearly $50 million worth of mainly junk bond loans.

With that $50 million, Ron proceeded to bulk up a spectacularly leveraged empire that *Forbes* eventually estimated to contain $1 of Ron's own money for every $2,300 he had borrowed from someone else—mostly the buyers of Drexel Burnham's junk bonds.[6]

In this collection of assets could be found a cigar company (Consolidated Cigar), a film developing company (Technicolor, Inc.) a supermarket chain (Pantry Pride, Inc.), and the crown jewel of his business—the Revlon cosmetics company, which he acquired following an ugly, public, and widely watched takeover fight during much of 1985.

Adding up the rapidly rising market value of the assets, deducting the debt, and eliminating the double-counting resulting from companies owning parts of each other, *Forbes* still concluded that by the start of 1986—which is to say in not much more than half a decade—Ron had gone from $1.7 million borrowed on his wife's signature, to a $4.7 billion collection of businesses that he owned almost 100 percent.

Against all that, what was $80 million in alimony to get a woman he'd tired of to go away?

Closing in on life's backstretch turn, a man with such a track record of triumphs already behind him might well think of himself as capable of any conquest. Yet woe to he who answers the call of the ultimate big game hunt, and shoves aside wife number two for that most beautiful, and dangerous, trophy of them all: the legendary and elusive *Shiksa Goddess of Wall Street*.

11

JACK MEETS CELEBRITY'S DARK SIDE

During his first several years as GE's chairman and CEO, the world at large barely noticed Jack Welch. He had fired plenty of people to be sure, and made plenty of news in the process. But the news was largely confined to the business pages, and not terribly flattering, typically portraying him as little more than a humorless and angry self-server, who didn't have an authentic business plan beyond firing people.[1]

But Welch's relative anonymity was soon to disappear. Not only did the acquisitions of RCA and Kidder Peabody & Company bring an instant eruption of public curiosity as to who this Welch person actually was,* but his increased visibility came just as the American

---

*In 1981, English language newspapers and magazines worldwide published just 40 stories mentioning the new GE chairman and CEO, and most were little more than perfunctory announcements of his appointment. In 1982, the number rose modestly to 59 stories, then to 86 stories in 1983, and 93 stories in 1984. But when the RCA deal was announced at year-end 1985, public interest in Welch exploded; the number of stories surged to 152 and continued to rise dramatically thereafter. In the last two years of his tenure as chairman and CEO, the number of stories topped 8,600, and nearly all were

media, having consigned the business leaders of the 1960s and 1970s to history, was searching for a new role model for business leaders of the 1980s.

In fact, scarcely had the 1980s begun when two young management consultants—Thomas Peters and Robert Waterman—sensed just such a yearning and coauthored a book entitled *In Search of Excellence* in an effort to define effective business leadership. The book offered faddish advice that often sounded self-contradictory, but readers ate it up, sending the book to the top of the nonfiction best-seller lists.*

Yet issue-oriented business books failed to satisfy Americans' hunger for a hero, and one detected exactly that hunger, still unsatisfied at mid-decade, in a January 1985 *BusinessWeek* cover story entitled "The New Corporate Elite."[2] Unable yet to identity any one individual as the new poster child for CEOs of the United States, the story did the next best thing and rounded up fifty of them, with Welch buried somewhere down in the list.[†]

Meanwhile, a Utah business consultant named Wess Roberts thought he had a better and more specific sense of what the public was after, and having failed to persuade sixteen different publishers that he knew what he was talking about, he self-published an eighty-five-page book of business advice bearing the title, *Leadership Secrets of Attila the Hun.*

---

adulatory retrospectives about his accomplishments. (During his retirement, media coverage of Welch has continued to run high, but the tenor of the coverage began to change as a result of the scandals that enveloped both Welch and the corporate world at the end of the decade.)

* Among the roughly 18 companies selected by the authors as "excellent," a third have gone out of business since then, and 3 others narrowly escaped collapse.

† Of the 50 individuals listed as "new corporate elites," 16 headed companies that eventually went out of business. Two others ran companies that are now traded in the OTC Bulletin Board for penny stocks. Only 16 of the "elites" ran companies that have survived in a respectable fashion to the present day.

The book offered a portrait of Attila as a "determined, tough, rugged and intriguing leader—who dared to accomplish difficult tasks and performed challenging feats against insurmountable odds. . . ." It suggested that the emerging new generation of American business leaders could learn the "leadership fundamentals" that had earned for Attila the sobriquet, "the scourge of God."

This message resonated with an outspoken Dallas computer salesman named H. Ross Perot, who had sold his company to General Motors in June 1984 and been given a seat on the GM board. From that perch he had begun clashing repeatedly with GM's doughy chairman, Roger Smith, over every management issue imaginable.

Seizing an opportunity to tug Smith's beard, Perot told him he planned to pass out 500 copies of a self-published book he had come across called *Leadership Secrets of Attila the Hun*. The remark not only shocked the GM chairman but found its way into a critical account of Smith's ineffective struggle to reform and streamline the company's Byzantine management structure.[3]

The publication of *Call Me Roger*, a critical look inside GM published in 1988, elevated the Attila book's visibility still more, reviving interest among publishers who had ignored it the first time around. Now, its central thesis seemed to express what Americans had been yearning for all along—a noble savage in the Darwinian blood sport of business.*

By mid-decade, the first of America's true "corporate elites" for the decade ahead was emerging in the person of Detroit auto executive Lee Iacocca—the trailblazer in a form of leadership that Americans had never before encountered: the CEO celebrity. Having been fired as president of Ford Motor Company in 1979, Iacocca had been hired

---

*The executive who acquired *Leadership Secrets of Attila the Hun* for Warner Books, Laurence Kirshbaum, had an apparent affinity for the celebration of the businessman as tough guy leader because he went on to acquire Jack Welch's autobiography when it became available a decade later.

by Chrysler Corporation a year later, thereafter engineering the corporate turnaround that saved Detroit's number three automaker from collapse. That alone had been enough to warrant a laudatory NBC prime-time profile of the man and his career in January 1984.

The program amounted to a curtain-raiser in the marketing of Iacocca as a business celebrity introducing the essential biographical elements in his iconography. They ranged from his Italian immigrant roots (complete with mom in the kitchen in her home in Allentown, Pennsylvania) to his tough-talking, "Hi ya, I'm Lee" demeanor, and his Real Man's vocabulary. It was the unfurling of Lee Iacocca as the all-American guy—a kind of John Wayne of big business. When Bantam Books published his autobiography nine months later, the book leaped instantly onto the bestseller lists and stayed there for years.

Not all reviewers fawned over *Iacocca: An Autobiography*, and the more they knew about the inner world of Detroit automaking, the less they seemed to like Iacocca's version of events. A reviewer for the Associated Press wrote that many business executives had engineered far more impressive corporate rescues than Iacocca had achieved with Chrysler, but had shown the modesty not to make bragging about it thereafter a full-time job. The AP writer quoted a management professor at Michigan State University as asserting that Iacocca's version of events was unfair and that his unrestrained ego would eventually bring him down.[4]

But the public dismissed such comments as mean-spirited carping, preferring instead the portrait of Iacocca offered by *Time*. That magazine described him as "A spunky tycoon turned superstar" and as "America's hottest new folk hero . . ."—a fellow who simply could not speak for thirty seconds without using the word "guys." Exclaimed a writer for the *Financial Times* of London, "[T]he virtues of individual charisma are back in vogue."[5]

The publishing industry had never seen anything like the Iacocca phenomenon, and agents rushed in to fill the demand for what appeared to be a whole new genre of biography: the businessman as celebrity. Books were soon emerging to celebrate Peter Ueberroth, Victor Kiam, T. Boone Pickens, John DeLorean, and many others.

Unfortunately, they all lacked the essential elements that made Iacocca's story so compelling: his humble origins and his street-smart savvy in overcoming seemingly insurmountable obstacles. His was the template for proven success in the fight of the individual against the entrenched forces of corporate bureaucracy, the status quo, and "the Establishment"; and no other CEO had the resume to pull it off except Jack Welch. And Welch had one thing more—which even Iacocca didn't have—control of the NBC television network, and in September 1986, he named himself its chairman.

〰️

As do most celebrities, Welch soon realized that the more the public's eyes were on him, the more important it became for him to make sure there were no points of conflict between his public image and his private life—a fact that now gave rise to one of the odder moments in the history of GE.

The date was September 27, 1986, and the occasion was the twentieth anniversary of the construction of the Plastics Division plant in Selkirk, New York.[6] This is where Welch had begun his climb to fame nearly a quarter century earlier when he had presided over the development of Noryl—that strong but flexible plastic that had become a ubiquitous component in everything from automobiles to office printers. Welch had led the engineering team that had overseen the development of Noryl and had also been responsible for seeing that the plant was completed on time and within its allotted $10 million budget.

Now more than two full decades had passed, and Welch had gone on to become the chairman and CEO of the entire company, presiding over a global enterprise stretching from Hong Kong to Latin America, Europe, and the Middle East. In the process, Welch had become an almost mythic figure for the employees of the Selkirk facility.

With the chairman himself having agreed to deliver the keynote address at the celebration, the men and women of the plant had been working hard for months to make sure that everything would be just as Welch would want it.

Two large tents had been set up on the factory grounds—one for refreshments, the other for a display of all the products in which Noryl was now being used. A speaker's podium had been constructed, with chairs arranged in an amphitheater-like semicircle in front. Outdoor loudspeakers had been positioned throughout the area, and a band had been hired to provide live entertainment.

The organizers had worked particularly hard to make sure that one potential embarrassment would not come up to spoil the festivities for anyone, least of all Jack Welch. The embarrassment was, of course, Selkirk's one-time top Noryl salesman—and Welch's bar-hopping soul mate—Tom ("Fitzy") Fitzgerald.

Since May, the newspapers of the mid-Hudson Valley had been brimming with stories about Fitzgerald's arrest during a homosexual liaison in a rest area off the New York State Thruway. The coverage, in turn, kept the rumor pot boiling about what had really been going on with the executives of Becker House behind the drawn curtains of the Selkirk plant.

And it hardly helped matters that although the only other man arrested in the case—a thirty-six-year-old mental health worker named John A. Rainville—had quickly pleaded guilty to a reduced charge of disorderly conduct and put the matter behind him, Fitzy Fitzgerald kept sending forth lawyers to protest his innocence.

What's more, their convoluted legal arguments seemed designed to keep Fitzy's actual behavior well hidden. When his lawyer said in mid-July that he intended to ask that the entire matter be examined in secret by a Saratoga County grand jury, public interest in the case simply ramped up yet another notch. Just what was the man trying to hide?

Something was going on here that the organizers didn't understand. Unsure of how to handle the matter, they thus did the only reasonable thing they could do under the circumstances and proceeded to erase all fingerprints of Fitzy Fitzgerald from the Selkirk plant's history that was about to be celebrated. All mentions of the man were excised from the eight-page folio brochure that was being prepared to chronicle the plant's twenty-year history. Speakers were told to drop any reference to him in their comments. No one was going to embarrass Jack Welch by bringing up the name of the strangest skeleton in his closet, who not only was still employed at the company but was actually continuing to run the Waterford Silicone Division.

Two weeks before the big day, the organizers got the biggest— and in some ways most perplexing—surprise of all. Fitzgerald abruptly reversed himself after nearly half a year of protesting his innocence and pleaded guilty to the same disorderly conduct charge that the other defendant had accepted so many months earlier. No one knew how to interpret the cave-in, and speculation ran rampant.

Yet there was at least one thing to be grateful for: Nothing more would be turning up in the newspapers about this bizarre situation to ruin the celebration. With the event now just two weeks away, the story had at last run its course. And to make sure that Fitzy didn't have any last-minute surprises up his sleeve, the organizing committee got word to him to stay away from Selkirk entirely on the day of the celebration.

Such was the prevailing climate to the celebration when, toward midday on Saturday, September 27, a GE corporate helicopter dropped from the sky and settled onto the tarmac at an airstrip abutting the plant. With the chopper's blades revolving slowly in the warm autumn air, the door to the aircraft dropped open, a ladder fell away to the ground, and Welch and his entourage emerged, then climbed into a waiting limo and departed the area. Minutes more and the limo came to a halt beside the speaker's podium on the plant's grounds, and the guest of honor stepped forth. There to greet him were various Selkirk town officials, a state senator, and an array of local GE officials.

By autumn 1986, Jack Welch's views regarding corporate management were widely known and discussed at every level of GE. His idiosyncratic opinion that fat people were lazy had already caused at least one fearful GE executive to undergo a stomach-stapling operation.[7] And he had also made it clear to one and all that he regarded the concept of "corporate loyalty" as nothing but a code phrase for "lifetime employment," which he viewed as encouraging underperformance and mediocrity.*

But when the concept of corporate loyalty touched Welch personally, his views on the matter seemed far less dogmatic. In fact, the assembled guests at the twentieth anniversary of the construction of the Selkirk plant were about to witness just how flexible his concept of loyalty really was—at least when it came to the personal corporate friendships of GE's chairman and CEO—as Welch rose to

---

* By the summer of 1988, Welch's opinions regarding corporate loyalty had burst free of GE's inner world and begun to surface in press interviews with the chairman. In an interview with the *Wall Street Journal*, Welch declared, "Loyalty to a company, it's nonsense." (See J. Guyon, *Wall Street Journal*, August 4, 1988.) But a reaction to the message had already begun to set in, reaching *Business Week* readers in an article that quoted a top GE executive as complaining, "Loyalty here is 24-hours deep. Welch has lost the dedication of a couple hundred thousand people." See "Jack Welch: How Good a Manager?" in *Business Week* (December 14, 1987), p. 92.

the microphone and proceeded to contribute his own two cents to the day's festivities by launching into an extended oration on that great business leader to whom GE owed so much—the one and only Fitzy Fitzgerald.

More than a decade and a half later, a man who had been sitting behind Welch on the podium during his speech remembered the scene as vividly as if it had happened just twenty minutes earlier. He said, "It was so quiet you could have heard a pin drop. And you should have seen the faces in the audience. The people were utterly stupefied."

〜〜〜

In fact, even as Welch rose to praise the accomplishments of a "business soul mate" who was now recognized as a sexual pervert, the GE chairman's personal affairs were presenting him with challenges from yet another direction: It was time to dump the wife.

The relationship between Jack and Carolyn Welch, married by now for nearly twenty-eight years, had been deteriorating steadily, as the rumors regarding Jack and his womanizing grew noisier and more persistent. By now, the situation with Carolyn had passed the point of no return, at least as far as Jack was concerned, and in December 1986, he finally served divorce papers to her, and squared off to fight her in court if things ever got to that point.

Documents in the case show just how lopsided such a struggle would have been, too, since faced with the biggest challenge of her adult life, Carolyn seems to have gone through her days in a traumatized fog, barely aware of the magnitude of the stakes involved. And certainly Jack wasn't about to spell out the situation for her.

During the previous twenty-eight years, the Welches had accumulated a family estate worth just under $12 million.[8] Yet none of it belonged to Carolyn except a half interest in their New Canaan,

Connecticut, home, a 50 percent share of their vacation place in Sun Valley, Idaho, and roughly $90,000 worth of cash, jewelry, and stocks. Everything else—more than $11 million worth in all— was held in Jack's name. And most of it sat beyond Carolyn's easy reach, though she had certainly contributed to Jack's ability to accumulate it.

In Jack's name were just under $5 million worth of municipal bonds, $12 million in GE stock options, and $2 million in real estate, including his own 50 percent stakes in their homes in New Canaan and Sun Valley. But Jack also owned $370,000 worth of properties in Florida, a vacation home on Nantucket, an apartment in New York, and some odds and ends, bringing his gross total to $19.2 million. Against that, he owed $1.7 million in real estate loans, and $6.3 million in potential tax liabilities, for a net personal estate of $11.2 million that his wife would have to fight hard to get even a piece of. And she hardly seemed ready to try.

Quite the contrary, financial documents in the case file reveal Carolyn to have been living an *extremely* modest lifestyle for a CEO's wife. Her total personal food bill, including meals in restaurants, averaged $175 per week, making clear enough (1) that Jack either rarely if ever took his wife to dinner or (2) that no one told Carolyn she could include those expenses in her estimated weekly food bill.

Carolyn's clothing outlays, of roughly $10,000 per year, was likewise modest for the wife of the chairman of the U.S.'s largest industrial and manufacturing enterprise. Compare $10,000 per year for Carolyn to the $15,000 per dress that designers like Galanos were by this time charging for evening gowns worn by trendsetters like First Lady Nancy Reagan at White House galas.

Carolyn's personal transportation expenses of $1,800 per year become nothing more than a rounding number when compared with the staggering $67,000 per *week* that Jack's second wife, Jane

Beasley Welch, listed in her own divorce against him fifteen years later, in 2002.*

Reading through the documents, one senses in Carolyn Osburn Welch a woman struck dumb by what was happening to her. In the entire case file, there is not a single assertion of her entitlement to the lifestyle she had presumably lived as the wife of GE's chairman and CEO. Instead, the file contains a "Defendant's Financial Affidavit" suggesting that on some level or other Carolyn was already preparing herself for a life of utter penury. On the affidavit, one finds anticipated weekly outlays for things like:

Garbage removal	$ 4.42
Driver's license, registration fees	$ 0.53
Parking	$10.00
Hairdresser	$20.93
Exterminator	$ 4.42

It is the list of a desperate and confused woman, seemingly unable to summon even one counterpunch to the haymaker that had just knocked her against the ropes.

---

*The comparison between the income levels and living standards supplied by Welch to the two women is astounding. The first wife, Carolyn Osburn Welch, listed total discretionary expenses of $766.82 per week, including food, domestic help, laundry, a visit to the hairdresser, hobbies, vacation and travel, and home entertaining. Fifteen years later, Welch's second wife, Jane Beasley Welch, listed travel alone at nearly $10,000 per *day*. Jane also listed $10,360 per month in jewelry expenses, $5,000 per month in petty cash, $4,000 per month for a chauffeured limo, $8,260 for wine, $6,933 for live-in help, and unspecified maintenance costs on six luxury automobiles. One sign of changing spousal attitudes in these matters is that Carolyn Osburn Welch was willing to settle, uncontested, for not much more than $3.2 million in cash plus a Toyota station wagon and the house she lived in. However, Welch's second wife, Jane Beasley Welch, demanded 50 percent of his net worth (by some estimates to have topped $900 million by the end of the 1990s)—a claim that represented a 30,000 percent escalation in living standard expectations from the first wife to the second, during a fifteen-year-period when Welch's actual employment did not change at all.

As for Jack, well, he just hung tough. With Carolyn seemingly incapable of fighting back, Welch agreed to give her the New Canaan house, while keeping all the others, including the place in Sun Valley, for himself. He also got to keep all four of the family automobiles, while agreeing in return to buy Carolyn a Toyota. He also agreed to let Carolyn keep the $90,000 in cash, stocks, and jewelry she already owned, while keeping everything else—roughly $11 million worth of assets in all—for himself. Out of that total, he agreed to pay her a lump sum of $2.2 million, plus $1 million in alimony spread over seven years.

With that—and a tip-of-the-hat—Jack was gone. And having already purchased a new riverfront home for himself in the nearby town of Weston, he began living out the babe-magnet fantasies to which he had aspired for so long. Welch was, after all, now a power in the media. The man he was soon to oust as president of NBC News, Lawrence Grossman, looked back on the matter years later and remarked of his former colleague, "Yes, he was really like that," adding discreetly, in the way men often do, "but you'll have to get the details from someone else."

Much as he may have wished in the end that things had turned out differently, what happened next to Jack Welch underscores just how reliable behavioral science often proves to be in predicting the sex-linked choices men make, whether the man is an entry-level employee at a plant like GE's Plastics facility in Pittsfield at the start of the 1960s, or the head of the entire corporation thirty years later.

To that end, data compiled by the U.S. Census Bureau show that the median age of white American males born in 1935 was 22.5 years when they married for the first time.[9] Welch, who was born in 1935, was just two days beyond his twenty-fourth birthday when he married Carolyn Osburn in November 1959. What's more, the data also show that men who had been married for more than twenty-five years at the time of their first divorce would typically remarry within the following two years—and that is exactly what Welch did.

In other words, far from being a creation of his own free will and personal choices, Jack Welch was just another testosterone-crazed guy, tugged along by the unseen grip of fate on his dong.

The woman with her hand on Jack's tiller was a New York lawyer named Jane Beasley, and she, too, had issues that made her life interesting. She had come to New York with a degree from the University of Kentucky Law School at the start of the 1980s, landing a job as an associate at the law firm of Shearman & Sterling. From that perch, she had caught the eye of Walter Wriston, a former chairman of Citicorp who was still serving as an outside director on the board of GE. Knowing that Welch was now divorced, Wriston had fixed Jane up on a date with the GE chairman, and as can be counted on to happen under such circumstances, one thing led to the next.

To begin with, Jane was good looking, which counts for a lot with a man who is over fifty, balding, and looking for reinforcement that he's actually six-foot-four with a full head of hair. What's more, Jane was energetic and tending toward the dirty blonde zone, which made the situation even better. And though she was seventeen years younger than Welch (hardly an obstacle so far as Jack was concerned), she had logged a few laps of her own on the "Dealing with Men" circuit, with an actual former husband rattling around somewhere in her past.

In fact, Jack Welch was putty in her hands, and by the second date, she had figured him out entirely. She showed up for dinner at an East Side Manhattan steak place called Smith & Wollensky's wearing exactly the outfit to knock him flat—not the heels and the thigh-slit skirt and braless crepe blouse with the top four buttons undone. Not this time. No "Easy Girl at the Drive-In" outfit from Annie Sez for this bag-the-bear date!

Jane and Jack Welch: Just a down-home girl with her hand on the man's tiller. A typo from farmer to lawyer, but can she play golf? (*Photo credit:* Marina Garnier.)

Instead she wore blue jeans and a leather jacket, like Olivia Newton-John in *Grease*. And Jack showed up in his own jeans-and-leather-jacket rig, suggesting a bald and flabby version of Olivia's co-star, John Travolta—that being the person he really seems to have thought *he* was.

Jack asked her about her family, and she told him she was just a down-home girl from Alabama, which he naturally lapped up, and they agreed to meet again.*

---

*Jack and Jane's first dinner-for-two appears in both the hardcover and softcover editions of his autobiography, *Jack: Straight from the Gut* (New York: Warner Books, 2001). But certain key facts regarding Jane's background and parentage were grossly altered in the softcover edition (published two years after the hardcover), underscoring the self-serving and often unreliable characterizations and recollections of persons and events found in Welch's autobiography.

During the two years between the publication of the hardcover and subsequent softcover editions, Jack's personal life went through a major upheaval in which he and Jane became embroiled in an ugly and public divorce triggered by Jack's romantic

One date led to the next, and finally Jack was ready to pop the big question: "Can you play golf?" To which she replied no, thereby reassuring him without actually having to say so that even if she learned to play and thereafter practiced real hard (which of course she quickly promised to do), she'd never be good enough to beat GE's king of all hole-in-one heroes. After that, there was nothing left but to draw up the prenuptial agreement, and eighteen months later they were married—just as the U.S. Census Bureau data had said would happen.

---

involvement with an editor from the *Harvard Business Review* named Suzy Wetlaufer, who thereafter became his companion.

In both editions of Jack's autobiography, he and Jane are shown discussing Jane's family background during their dinner-for-two at Smith & Wollensky's. In the hardcover edition, Jane is portrayed describing her childhood as it actually was—the life of an impoverished Alabama farm girl, who worked at 5:30 A.M. in the mornings in stoop-labor, picking beans on her father's dirt farm.

But in the softcover edition two years later, all references to her father as an Alabama dirt farmer, and to her childhood as a stoop-laborer, are removed and replaced with the false characterization of her father as "a lawyer." Thirty-three words in all were changed, as well as several entire sentences, to accomplish the alteration of his second wife's childhood into out-and-out fiction. The change itself, which bears the skillful touch of a professional editor, seems to have had but one purpose: to improve and upgrade the backgrounds of the women Jack chose as wives, suggesting that the likely culprit was Suzy Wetlaufer, who declined to be interviewed for this book. For his part, the autobiography's co-author, John Byrne, said he knew nothing of the change when questioned about it for this book, and expressed anger and bewilderment over the fact that it had been made. Requests for an explanation from the publisher of the book, Warner Business Books, brought only a vague response that the change had been nothing more than an inadvertent "typo."

In yet another—and separate—re-editing of his past, a bedroom scene in which Jack and Jane discuss golf was deleted from the softcover edition in its entirety.

12

THE SHIKSA GODDESS OF WALL STREET

Jack Welch was not the only business leader for whom the 1980s had become a time of new beginnings, as rising wealth and advancing middle age brought an entire generation of business leaders to the portals of new opportunity—both at the office and at home. And without missing a beat, they began one after the next to step through—as if by doing so was to say that wealth, sex, and power had been their natural entitlement all along.

Leading the parade: Ronald Perelman, his coffers now bulging with billions from his early use of Drexel Burnham junk bonds. With interest rates falling and his riches rising, he seemed a financial genius and clairvoyant. And with the fame came the women, more glamorous and seductive than ever.

Alas for Ron Perelman, not every woman who came his way was ready simply to decorate his arm—and one in particular saw things quite differently. Ron Perelman may have thought of himself as being entitled to the most beautiful woman on earth as his reward for being rich. But Patricia Duff Medavoy viewed the matter from the opposite perspective and had been eyeing the richest man on

Wall Street as her reward for simply being beautiful. The clash of these two egos was to usher in the final and most egregious chapter in the escapades of CEOs gone wild.

Patricia Michelle Hoar was born in Los Angeles in April 1954, the third of four children of a former Navy pilot, named Robert Hoar, and a stay-at-home mom named Mary, who seemed to go through her days in a permanent pout at her husband over one thing or another.[1] When Patricia was born, the Hoars were living in Woodland Hills, California, amidst the tract homes of the San Fernando Valley about eighteen miles west of Burbank, where Robert Hoar worked as an executive for the Lockheed Corporation. In 1960, Robert changed the family name from Hoar to Orr—apparently to help his three daughters avoid growing up with a name that invited teasing by schoolmates. After taking a job at Hughes Aircraft, he relocated his family to Bonn, West Germany, in 1964 and thereafter to Brussels, Belgium.[2]

It was the 1960s, and the Cold War was giving way to Détente. As contacts between East and West multiplied, the West German capital of Bonn—made famous in the John Le Carre novel, *A Small Town in Germany*—became a magnet for spies, informants, and double agents representing virtually every espionage service on earth. Whether Robert Orr was part of that demi-world is not known, though it certainly would have been difficult for an American businessmen in the aerospace industry to have avoided being at least approached for information at one point or another. Bonn was, after all, a city that swarmed with government agents and operatives—usually working under cover as commercial attachés—and always on the lookout to make contact with businessmen such as Robert Orr.

Be that as it may, the world of Bonn in the 1960s was by its very circumstances both wary and scheming—a place where friendships formed quickly, remained shallow, and were easily shed when necessity dictated. Arab diplomats arrived dripping with money, threw a few parties, and then disappeared. Everyone knew at least one former

Wehrmacht *obergruppenführer* who had done something frightful on the Eastern Front. But nobody mentioned names, and nobody had the full details. It was the way Bonn was—and it was the first world beyond her own home that Patricia Duff ever really knew.

Thereafter, Robert Orr was relocated to Brussels and the family moved again. Patricia and her siblings attended the International School in Brussels, which served the city's rapidly growing international community. By all accounts, Patricia was a good student and enjoyed participating in the life of the school, including such extracurricular activities as the school's student council, where she served as vice president. She was also very good looking—tall and trim, with clear skin and intense gray-green eyes that bathed her with a kind of "notice me first" aura whenever she walked into a room.

The only place where Patricia didn't seem to hold the spotlight was in her own home, where family life seethed with an undercurrent of bickering and tension between her parents. Often, Patricia found herself playing the role of peacemaker in their conflicts.[3]

Patricia graduated from the International School in 1971, and because her grades had been good, she was accepted as an undergraduate at Barnard College in New York, a prestigious "Seven Sisters" college for women that is affiliated with Columbia University.

Pat brought with her a head full of ambition to make both a name and a career for herself in the world of men. This inspiration appears to have originated with her mother, Mary, who seems to have spent a lot of time griping that her own career had been sacrificed to advance her husband's, and encouraging Patricia not to make the same mistake.

A bachelor's degree from Barnard College would certainly have aided Patricia greatly in pursuing her goals, which at this point seem to have been focused on a career in either journalism or the diplomatic corps. Yet midway through her freshman year, she suddenly dropped out of Barnard and returned to Europe, resurfacing a year later in Washington, D.C., as a student at Georgetown University.

It was an odd detour to say the least, and when she subsequently became famous as the Democratic Party's reigning bicoastal Cleopatra and magazine writers began to chronicle her life, they discovered the puzzling moment. But she waved their curiosity away. And when they persisted, she engaged in manipulative little negotiations to arrange the facts of the period in the way she wanted. Her principal goal appears to have been to sidestep her way around any mention of a person named Thomas Zabrodsky and the brief but seemingly bizarre role he played in her life.

In fact, it wasn't just Zabrodsky but what he represented that Patricia was actually trying to keep hidden; Zabrodsky marked the start of a lifelong pattern of self-destructive choices in husbands, with each new misadventure causing Patricia to suffer the ravages of her poor choice more piteously, even as she scanned the horizon for someone new to rescue her from her misery.

Zabrodsky was the first; though many facts are missing to explain how it happened that this individual—who was several years older than she, yet seems to have been her boyfriend at the International School in Brussels—should have conveniently materialized at her side in New York at just the moment when she ostensibly learned, midway through her freshman year at Barnard, that her parents were divorcing and would no longer be able to afford her college tuition.

A 1996 profile in *Los Angeles* magazine suggests that her father may have played a role in triggering her behavior, for the article quotes an unidentified longtime friend as saying that Patricia held her father responsible for no longer being able to pay her tuition at Barnard so that she had to drop out of college.[4]

According to a psychological report covering Patricia's early years, prepared by a Canadian research expert on domestic violence, Donald Dutton, as part of Patricia's divorce fight with Ron, she reacted to her father's failure to pay her tuition by hooking up with Zabrodsky. As explained in the so-called "Dutton Report," Patricia's life at the International School had left her unprepared for the challenges of urban life as a college student in a city like New York, and she had become involved with Zabrodsky in a search for support. Her dependence on Zabrodsky thereafter increased, says the report, after she was hit with the news of her parents' collapsed marriage and the termination of their tuition support.

According to the report, at the same time that Patricia was being informed *"by her father"* [emphasis added] that "she could no longer attend Barnard College, she came into contact with an old boyfriend named Tom Zabrodsky." The report states that she had known Zabrodsky during a period when they had both been students at the International School, and that she now "found herself gravitating toward him as a substitute for her parents."

Precisely *how* Duff "came into contact" with Zabrodsky at this pivotal and anxious moment is not discussed, though it seems improbable in the extreme that it was quite so coincidental as Patricia appears to have made it sound. Zabrodsky was a boyfriend she had last seen in Brussels, and it simply challenges common sense to imagine her walking across the Columbia University campus one day and suddenly finding herself face-to-face with this individual, who had presumably never told her he was in town.

More likely, Zabrodsky either accompanied Patricia to Columbia at the beginning of the semester, or she reached out to him as a rescuer after her father cut her off—if indeed her father did so. The likelihood that any such thing happened is itself doubtful since Patricia returned to college in the United States the following September—this time at Georgetown University in Washington, D.C., where tuition costs are as high as at Barnard.

Whatever the precise scenario, the Dutton Report reveals that not only did Duff immediately drop out of Barnard, but that she proceeded to accompany Zabrodsky back to Europe, where "she lived with Tom in Switzerland for about one year."

According to the Dutton Report, this led to yet another round of Rescue Pat adventures—only instead of Zabrodsky rescuing Patricia from her father, Dad was now to rescue her back again from Zabrodsky. As proof, the Dutton Report describes what happened when, according to Patricia, her father at last made arrangements to get her out of the country, away from Zabrodsky, and back to the United States. The Report describes a melodramatic scene in which Zabrodsky somehow blocked her from reaching the airport, not just once but several times, leading her father to help her escape "surreptitiously . . . via an indirect route."

In the escape yarn, steeped as it is in the images of a CIA novel, one finds Patricia in the first of her Fay Wray roles as a real-life drama queen, eternally doomed to be rescued by Bruce Cabot from the clutches of the tall dark stranger who marries her then proceeds to morph before her horrified eyes into the world's biggest gorilla.

And the bizarre entanglement didn't end there because, according to the Dutton Report, Zabrodsky followed her back to the United States, tracked her down to Washington, D.C., and took up with her all over again. What's more, he began "repeatedly and forcefully" pressuring her to marry him. Claiming to have felt "emotionally blackmailed"—the identical excuse she would give for marrying Perelman almost twenty years later—she succumbed. The Report says the marriage ended with an uncontested divorce sometime later but doesn't specify exactly when.

Whether or not Zabrodsky was quite the control freak portrayed in the Dutton Report is hard to know. He subsequently acknowledged in a magazine interview that their marriage had been "turbulent," and that it involved a "battle for dominance."[5] But even allowing for that, at least one published account of their relationship includes a reported tidbit from Rescue Number Two that sounds wholly improbable to say the least—that when Patricia's father came to rescue her from Zabrodsky he found her literally "chained to a radiator."[6]

How Patricia got her foot in the door in Washington, D.C., Democratic Party circles is itself a story of Rashamon-like variability, though it seems that much of the emotional inspiration for at least making a stab at politics came by way of her mother, Mary, who had been struggling with her own frustrated career opportunities as a Kennedy-era liberal. That struggle was undoubtedly intense, with the drama of the 1960s unfolding back in the United States and beyond Mary's reach while she remained shipwrecked in Europe in a bad marriage to a man who may or may not have had ties to the world of covert intelligence.

So it's not surprising that we hear echoes of Mary's plight in Patricia's interviews once she became newsworthy in her own right, and reporters began to explore her ties to Democratic politics in the Carter era. Thus, when a reporter for *Esquire* asked Patricia to reflect on the reasons for her interest in politics, she cited her mother, saying, "She was totally committed. She believed you had to do something, whether it was civil rights or women's issues or whatever."[7]

No one seems to have greased any rails for Pat in her job search. She just knocked on doors for interviews and was immediately invited in—especially if the person who answered the door was a man. At the age of twenty-three, she had already acquired the swanlike looks of a timeless and classical beauty, from her ripening and sensuous frame to her drowning pool eyes and graceful neck, which she displayed by piling her hair atop her head in billowing folds. In this way she wound up as a staff researcher on a congressional committee set up in 1977 to investigate the assassination of President John F. Kennedy.*

---

*The so-called House Select Committee on Assassinations was established by an act of Congress in March 1977 and submitted its final report two years later, in March 1979, after which it disbanded. The committee's principal work focused on the assassination of President John F. Kennedy in Dallas, Texas, November 22, 1963, and was directed toward addressing concerns as to whether evidence of a conspiracy to kill the president had been either ignored or overlooked by the so-called Warren Commission that had

Much of the committee's work involved exploring the conspiratorial ties, both rumored and imagined, between organized crime figures such as Sam Giancana of the Chicago Mafia, and anti-Kennedy groups ranging from the right wing of Texas politics, to the Fair Play for Cuba movement in Miami. Assigned to research linkages between these various groups, Pat fit right in and was soon on the radar screen of every male working on the committee.

By the time the committee disbanded at the end of the decade, Pat had acquired an aura of glamour and mystery that loomed all out of proportion to her job as a mere staff researcher. She also had become a frequent—and much gossiped about—companion of Connecticut Congressman Christopher Dodd, a member of the committee.

The trail of slack-jawed men she left in her wake ranged from political commentator John McLaughlin, then beginning his career as a professional TV talk show yeller, to Democratic pollster Pat Caddell and virtually every male member of the House Select Committee and all their staff aides. Yet of them all, she next married an obscure government lawyer named Daniel Duff—a fact subsequently sighted by herself and various friends in her divorce fight with Perelman as evidence that she really wasn't a gold digger and was actually just a normal down-home girl at heart.

Down home or not, her interest in Duff lasted just four years—from 1980 to 1984—coming to an end when she moved out and headed for Los Angeles in hopes of re-inventing herself as a Hollywood actress. That effort went nowhere, and instinctively she returned to politics, drifting into the glamour and showboating end of Democratic Party fund-raising on the West Coast.

---

been appointed to investigate the matter. The resulting report asserted a "high probability" that the "lone gunman" theory put forth by the Warren Commission had been wrong and that a second gunman, in addition to Lee Harvey Oswald, had fired on the president in Dealey Plaza.

Patricia Duff Medavoy Perelman. She looked great, and she moved great, and she smelled great, and she sounded great. And Ron thought, this is great, as into the room she would sweep, trailing her fur coat and done up top-to-toe in Valentino. What else could one do but fall silent and simply stare? It was Fay Wray Patricia versus Rescuer Ron. Her *Leave It to Beaver* house? (*Photo credit:* Marina Garnier.)

In this way, she wound up catching the eye of a motion picture producer named Michael Medavoy. Having divorced Daniel Duff in 1984, she married Medavoy two years later and began what amounted to a whole new career for herself in Hollywood. Then one day toward the end of 1992, Ron Perelman turned up in her life.

The scene was the lobby of the Ritz Hotel on Paris's Place Vendôme. A decade had passed since Ron Perelman had committed matrimonial *hara-kiri* with his flower girl honey, Susan ("Suzie Cream Cheese") Kasen in the Hotel Plaza-Athené, and now he was back—this time with wife number two, gossip columnist Claudia Cohen, in tow.

The intervening years had been good for Ron, at least in business terms. Falling interest rates had driven up the value of everything he held, even as the savings and loan crisis that followed the 1987 stock market crash created enormous investment opportunities for anyone with enough cash to take advantage of them. And since Ron had built his empire almost entirely out of borrowed money— much of it backed by Drexel Burnham & Company junk bonds— he had been able to save his cash rather than spend it. In this way, he wound up perfectly positioned to take advantage of the S&L deals that appealed to him.

Key among them was a deal he worked out with the Federal Savings and Loan Insurance Corporation to put up $165 million of his own cash in return for a 77 percent ownership stake in five Texas-based S&Ls that had $13 billion of combined assets on their books. The investment thereafter generated huge tax benefits that sheltered income throughout the rest of the Perelman empire.

Scarcely was the ink dry on that deal than Ron paid $82.5 million to acquire ownership of the Marvel Entertainment Group comic books publishing house, then paid $120 million to acquire the television company that had sold it to him (New World Entertainment), while buying the Coleman Co. camping goods company for $545 million more.

But Ron wanted more . . . more money of course—and more, as well, of what money could buy. And that is pretty much where things stood when he took a trip to Paris, with Claudia in tow, and they happened to run into the actress Melanie Griffith and her husband at the time, television actor Don Johnson.* Both Melanie and

---

*Both couples have had successful, and at times colorful, careers. The two were married briefly in the late 1970s, then divorced, then remarried in 1989. Melanie Griffith, the daughter of Hollywood actress Tippie Hedrin, underwent well-publicized bouts of alcohol and drug abuse in both the 1970s and 1980s, and has not been a marquee name in Hollywood since she costarred in *Working Girl* in 1988. Don Johnson has also had well-publicized alcohol and drug problems and was admitted to the Betty Ford Clinic for treatment in 1994. In November 2002, he was stopped while crossing by automobile from Switzerland into Germany and found to be carrying documents reflecting $8 billion of credit transactions. An investigation was opened, Johnson denied any wrongdoing, and the matter remains unresolved as of this writing.

Don had already worked for Perelman in a 1989 magazine ad campaign for Revlon, and Melanie would soon be signing with him as a Revlon Girl model.

The four had agreed to meet for dinner that evening at a Parisian restaurant called Taillevent, on Rue Lamennais.

Later that day, as Don and Melanie were leaving their hotel on an errand, they unexpectedly encountered Mike Medavoy and Patricia entering to check in. Surprised greetings were exchanged all around and Melanie, who was a better friend of Patricia's than Don was of Mike's, suggested the couple join them for dinner with "the man who owns Revlon . . . you know, Ron Perelman." They agreed.

How Ron reacted to the news that Medavoy and his attractive wife would be joining them for dinner that evening isn't known. But his curiosity to meet Medavoy's much talked-about wife, Patricia, is not hard to imagine.

One may view the matter through the subtext to a marketing poster that had begun turning up in California and Florida luxury automobile speed shops as the 1990s progressed. The poster featured a vertical shot, from a height of perhaps twenty feet, of a red Porsche Cabriolet convertible with the top down, under which appeared the caption: "Everybody Wants One."

In fact, the poster's appeal went well beyond the automobile itself, even allowing for its ruby lacquered finish—as luscious and wet as the lips of Claudia Schiffer—and the black-on-black lambskin leather seats that could swallow you in their embrace. No, the appeal involved something more, for once a man possessed all that—once he had acquired the summer place in Bar Harbor and the getaway cottage in East Hampton; once he owned the 110-foot aluminum hull Feadship, and the Gulfstream IV at Teterboro—there was still (and always) one thing more to want.

Beyond the Guardsman red Porsche Cabriolet, with its 1,400 pounds of oiled and thrusting steel, came the promise of what owning

EVERYBODY WANTS ONE

After the Porsches and the Feadships and the owner's box above home plate, Oh God, please, just this one more thing. (*Photo credit:* Copyright 1986. Auto Trend Graphics poster available at www.autotrend.com/6969.html.)

one was really all about. And there in the poster was the promise: The man in a dinner tux behind the wheel, his tie yanked off in exhaustion and his head slumped back, and next to him the blonde, in her slit-to-the-thigh evening dress, her milk-white skin glistening in the evening dew, and her head bent over, face down in his lap, her golden hair spilling discreetly over him in waves of desire.

That is what every man wanted: After the Porsches and the Feadships and the owner's box above home plate—there was still (and forever) that one last thing to desire . . . that one last moment to complete the mightiest conquest: *Oh God, please, just this one more thing . . . !*

And at the start of 1993, no billionaire businessman could have asked for more than to take a ride in a Porsche Cabriolet, or a Gulfstream IV, with Patricia Duff Medavoy at his side. She had what they refer to (when the women aren't around) as "the complete package"—the face of Greta Garbo, the brains of Brooke Shields, and the body of Heather Locklear. Unfortunately, when Ron unwrapped the package and looked inside, he found smiling back to embrace him, the one they call Lilith, the golden-haired demon queen.*

---

*The origins of the myth of Lilith the Dark Goddess are lost in antiquity, with elements of the myth appearing almost simultaneously in several pre-Christian cultures, suggesting either a common source that has yet to be uncovered, or that the imagery is powerful enough to find original expression in many cultures at once. In Mesopotamian mythology, Lilith appears as both a fertility goddess and a demon. She appears in myths of ancient Sumeria, Persia, and many other cultures as well, embodying the most potent fantasies—and deepest fears—of men in each culture. In Etruscan mythology, she guards the gates of Hell. In other myths, she is the bride of Satan and the mother of all plagues. In early Christian astrology, she is known as the "Black Moon." Biblical scholars say she appears in the Old Testament as a "screech owl" (Isaiah 34:14) and in Hebrew folk mythology as Adam's first wife, who leaves him to become the concubine of demons.

In *Changing Literary Representations of Lilith and the Evolution of a Mythical Heroine* (Pittsburgh, PA: Carnegie Mellon University, 1999), Amy Scerba traces the threads of the Lilith myth from the Sumerian epic poem of Gilgamesh, fifth king of the first dynasty of Uruk (2000 B.C.), through the early-nineteenth-century Romantic writers of Europe (Goethe and Keats), and finally into the modern era's image of Lilith as the ultimate *femme fatale* in the poetry and painting of Dante Gabriel Rossetti, who wrote:

> Of Adam's first wife, Lilith, it is told
> Her enchanted hair was the first gold.
> Who draws men to watch the bright net she can weave,
> Till heart and body and life are in its hold.

In *Popcorn Venus, Women, Movies and the American Dream* (New York: Avon Books, 1973), film critic Marjorie Rosen discusses the motion picture industry's creation of feminine stereotypes. One result: American pop culture's deification of blondes, which can be traced to the sexual fantasies of Hollywood's early studio bosses, who projected their own yearnings of one face of Lilith—the blonde, blue-eyed ingenue—onto the silver screen, further solidifying the modern stereotype of beauty as the woman with the hair of gold.

In 1967, author Philip Roth's lead character in the novel *Portnoy's Complaint* simply reflected that conditioning when he came upon a group of girls in Central Park and

Certainly the dinner revealed only Lilith's more beguiling charms, as Patricia (she pronounced it Pah-tree-sha) exuded precisely the sort of approachable appeal that must have driven Ron wild. She was Hollywood's most heavenly angel—all light and fresh and new, with none of the Levantine subtext Claudia brought with her. She seemed to say, I am confident about who I am, and you can be confident, too. Her voice was clear, but low, and it came from somewhere deep within her, with the throaty timbre that suggested a woman who knew her own mind. He seemed to stay cool, and keep everything dialed back and low key. But did she notice, in that instant when their look-away eyes met for a second, that his gaze may have lingered just a beat longer?

It was a dinner with subtext messages running in many directions. Melanie and Don had been married and divorced once already, in the late 1970s, and now they were back together again, like a B-list version of Elizabeth Taylor and Richard Burton. And true to the Liz-and-Dick script, tensions were once again building between them—much of it rooted in Don's substance-abuse issues. And all of this was part of the subtext to the dinner.

For that matter, so was Melanie's separate situation with Ron, which traced back to her work as a Revlon magazine advertising model and a deal that was now in the works to sign her to a much more lucrative and high-visibility contract as the first "over 35" Revlon Girl for a TV advertising campaign. As part of such deals, Revlon Girls were rumored to get some quality time with Ron, and Melanie was no exception—at least so far as the rumors were concerned.

---

swooned: "I am so awed that I am in a state of desire beyond a hard-on. My circumcised little dong is simply shriveled up with veneration. Maybe it's dread. How do they get so gorgeous, so healthy, *so blond?*" See P. Roth, *Portnoy's Complaint* (New York: Random House, 1967), pp. 144–145.

In addition, there was the relationship between Ron and Claudia. Signs of trouble had begun seeping into print more than a year earlier when Ron had walked out of their Manhattan townhouse and took up residence in the couple's newly acquired East Hampton estate.[8] The departure was followed by Claudia's reported admittance to Memorial Sloan-Kettering Hospital for an undisclosed treatment, and the gossip mill cranked overtime regarding her health. Not long after, Ron began surfacing in gossip columns in both New York and Hollywood, typically linked to boldface names like supermodel Claudia Shiffer and *Vogue* magazine editor Elizabeth Saltzman. By now, the marriage between Ron and his second wife was said by friends of the couple to exist pretty much in name only, yet there the two sat as well, adding their own piquant tension to the proceedings.

And, of course, the dinner included Mike and Patricia Medavoy. Born in Shanghai in 1941 where he remained throughout the whole of World War II, Medavoy was barely a decade older than Pat, to whom he had been introduced by Congressman Christopher Dodd. And though they had quickly become a Hollywood glamour couple, the two really seemed to have little in common. The biggest issue dividing them: Pat's increasing fixation on having a baby before her biological window of opportunity closed forever. This is something that Pat hadn't explained as one of her life-agenda items when the two were married in 1986, but six years later it was the subtext to everything between them.

Medavoy's Hollywood credentials were considerable. He had begun his career in the mailroom of Universal Studios, then became a talent agent, helping package a number of 1970s hits, including *The Sting* and *Jaws*. In 1974, he and four associates founded Orion Pictures, where he was thought to have developed an almost Midas touch, launching seven "Best Picture" Oscar winners in a row, beginning with *One Flew over the Cuckoo's Nest* in 1975, to his most recent

Mike Medavoy and his doll-face. On Oscar night, she and Ron walked the floor while Mike felt sick and went to sleep. Best Performance by a Drama Queen? (*Photo credit:* Marina Garnier.)

accomplishment—*The Silence of the Lambs* (1991)—which he had green-lighted from his new post as chairman of Tristar Pictures.[9]

But lately, Medavoy's hot hand had cooled, in large part because of the unsettled corporate politics of Tristar itself. Originally a joint venture of CBS, Home Box Office, and Columbia Pictures, Tristar had been effectively owned and controlled by Columbia since 1987. Then in 1989, Columbia was taken over by Sony Corporation of Japan. Into this confused situation wandered Medavoy in 1990. Though he held the title of Tristar Pictures' chairman, his real power was circumscribed by the bizarre role of the executive above him: a one-time hairdresser named Jon Peters. This individual, who did time in reform school and had dropped out of junior high school after the seventh grade, got his big break in Hollywood when he was invited to cut and blow-dry Barbra Streisand's hair for the 1974 movie, *For Pete's Sake*.

The movie bombed, but Peters was nonetheless able to parlay the cut-and-blow-dry assignment into a romantic relationship with Streisand, and after that, into the co-chairmanship of Columbia Pictures along with his sidekick Peter Guber. Together, the two nearly bankrupted the studio, departing in 1991 with the place in shambles.*

A year later, the situation at Columbia had deteriorated still further, and the Hollywood gossip mill was beginning to churn with speculation about how much longer Medavoy would be able to hang on. Yet in the midst of all this, his wife kept bringing up the one subject that he really didn't want to hear about: "the baby" thing.[10] It was driving him nuts. Now this, too, was part of the background hum to the evening's dinner table festivities, as six individuals

---

*For more on the Peters and Guber era at Columbia Pictures, and Medavoy's role at Tristar, see K. Masters and N. Griffin, *Hit and Run: How Jon Peters and Peter Guber Took Sony for a Ride in Hollywood* (New York: Simon & Schuster, 1996). The story contains an entertaining series of fly-on-the-wall accounts of how Peters and Guber conducted business at the studio. In one typical scene, a meeting is under way in a conference room at Sony's New York headquarters to firm up the Japanese electronic giant's $4.8 billion takeover of Columbia—the largest such deal up to that time in Hollywood history. A solemn occasion? Don't bet on it. Behind the closed doors of this particular ten-digit deal are a room full of media and investment banking executives engaged in the rough equivalent of a food fight—at the center of which is Walter Yetnikoff, the head of Sony's record division, lately acquired from CBS, with Yetnikoff coming along as part of the deal. In the final throes of drug abuse hysterics—and soon to be admitted to the Hazelden Clinic for detox treatment—Yetnikoff is puffing furiously on a Nat Sherman cigar while verbally abusing his own top investment banking advisor, Pete Peterson, chairman of the Blackstone Group, at whom he screams, for no apparent reason, "You're a fucking asshole." At which point, more or less—and again for no discernible reason—one of the two men who are destined to run the studio once Sony acquires it, Jon Peters (but who is being kept out of the room so that none of the Sony brass will see that he sports a pony tail), bursts through the door like a kind of acid-crazed Rambo to join the proceedings. Through it all, the Japanese executives sit agape at the spectacle of how business is conducted in what is alleged to be the world's most glamorous industry.

who seemingly did not want to be paired up in matrimonial bliss the way they were, made small talk while at least one of the three men, having already enjoyed some personal recreation with the second man's wife—at least according to the rumors—was now beginning to covet the wife of the third man at the table . . . a fact that would quickly move beyond the rumor stage.

Back in New York, Ron was beside himself, and began describing Pat to anyone who would listen. "She looks at you with those eyes," he explained, groping for the words that would capture her witch-craft. "And she looks great, and she moves great, and she smells great, and she sounds great. And I thought, this is great."*

The best description of what Ron thereupon proceeded to under-take came from one of Pat Duff's more than twenty different lawyers in the divorce suit that climaxed their short and surreal marriage. In the words of the lawyer, Patricia became the target of a Ron Perelman takeover campaign. He began phoning her from his office in New York—one or two calls a day. Then the frequency increased.

He was still married to Claudia, and he barely knew Patricia, but before the grass had turned green in Central Park he was phon-ing her up to twenty times a day, reaching her in the Coldwater Canyon home that she and her husband shared.[†] And never once

---

*See M. Williams, "Dangerous Beauty," *Vanity Fair* (August 1999), p. 132. A source close to Perelman at the time says that after meeting Duff, Perelman confided his frus-trations to Hollywood producer Keith Barish regarding Duff's allure and the fact that she was married to Mike Medavoy while he, Perelman, was still married to Claudia Cohen, saying "I've just got to have her," at which point he began to choke up and tears welled in his eyes.

[†] In 2002, the *Wall Street Journal* editor Laura Landro wrote of their home, "Mike and Pa-tricia built a massive vanilla-colored house in Coldwater Canyon. It received a full-color spread in the November 1992 issue of *W*." The article described the mansion as an intellectual salon in pagan Hollywood. "Years from now, when they talk about the Medavoy house—and they will—it's quite likely to be listed alongside those other cel-ebrated Hollywood salons where art, commerce and style mixed." L. Landro, "You're Only as Good as Your Next One," the *Wall Street Journal* (February 15, 2002), p. w6.

did she tell him to stop. Instead, they gossiped about their personal lives, back and forth. Ron would tell Pat about Claudia, and Pat would tell Ron about Mike. Sometimes Ron would call up and not say much of anything. He'd get her on the phone, they'd talk briefly, then fall silent. Minutes would pass, and finally one or the other of them would speak.

Ron would ask, "What are you doing now?" And Pat would answer, "Nothing. What are you doing?" And Ron would answer.

"Nothing."

It was the mating ritual of two fourteen-year-olds in junior high school. Only they weren't fourteen-year-olds. The man was the fifty-year-old chairman of the Revlon cosmetics empire and was reputed to be a multibillionaire. And there he was on the phone, "doing nothing" . . . if you don't count trying to seduce the wife of the head of Tristar Pictures because she looked great, and moved great, and smelled great, and sounded great, and he thought, "This is great!"

Pat later tried to convince the court in their divorce case that Ron had simply overpowered her with his charm. Yet if this is so, she hardly seemed to put up a struggle, and in fact appeared to welcome and even encourage his constricting embrace.

"He's so charming and thoughtful," she said to friends, after he flew with her in his Gulfstream IV business jet to Washington, D.C., to meet her mother, and to Texas to meet her brother. And Ron certainly knew he was making headway when, in the summer of 1993 she moved out of the Medavoy home and into her own West Los Angeles apartment, and from there into a house of her own, after which she filed for divorce.

And when she spent time with Ron at his townhouse, she was suitably dazzled at his possessions. The artwork alone rivaled anything in the Museum of Modern Art or the Guggenheim. There were paintings by Matisse, Jasper Johns, Warhol, Picasso, Rothko, and de Kooning. His dressing room closet contained hundreds of pairs of shoes. And the suits—over a hundred of them as well—were all handmade Italian wool, each with a label showing its date of creation.

It was like the closet of Jay Gatsby, and she was his Daisy, awed by a billionaire's socks drawer: *Look on my works ye mighty, and despair!*

⚞⚟

During all this Ron had a business to run, and the glamour of the woman he was pursuing seemed to energize him on that front as well. That was particularly so in Hollywood and Washington, the two cities into which the cultural energy of the whole nation seemed to be flowing, buoyed by the rising tide of riches from Wall Street and the charm of the sax-playing young president who had led the Democratic Party back to the White House after an absence of more than a decade. These were the arenas where it was coolest to be connected, and wherever Ron looked, Patricia was already wired right into the heart of the action. What a prize she would be for him!

Ron was doing well enough in Hollywood already. But his position in Washington was less settled, and as was the case with almost anyone whose political base consisted of little beyond money, the price of staying connected never went down. What's more, in the relentless maneuvering for advantage that defined Washington politics, Ron could never be sure when a problem might erupt that all the money on earth couldn't solve.

To maneuver effectively in this environment, Ron needed help, and he seemed to have just the right man when one of his own Revlon board members—a politically-connected Washington, D.C., lawyer named Vernon Jordan—was tapped by the incoming president to head up the transition team for the new administration. Here was a man who not only knew his way around Washington as well as anyone alive, but was now set to become, in effect, the obstetrician for the birth of a whole new presidency. And by the fortune of the Gods, he was already working for Ron!

In September, Ron flew to Los Angeles to meet Patricia at the Bel Air Hotel. It was the turning point for both, with Patricia ready, whether or not she quite realized it, to sink the gaffing hook into him, and Ron ready to do the same back to her. Each now had the other's number. Patricia was going to play to Ron's vanities as the king of all Type-A control freaks, and stand before him in her ultimate helplessness and vulnerability. And Ron was going to rescue her from the fate that otherwise promised her doom. All that was needed was for one or the other of them to throw a bit of chum off the stern to get the feeding frenzy going.

In human relations, people often as not wind up seeking out the type of life situations for the future that they are most familiar with from their past: The problem father who becomes the husband, the problem mother who becomes the wife. And if they cannot find them ready-made and off-the-shelf—and if their needs are desperate enough—they will take whomever they can find and turn him or her into the person they need him to be. And here in the Bel Air Hotel, on a September day in 1993, the richest billionaire in New York and the dream goddess of his desires, were about to drag themselves down that very rat hole, oblivious to what awaited them.

It was Patricia who provided the chum, as she rolled up her sleeve and displayed a welt-covered arm, and said, according to Ron's subsequent court testimony in his divorce from her, "Mike hit me."*

And in that instant their fates were sealed, as Sir Ron eyed the bruises, then barked out the command that put him in charge. He wanted photographs taken, and he wanted eyewitnesses. Nobody was going to get away with a stunt like this!

---

*The scene, and Patricia's quote, come from court testimony by Ronald O. Perelman, in *Anonymous v. Anonymous* Supreme Court of State of New York, New York County, Civil Term, Index No. 310754/96, May 2000. Patricia later insisted that the incident never occurred, though Ron's testimony on the matter stood unchallenged throughout the trial. For Medavoy's view of Duff, see D. Shah, "Beauty and the Billionaire," *Los Angeles Magazine* (December, 1996), p. 62, in which he is quoted as saying of his ex-wife, "I'm sorry I ever met her."

What followed thereafter was of course entirely predictable, as both parties—having at last bagged their respective quarries (namely each other)—began to devour each other alive, with Patricia soon wailing for someone to rescue her, even as Rescuer Ron grew more and more insistent that she just shut up and do as she was told.

Court records show the two teetering on the knife-edge of fist fights and brawls before they were even married.[11] In the wake of the scene in the Bel Air Hotel, Patricia filed for divorce from Mike Medavoy,* then flew to Hawaii to be alone and "to think." But, according to her subsequent court statements, Rescuer Ron was hot on her tail and showed up unannounced, demanding attention. The situation deteriorated into a pushing, shoving, hair-pulling fight over whether or not to go out for New Years Eve, and if so, where.

Back in Los Angeles, Patricia rang up her friend Melanie Griffith for some advice on how to escape the clutches of this Jewish King Kong. Melanie had a suggestion: Go see her personal therapist, Dr. Deborah Phillips, who had helped Melanie escape the clutches of her own issue-drenched husband, Don Johnson, in their first failed attempt at married life.

But when Patricia thereafter did so, and sat down for a therapy session in Dr. Phillips' Los Angeles office, Ron burst in and dragged her out, declaring that everything would be fine between them if she'd just do everything he said and stay with him twenty-four hours a day.[12]

Over the Presidents' Day weekend of February 21, the couple flew to Aspen for some skiing, and according to Patricia's court documents another argument erupted. This one climaxed when Ron

---

* In her divorce affidavit from Perelman, Patricia stated that after she separated from Medavoy in August, Ron threatened to have both Medavoy and herself "whacked" if she went back to him, and that he shortly thereafter "marched" her into his lawyer's office in Los Angeles and "pushed" her to sign a divorce action against Medavoy.

threw Patricia's toiletries against the wall of their guesthouse, tore her sweaters and pants, and "bent [her] hand back."[13] Reason? She had forgotten to meet him for lunch. A month later, the couple flew to Los Angeles to attend the Oscars, and another and similar fight broke out.*

Somewhere in the midst of all this, Patricia did her ingénue number and fretted that she wasn't pregnant. So Ron arranged for her to have some in vitro fertilization treatments, which worked, and in mid-April 1994—most likely during the week of April 10 to 16[†]—she got pregnant.

Just how happy Ron was at this news is not known, though he does seem to have been willing to cope with his feelings long enough to throw Patricia a party for her fortieth birthday. In retrospect, the event is of interest because of one unexpected development: the brief and surreal return to the Pat and Ron storyline, of one of its walk-on characters from the opening scene, Don Johnson.[14]

A bit over a year had now passed since Don and his wife Melanie Griffith had sat down for dinner with the Perelmans and the Medavoys that night in Paris, and for Don, well, it looked as if ole demon substance abuse was back in the driver's seat.

Until lately, everything had been going great for the Johnson-Griffith duo—Melanie had her gig as a Revlon (older) gal, and Don . . . well, that was just it. All of a sudden it seemed Don had a woman

---

*The happy couple was all smiles at the actual awards ceremony. But Mike Medavoy, who had greenlighted the movie that brought Tom Hanks a 1994 Oscar for Best Actor, was no where to be seen. While Ron paraded around proudly with the woman who was still Medavoy's wife affixed to his elbow, Medavoy watched the proceedings glumly on TV from a hotel room in Palm Springs. When Hanks rose to accept the award and gave an emotional speech in which he singled out Medavoy for playing a key role in getting the movie—*Philadelphia*—made, Medavoy switched off the TV and, feeling sick, turned out the light and went to sleep. See A. Citron, *Los Angeles Times* (March 25, 1994), p. 4.

[†]This is a reasonable assumption since the child, Caleigh, was born December 13, 1994, and Patricia stated in her court affidavit that the child arrived a month early.

in Canada who was claiming he was the father of her seven-month-old baby, and out of the blue Don was turning up at celebrity parties blotto and slobbering all over the women . . . which is how he arrived on the evening of the 12th for Patricia's party—stumbling drunken from the limo, falling all over the women inside, then staggering back out and somehow winding up the next morning, still drunk, cursing on the radio with some deejays in Miami.

For her part, Melanie had seen it all before, and by the end of the week she had divorce papers in his hands, meaning that of the six frustrated and unhappily married people who had come together for dinner in Paris the year before, each was now decoupled and, it would seem, no happier than before.

⬩⬩⬩

Ron at least had a ready distraction, and a week later he was sitting down to dinner with a roomful of business world luminaries to celebrate the redemption, resurrection, and return to respectability of the man who had made them all rich.

The setting was New York's swankiest restaurant for these sorts of things—the 21 Club—and the man to be honored was the one-and-only Michael Milken, marketing wizard of the junk bond, whose genius for promotion (and whose card-counter's knack for keeping track of a lot of numbers in his head) had made multimillionaires, and even billionaires, out of nearly everyone in the room. They ranged from casino operator Steve Wynn, to corporate raider Carl Icahn, to underwear king William Farley, and of course Ron Perelman.[15]

And there was someone else there as well—or at least let us say, his disembodied voice was there, emerging Oz-like from a loudspeaker at 9 P.M. to grovel as well before the riches and genius of this recently released white-collar felon, now seeking a passport back into the world of the law-abiding by leading a fund-raising drive to fight prostate cancer.

For arranging this grand affair, all in the room—including Milken and (especially) Ron Perelman—knew there was but one man to thank: the organizing committee's co-chairman and spark-plug, who was also in the room. This was the man who made sure everything would shine with just the right Wall Street luster, then reached out for the "the voice" that would be its crowning moment.

The organizer? Who else but Washington's—and Ron Perel-man's—ultimate new Mister Fixit, the super-connected Vernon Jordan. And if Perelman harbored even the slightest of doubts that his Revlon board member had his hands on Washington's *real* levers of power, what happened next put those doubts totally to rest, as the loudspeaker crackled to life, and from out of it came the voice of the president of the United States, William Jefferson Clinton, praising the fight against cancer, lauding the work of Milken, and ending with his familiar "come together" flourish—in this case re-garding the "private sector" and the "health care folks."

A drop-dead evening? To be sure. But for a select few it was now going to get even better, and Ron had a ticket of admission to this one, too. Granted, the voice of the president of the United States was one way to enjoy an after dinner cigar and a snifter of cognac. But in the world of the truly smooth, only one voice could stand alone, and it didn't belong to some piece of Arkansas white trash who couldn't finish a sentence without biting his lip and saying the word "folks." It belonged to the man from whom true coolness really flowed, who was now upstairs for a private party all his own. After the president of the United States, there really was only one step up still to take . . . and that's where Ron Perelman was headed next, from the president of the United States, it would be one more flight up, to finish off the evening with Frank Sinatra.

A few days later, Ron Perelman's top lawyer at MacAndrews & Forbes—a man named Barry Schwartz—picked up the phone to find Vernon Jordan on the line.[16] It seemed Jordan had a problem that he thought Schwartz might be able to help him solve. A man named Webster Hubbell had just resigned from his post as Associate Attorney General in the Clinton administration and would be setting himself up in private practice. The problem was, Hubbell needed some consulting clients to get going.

Schwartz said he'd see what could be done, and after checking with higher-ups, a meeting with Hubbell and the brass at MacAndrews & Forbes was set up in New York for April 29, after which Revlon hired Hubbell on a $100,000 consulting contract, handing him an initial $25,000 payment in the form of a check that had been issued and dated the day before the man was even interviewed. In the real world of Washington politics, it was just a little deposit in the favor bank, to be sure, but it was how the game was played, and no one was better at it than Vernon Jordan—as Ron Perelman had now seen for himself not once but *twice* in recent days. Vernon Jordan, what a *macher*.

While all this was going on, Ron still had his shiksa doll-face to contend with, and she was turning into a bigger problem than maybe even Vernon could handle. In fact, by the time they got married, in a private ceremony at the end of January 1995 in New York, they basically seemed to loathe each other—which is probably why they went through with the marriage at all.

Originally, the wedding had been scheduled for December 28, 1994—so that the baby, who was due in mid-January, wouldn't be born out of wedlock. But this meant that time was running out for Ron to get Patricia to sign a prenuptial agreement to keep her away from his money. And the problems grew worse when Patricia developed toxemia and was admitted to Lenox Hill Hospital on Manhattan's Upper East Side at the start of December to keep her under observation in case of complications. So, realizing the stakes involved, Ron and his lawyers pursued her right into the hospital with the prenup and a pen (or at least that's what Patricia later claimed to her friends).

On the other hand, the record is fairly clear that she fought him on signing it right to the end. The baby, a girl named Caleigh, was born on December 13, 1994, a month early, and still she didn't sign. But he wore her down, and finally, a week and a half later she gave up, apparently realizing that she had overplayed her hand and that the mere fact of having given birth to their child wasn't going to make him marry her at all.*

Yet, she still had one last parting shot in her: She failed to show up for the December 28 ceremony, which Ron had arranged to take place at the private residence of his rabbi. Finally, she gave it up on that front, too, and having signed the vile prenup, which gave her but a fraction of the $80 million that his second wife, Claudia Cohen, had wrestled out of him, the two were finally married in a private civil ceremony on January 25, 1995.

Thus, began the short and surreal marriage of Ronald Owen Perelman and Patricia Hoar Orr Zabrodsky Duff Medavoy Perelman—in a mutually shared state of revulsion at the mere thought of the other's name . . . and things went downhill from there.

---

*The prenuptial agreement, dated and finally signed by the parties on December 22, 1994, nine days after the birth of their daughter, provided in the event of a divorce for maintenance and property distribution, but not child support. Under the terms of the agreement, Ron was to pay Patricia $1,131,744 annually until January 1, 2011, as well as transfer and deliver to her, free and clear of any encumbrances, a Westport, Connecticut estate that he had bought for her. In addition, he agreed to pay $150,000 annually toward taxes, utilities, and upkeep on the property until July 15, 2001, as well as let her keep any jewelry he had given her during the marriage (it wound up totaling $5 million in value). He also agreed to let her keep any unspent cash he had given her (total cash from Ron to Patricia topped $8 million by the time of the divorce). The highly contentious divorce case that followed centered on the question of child support by Ron, which had not been stipulated in the prenup.

13

JANE BEASLEY AND THE SPOOR
OF AN OLDER MAN

By the start of the 1990s, Jack Welch had begun to emerge as a recognizable business leader not just among his peers but to the public at large, with ten times as many newspaper and magazine articles quoting or mentioning him in 1992 (410 in all) as had been the case in 1981 when he had been made chairman of GE. And increasingly, the stories were quoting him as a voice of authority not just on GE but on business in general, on the economy, and even on presidential politics. When Welch worried aloud at a business conference in October 1992 that a Clinton victory in the upcoming presidential election, then only weeks away, would bring a return to Washington of "flat earth" thinking, the comment turned up in newspapers from Los Angeles to Toronto the next morning.*

_____

*In its January 1993 issue, the *Harvard Business Review* felt comfortable referring to Welch as "one of the nation's highest profile managers." The Associated Press now referred to him as "forward looking." And *Newsweek* called him "a consummate American executive . . . who became lean and mean before everyone else, and now profits from it," *Newsweek* (November 30, 1992).

So it is hardly surprising that Welch's increasing visibility and prestige had already aroused the press to begin the search for others like him. In the new world of business in the 1990s, Welch represented a new model for the American CEO—the "bite the bullet" leader who had "the right stuff" and could "make the tough choices" on behalf of "maximizing shareholder value." But where were all the others—the officer corps of Attila the Hun CEOs ready to lead American business into mortal combat in pursuit of profit?

In Albert ("Chainsaw") Dunlap, the press found an answer. Big Al was, among other things, actually and literally *bigger* than Welch, giving him a domineering presence in almost any setting. And it also helped that he was better looking, with a lantern-jaw profile that suggested an early Al Haig.* And he was noisier than Welch (if that was possible), with a repertoire of nonstop sound bites that made him good copy and fun to cover. And more than anything else, he was a genuine Original, completely comfortable at being cast as the new Barbarian Leader of American business.

Through his work at Lilly-Tulip at the start of the 1980s, Big Al had begun to develop a name for himself as a corporate turnaround executive. But in 1986 he moved abroad, going to work in Britain for the Anglo-French financier, James Goldsmith. After that, he worked in Australia for Kerry Packer, a Goldsmith associate who owned a company called Consolidated Press Holdings. Thus, removed from the day-to-day action back in the United States, Dunlap quickly dropped off the radar screen of the American media and was forgotten.

---

* A 1999 study by four researchers at the University of Liverpool linked jaw size to testosterone levels in males. The study is cited in J. Dabbs, *Heroes, Rogues and Lovers: Testosterone and Behavior* (New York: McGraw-Hill, 2000) in connection with research at Georgia State University showing that male "preening" is often a testosterone-linked activity designed to assert dominance in social settings as an alternative to fighting and aggression.

But halfway around the world, he continued to pursue the same angry and vainglorious management style that had marked his career in business from the start, and it was only a matter of time before his abusive and bullying approach to leadership got him in trouble all over again. Summed up one of his subordinates at the time, "The way Al Dunlap impacted my career was very vividly to show me how not to do things. He showed me how a totally dysfunctional leader operates."[1] In 1993, Dunlap abruptly exited Consolidated Press and returned to the United States three years before his contract was up, stirring gleeful rumors that Packer had fired him.

But the details of his departure from Consolidated Press were apparently of little interest to a search committee from Scott Paper Company when it interviewed him in the spring of 1994 to succeed Philip Lippincott as chairman and CEO of the troubled Philadelphia paper products company.

In fact, the committee had its back to the wall, having been searching in vain since November 1993 for a successor to Lippincott, who had announced his intention to retire on April 1, 1994, following a string of deepening losses that culminated in a $381 million write-off in the fourth quarter of 1993. No one could be found who wanted to take on what looked like a doomed struggle to turn the company around. Lippincott had already announced plans to cut Scott's workforce by an unheard of 25 percent, letting go more than 8,300 employees over the following three years. What CEO wanted to preside over a bloodletting of that magnitude![2]

Answer: Chainsaw Al! And when he agreed to take on the task, the search committee had heard all it needed—and evidently didn't need to bother looking at his troubled early years at Max Phillips & Sons and Nitec Paper Corporation, which he had long since managed to erase from his resume in any case. So the general level of understanding about the career history of Scott's new chairman and CEO seemed to boil down to the breezy comment of a Salomon Brothers analyst, who said of him, "I understand he's very much a nuts and bolts, results-oriented manager. And that's just what this company needs right now."[3]

Instead, what Scott Paper got was Al Dunlap, human chainsaw. Lippincott's plan had been to cut the payroll by 8,300 employees over three years, but Big Al added 9,600 more to the hit list and chainsawed every one of them during his first eight months on the job. He also sold off the company's publishing and printing businesses, dumped Scott's health care business, its U.S. timberlands, its Nova Scotia, Spanish, and Chilean paper mills, and then sold off its world headquarters, and moved what was left to Boca Raton, Florida, where he had recently bought a $1.8 million home.[4]

Because of all this, Scott's operating costs instantly plunged by nearly 20 percent, turning a 1993 net $277 million loss into a 1994 net gain of $210 million, while adding roughly $1 billion of cash to the balance sheet through the proceeds from the sale of assets. "Rambo In Pinstripes," gushed the *Wall Street Journal*, awestruck at Dunlap's apparent success in pulling off "one of the fastest turnarounds in corporate history."[5] His secret? According to the *Journal*, the winning formula boiled down to "clear vision, charisma, and decisive leadership."

In fact, Al's eviscerating chainsaw had sent Scott's business into a tailspin, causing operating cash flow—the best measure of any business's health—to plunge by a third in 1994 from the level that had prevailed the year before. By the third quarter of 1995, the business had been weakened to the point that cash flow fell into the red for the first time in memory, spelling the company's eventual doom.

But this was the mid-1990s, marking the start of the final, blowout phase of the bull market that had begun in the summer of 1982. And with the Dow Jones Industrial Average already rising at a pace of nearly 20 percent yearly, even the most cautious of investors were looking for reasons to *buy* more stock, not *sell* what they already had. It was a mind-set that quickly made Scott Paper seem like an under-valued opportunity.

Ecstatic at the company's rising earnings, investors bid up the price of Scott Paper by 75 percent, from less than $40 per share at the end of 1993, to nearly $70 by the end of 1994, then added another $30 to the price (adjusted for a two-for-one April 1995 stock split) in the six months that followed. And since Dunlap's compensation deal was based on how much he succeeded in making Scott's stock price rise, the resulting gain wound up putting roughly $100 million in his pocket when he succeeded in selling the business to a rival company, Kimberly Clark, in July 1995.

The actual terms of the deal still had to be worked out with lawyers, a process that could take months. But psychologically, Big Al had seemed to put Scott Paper behind him the very second he had negotiated the basic agreement, and as the *Wall Street Journal* reported before the ink on the deal was even dry, Dunlap was already looking for his next mountain to climb.[6]

When a television interviewer asked him a question that was beginning to become just a touch familiar—how does it feel to be earning so much money from a job that basically boiled down to the firing of employees?—Big Al just waved the concern away. Pointing to the rising price of Scott's stock, he declared, "I created $6.5 billion of value. And for that I received less than 2 percent." Then basking in his newly found fame as the CEO of the moment, he added, "There are only a handful of superstar executives. You've got to compare them with the other superstars. You can't compare them with the worker on the floor."[7]

And Big Al was lucky in yet another way. Not only did he arrive on stage at just the moment when his bullying behavior was easily misread as a new form of tough-love leadership for businesses in distress, but scarcely had he stepped into the spotlight than GE's Jack Welch—the media's original model for that role—began for the first time to stumble.

Welch's problems could be traced in part to the sudden departure, in 1991, of his right-hand man at GE, Larry Bossidy, who left to become the chairman of AlliedSignal Corporation, which competed with GE in markets everywhere.

In many ways, Bossidy had been the glue that had held Welch's management team together, especially in his role as blocking tackle between Welch and Gary Wendt at GE Capital in Stamford. As the day-to-day operating chief of GE Capital, Wendt was the man most directly responsible for the continuing growth in GE's earnings, and it was that growth that was driving the price of GE's stock on Wall Street and making Welch a hero.

So Welch really depended on Wendt—a fact that seemed to make him resentful of the man, and Wendt clearly sensed it. As a result, though he was openly awed by the GE chairman, Wendt was also wary of him. Like everyone else, except perhaps Bossidy, he feared Welch's bullying tactics and abusive, scolding tongue, which he knew could be turned at any minute against Gary or anyone else—especially in front of colleagues at meetings. Fortunately, that rarely happened, and for that he had thanked Bossidy, the vice chairman, to whom he reported instead of to Welch directly.

But with Bossidy now gone, Wendt suddenly found himself face-to-face with the Dreaded One himself. And seeming to sense Wendt's vulnerability, Welch began what appeared, to Wendt at least, to be an ongoing effort to torment him. Typical stunt: Force the GE Capital executive to come from Stamford to Welch's Fairfield office for face-to-face meetings on any GE Capital investment Wendt proposed to make if it involved more than a million dollars.

Thus, began a daily ritual of forty-mile round-trips up the Merritt Parkway—sometimes twice and even three times a day—that Wendt now had to make, to present Welch with deals that were sometimes so small that even Welch seemed to wonder why he was listening to them. There were car loans in Czechoslovakia, aircraft loans in China, loans for power generators in Brazil—and Gary had to sell every one of them personally to the boss.

Back and forth he would go, up and down the Merritt Parkway, hour after hour, day after day, until the weeks became months and the months turned into years. It was crazy. To make some fathomless point that probably not even Welch grasped, the highest paid and most important executive in GE's most important line of business—the borrowing and lending of money—was being turned into little more than an interdepartmental messenger boy. But who could he turn to? Who would understand? The wife? Gary would phone home and tell her to be ready at 6 P.M. for a dinner in New York, and by the time he saw her, she'd be wearing her *attitude* face. No support from that direction!

With Bossidy's departure, Gary's dream job of all time had become a dreadful, enervating burden. In fact, everything had: the office, the job, the wife. And behind them all loomed the ghoulish and grinning face of the Dreaded One, his evil eyes following Gary wherever he went. Thinking that way on his return from a business trip in the company jet, Gary felt waves of self-pity wash over him; and alone at 30,000 feet, he broke down and cried. Who could he turn to? Who would understand?

One day, Wendt met a good-looking, trim, dark-haired travel consultant named Rosemarie, who looked at him with big, dark, and welcoming eyes that seemed to murmur, "I understand . . ." and for Gary Wendt, a little ray of sunshine broke through the gloom.

For Jack Welch, things were not so simple. His romance with Jane Beasley had started off smoothly enough—too smoothly, in fact, almost as if it amounted to a contract negotiation. Instead of love, he spoke of "getting serious," which they dealt with by having a "why it won't work talk" about marriage. As described by Jack, the talk appears to have been astonishingly ephemeral, focusing not on Jack and Jane and their individual needs and wants as human beings but on non-issues like the fact that it "bothered" Jack that Jane did not ski or play golf, and that it "bothered" Jane that Jack did not enjoy the opera.[8]

When Jane agreed to learn golf, and Jack agreed to attend the opera, the "why it won't work" issue was put to rest, and they proceeded to step two: settling on the terms of a standard, ten-year prenuptial agreement. This was an increasingly accepted way for the men at the top in business to protect their soaring net worths while trading in one wife for the next in a quickening bull market.

After that, there was just basically just one thing left to do—get married—which they did in April 1989 in Nantucket. Yet right from the start, one could see the first spider-like veins of future trouble beginning to spread. Though Jack's four children attended the wedding, Jane's own family members did not, and her uncle, Jere Beasley—an influential Alabama judge and former lieutenant governor of the state—later said he never even knew about the wedding until after the fact.[9]

In fact, had any of Jane's immediate family members attended the wedding, they certainly would have felt out of place, for the family that Jane Beasley grew up in made the circumstances of Jack's own financially stressed upbringing in North Salem, Massachusetts, look positively Bourbonesque by comparison.

The Beasley home, set back off the state highway on the outskirts of the Alabama farming village of Pratt's Station,* was not a whole lot

---

*Until Jane Beasley Welch became its most famous citizen, the town of Pratt's Station was best known for being mentioned in *Ripley's Believe It or Not* because a tombstone for a local had been cut in the shape of a whiskey bottle to honor the man in the grave beneath it, who had drunk himself to death. See D. Jones, "Jane Welch Seeks Half of Couple's $1 Billion Fortune," *USA Today* (March 19, 2002), p. 3B.

better than a shack with a front porch. Jane's father, Durwood, worked as a county highway department maintenance man, supplementing his income by some part-time farming. Jane's mother, Marion, worked as a local schoolteacher to bring in a few dollars more. Marion died in 1984, and Jane's three brothers—Bill, Bob, and Ben— had stayed pretty much close to home.

It was Jane who possessed the spunk—and the winning smile— to help her open doors to the world beyond Pratt's Station. But there was never enough money to provide for everyone's needs in the meantime, and as the girl, Jane stood at the end of the line. Jane's best friend from high school, Regina Littlefield, recalled the Beasley family's circumstances thusly, "They weren't downright poor, but money sure was tight."* And the lack of it seemed to be constantly on Jane's mind. "She was always talking about getting out of town and making sure she had money someday in her life," Regina recalled. "She talked about it a lot."

After high school, Jane went to college, on a scholarship, at nearby Troy State University. Afterward, she got a job as a high school teacher and prepared to follow in her mother's footsteps through a life of impoverished obscurity. But the prospect drove her nuts, and after a semester she quit and moved to Atlanta, where she landed a job as a secretarial assistant in a local law firm.

By and by, she picked up the spoor of an older man named Charles ("Bo") Cole, a law professor at the Cumberland School of Law. Cole found her charm irresistible and they were married, and she headed for law school at the University of Kentucky. But five years later they were divorced, and with her sheepskin in hand and some divorce settlement seed money from ole Bo in her purse, she

---

*Four decades later, Jane was still picking at that scab. In unpublished comments during an interview with a Connecticut magazine writer, Leslie Feller, Jane recalled that while growing up in Alabama her living conditions were so financially stressed that the Beasley home didn't even have a television set.

headed for New York where, in the fullness of time, she caught the spoor of another older man and began to close in on Jack Welch.

Meanwhile, stories from Jack's past had already reached a reporter from the *Wall Street Journal* named Thomas O'Boyle, creating a whole new set of complications for Jack when O'Boyle decided to include them in a book he wanted to write about GE under Welch. When a GE official managed to obtain a six-page proposal that O'Boyle's literary agent had put out for auction, Welch apparently read it and hit the roof. Barely two weeks passed before the first of a series of angry and threatening letters went out from GE's lawyers in an effort to halt the book's publication.

Jack faced problems on other fronts as well, and without Bossidy as his consigliore in moments of crisis, he needed a shoulder to lean on. So, he reached out to GE's top executive ranks in Europe, and reeled in one of his long-time confidantes—a suave-looking Italian-born executive named Paolo Fresco, who headed GE's international operations—to become Bossidy's replacement.

But Fresco, who enjoyed displaying his trim figure to the world in hand-tailored Italian suits, was of little apparent help in counseling Welch about the next big problem to roll down on him: a financial crisis at Kidder Peabody.

The Wall Street firm had in fact been a ticking time bomb inside GE from the moment the company bought it in April 1986. Distracted and exhausted by the completion of the RCA acquisition only weeks earlier, the GE executives were in no shape—psychologically or even physically—to take on another such deal so soon. But Welch, believing in his own invincibility, simply ordered that the deal be done. So GE wound up taking over a severely troubled and undercapitalized investment firm for $600 million, promising to pump in $130 million more on the basis of less due diligence than someone might be expected to conduct before investing in a Poconos time-share.

The first sign of trouble came only a few months after the takeover. In February 1987, Kidder's former star trader, Martin Siegel, told federal prosecutors that he had been taking bribes from financier Ivan Boesky to leak him inside information on pending Kidder deals and had even set up secret trades whereby Kidder could profit from its own inside information.[10] This led to a GE-ordered reshuffling of Kidder's top management and not much else, triggering the mass resignation of seven of Kidder's top officials two years later in a warning sign of troubles to come that the GE brass simply ignored.

A lot of the trouble with Kidder came from personality conflicts and friction between the Kidder brass and their counterparts at GE Capital. Though Bossidy had regularly been able to smooth things over, he was now gone. This set the stage for the eruption of generalized corporate-wide hysteria at GE headquarters when, late in the afternoon of April 14, 1994, Welch got a call at his office in Fairfield from a one-time management consultant named Michael Carpenter. He had won Welch's confidence and been assigned to serve as his eyes and ears at Kidder following the firm's mass resignations in 1989. Carpenter's news, which he presented in a way that made sure Welch understood that Carpenter himself was blameless: Some $350 million was missing from the account of a Kidder bond trader named Joseph Jett, and Jett himself had "disappeared" as well.

The "missing" Joe Jett, the only African American trader on the Kidder payroll, was in fact the same Joe Jett who had gone to work as a trainee engineer in Welch's old haunt—the GE Plastics Division headquarters in Becker House—more than a decade earlier. He wound up quitting from frustrations that began to build after his boss told him to stay out of sight because the company's new chairman and CEO (Welch) was making a visit to the plant and might not like seeing a black employee working at a management level job. Thereafter, Jett enrolled at the Harvard Business School, earned an MBA, and went to work as a bond trader at Kidder Peabody—just in time to wind up working for Welch all over again when GE acquired the firm in the spring of 1986.

In his autobiography, Welch claimed that the missing $350 million was the result of a pattern of fraudulent trading activity confined to Jett alone, citing a Securities and Exchange Commission administrative judge ruling that Jett had "intentionally deceived his supervisors, auditors, and others with false denials and misleading and conflicting explanations."[11] Yet there was more to the matter than that since Jett's superiors had every reason imaginable to *want* to be deceived. Jett's trades had alone generated more than 25 percent of his department's profits the year before. In appreciation, the firm had bestowed on him, only three months earlier, the designation of Kidder's "Man of the Year" for 1993—an award that made both his superior, a man named Edward Cerullo, and the top man overseeing them both, Mike Carpenter, look like heroes to Welch.

Jett, who had not in fact disappeared at all, was nonethess immediately fired on Welch's orders and wound up spending the next ten years protesting that he had only been doing what his bosses had told him to do. By contrast, Jett's superiors succeeded in arguing that Jett had hoodwinked them all, and none was charged with anything in the affair.

From the moment the news of the Kidder debacle first broke, Welch began behaving like an escaped hysteric at the thought that the media might decide to blame *him**—and for very good reason: He *deserved* to be blamed. It was Welch, and Welch alone, who had set up

---

* Welch's autobiography contains a revealing—and unintentionally hilarious—passage in which Welch rails at the Kidder brass for trying to duck responsibility for what had happened, then turns around and advises his wife Jane to "hang on for a very long and tough ride" because the media was likely going to jump to the "ridiculous conclusion" that "poor GE management" was somehow to blame.

the confused chain of command that had allowed the situation to fester undetected. As part of the reassignment of executives that followed GE's rapid-fire acquisition of RCA and then Kidder, Welch had not only promoted Bossidy to the job of vice chairman, while leaving him with oversight of GE Capital, but he had simultaneously assigned Michael Carpenter, who had been working in GE Strategic Planning on the RCA deal, to GE Capital as executive vice president under Gary Wendt. And it took about an hour before Wendt and Carpenter were at each other's throats.

The situation festered unresolved for years as the two Alpha-male personalities clashed repeatedly over who would dominate and control the other. At one point, the tension got so bad that the company brought in an industrial psychologist to try to mediate between the two, but his efforts resolved nothing.

Hardly fond of Wendt to begin with, Welch made the situation worse when he appointed Carpenter to the presidency of Kidder in 1989 and to the job of chairman in 1990. This gave Carpenter a line of direct reporting responsibility to Welch, looping around Wendt and Bossidy as well, eliminating all possibility for Welch to claim that he didn't share at least somewhat in the fiasco. Either Carpenter knew what Jett had been doing and hadn't shared the knowledge with Welch, or he didn't know but should have. Whichever way one looked at the matter, the buck stopped with Welch and no one else.

Welch seemed to sense as much, and his angry flailing about simply betrayed his fears. When a reporter for the *Wall Street Journal* asked him whether rumors that he had lost his management touch were true, he shot back angrily, "Who says that? Be sure and quote them by name."[12]

With the company's entire top management in seeming disarray, the press came running, for as everyone knew, nothing could be stabilized until someone could be found to take the heat for Welch. And though Welch proved predictably quick to pronounce his unwillingness to fire Carpenter, few doubted that the ax would soon fall—and on no one else but Carpenter himself.

In the end, only Carpenter seemed not to realize the fate that awaited him. In one of the more foolish moves of his career, he appeared for an interview with journalists at the offices of the *Wall Street Journal* in early May and was quoted as saying that he certainly didn't think Welch would fire him—a statement that amounted to calling the chairman's bluff and making his ouster certain.

Eight weeks later, Carpenter was gone, and not long after that so too, was Kidder Peabody & Company, sold to PaineWebber & Company for $670 million, or less than half the reported $1.5 billion that GE had poured into it during the eight years it had owned the firm.[13]

Six months after that, Welch gave a talk to students at New York University's Stern School. The host of the event was the former managing editor of *Fortune*, Marshall Loeb, now easing into retirement by way of a stint as editor of the *Columbia Journalism Review*.

"Geez," thought Loeb, as he eyed the man at the podium, "he looks kind of tired." Welch finished his speech, took questions from the audience, and left. A few days later, Welch collapsed in his bathroom, struck down by the first of two back-to-back heart attacks, in what looked to be the grim finale to a year of stressful and worsening setbacks.

14

MARVIN HAMLISCH MEETS THE
WORLD OF SIX SIGMA

Perhaps it was the accelerating rise of the stock market, or maybe it was something else. Whatever the cause, an undeniable sense of impatience seemed to be spreading everywhere.* And few CEOs seemed more perfectly attuned to the times than Big Al Dunlap: quick, glib, and boasting the attention span of a gnat. When critics of his tactics brought up squishy questions like company morale and labor relations, Big Al just fired back with another machine-gun burst from his inexhaustible supply of snide but entertaining one-liners. "Want a friend?" he'd ask with a sneer. "Then get a dog!"[1]

---

* Between 1990 and the start of 1995, the Dow Jones Industrial Average rose at an average annual rate of just 6.8 percent. But during the first five months of 1995, the market caught fire, and on the day of Jack Welch's heart attack, it was rising at an annualized rate of more than 26 percent.

It was a comment that perfectly mirrored the moment, as thirteen straight years of nearly uninterrupted economic growth and rising stock prices seemed to be proof enough that cynicism was its own reward. It seemed especially appropriate because the ruggedly handsome warrior champion of this new and pitiless morality was about to be rewarded with a $100 million payout for firing half the employees of the company he ran (Scott Paper), and selling what was left of the business to a rival. When CBS Evening News' economic correspondent, Ray Brady, asked Dunlap how he felt about pocketing so much money from his brutal and indiscriminate downsizing at Scott Paper, he answered, "They had two choices: It was either me or Dr. Kevorkian . . . and I'm a lot more fun than he is."[2]

Faced with the seemingly irrefutable evidence of his success, the press simply cheered him on. Looking for fresh ways to bring up his name, the *Wall Street Journal* discovered him as the driving force behind a whole new business "trend"—all-but deifying the man in a July 1995 story that celebrated the arrival of "the rapid turnaround" in American business.[3]

In a sense, speed itself had begun to emerge as a cultural theme, captured in the titles of such business books as *The Second Curve: Managing the Velocity of Change,* by Ian Morrison, and *Value Migration: How to Think Several Moves Ahead of the Competition,* by Adrian J. Slywotzky. In fact, even as Jack Welch and his aides reeled from the summer-long aftershocks of the Kidder Peabody crisis and the firing of Joe Jett the previous April, the Hollywood film industry was already abuzz with talk of an upcoming Twentieth-Century Fox release that promised to become a metaphor for the state of the stock market, the state of business, and even the frenzied, can't-slow-down state of life in the United States.

The film featured three of Hollywood's most bankable actors: Sandra Bullock, Keanu Reaves, and Dennis Hopper. But the movie's real star was an out-of-control municipal bus that raced through the streets of Los Angeles, unable to slow down without blowing itself up. The movie's title: what else but *Speed*.*

And speed was what Big Al Dunlap was all about—speed and control—the blitzkrieg strokes in which you take no prisoners and shoot the wounded; and the control that comes from eliminating layers of management, flattening bureaucracies, removing contrary voices. One leader, many followers.†

In December 1995, Big Al pocketed his $100 million payday from the Scott Paper turnaround, and taking some brief R&R with his wife, Judy, and their twin German Shepherds, Brit and Cadet, in the couple's newly purchased estate in Boca Raton, he paused (but only briefly) to reflect on the opportunities that beckoned. What new landing beach would he be storming up next? Who would be the next corporate slackers to feel the wrath of Chainsaw Al?

---

*Befitting the accelerating pace of life and business, as the United States approached the millennium's end, only 36 months were to pass before the movie's sequel, *Speed II*, reached theaters. On its opening day, Dunlap had been in his latest turnaround job as CEO of Sunbeam for barely 9 months and had already fired half the employees.

†Dunlap and Welch shared similar views about business and management and even expressed them in similar ways, from their eagerness to make snap judgments about people, to their bizarre and authoritarian notions of leadership. Here is Dunlap, from his business memoir, *Mean Business* (New York: Times Books, 1996), p. 159, on the subject of snap judgments: "Any factory worker can spot a phony a mile away." Here is Welch, from his business memoir, *Jack: Straight from the Gut* (New York: Warner Books, 2001), p. 4, on the same subject, referring to his mother Grace as the person from whom he learned the skill: "She could 'smell a phony a mile away.'" Here is Dunlap, in a 1994 interview with Alenn Collins of the *New York Times* (August 15, 1994), p. D1 on purging organizations of people who don't agree with you: "You must get rid of the people who represent the old culture, or they will fight you. And you have to get rid of all the old symbols." Here is Jack Welch, from an interview in *Industry Week* (May 2, 1994), p. 13 on the same subject: "Distasteful as it is, the only response to bad leadership is to take them out and clear the forest."

In fact, Dunlap could hardly afford to dally for long because deal fever was in the air, and in New York's race for the big bucks, it simply wasn't wise to take a pit stop to count your winnings: Linger too long and you could be lapped right out of the competition.

As the stock market roared ahead, the moneymen of Wall Street were discovering opportunities at every turn, and the more glamorous the investment the greater its appeal. That was particularly so in the media, where the phrase "content is king" was all it took to adjust eager executives to the idea of prices that would have seemed unthinkable a year earlier. In August, the Walt Disney Company agreed to pay $19 billion to acquire the CapCities/ABC television network. The very next day, the Westinghouse Company—for generations a second-place rival to GE in markets like power generation and home appliances—announced plans to pay $5.4 billion to acquire ABC's network rival, CBS, just three blocks to the south on Manhattan's Avenue of the Americas.

Weeks later, and the Time Warner Company, with its headquarters in Rockefeller Center two blocks further south, announced a $7.5 billion deal to acquire the Turner Broadcasting Company of Atlanta, pushing the total value of the deals these three midtown Manhattan media companies had done in just the past month to nearly $32 billion.

Even Ron Perelman had gotten into the act, going fifty/fifty with the U.S. arm of a French-owned publishing company, Hachette Filipacchi, to acquire a struggling monthly magazine called *Premiere* that was devoted to the movie industry. The magazine, which had been owned by a media buyout fund backed by financier Henry Kravis, was hardly a television network or film studio. Yet for just $10 million (that being his share of the $20 million purchase), Ron had acquired a media soapbox from which he could influence the entire industry as well as promote his own interests.

Thirty-five miles north of midtown Manhattan in Stamford, Connecticut, another CEO also had his thoughts on the future, and at almost exactly the same time. But unlike Ron Perelman or Big Al Dunlap, who were both rich already and expecting to get even richer, the head of GE Capital, Gary Wendt, faced the challenge of hanging on to what he already had. The issue: a woman—specifically, the wife.

It was December 1, 1995, and Wendt had finally made up his mind. After thirty years of marriage, he had decided at last to divorce his wife, Lorna. He was in love with Rosemarie now, and thank God for that. He was going to do the right thing . . . at last—for himself, for Rosemarie, and for Lorna, too. It was over.

Yet of the many challenges he knew he would face, one in particular had trouble written all over it: How much of his money—which by some estimates could have topped $100 million—would he wind up having to give Lorna in a settlement?*

By 1995, the Wendts were not simply well off, but very, very rich. And as Gary viewed the matter, he had earned that money, and Lorna had not. As Gary viewed things, Lorna had been a housewife, and that was it. Sure, she had helped bring in the money when he was going to business school at Harvard, but after that, well, as Gary could very distinctly show if push came to shove, she hadn't worked a damned day in her life. Here's how things were arranged (and for three long decades if you wanted to know the truth): Basically speaking, Gary earned the money and brought it home, and then Lorna spent it. That was the division of labor in the Wendt house. According to Gary.

---

*Estimates of the Wendt family's wealth ranged widely, depending on when the estimate was made, the party making the estimate, and the assets included in the calculation. Nearly all estimates have ranged between $50 million and $100 million.

Gary knew this wasn't going to be easy, and he knew that Lorna had an entirely different view of the matter. As Lorna sized things up, she'd been a great GE wife, supporting her husband in every aspect of the job. Gary could imagine all the nonsense she would bring up if the divorce ever got to court—everything about how, as a GE wife, she had read newspapers front-to-back, every day of her life, just to be able to talk to him about the hideously boring stuff that was in them. She would carry on about being more than your typical "corporate wife," and how her responsibilities had gotten so burdensome once he began to rise up the corporate ladder. He could hear it all now, about how she was always having to drop everything in *her* life on a moment's notice to rush to New York and have dinner with a bunch of clients in *his* life. Sometimes she'd have to do something like that once every ten days, poor baby.

In reality, Lorna had done more for Gary and his career than Gary wanted to admit. In 1986, shortly after he became CEO of GE Capital, they sold their home and moved to a bigger place—a four-bedroom, center hall colonial, also in Stamford. Then two more years passed, and they bought a piece of vacant land, also in Stamford, and for the following two years Lorna oversaw the building of a massive 5,068-square-foot home with 3½ baths and 4 bedrooms, a family room, an exercise room, and a bathroom in the basement.*

In fact, in many ways Lorna was the engine that kept the Wendt family running. She was the mother of their two daughters, she was the cook, the homemaker, you name it. In the summers, it was Lorna who took the children to camp. In the winters, it was Lorna who

---

*One sign of their deteriorating marriage was built right into the house's architectural design. Gary liked contemporary, and Lorna liked traditional styles. So as a compromise, the home was constructed with a traditional Colonial front facade and a contemporary style facing the rear. See the testimony of Lorna Wendt, December 3, 1996, in the matter of *Lorna J. Wendt v. Gary C. Wendt*, Superior Court of Connecticut, Stamford-Norwalk Judicial District.

helped with their homework. Gary didn't change their diapers, Lorna did that. In fact, it was Lorna who did the family's annual income tax returns, not Gary. She might be smack in the middle of doing exactly that—going over the taxes (with the accountant whom Gary had never met but once in fifteen years, thank you very much)—and he'd phone from the office and say, "I need you on this California trip," and that would be it, she'd have to drop everything and go.

So okay, maybe Gary was the one who brought home the money. Maybe he brought home truckloads of it, too. But so what? If Lorna hadn't been doing her job, who would he have been bringing it home to? Why would he even have been earning it? What had this whole thing called their married life been about anyway, if not that?

Lorna Wendt. She played the oboe, sang in the glee club, and made sure Mr. Wonderful always had ironed shirts to wear. But could she swing an LBO? (*Photo credit:* David Rentas, *New York Post.*)

Their older daughter was now twenty-eight and a graduate student at NYU. The younger one, twenty-five, was a graduate of a private eastern college and had her master's degree in human resources. Wasn't Gary proud of them? Of how they'd turned out?

Gary knew that if push came to shove, Lorna would be able to produce a parade of witnesses about how good a mother and homemaker she'd been—about how she'd cooked and housecleaned, and even did the windows . . . how she'd paid the household bills, arranged for the auto repairs and maintenance, for the grocery shopping, the feeding, the driving, the music lessons, the school teacher conferences, the church activities, the clubs, the concerts and recitals, the after-school activities, the car pools, the doctors' appointments—the whole bloody nine yards . . . and through it all she'd never know when the phone might ring and Mister Wonderful would be on the other end telling her to get a move on because there was something she'd have to be attending that night. Then four hours later, she'd be talking to people she'd never before met, trying desperately to remember the details of their lives to debrief Gary on them afterward. She would be pleasant and would mix confidently with total strangers, and put everyone at ease. And if the children came out to say hello, they'd always be neat and polite and never have any dirt on them, and the house would always be immaculate, and her husband would always have ironed shirts to wear, and the girls never went to school wearing something that needed to be sewed, and she was an excellent cook and everyone said so, and she was an important and hard-working member of the Stamford Lutheran Church just like her father would have wanted her to be, and every time Gary bowed out, she would cover for him and do it so smoothly no one would even know why he wasn't there.

Gary knew that all that was true. And he could imagine full well that when everyone arrived for the Wendts' annual Christmas party, which was now only a couple of weeks away, Lorna would be the perfect hostess, behaving as graciously as you please, so that no one would have the slightest idea that he wasn't even living there anymore.*

So, sure, Gary knew all of that. And he was certainly ready to admit it, too. But he also knew that everything Lorna had contributed in the way of honest-to-God actual *work* didn't amount to squat compared with what he had done. To listen to Lorna talk, it was like running the Wendt household was as big a job as running GE Capital! And hey, if she wanted to be that way about it, well Gary had plenty of his own witnesses to call!

He could produce witnesses who had worked with him every day for years at GE Capital. Witnesses who would explain what he'd really done with his life. And they could make it all nice and simple for the judge to follow. Like for example, the Tiffany's deal—the first time in the history of the lending industry when a major player like GE Capital had lent money on nothing but a brand name. Gary had priced out that deal, and now it had become a model for the whole industry. He could produce witnesses who'd say he was the one—little old Gary Wendt—who'd invented the whole idea of the leveraged buyout . . . and frankly, what would you rather have, holes in your socks, or a $200 million leveraged buyout? Everybody knew it: When it came to the lending game, Gary was a genius. He knew the details of every deal (actually, he had to because of Jack Welch). He knew the strategic side, too. He could spot the leverage in anything. If there was something to lend against, Gary could find it.

And frankly, it wasn't as if Gary was *totally* disengaged from community affairs either. Didn't the Stamford Boys and Girls Club need a trailer back in 1989? And didn't Gary get them one? And

---

*In trial testimony, witnesses for Lorna Wendt stated that the couple's 1995 Christmas party went off smoothly even though Lorna had confided beforehand to a friend that, with dissolution papers then in the process of being filed, "I do not know how I can go through with this party because of my marital problems."

didn't he wind up financing the construction of a whole new center for the Club? And didn't he design a development plan for the Stamford Public School system? And hadn't he served as the director of the Regional Planning Network for the entire tristate area? And didn't he do plenty of actual goddamn real work for the Network and not just lend them his name? And didn't he create a "Reach Out" program for the Stamford Center for the Arts? So, again: What would you rather have, the Stamford Center for the Arts, or holes in your socks?

And while he was on the subject, just how tough were all those "perfect hostess" jobs anyway? Gary could remember times—plenty of times, in fact—when GE wound up catering the whole thing, and all Lorna had to do was be standing upright at 6 o'clock. Hey, it wasn't Lorna who'd arranged for last year's Christmas bash, was it? . . . the one with the pianist and the harpist and Marvin Hamlisch for God's sake. This was first-class stuff, and GE handled it all. And now she was sounding like her life with him had been some gigantic three-decade-long crucifixion.

Just how tough was it to fly first class to some fancy resort and wear yourself out shopping! Just last year they went to northern Europe twice, and to Florida, Singapore, California, India, and even Asia, and all she did was shop, shop, shop. One year they went to Egypt, Greece, Turkey, Singapore, Bali, Malaysia, and Vietnam. And you know what? She shopped! Sometimes she shopped right from the boat. Last summer they went to Sorrento on a GE cruise and she stayed aboard having her hair done and getting an aromatherapy treatment. Next day in Capri, it was the same thing. The whole boat goes ashore, and Lorna stays on board and gets a facial, a massage, and has her hair done again.[4]

Gary knew all those things about Lorna, and more things besides—just as he knew that Lorna knew things about him. Yet, he also knew something else: Jack Welch wasn't going to like this, and if it got out of hand, he was going to like it even less. But he obviously had to tell him—and soon—lest he read about it in the newspapers first. For as everyone at GE knew, the all-seeing Dreaded One hovered ever nearby, and woe to anybody who tried to keep him in the dark.

~~~

In fact, Jack Welch had bigger concerns on his mind than Gary Wendt's marital issues when the GE Capital man telephoned him the next morning and broke the news. "Look," said Jack, sounding anxious to get the annoying Wendt off the phone as quickly as possible, "you just let me know if there's anything I can do to help." And with that the conversation ended, and the GE leader turned back to the weightier matters at hand.

By now Jack had recovered from the angioplasty and bypass surgery he had undergone in mid-May, and had returned to work, where a strange new project was now consuming his attention day and night: the establishment of a quality control program for GE that bore the somewhat off-putting name of "Six Sigma." To Jack, it offered GE's best hope for prospering in the global marketplace of the twenty-first century. In reality, it had the earmarks of a cult.

During his first five years as GE's chairman and CEO, Welch's list of accomplishments had been remarkable. He had chopped back one of the most change-resistant bureaucracies on earth. He had shed nearly every slow-growth business the company had and moved the resulting freed-up capital into high-growth arenas, in particular financial services. His acquisition of RCA, and the resulting spin-off of all its businesses except NBC had in effect given GE a TV broadcast network for free. Between 1981 and 1986, the company's resulting profitability per employee from all this had jumped by 50 percent, to $6,681 per worker.

But what could he do for an encore? In recent years, he had given plenty of speeches and engaged in a practice that he liked to call "deep diving," in which he'd shove his way into the most obscure and remote recesses of the company's operations and start telling the employees how to do their jobs. He knew it made him a pest and a meddler, but at least it was a way for him to keep reminding people who was really in charge.

Welch's basic problem was that GE was a conglomerate—a company that by definition would engage in any legal form of commerce imaginable as long as the end result was increased profitability. And since he couldn't quite put into words what the job of a conglomerate's CEO actually was—except perhaps to make the company's stock price go up—he seemed constantly trying to explain how the company amounted to "more than the sum of its parts . . . more than a conglomerate . . . more than a portfolio of disconnected businesses."

But what else was it really? Since it wasn't the products and services that set GE apart from its competitors in the market, given that the company would (and often did) sell just about anything, Welch was left in the end with little to talk about except the "values" around which the company organized its efforts.

Yet the values he wound up articulating—the same ones he had learned from his mother, Grace, as a boy growing up on the streets of North Salem, Massachusetts—were hardly unique to GE but instead turned out to be so unexceptional and commonplace as to be part of the shared value structure of the United States itself. Who could object to the values of *quality* and *excellence*, for example, when as Welch understood the words, they meant taking pride in your work, and working hard?

To make them uniquely *GE's* values as opposed to everybody's, Welch somehow had to insist that his employees embrace them more fervently than anyone else did. If being an American meant working hard and taking pride in your work, then a GE employee had no choice but to work *harder*, and take *more* pride in his or her work—or settle for being no different from anyone else.

That became Jack's message to GE. And just as Grace had harangued him with the identical message through her desperate and angry expressions of love, Jack now set out to browbeat GE the same way. Using the company's executive training center in Crotonville, New York, as his soapbox,* he lectured incessantly on one aspect or another of the "GE Way." He was always on the lookout for ways to weed out the middlemen, flatten the bureaucracy, and reach more of the company's employees more directly, with a message that became ever more insistent, fervent, impassioned, and shrill—more, more, *more*—for it was, in the end, the only message he had.

From 1986 onward, and with the successful completion of the RCA deal, Welch began a seemingly relentless hunt for the right slogan or gimmick to ram home his message, and when he stumbled on one, he'd embrace it with an enthusiasm that at times seemed almost scary. In 1988, he and an aide came up with an idea he called "Work-Out," which basically boiled down to a way to encourage rank-and-file employees to speak out publicly against bureaucratically minded bosses. Within a year, Work-Out had morphed into another non-word idea: the so-called "Boundaryless" concept. The premise was that every person at GE should be willing to share every idea he ever had with everybody else, thereby—as Welch explained it in almost fascist-like imagery—"focusing the brainpower of 300,000-plus people into every person's head."[5]

---

* In a remarkable, if unintended, insight into the powerful grip his childhood still held on him a half century later, Welch ordered a renovation of the main lecture hall of the Crotonville training center, then christened it "The Pit"—the same name he had given the makeshift playground in North Salem where he had ruled supreme as the leader of his neighborhood gang.

Yet, for all the Billy Sunday enthusiasm that he packed into delivering this strange gospel, the one thing it couldn't do was the only thing that really mattered: make people more creative. For all GE's fine talk about creativity and product innovation, the company's track record in those areas had been rather ordinary under Welch. By the mid-1980s, the innovative initiatives of the Reg Jones era had largely either led to marketable products or been abandoned, and the company began taking bows for accomplishments like:

1986: New lights for the Statue of Liberty.

1989: The launch of CNBC.

1994: The launch of the company's first web site.

1996: The launch of MSNBC as a joint venture with Microsoft.

1998: Insurance for hospitals.

1999: An oven that cooks food with light.

1999: Generation of 1 percent of revenues via Internet sales.

2001: A kitchen refrigerator that can chill a bottle of wine "in minutes."

2001: A light bulb that gets the yellow out.

With the company's top-line revenue growth coming either from acquisitions or Gary Wendt's GE Capital operation (which increasingly was accounting for both), Welch wasn't going to be able to show continuing growth in bottom-line earnings without cutting out yet more of the fat in the middle. Then, in 1995, the GE chairman discovered "Six Sigma," a mathematically expressed concept for implementing and tracking quality control at corporations, and all his problems seemed to vanish.

Developed in the 1980s by a group of engineers at Motorola Corporation, the Six Sigma methodology had spawned proselytizers who helped spread the concept to other corporations. One of them turned out to be AlliedSignal Corporation, which was by then headed by Welch's one-time consigliore, Larry Bossidy. When Bossidy thereafter suggested that Welch take a look at the idea as a way to put some money on GE's bottom line, Welch quickly did so.

As a program for measuring and tracking manufacturing defects, the Six Sigma program had a certain utility in lowering operating costs and thereby improving a company's cash flow and net income. But Welch saw more in Six Sigma than just that. As packaged and sold to companies in training courses by consulting firms like the so-called Six Sigma Academy, the program contained elaborate and mathematically complex instructions regarding how to implement cost controls, reduce output defects, and track the results over time.

In addition, graduates of the program could go on to advance upward within the world of Six Sigma itself, as they mastered its increasingly arcane and abstract "knowledge" and the "language" used to communicate its ideas. And in keeping with the idea of business as combat, there was even the Six Sigma equivalent of campaign ribbons for these Samurai of the bottom line: One could begin as a Six Sigma "Green Belt" (ten days of training) and wind up an actual Six Sigma-certified "Black Belt," whacking away at corporate waste on a two-year-long Six Sigma project.

For Welch—and in fact many other business leaders, steeped as they were in the Attila the Hun values of business as combat—the appeal was overwhelming. It was as if they had come to work one morning to find their lives filled again with secret handshakes, decoder rings, and GI Joe paratrooper boots from the Army and Navy Store.

With Bossidy endorsing the idea, Welch quickly became Six Sigma's biggest proselytizer, for this wasn't just a cost-cutting program. As he put it in his business memoir, Six Sigma was "more than statistics for engineers," it was "for the best and the brightest in any function." Six Sigma was "the most ambitious undertaking the company had ever taken on," and it could make GE into "absolutely the greatest company in world business." It could be the glue that held GE together, the "universal training program" for everyone . . . the "universal language" that would reach around the world, to GE operations in "Canada, Mexico, North Africa, Morocco, Bangalore, Korea, Taiwan . . ." Six Sigma could be what "ties all the pieces to together."*

---

*See J. Welch and J. Byrne, *Jack: Straight from the Gut* (New York: Warner Books, 2001), pp. 185, 330, 338, 339, and 432. Yet even among those closest to Welch, not all believed in his over-the-top proselytizing on behalf of this so-called revolutionary program. In her own memoir as Welch's personal secretary, Rosanne Badowski dismissed the program as little more than a joke, saying that she personally did not feel the need to "chop, kick, and block" her way to "perfection as a Six Sigma Black Belt [and] alas, not even a Green Belt." Badowski questioned "the utility of a nearly across-the-board training model that takes people away from their jobs for long stretches, when they may never use those skills when they return." She also argued that Welch applied a double standard when it came to Six Sigma, ordering all salaried employees to be trained in the concept or to kiss their opportunities for promotions, stock options, and bonuses goodbye. But Badowski reports that the edict didn't apply to her because Welch didn't want to lose her services while she was taking the course. When she asked him if she could attend the course, Welch answered, "You could *teach* that course," and walked away. See R. Badowski, *Managing Up: How to Forge an Effective Relationship with Those above You* (New York: Doubleday, 2003).

15

CEO IN BANJO-LAND

t was the spring of 1996, and a problem was brewing for Ron Perelman. It all had to do with that 50 percent stake he had acquired in *Premiere* magazine the year before. Ron had seen *Premiere* as a way to stay in the loop in Hollywood, and the $10 million he had paid for his one-half interest in it hardly seemed exorbitant.

There was even a side bonus: Owning half the magazine gave him a way to throw a bone to Patricia, who'd long since gone in his eyes from shiksa goddess to shiksa ghoul. Thanks to his stake at the magazine, he'd been able to get her a job as *Premiere's* roving "editor at large," and the magazine now planned to list her for the first time on the masthead, in the very next issue.

The problem was, Patricia had become as much of an annoyance to the magazine's editors as she'd become to Ron; and Ron had become an embarrassment in his own right. None of the staff actually had to deal with him, but they could feel his constant hovering presence as the 50 percent owner. Things like requests—which somehow seemed to materialize out of nowhere, and prove traceable to no one—to run photos of bevies of Revlon girls who would turn up at film industry glamour-events like the Oscars. It cheapened the whole magazine to find a photo spread like that in its pages. It seemed to say, this is Ron Perelman's personal vanity press—and you didn't need the finely tuned sensitivities of a writer or editor to realize it either. Everyone in Hollywood and everywhere else knew who owned *Premiere*—just as everyone knew who owned Revlon. It just looked bad.

On top of that, the staff now had to deal with the presence, not simply on the masthead but at their actual story conferences, of "editor at large" Patricia Duff—an even bigger Ron Perelman smudge on the magazine's credibility than photos of his Revlon honeys. One of the magazine's top editors, Nancy Griffin, whose much anticipated Hollywood exposé, *Hit and Run*, was about to be published, felt particularly incensed. The book, coauthored by an equally talented former *Washington Post* reporter named Kim Masters, peeled back the hidden world of life inside Columbia Pictures under out-of-control studio moguls Jon Peters and Peter Guber. And awkwardly, Duff's ex-husband Mike Medavoy figured prominently in the storyline. There were even walk-on parts for Duff and, most embarrassing of all, for none other than Perelman, who was painted as a liar for having been spotted in a secret rendezvous with Duff in Hawaii while she was still married to Medavoy, then claiming that he was actually in Hawaii alone.*

---

*Four years later, in April 2000, Patricia Duff filed an affidavit in New York State Supreme Court that suggested her own role in the matter. According to Duff, she had been the one who had wanted to keep Perelman's presence in Hawaii quiet, and it had been Perelman who had wanted to draw attention to himself. According to the Duff affidavit, filed on April 11, 2000, in connection with her divorce proceedings against Perelman, she had flown to Hawaii over the Christmas holidays of 1993 to escape Perelman's hovering presence only to find that he had followed her there. According to the affidavit, this led to a quarrel over whether the two should be seen publicly on New Year's Eve. The quarrel allegedly escalated to the point that, according to Duff, Perelman grew violent, pulled her hair, and threw her to the ground.

Now Griffin, whose journalistic credentials were impeccable and whose book was clearly headed for best-seller status, found herself at story conferences sitting next to the very person whom the world would soon be reading about in *Hit and Run*. It was hard to imagine a more awkward—or conversation-stifling—situation, as Patricia's arrival at each story conference was always the same, beginning with the distinctive click-click-click of her stiletto heels approaching in the hallway, followed by the sweep into the conference room of Patricia herself, trailing her fur coat and done up top-to-toe in Valentino. In the grimy, ink-stained world of the magazine's editorial offices, what else could anyone do but fall silent and simply stare—awed not merely by the grandness and sheer theatricality of her entrance, but more than anything else, by how utterly and impossibly *clean* she looked. Then, in the enveloping silence, and with the eyes of the dumbstruck upon her, she would settle into her seat and draw forth from her purse the now-familiar pen and notecase, and the meeting would begin. Meanwhile down on the street, the stretch limo would sit idling at curbside, to take her next to lunch or perhaps for an hour with her personal trainer.

By the spring of 1996, the staff's anger had reached the boiling point over the way Perelman seemed to be allowing his personal affairs to seep into so much of the magazine's editorial product. And the problem passed the point of no return when the magazine's top editor, Chris Connelly, tried to schedule an investigative story involving actor Sylvester Stallone and the Planet Hollywood, Inc., fast-food restaurant chain, only to have higher-ups kill it. The rumors were that Perelman was negotiating with Planet Hollywood to start a restaurant chain of his own.

Connelly was right to be suspicious because Perelman's ties to Planet Hollywood were deep and extensive, and had already developed beyond the talking stage. Indeed, by the time the editor attempted to schedule the story, Perelman had agreed to a deal with the chairman and CEO of Planet Hollywood, Keith Barish, to invest $36 million in the corporation. Their intent was to open a chain of fast-food restaurants based on action hero characters in the Marvel comic book series, to which Perelman owned the rights.

This was an important deal for Barish, whose Planet Hollywood chain was facing deepening financial problems. And it was an important investment opportunity for Perelman as well, who knew that his financial resources would give him great leverage in any future transactions with Barish if Planet Hollywood's own finances deteriorated further. So, although no evidence ever surfaced of intermeddling by Perelman to get the story killed, he undoubtedly stood to benefit financially if the story were spiked.*

With that as the backdrop, Connelly and Griffin both abruptly quit on May 7, citing the magazine's "drastic change of direction." Normally, such actions would not have made much news. But this time the stars had lined up in a way to catch the attention of media people everywhere. Not only did the story involve Hollywood and the possibility of financial scandal lapping at the feet of both the Planet Hollywood restaurant chain and one of the film industry's biggest stars, Sly Stallone, but the man who seemed to be pulling the strings in the whole affair was who else but Ron Perelman, America's most glamour-crazed billionaire.

---

*Though the editors didn't realize it, Patricia Duff was a factor of sorts in the matter as well. Her role derived from her ties to Barish, which functioned independently from Barish's ties to Perelman. Barish, a sometime Hollywood producer with screen credits that included The Fugitive and Sophie's Choice, had a background in Democratic Party politics that closely paralleled Duff's. Barish had been a White House intern during the Kennedy administration, after which he became a business partner of JFK's press spokesman, Pierre Salinger—a period during which he lived in the same building (740 Park Avenue) where Perelman lived with his first wife, Faith. When Perelman first met Duff in Paris and thereafter began raving about her captivating charm, one of the people he confided in was Barish, who relayed Perelman's feelings back to Duff, thereby giving her valuable back-channel intelligence to help her steer the course of her developing relationship with the billionaire.

In the days that followed, stories appeared in the *Washington Post*, *Atlanta Journal-Constitution*, *Hollywood Reporter*, *Variety*, *Newsweek*, *Time*, *Chicago Sun Times*, *Wall Street Journal*, *New York Times* and elsewhere. Nearly all of them expressed the sentiment of the headline in the *Washington Post*: "Top Editors Quit; Movie Magazine *Premiere* Staffers Refuse Corporate Order to Kill Column."[1] The stories marked the start of a new and less reverential view of Ron Perelman in the media, and he could not even begin to imagine how quickly his problems would mount.

———※———

Jack Welch's problems were also about to take a quantum leap upward. It was Thursday, the Fourth of July, 1996, and instead of enjoying the ocean breezes from his home in Nantucket, he was somewhere over the southeast Alabama countryside. What awaited him below would not be pleasant, and he obviously knew it. But as he and his wife Jane buckled their seatbelts for the GE corporate jet's final approach into Eufaula Airport, he could never have imagined the forces that were already gathering against him. He was on a collision course with fate, and with the woman seated next to him.

Twenty-four hours earlier, he had been Jack Welch, king of the CEOs, standing before the throng to unfurl yet another wonder from the mind of GE—a joint venture with the Boeing Corporation to build a new corporate jet the size of an entire Boeing 737. They were going to call it the 737-700, and it could be configured differently for every business trip, for any imaginable purpose: as a meeting center, a communication post, a traveling hotel, you name it. The planes were going to cost $35 million each, and GE and Boeing figured to sell a hundred of them by 2006, which is to say $3.5 billion worth of a whole new kind of aircraft so that CEOs like Jack Welch could take their entire offices and support staffs with them when they traveled. You want to talk command and control? Well this was the 360-degree power-view on steroids.*

And now here he was instead, one day later, putting his seat-back in the upright position for a crisis visit to Deliverance Country, down there along Highway 51, midway between Clayton and Louisville and a mile east of Pea Creek, to the farmhouse where Jane had grown up, where the old lady named Warine still worked in the fields for Jane's daddy, Durwood, who used to raise hogs, and grow peanuts and corn, and drive a backhoe for the county until he got too old and worn out . . . to whom Jane and her brothers had been providng the money—month after month—so he could pay the old woman, Warine, who did the cooking and the cleaning and the hoeing and the weeding. And now this?

To call the situation that awaited Jack and Jane Welch macabre hardly got it, for somewhere down below—in Alabama's red earth world of crickets and tree frogs, where the bougainvillea covers everything and the greatest crime of all is betrayal—the old woman, Warine, had been standing in the doorway not twenty-four hours earlier, shrieking at the Chief of Police: "He chopped himself in the head . . ." while behind her on the floor, with the back half of his skull

---

*Many executives at GE advised Welch against pursuing the B 737-700 project, arguing that the corporate boards of the companies that were the plane's most likely customers would balk at authorizing purchases for fear of being seen by shareholders as showering their CEOs with unnecessary extravagances. Yet Welch pushed ahead with the project anyway, arranging for GE to buy the first 737-700 to roll off the production line. When the plane was finally delivered in 1997, GE kept it at the company's facility at Westchester County Airport north of New York City, where Welch made regular use of it for himself and his wife's travel needs, charging the operating and maintenance costs to the company. Doing so came back to haunt Welch in a big way when Jane Welch subsequently seized on that fact to claim the plane's costs ($291,667 per month) as one of numerous itemized expenses in her demands for spousal support in her divorce. The claim helped portray Jack in the media as living the life of a latter day King Farouk at the expense of GE's shareholders. And the program came back to haunt GE as well. According to executives at the company, by the end of 1999 only eleven of the aircraft had been sold.

missing and his brains spilling out, lay the father-in-law of the chairman and CEO of the General Electric Company.[2]

And Jack Welch was going to handle *this?*

The sequence of events leading to that bizarre moment began at
some point in the early morning hours of July 3, 1996. There is much
confusion as to precisely when it was that police from the town of
Louisville, Alabama (pop. 1,475), which sits about six miles south of
Pratt's Station on Highway 51, were summoned to the Beasley farmhouse, or even why. Was there a domestic altercation? A burglary? A
murder? The record is unclear as to when the call came in, who it
came from, or even the nature of the complaint.*

On the available evidence, and from the statements of those willing to talk, it appears that an incident of some sort may have occurred
at the Beasley farmhouse shortly after midnight and that two police
cars from Louisville wound up being dispatched in quick succes-
sion—the first at 12:45 A.M. followed by a second at 12:50 A.M. The
so-called Patrolman's Daily Reports of that shift describe the incident
both as a burglary and as a murder, and show that the incident was
not closed out until 8 A.M.[†]

What happened during these long overnight hours is unclear.
Mack Houston, the Louisville chief of police, claims that he first

---

* At various times, the major law enforcement officials in the case have made statements
to the author and/or his research colleague that have been in significant conflict with
the statements of other officials. Some of these inconsistences have proved impossible
to resolve.

† The "Patrolman Daily Reports" of the Louisville Police Department were obtained
from the Louisville PD file and read to the author line by line and verbatim during an interview with the Louisville, Alabama, Assistant City Clerk Deborah Vincent on December 12, 2003. These reports show conclusively that report entries placed two Louisville
PD police officers at the Beasley home beginning at 12:45 A.M. and 12:50 A.M. The
logged mileage on one of the vehicles suggests two round-trips from Louisville to the
farmhouse took place during the period. The Barbour County investigator for the Alabama Bureau of Investigations on the case, Barry Tucker, said, during a separate interview with the author on December 12, 2003, that he had never seen the "Patrolman
Daily Reports" but insisted that if they contained the information stated in the interview, then the reports are "wrong."

learned of trouble at the Beasley place when he received a call from the city clerk on his police band radio at around 8 A.M. According to Houston, the city clerk thought Houston needed to get to the Beasley farmhouse quick. It seemed a woman named Warine Casey who lived in the nearby town of Clio and worked at the farm, had just arrived for work at the farmhouse to find her employer, Durwood Beasley, dead on the floor, apparently from a suicide.*

Like just about everyone else in Louisville, Mack Houston knew the Beasley family, which was enormous, with dozens of cousins scattered all over Barbour County, many in prosperous and influential positions in business, the law, and government. And he also knew the farmhouse of Durwood Beasley, one of the few members of the clan who had made next to nothing of his life and was now just passing the time in retirement out there on the state highway, knocking back Jack Daniels by the glassful on his front porch.

Why Houston's department became involved at all is yet another of the murder's mysteries, since the department's jurisdiction extended only to the Louisville city limits, which stopped short of Pratt Station (pop. 612).

Real authority over the case belonged to the Barbour County Sheriff's Department, which had its headquarters in the town of Clayton (pop. 1,012), twenty miles up Highway 51 to the *north* of Pratt Station.† And even the county sheriff's jurisdiction was somewhat

---

* In an interview with the author on December 12, 2003, Barbour County Sheriff John Hamm agreed with Louisville, Alabama, Chief of Police Mack Houston that Warine Casey had initially described Beasley's death as a suicide. But he said, Warine's first phone call after coming upon the body had been to her son, Ken. This differs from Houston's statement that her first phone call had been to the Louisville City Clerk. In an interview with the author's research colleague, D. Bertaccini, Warine Casey said her first phone call had been to a third individual, her preacher, Curtis Rich.

† Officials in the Barbour County Sheriff's Department declined to discuss any aspect of the Beasley murder, including the possibility, suggested by an official at the Louisville PD, that Louisville had assumed jurisdiction on a courtesy referral from Barbour County.

confused, for although the department's headquarters was legally in Clayton, the sheriff, a man named John Hamm, worked out of an office twenty-five miles to the east in the town of Eufaula, which is where he lived.

Eufaula, which sits on the banks of the Chattahoochee River that forms much of the border between Alabama and Georgia, is hardly the Paris of the South, but its 13,000 residents make it the largest community in Barbour County, and more than ten times the size of Clayton. Situated at what were once the navigable headwaters of the Chattahoochee River, the town had prospered as a mid-nineteenth-century commercial port. Visitors today can still stroll along streets lined with well-preserved Georgian homes that remind one of Eufaula's roots in the world of cotton and slaves.

On the basis of its size alone, Eufaula was the most practical place for the Barbour County Sheriff to keep his office, so it was there, in a first-floor office in the county courthouse, that Hamm worked. Unlike Clayton, which boasted an airport that consisted of little more than a strip of asphalt in the fields, Eufaula had an actual, functioning commercial facility, complete with a fueling pad and a repair hanger.

So, with the lines of authority confused already, Houston says he radioed the Barbour County Sheriff's Department to pass along what he had just been told, then left for the farmhouse to see for himself. Whether Houston's phone call caused the Barbour County dispatcher to radio instructions to a sheriff's deputy named Don Granger to get to the scene also isn't clear because the Barbour County Sheriff's Department hasn't been eager to discuss the matter.

In any event, though Houston claims he was the first law enforcement official to arrive at the farmhouse, his own department's files show that at least two of his own men might well have been there hours earlier. And even as Houston was heading toward the farmhouse, Warine Casey's son, Ken, was speeding there, too, in his red pickup truck, with his wife Martha at his side.

Soon enough, all three vehicles converged on the Beasley farmhouse. First came the Ford pickup containing Warine's son and daughter-in-law, followed by Mack Houston in a Louisville PD police cruiser, with a Barbour County sheriff's cruiser driven by Deputy Sheriff Don Granger bringing up the rear.

What they saw made it instantly obvious that this was no suicide: Durwood Beasley was missing the whole back half of his head, and had plainly been murdered. And given the fact that Warine Casey was not simply his domestic employee and had worked for him for years, but had been the first person on the scene—and, according to Houston, had absurdly described it as a suicide—it was hard not to see her as a suspect.*

But the situation was confused already, with at least five people milling about in the blood-drenched crime scene, and it was soon to get even more confused as yet another individual became involved. That person was Barbour County's district attorney, Boyd Whigham,

---

*In an interview with the author's research colleague, D. Bertaccini, January 17, 2004, Warine Casey gave her story, speaking publicly on the matter for the first time in seven years. She said that the first phone call she placed the morning of Durwood's murder, July 3, 1996, was to her minister Curtis Rich "around 8:00 A.M." She said, "I called him at the hardware store where I knew he worked." She said she had come to work at the farmhouse that morning at her usual time and there was no sight or sound of Durwood, so she proceeded to look through the house. On her way to his bedroom, she passed the room that she normally would stay in when she would stay overnight. It was the room next to his. She noticed that the "foot of the bed was turned up like someone had been doing something," which was unusual since she'd not been there to have made the mess herself. She said that was the first indication to her something was different. Then she proceeded to Durwood's bedroom and found him "on the floor of the bedroom by his bed in a pool of blood." She said she "was in a state of shock" and she doesn't remember calling the police or Louisville City Clerk's office. She said she "may have, but I really don't recall doing so." She said, "I also called my son Ken. I was too scared to be out there at the house alone. I wanted someone to be with me so I called my son Kenny." She said that Mack Houston was the first policeman there. She does not know how Mack Houston was notified. . . . She doesn't know if Curtis was the one who got in touch with Mack Houston or if it was someone else. She said, "I really hope some day they find the person that did that to Durwood. He was a really fine man and he didn't deserve that. He was a really good man."

who lived in the town of Louisville and at that very minute happened to be driving north along Highway 51 en route to his office on the second floor of the Eufaula County Courthouse.

The trip from Louisville to Eufaula took roughly thirty minutes, and Whigham had made it many times over the years, so it was not surprising that he noticed the commotion swirling about the normally quiet Beasley farmhouse, set off by itself in the fields. So, once he reached Eufaula and headed for his office in the courthouse, Whigham first stopped by the ground floor office of Barbour County Sheriff John Hamm to see if he knew what was up at the Beasley place.

Hamm was wondering as well. He always kept a police band radio switched on in his office and had trained himself to listen to it out of one ear as he went through his workday. And for the last half an hour or so, he'd become aware of some background chatter

The Beasley's home, Pratt's Station, Alabama, where the bougainvillea covers everything, and betrayal is the greatest crime of all. Burglary? Murder? Some Giorgio through the skull?

between his deputy, Don Granger, who was apparently at the Beasley place, and the sheriff's office in Clayton. Hamm thought it had something to do with a self-inflicted wound. But then Whigham stuck his head in the door and said he'd just passed the Beasley farmhouse and that there seemed to be a fair amount of commotion going on, and asked if Hamm knew anything about it.

So Hamm figured he'd better pay a bit more attention, and reaching Granger on the police band radio, he asked what was up. The very vagueness of Granger's reply didn't sound right, so Hamm told his deputy to call him back on a landline where he could talk more freely. Moments later Hamm was back on the phone, and when he heard what his deputy had to say, Hamm too was sliding behind the wheel of a Sheriff's Department black-and-white and speeding to the scene.

Back at the farmhouse, Granger and Houston had noticed that, incredibly enough, old Durwood wasn't actually dead. Though unconscious and almost motionless, the man was still breathing, though barely. So they had called an ambulance, which had already arrived and departed for the Lakeview Community Hospital in Eufaula with the all-but-lifeless body by the time Sheriff Hamm arrived at 9 A.M.

Houston says that it was by now clear to him at least that Warine had done the deed. For one thing, there was blood splattered on her sneakers, and what was it doing there if Beasley had already been assaulted by the time she had come upon him?

Moreover, the murder weapon—a full-sized woodchopper's ax—was not only lying on the floor nearby, but it was an ax that Warine certainly knew how to use because she regularly used it to chop firewood for Durwood.

And perhaps most important of all—at least so far as Mack Houston was concerned—was the low height of the ceilings in the farmhouse. This meant that the fatal blow had to have been struck by someone much smaller than Durwood, who stood nearly five feet ten inches tall. With the entire back half of Durwood's skull having been severed, the force of the blow had to have been considerable. If a person of average height had swung it, the ax blade would have slammed into the ceiling before beginning the downward arc into the skull. But Warine—whose weather-beaten face and tough hands betrayed her life of rough physical labor and the remarkable strength that came with it—was in fact not a whole lot more than five feet tall . . . short enough for the full arcing blow that sent Durwood to his reward.*

Yet Houston had lacked any real role in the case from the start, and now that officials from the Barbour County Sheriff's Department were on the scene, he could do nothing but offer a polite opinion and then leave, which is what he did. By contrast, John Hamm, who was younger and less experienced in law enforcement than Houston, disagreed with his colleague from the Louisville Police Department. Seeing no reason to view Warine with suspicion, he let her go home with her children, wash up, and change her clothes.

Later that day, Warine returned. It was past four o'clock, and a new team of sheriff's deputies was guarding the crime scene. When Warine asked to be allowed in to inspect the premises to make sure that nothing "had been disturbed," the officers permitted her to do so. They watched her mill about momentarily, then disappear into the bedroom. When she didn't come right back out, they followed

---

*In an interview with the author, Barbour County Sheriff John Hamm said he eventually came to believe Warine Casey to be the most likely suspect. In a separate interview with the author's research colleague, D. Bertaccini, Louisville, Alabama, Chief of Police Mack Houston said he has always viewed Warine Casey as the most likely suspect. And in separate interviews with both the author and D. Bertaccini, Investigator Barry Tucker of the Alabama Bureau of Investigations said that he also views Casey as the most likely suspect. Barbour County District Attorney Boyd Whigham declined several requests for interviews on the matter.

her and found her removing $1,400 in cash from the pocket of one of Durwood's shirts in his closet. Seeing the police eyeing her, she explained that Durwood would have wanted her to have the money, and when they wouldn't let her take it, she left in a huff.

～～～

All this and more had transpired when Jack and Jane Welch met for the first time with Hamm, at about 11 A.M. on the morning of July 4, for a hurried and somewhat chaotic briefing on the situation. In keeping with the uncertain status of the case, the meeting took place in a conference room that was still under construction as part of a new jail facility being built in Clayton for the Barbour County Sheriff's Department.

In some of the rooms, the walls had been painted and carpeting installed. In other rooms, the raw flooring and sheet-rocked walls were still exposed. Construction debris was scattered everywhere, along with discarded coffee cups and sandwich wrappers. Whatever the state of completion of the individual rooms, everything was coated with a fine, powdery layer of dust.

In this setting of a building in progress, Jack and Jane Welch were now to be brought up to speed on John Hamm's investigation. It was a remarkable moment indeed, for it should have taken Welch, who prided himself on his cut-through ability to master any problem no matter how sensitive or complex, less than five minutes to drill through to the most likely suspect Sheriff Hamm ought to have been focusing on: Warine Casey.

This was, after all, Jack Welch, the man who had become a living legend for *never* coming to a meeting unprepared, or *ever* letting anyone but himself dominate every aspect of what transpired once he was in the room. This was Jack Welch, the Torquemada of the executive conference room, who had built his entire career out of parboiling and roasting any executive who could not instantly answer the most complex and technical questions on any topic under the sun. And if ever there had been a moment for him to show his stuff, this was it. Twenty-four hours after the murder of his wife's father, bureaucratic and jurisdictional confusion and executive inexperience—the very subjects he had spent the past forty years railing against most ferociously—were already conspiring to let a murderer go free.

Twenty penetrating questions would have been all that it took to put the spotlight of suspicion where it belonged. Maybe not even that many. Maybe fifteen questions. Maybe ten.

But Jack Welch said nothing. Presented with what seemed to be an obviously bollixed investigation, conducted by a well-meaning but inexperienced investigator from banjo-land Alabama—the chairman and CEO of GE, and America's soon-to-be-anointed "CEO of the Century"—sat silently by and, so far as Hamm could recall, neither asked a single question, nor offered a single opinion, on anything.

Forty-five minutes later, Welch simply got up and left, and with him went his stunned wife, Jane—the task of tracking down the murderer of her own father having been effectively dumped in her lap by a husband who had obviously wanted no part of it from the start.

Soon enough, Jack would discover that Jane wanted no part of him either—though she did intend to take half his money with her on her way out the door. And she certainly didn't expect she'd have to chop off the back of his head with an ax to get it either—though given what lay ahead for them both, it might have been a neater solution.

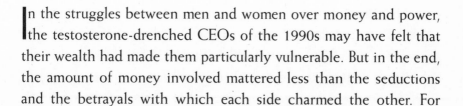

In the struggles between men and women over money and power, the testosterone-drenched CEOs of the 1990s may have felt that their wealth had made them particularly vulnerable. But in the end, the amount of money involved mattered less than the seductions and the betrayals with which each side charmed the other. For

where in the final reckoning is there all that much difference between what Patricia Duff had planned for Ron Perelman, or why she
had planned it—and what Jane Welch would soon be cooking up for
Jack (or what Jack would throw back in her face)?

And in either case where is there much difference from what
private investigators hired by Jane would eventually discover to be
the themes of money and betrayal that might well have lurked at
the heart of Warine's behavior as well? Durwood "worked her like a
slave," said Investigator Barry Tucker of the Alabama Bureau of Investigations, who suggested that one possible motive might have
been out and out anger. Tucker said Jane and other family members
had been covering Warine's wages, which didn't seem to amount to
very much, and that maybe to string her along, Durwood had recently promised to buy her a truck, then backed out at the last
minute.

But still he expected her to come to the house everyday, and
wash and clean, hoe the vegetable garden, and chop the firewood.
And sometimes, according to stories around town, he expected more
than that, and she'd wind up spending the night.

And where in the end is there much difference from *that* and what
the gang at the GE Plastics Division seem to have expected from *their*
female aides and assistants, such as Regina Paulsen? Over Regina's
high school yearbook picture is written: "Office Aide, Private Secretary," expressing to her classmates at Forest Hills High School, Class
of 1960, what was apparently her greatest career ambition . . . until
she discovered that on the dark side of seduction lurks betrayal, and
the pain of that discovery became so deep and writhing that she
ended her life.

Why wasn't Warine Casey ever tried, or even charged with the
crime? One answer comes from John Hamm, who did not stand for
re-election as Barbour County sheriff, and left to travel the world
when his term was up, returning eventually to take a job in juvenile
law enforcement in Montgomery, Alabama.

Hamm says he eventually came to believe that Mack Houston, chief of police for the Louisville Police Department, was right and that Warine was indeed the most likely suspect. Yet perhaps somewhat defensively, he says his office was just never able to develop enough evidence to go before a grand jury. For one thing, the ax handle was rough hewn, and forensics investigators were unable to lift identifiable fingerprints from it. And by the time the Sheriff's Department did turn its attention to Warine, she'd gotten a lawyer who refused to let her be interviewed, so investigators didn't even have a statement from her.

After a brief flurry of excitement when Mack Houston's office in Louisville arrested a man in the case on what turned out to be a false tip from a girlfriend, much of the impetus behind the investigation began to peter out. After his first visit on July 4, Jack never contacted Hamm or his office again, and once old Durwood was laid to rest, he left town and has never been seen in Barbour County again—so far as is known.

In the beginning, Jane called Hamm's office on an almost daily basis to stay updated on the investigation, and made repeated trips from Connecticut to meet with him personally.

Yet in time, her visits grew less frequent, as did the phone call contacts, and after about a year they ceased altogether. Hamm says that along the way Jane began to get pressure from Jack to let the private investigators go because of the costs involved, and by and by their involvement ended, too.

For her part, Jane's interests began to move in new directions, including learning how to speak Italian—the knowledge of which led not only to regular shopping junkets to Rome and Florence, but in the fullness of time to her own version of a score-settling ax through the skull—namely, Jack's—as she began a torrid transatlantic love affair with a man who seemed to embody everything Jack wasn't.

The new lover was tall (six foot two inches), he was trim, and he had movie star looks and a full head of hair. His name was Giorgio.

And to complete the picture of this new Fernando Llamas figure in her life, Giorgio wasn't some dashing European industrialist, or even some ne'er do well Florentine art collector with a villa in Tuscany and one of the Borghese women in his recent past. No, if Jane's goal had been to humiliate and enrage her husband beyond all reckoning in her selection of a lover, she could not possibly have made a better choice than the man she picked, since Giorgio was the limo driver for Jack's nattily suited best friend at GE, Paolo Fresco.

As a long-time Beasley family intimate put it not long ago, reflecting on how people deal with betrayal in that part of the world, so as to make the scales of justice balance evenly in the end: "They have a strange way of doing things down there in Barbour County . . ." and in the end it seemed pretty much all there was to say.

16

BIG AL GOES AWOL

I f the themes of money, sex, and power were what the bull market drama of the 1990s was ultimately all about, then the autumn of 1995 was when the actors took their marks, and the final act began.

In Beverly Hills, California, five floors of the Barney's New York department store on Wilshire Boulevard had been emptied of clothes racks and display stands, and the store had been turned into the setting for the annual Fire & Ice Ball. The event's purpose was to raise money for breast cancer research. But over the years, the affair had developed into a major "see and be seen" event for Ron, and this year's ball was no different.

It was Monday evening, November 13, 1995, and it seemed as if all of Hollywood had turned out—some for no other obvious purpose than to get their names in the gossip columns. Actor Christian Slater had arrived escorting actress Courtney Cox, stirring rumors that the two, who had not been seen together before in public, were an item. This, of course, gave them an opportunity, through their press agents, to deny that they were anything more than long-time "good friends," thereby keeping their names in print for a second day of follow-up coverage.

Actor Jim Carrey "dropped by," and so did country music singer Lyle Lovett. Jack Nicholson was there, and so were Dustin Hoffman, George Clooney, Faye Dunaway, Dennis Franz, and Sharon Stone— along with more than 1,000 men and women who were connected one way or another to either the entertainment industry or breast cancer research.

For Ron, the evening had a special significance for yet another reason since it marked one of the last occasions in which he and his wife for the previous ten months, Patricia, were to be seen together in public. Still outwardly cordial to each other (at least when others were around), the two had fought incessantly from the day they were married, often over the most preposterous of things. Pat would complain that he was intentionally hurting and abusing her by squeezing her hand too tightly when he was holding it in public. She complained of his hectic schedule and that he would never spend "a quiet night at home."

Some of her complaints seemed to suggest that their bizarre relationship had deteriorated into a mutually self-destructive game. She complained that when they were indeed alone he might begin to rage at her and rip off a piece of her clothing—for example a nightgown if they were preparing for bed. She would then put something else on and he would rip that off, too. She would then appear "terrified," and he would "turn off" and threaten to have his bodyguards throw her into the street. This didn't go on once, or even twice, but appeared instead to have become almost a ritual element in their lives together as husband and wife.

Meanwhile in Washington, a situation was developing that would soon enough give Ron yet more reasons to despise his politically connected wife and her ties to the Democratic Party.

It was the evening of November 15, two days after the Fire & Ice Ball, and in the White House an extraordinary scene was about to unfold. The setting was the Oval Office—by general agreement the ultimate inner sanctum of power on the earth. Yet given the climactic moment at hand, one could not be entirely sure where the power really resided, for even as the president of the United States stood by the desk in his personal study off the Oval Office, seemingly deep in a telephone conversation with a member of Congress, a twenty-two-year-old White House intern named Monica Lewinsky was on her knees in front of him, engaged in an activity that any man would find distracting—though the president himself would eventually insist under oath that it hadn't been sex.*

Aside from the two people in the room that night, no one yet knew what the 42nd president of the United States meant by "not having sex"—an activity he was to engage in with Ms. Lewinsky on eight separate additional occasions over the following fifteen months at various locations in and about the Oval Office. There would also be thirty-four instances of not having phone sex, and even an instance of not having a hitherto unheard-of activity known as cigar sex.

Nonetheless, Ron Perelman would soon find himself pulled into a strange supporting role in these matters. What's more, the process destined to summon him on stage had already begun even as the president was zipping up his fly. And for that he could thank his super-plugged-in Mister Fixit, Vernon Jordan, who had put the touch on Perelman more than eighteen months earlier to help ease

---

* In several respects, the life experiences that brought Bill Clinton to this moment are not much different from those that shaped the sexual appetites of Jack Welch. Both men were the firstborn sons of overbearing and dominant mothers in stressful family settings. Both developed difficulties relating to women. And in both cases, the problems worsened following the death of the mother.

Webster Hubbell out of the Clinton administration and into private practice as a consultant to Revlon Corp.

For his part, Hubbell had been a minor player in the so-called Whitewater land scandal, which traced back to the president's early political career in Arkansas and had dogged both Clinton and his wife Hillary from their first days in the White House. In January 1994, the president's Attorney General, Janet Reno, yielding to calls for a probe of the affair, appointed a Special Counsel named Robert Fiske to investigate Whitewater.

Fiske's investigators thereafter sought information from Webster Hubbell, a one-time partner of Clinton's wife in a Little Rock law firm, who had been appointed Associate Attorney General under Reno in the new administration. When Hubbell began stonewalling the investigators, they grew suspicious and escalated their efforts. This led to Hubbell's resignation in March 1994,[1] launching Vernon Jordan and a small group of Clinton insiders on a mission to line up business contracts for Hubbell so that he could open an office* as a corporate consultant in the private sector.[†]

Between March and December 1994, Jordan and others secured seventeen different consulting clients for Hubbell, bringing him business worth more than $500,000.[‡] But investigators from the Office of Independent Counsel continued to pursue Hubbell, and his

---

* Hubbell set up an office for his short-lived consulting business at an address on 19th Street NW in Washington.

[†] In August, a three-judge panel ruled that Fiske's Whitewater probe could not properly operate under the control of the Attorney General, and thus replaced it with an Office of Independent Counsel headed by Kenneth Starr and answerable to Congress.

[‡] Jordan was one of at least four Clinton intimates engaged in securing consulting contracts for Hubbell when he left the administration. Altogether, the group brought Hubbell contracts from seventeen different individuals and organizations, including Revlon, the Sprint Corporation, the American Income Life Co., Pacific Telesis, SunAmerica Inc., and Time Warner, Inc.

business collapsed in December 1994 when he pleaded guilty to mail fraud and tax evasion in connection with bilking his former Little Rock law firm partners out of at least $394,000.[2]

From its inception, Hubbell's consulting business looked fishy, and once he pleaded guilty to swindling and tax evasion charges, it looked even fishier.* Yet from the moment Hubbell opened his doors, not a word was said publicly about any of it, by any of the companies that had hired him, even after he stood revealed as a confessed felon. Instead, they all quietly cancelled their contracts in the wake of his guilty plea and turned to other matters.

Now, more than a year and a half had passed since Hubbell's resignation, and with the back-story to his departure still well hidden, the president of the United States was in his Oval Office private study, seeking the sort of personal gratification that would soon enough lead to yet another mission for his trusty Mister Fixit, to say nothing of the woe that Mister Fixit would in turn bring to his own billionaire buddy in New York, Ron Perelman. Yet engaged as the president was at that moment, in pursuing the one thing that every man wants, we may wonder whether even a glimpse into the future

---

*News of Hubbell's financial problems involving his former law firm first surfaced publicly in the *Washington Post*. See S. Schmidt, "Law Firm Probing Hubbell," *Washington Post* (March 2, 1994). Eleven days later, on March 13, Clinton's chief of staff, Mike McLarty, met with Clinton and the First Lady and said, "We're going to try to be supportive of Webb," to which Ms. Clinton responded, "Thank you, Mack. I appreciate that very much." Later that day, McLarty spoke with Vernon Jordan and at least one other Clinton insider with known business ties (Truman Arnold), and asked them to help secure some consulting business for Hubbell. The next day (March 14, 1994), Hubbell submitted his letter of resignation to the president. He subsequently told investigators for the Office of Independent Counsel that he was unaware of any efforts on the part of the White House to ease his transition to private life, and that he could not say why they may have wanted to help him and that he never asked anyone about it in any case. See "Webster Hubbell's Billing Practices and Tax Filings," *Report to Congress by the Office of the Independent Counsel*, Part C. (September 11, 1998), p. 17.

and the nightmare destined to engulf them all would have been enough to cause him to stop and think where his actions might lead.

~~~~

And what of Al Dunlap through all of this? So far, Big Al's testosterone-stoked behavior had been channeled largely into the business equivalent of extreme fighting in the boardroom. Now it was about to unleash the biggest and most out-of-control brawl of his life, destroying not only his career in business, but dragging Ron Perelman into *that* fray as well.

As 1995 drew to a close, few CEOs in American business seemed better known—and in at least one sense, more admired—than Al Dunlap. That was certainly the view of many in the media, which had by now pretty much settled on him as the CEO who actually brought home the bacon.

In the corporate world, the enthusiasm for Chainsaw Al was more circumspect. In fact, the closer one got to the men at the top the fainter grew the applause, for these were the individuals who stood the best chance of actually encountering Dunlap close up and personal, in his natural default state as an ogre.

Yet the press kept celebrating him anyway, and he kept rising to the bait, providing the sound bites and photo ops that kept his name before the public as America's "Real Man" CEO. He was the man who shunned weak-speak and the language of political correctness, and simply said what he thought—the Jackie Mason of the corporate boardroom.

Big Al had an opinion on anything—and usually you didn't even have to ask to get it. By early November 1995, his time at Scott Paper was almost up. So, looking for ways to keep his name in the news, he led a reporter from New Jersey's *Bergen Record* and some students at a local engineering college on a walking tour of his old neighborhood in Hoboken, New Jersey. While pointing out the sights, he pontificated on the current state of American business. Predictably, the tour soon developed into a typical Al Dunlap rant on the stupidity and incompetence of everyone in business but himself. Eventually, an exasperated member of the group could take it no longer and asked Big Al a question: Who, if anyone, did he actually admire? Wasting no time to make clear the type of leader he hoped to be viewed as, Dunlap answered: Jack Welch of GE and Bill Gates of Microsoft. As for the rest, his basic judgment boiled down to two words: Forget it.

Not everyone in business viewed Dunlap as disparagingly as he seemed to view others. On Wall Street, a successful mutual fund manager named Michael Price faced a problem that he thought Big Al might be just the man to solve. Price ran a Wall Street investment group under a company called Heine Securities Corporation, and over the years he had done well for his investors, with an average annual return in the high teens or better since the mid-1980s.

But mixed in among his successful investments was the occasional bad choice, and one in particular now haunted him: his 21.4 percent stake in Sunbeam Corporation. Seven years earlier, he and another fund manager, Michael Steinhardt, had jointly paid $130 million to take over a bankrupt conglomerate called Allegheny International Corporation, which in turn owned Sunbeam, a well-regarded but money-losing maker of consumer products for the home. They had then hired a man from Goldman Sachs & Company named Paul Kazarian to run it for them, and he had turned the company around and made it profitable.

In 1992, the two sold a 40 percent block of Sunbeam stock to the public, gave some more to the company's management, and kept two 20+ percent blocks for themselves. But a dispute developed with Kazarian over his compensation and various management-related issues, and the two brought in a successor, whose weak, hands-off approach to management was the polar opposite of his predecessor's.

With Sunbeam's stock sliding, Price's eye fell on Dunlap, who seemed to possess exactly the qualities Price figured the company needed. In certain key respects, those qualities mirrored what Price thought he saw in himself. Like Dunlap, Price possessed a mercurial temper and a habit of yelling at people who annoyed him. He insisted on quick, cut-through answers to complex questions, and believed that he had the right as an employer to criticize employees harshly, and publicly, if he wanted.

So Price hired Dunlap, and on July 18, 1996, Big Al began as Sunbeam's newest savior—with a far more lucrative pay package than he had gotten out of Scott. The earlier company had offered him 50,000 shares of restricted stock up front, plus 750,000 more shares in the form of options. But Sunbeam now gave him, in addition to a base salary of $1 million per year, fully twenty times as much stock up front as he'd gotten from Scott (one million shares in all) plus nearly four times as much in the way of stock options (an options package of 2.5 million shares in all). In addition, the company agreed to an astonishing array of seemingly niggling demands from Dunlap, including a demand that the company agree to fly him first class wherever he went, as well as provide him a full-time bodyguard and chauffeur, and to buy back the Mercedes car he owned and get him a new one, and to replace the new one every two years thereafter. To lighten his financial burdens still more, the company also agreed to pick up all his country club expenses and to let him expense any personal financial planning advice he required, and any tax planning and preparation costs as well.[3]

The idea behind all this largesse was to make sure that Al wouldn't be distracted with any personal financial worries, so he could therefore stay 100 percent focused on what he was supposed to be doing—orchestrating the turnaround that would make Sunbeam's stock price, which had fallen from $20 to barely $12 in the preceding year, go back up again.

The more that Sunbeam agreed to his demands, the more self-absorbed Big Al seemed to grow, for if he wasn't really a figure of such gigantic importance in American business, then why was the company willing to pay him so much? Dunlap had already decided to share his life story with the world, and with little else to do since leaving Scott Paper in December 1995, he had been plowing ahead with a writer from *Business Week* to finish it up. The title said it all: *Mean Business: How I Save Bad Companies and Make Good Companies Great*. Now, the deal with Sunbeam meant he'd soon be able to capitalize on a whole new escalation of his fame, and with the book set for release by its publisher, Times Books, in September, he made sure it got prominently mentioned in the press release announcing his hiring.

The stock market's reaction to the news of his hiring simply strengthened his belief in his greatness. The release was distributed at nearly the end of trading on the afternoon of July 18, 1996, and its impact wasn't really felt on Wall Street until the next morning. But when the news finally broke, it hit like an earthquake.

"This is like the Los Angeles Lakers signing Shaquille O'Neal," gushed an analyst at the investment firm of Oppenheimer & Company, when the opening bell rang at 9:30 A.M. and Sunbeam's stock price instantly soared 50 percent in value, from $12.50 per share, to $18.50. With more than 82 million shares already issued and outstanding, the $6 per share spurt in price meant, in effect, that the mere mention of Big Al's name had been worth nearly $500 million to the company's shareholders—and he hadn't yet done even one day's work.[4]

Pumped up and ready to go, Big Al headed forth to earn his keep. Telling reporters that he planned to have the turnaround completed in less than a year, he promptly fired Sunbeam's chief operating officer, followed several days later by three more executives he didn't like, then two more after that.

Then suddenly, everything stopped. No more firings, not even any rumors of firings. Was something wrong? Had Big Al lost his nerve? Worst of all, the stock wouldn't budge. There it sat, in the low $20s, as the days turned into weeks, and the weeks turned into months. Labor Day passed, and then Columbus Day. Soon it was the start of November, and still no news—still no movement in the stock. Where were the mass layoffs, the gutters soaked with the blood of the disemboweled?

In fact, there was nothing wrong at all. Having reassembled the clique of trusted aides who had been with him at Scott Paper, Big Al had been secretly preparing the biggest, most horrifying massacre of his career.

The planning, which he eventually likened to preparations for the Allied invasion of Normandy in World War II, had involved seventeen different management teams reporting to Big Al's cronies,

Albert J. Dunlap Jr. From Day One he was life's angry young man, defiant and raging at all that came his way. But in Niagara Falls, New York, one local businessman played Al like a yo-yo—by stroking his preening sartorial vanity. He'd say "Jesus, Al, that's the most spectacular suit I've ever seen . . ." at which Al's chest would puff out and his head would tilt back to display the full and glorious profile of this one-of-a-kind business leader in his one-of-a-kind suit. Wondering what human flesh tastes like? (*Photo credit:* AP/Wide World Photos.)

with everything being coordinated by a trusted Dunlap advisor
from the Coopers & Lybrand accounting firm. The work had gone
on right up until the night before the announcement, when a special
meeting of Sunbeam's board of directors was convened to approve
the plan. (Approval was hardly in doubt since the board had by now
been purged of anyone who might have objected.)

The next morning at 9 A.M., Big Al hit the beach. It was H-Hour,
Tuesday, November 12, 1996, and in a conference call with Wall
Street analysts, Big Al fixed his bayonet, tightened the chinstrap on
his helmet, released the safety on his weapon, and charged. First bulletin from the front? Big Al was going to:

1. Fire half the company's 12,000 employees, effective immediately,
2. Close nearly two-thirds of its sixty-one warehouses,
3. Eliminate more than half its twenty-six factories,
4. Get rid of 75 percent of its field offices and other facilities,
   and
5. Scrap 87 percent of its entire product line.

Big Al said the whole bloodbath would be over in forty-five
days, and the business would be shipshape and fixed within a year.

Al clearly expected applause for the havoc he proposed to wreck,
since applause was what he had gotten for every previous such
bloodletting. But this time the reaction seemed more like stunned
disbelief. Firing a lot of people was one thing, but . . . *half the entire
workforce? Of a 1.2 billion dollar consumer products company?*

On Wall Street, where the stock market was closing in on its best
year in memory, any doubts about Big Al's ability to deliver the
goods should have been easily enough brushed aside. Something
called "day trading" had begun sweeping the country, causing stocks
to soar dramatically in hours and sometimes even minutes if they

developed a following and "momentum" on the Internet. In Newport Beach, California, a company called Comparator Systems Inc., had already soared nearly 3,000 percent on the wings of "Big Mo," to a market value of nearly $1 billion even though the balance sheet showed barely $4,000 of actual cash money and the income statement showed no revenues. And plenty more stocks were doing exactly the same.

But in spite of Big Al's promise of carnage, the price of Sunbeam didn't budge, and in the wake of his announcement, the shares actually slipped a few cents. Were people beginning to wake up to what this man was all about? It was hard to say. In Washington, the Clinton administration's Secretary of Labor Robert Reich ventured forth with a timid observation: "I do think it's unfortunate to view a company's employees as costs of production rather than assets."[5]

By contrast, a *Money* magazine writer named Duff MacDonald felt emboldened to be less circumspent and more to the point when he phoned Big Al later in the day for an elaboration on what seemed the man's over-the-top plans. After hearing the man out, MacDonald immediately scrapped his own plans for a Sunbeam turnaround story and began work on a story advising *Money*'s readers to sell any stock they might be holding in Sunbeam, and move their money to Black & Decker instead. Why?

"He came across like an idiot," MacDonald explained later. "He couldn't put two ideas together back to back that made any sense."

For his part, Big Al put on his characteristic show of bombast and bravado. Two days after the restructuring announcement, America's self-styled champion of the shareholder sat for a series of promotional photographs for *Mean Business*. Taken by a Miami-based wedding photographer named Andrew Itkoff, the photos caught Dunlap in a pose that he plainly thought would show him off at his manly best, and thereby help him sell the most books—a portrait of what *Mean Business* was really all about.

Thirty years earlier, Dunlap's horrified young wife Gwyn had filed divorce papers complaining that Al kept an arsenal of guns in their apartment and would take them out and clean them in the evenings, then wave them at her menacingly. Three decades later, Al was now ready to charm the whole of America in exactly the same way, presenting himself scowling before Itkoff, wearing twin belts of 50-caliber machine gun bullets crisscrossed on his chest bandolier-fashion, and with camouflage paint smeared under his eyes. To complete the picture of this Rambo in the boardroom, he held two machine pistols before him, their barrels pointed menacingly at the world. Al was ready to roll.

❧❧❧

Bizarre? Not half so much as what turned up three months later, on Valentine's Day, 1997, in the "Personals" section of the *Washington Post*. Appearing as it did on America's official Day of Romance, the unsigned message hardly seemed notable in any way, from the person to whom it was addressed—identified simply as "Handsome"—to its puppy-love sentiment in a couplet from *Romeo and Juliet*.

Yet behind that seemingly unremarkable message and its salutation of "Handsome" loomed not just Bill Clinton and his girl-on-the-side, Monica Lewinsky, but all the Ron Perelmans and Jack Welches, and all the shiksa goddesses there ever were. For when it comes to the really big issues in the life of a man . . . beyond the bull markets and the billionaires and peace on the earth, there's always just one more thing: *Hi ya, handsome, want to come upstairs?*

In the second scene of the second act of *Romeo and Juliet*, Romeo is beside himself to see again the enchantress of his dreams, and leaping the wall that separates his world from hers, he comes upon Juliet in the Capulet family's orchard. It is the balcony scene, in which Juliet asks the great question for all lovers everywhere: "Romeo, Romeo, wherefore art thou Romeo?"

And from beyond the gulf of social convention—and all the laws there ever were—comes the answered cry of all the men who ever lived, for whom all the Porsches, and all the estates, and all the Gulfstream IVs are never enough and never will be. *Oh God, please, just this one more thing . . . !*

For what else was Monica Lewinsky trying to do with that couplet but to plead with her lover for just one more chance: *"Don't dump me now, Bill, I'm sure we can work things out . . ."*

What else was that couplet in the newspaper there for but to try to get him to see it her way?

> *For stony limits cannot hold love out*
> *And what love can do that dares love attempt.*

And what else had really been going on between these two people—over and over for the past fifteen months—but Bill's schemes for jumping that wall, followed by his guilt and self-loathing afterward, as he climbed back over to his proper side, followed by her efforts to seduce him back into her orchard again.

During all this, here are some of the things that were going on elsewhere in the world:

- The Russian government was caught shipping armaments to Iraq.
- Iraqi strongman Saddam Hussein assassinated the West's top weapons program informant in Baghdad.
- United Nations weapons inspectors were repeatedly frustrated in their efforts to inspect potential weapons sites in Iraq.
- Nineteen U.S. servicemen were killed in Saudi Arabia's Kobar Towers bombing by a little known terrorist group calling itself the al Qaeda network.
- Israeli Prime Minister Benjamin Netanyahu developed a secret plan to annex the West Bank.

- Iraqi forces launched an incursion into the northern No-Fly Zone and began slaughtering Kurds.

- The Al-Jazeera news channel began broadcasting anti-Western news in Qatar.

- The Taliban army captured Kubal and took over Afghanistan.

Despite all that, Monica managed to lure Bill back into the Capulets' orchard eight times for (not) oral sex, fourteen times for (not) phone sex, and once for (not) cigar sex. And, as the Starr Report on the matter subsequently showed, on nearly every occasion Bill climbed back over the wall promising never ever to do it again (before he returned to the orchard for *just this one more time . . . oh God please*).

And now, on Valentine's Day 1997, there was that Personals note in the *Washington Post:* "Hey, handsome, want to come upstairs?" And two weeks later, the president of the United States was back over the wall, getting semen on the young woman's pretty blue dress—underscoring that if even being the president of the United States isn't enough to satisfy a man, then the biggest bull market in American history is not likely to do the job either.

17

RON'S NEXT DEMOCRAT

Altogether, it took Al Dunlap little more than six months to implement his restructuring plan for Sunbeam. By Thanksgiving 1996, he had cut Sunbeam's payroll by 50 percent—half through outright firings, and half through the sale of subsidiaries. And by year's end, eighteen of the company's twenty-six factories had been closed and padlocked as well. As an added bonus, he had even ended all charitable giving by the company to conserve cash.

Unfortunately for Al, his act was growing stale. By year's end, a writer for *BusinessWeek* magazine named John Byrne was on his tail, and in December he produced a devastating portrait of Dunlap that gave the world its first glimpse into the bizarre individual who bore the name "Chainsaw Al."[1]

What's more, though Sunbeam's stock had inched up to the low $30s by April 1997, the whiplash energy that Dunlap had been able to transfer into his earlier turnarounds by way of his self-promotional grandstanding was pretty much gone. In Dallas, a newsletter publisher named David Tice just about finished it off, issuing a report on Sunbeam that judged Wall Street to be under some strange "Dunlap spell" and that if analysts were able to look beyond his hype they'd see how foolish and unworkable his turnaround strategy really was.

A *Fortune* columnist named Herb Greenberg ticked off the high points of Tice's report in a column of his own, and before long one could begin to sense the slow but inexorable shift in public opinion, begun by *Business Week*, and now moved along by others, as the winds that had been blowing at Big Al's back began to swing around and blow in his face.*

So it's hardly surprising that even as the media's more critical new view of Dunlap was beginning to take hold, Dunlap himself had already begun quietly, but unsuccessfully, to shop Sunbeam around. When it came to Al Dunlap Turnaround King, the jig was up, and he seemed to know it.[2]

Obviously, Dunlap needed a new schtick—and fast. But what? If *Al The Destroyer* wasn't working, then maybe he'd have more success with the opposite. How about *Al the Builder?*[†] When a reporter from the *Wall Street Journal* asked him whether he regretted posing for those promotional photos as a boardroom Rambo the previous November, Al answered, "That was a dumb idea," and switched to his new riff as a one-man Marshall Plan for ruined companies. Conjuring up the kind of destruction-filled landscape where his imagination seemed to

---

*Greenberg's column, citing the Tice report, pointed out that margins in consumer small appliances were being squeezed already by mass market chains like Wal-Mart and Target, which were bringing more and more of their own house label products to market. In this environment, the most valuable asset a company like Sunbeam had was its access to retail shelf space. But by chainsawing Sunbeam's product line, Dunlap was simply surrendering that shelf space and, in effect, dooming the company.

†The tactic recalls an almost identical message that Ron Perelman began promoting in 1985 as he stalked Revlon Corporation in a hostile takeover. Fearful of mounting criticism that he was little more than a "bust-up artist," he described himself in a *New York Times* interview as, in reality, "a builder." See S. Prokesch, "Pantry Pride Chairman Hunts Biggest Prey Yet," *New York Times* (August 28, 1985), p. D1. By 1990, Perelman's publicist, Linda Robinson, was routinely correcting writers to refer to Perelman not as a corporate raider but as a "builder" or "industrialist." See R. Smith and D. Wessel, "New Look: The '80s Are Over," *Wall Street Journal* (March 27, 1990), p. A1.

keep returning, he said, "You can't make money just firing people. Mickey Mouse can do that. You must take something that's totally destroyed and in rubble and build it back into a powerhouse."[3]

Al's confused imagery didn't seem to catch on with anyone. But his comment about perhaps putting Sunbeam up for sale was a different story, automatically stirring speculative interest in the stock as a takeover play. And that, plus the relentless upward surge of stocks in general, at last got Sunbeam's shares moving.*

And there was one other factor that also provided lift: the sudden and startling improvement in Sunbeam's financials from about mid-spring onward. "The turnaround is on track!" squealed an analyst named Constance Meneaty, who worked for a Wall Street investment firm named Bear Stearns & Co.,[4] and plenty of her colleagues agreed.

Only the press remained negative on Big Al, with the result that it was business writers—and not Wall Street analysts—who took the first critical look at the Sunbeam numbers, and what they saw was horrifying.

At *Barron's*, a writer named Jonathan Laing produced a 4,300 word story in mid-June that dismissed Wall Street's starry-eyed coverage of the vaunted Sunbeam turn-around as "uncritical, stenographic, even fawning . . ." and laid a lot of it at the feet of Dunlap's "almost cultlike following" among analysts. By September, Dunlap had emerged as a subject of out-and-out media ridicule, paraded through the funny pages in the syndicated *Dilbert* comic strip as "Buzz Saw Dogbert," an imperious beast that shooed away downsized workers disdainfully. When someone asked Dunlap for a comment, he behaved exactly like Buzz Saw Dogbert and sniffed, "I don't think he's funny."[5]

Al's big problem wasn't his disappearing sense of humor, it was the increasingly fishy smell that had begun to emanate from Sunbeam's

---

*Between early spring and mid-summer of 1997, the Dow Industrial Average climbed at an annualized rate of more than 50 percent, one of the sharpest such climbs on record.

financial reports to its shareholders and the Securities and Exchange Commission. The company's reported profits were surging, quarter after quarter—of that there seemed little doubt—and those surging profits were what the analysts had gotten so excited about, for they seemed to be proof positive that the turn-around was working.

But the actual cash money that was winding up on the bottom line had begun to disappear. Where was it going? The press had begun to catch glimpses of the problem as early as the spring of 1997. In late April, the *Wall Street Journal* reported that "shipping and billing snafus" had "strained relations with customers." A Green Bay, Wisconsin, distributor was quoted as complaining that Sunbeam kept pressuring him to stock up on more and more products when his warehouse was already overflowing with Sunbeam merchandise that he hadn't yet sold.

Behind these complaints lurked a problem known as *channel stuffing*, and anyone looking carefully at the impressive-seeming turn-around numbers the company had begun producing would have spotted it right away.

Sunbeam was shipping merchandise all right, and reporting the shipments as revenue. But the distributors weren't yet paying for it, and the result was an explosion in a red ink item known as "Receivables." Between 1996 and 1997, those unpaid "check is in the mail" Receivables surged more than 500 percent. And so did the company's unsold inventories, which also hadn't yet generated any cash.

In other words, Sunbeam Corporation appeared to be experiencing a dramatic surge in profitability, but it was actually going broke—the same type problem the Nitec Paper Co. had encountered when Dunlap had been in charge more than twenty years earlier.[6] It would be nice to think that the analysts of Wall Street missed all this because it was too hard to detect—and plenty of folks on Wall Street offered exactly that excuse in the wake of Sunbeam's eventual (and

RON'S NEXT DEMOCRAT   269

inevitable) collapse. But the truth was exactly the opposite, for the situation at Sunbeam was in fact hiding in plain sight.

~~~~

Meanwhile, 1,200 miles to the north in Stamford, Connecticut, the head of GE Capital Corp., Gary Wendt, faced a different situation entirely, for even as Al could see his financial prospects brightening, the future for Gary looked to be clouding over rapidly. The problems all had to do with his estranged wife, Lorna, and her diabolical scheme to accomplish the one thing he'd never expected in the divorce: demand half his money in a settlement.

In their negotiations, Gary had been plenty reasonable, he thought, and offered Lorna $8 million up front, plus $250,000 a year in alimony for the rest of her life. And so far as Gary was concerned, that was more than enough. But Lorna had come back with a counterclaim in which she had begun by insisting that his net worth was $98 million and then demanding half of it, or $49 million.

Previous divorce case law seemed to say that Lorna would never get anywhere near that amount in a settlement. But Gary wasn't so sure, and the persistence with which she stayed at it had begun to make him uneasy. There had already been a big and embarrassing story on the Wendt divorce in the *Wall Street Journal* and Gary was sure Lorna had stirred it up. For all he knew she was already planning more.

The most infuriating thing of all was how Lorna had somehow managed to gain the high ground psychologically in the struggle. By including Gary's future income from his GE retirement plan and stock options in her estimate of his current net worth, and then demanding half of it as her settlement pay-out, she was in fact asking for more money than Gary could argue he even had.

Doing so put Gary in the awkward position of having to talk *down* his net worth when his entire career had been spent struggling to

Gary Wendt and Rosemarie. Alone at 30,000 feet, he broke down and cried. Then he met Rosemarie and some sunshine pierced the gloom. (*Photo credit:* Susan May Tell, *New York Post.*)

make his net worth go *up* instead. It was a humiliating position for any corporate executive to find himself in—especially in the money-obsessed 1990s, when a man's net worth was judged by many to be the best measure of not simply his success in business but even the very measure of his manhood. Here he was, having filed for divorce, and suddenly his wife was making settlement demands that threatened to bankrupt him—then leaking it all to the press. This was impossible, and Gary knew he had to do something about it, and fast.

In the end, there seemed but one course of action open: He had to fight fire with fire, and strike back via the media. But rather than just give a tit-for-tat interview, Gary decided to fire a bigger weapon. He'd go on TV.

Unfortunately, Gary hadn't done much TV in the past, and he thus did not seem to grasp the fact that anyone who shoots back challenging responses to questions in a live interview is asking for trouble. One might be able to intimidate the interviewer, to be sure, but it would never be possible to intimidate the camera, which would simply record it all for posterity.

Nonetheless, Gary agreed to an interview with ABC News' 20/20 television newsmagazine program. The plan: To hit Lorna with a counterpunch she'd never forget.

The program's producers had taken an interest in the Wendt divorce following the *Wall Street Journal* story because it seemed to crystallize an important new concern that had begun spreading through the offices and homes of America's corporate executives: the value of a corporate wife.

For nearly the whole of the past twenty years, the wives of American business leaders had stood by in silence while their husbands converted the gains of the Wall Street bull market into a theory of executive entitlement that granted the successful CEO the presumed right to trade in his wife for a newer and younger model whenever the spirit moved him—and for a pay-out that rarely climbed to more than $8 million to $10 million no matter how much the family was worth.

But soaring stock prices had escalated the value of executive compensation packages, as well as the family estates that had evolved out of them, to levels that would have seemed unimaginable a decade earlier. New and exotic kinds of assets, like stock options and so-called SARs (for Stock Appreciation Rights) were acquiring enormous value in the booming economy, making them suddenly worth fighting over in divorce court.

And women had begun doing exactly that. In New York, the wife of a financier named Robert Goldman had lately filed divorce papers demanding 50 percent of his $100 million estate. A similar case was already before the courts between a billionaire telecommunications executive, Craig McCaw, and his wife. Still more cases had been filed in Florida, Massachusetts, Texas, and California.

Unfortunately for Gary, the resulting ABC News 20/20 interview, which was taped for airing at an unspecified future date, did not go as well as he might have wanted. Under the skeptical stare of the program's on-air correspondent, Lynn Sherr, Gary came across as angry and resentful at the claims of his estranged wife, insisting that while he himself had worked hard throughout the whole of his career, she had not—essentially because being a mother, wife, and homemaker was really not hard work.

As the interview progressed, Gary seemed to grow increasingly contentious, and at one point actually began challenging the interviewer. When Sherr said that Lorna claimed that what she did was indeed hard work, Gary retorted, "Do you think having to get dressed up to go to dinner in New York is hard work? Tell me, please." Next, he took on feminism itself, saying, "Do feminist causes now want equality without effort? Is that the new battle cry?"

By contrast, his wife Lorna—who was also interviewed, separately, for the show—came off as polished, poised, and completely comfortable with her position. "I've been fired," she summed up. "I didn't ask to be fired. He fired me from my job. I'm fifty-three. I may never get another job." Then raising a standard to which corporate wives all over America would soon be rushing, she said, "This is the issue that affects all women at whatever economic, socioeconomic level. I want to know that I tried for what I believe was my right."

Gary, of course, had no way of knowing what Lorna had said in her own interview. And neither did he know what portions of his interview would be used for the show. But since his divorce trial was still under way, and the judge hadn't yet rendered his decision, Gary went back to work and basically tried to put the entire experience out of his mind.

Unfortunately, by doing so Gary only compounded the mistake he'd made in giving the interview in the first place. For starters, he had now handed ABC News (NBC's chief network rival) an extensive and probing interview, to be used whenever it chose, on a highly sensitive matter in which he was personally and intimately involved. And worse still, he had failed to clear the matter before-hand with GE's chairman and CEO, Jack Welch, or even to brief him on the situation after-the-fact. So Welch knew nothing of Gary's performance before the cameras of ABC News . . . just as Gary had no idea how he had come across either. Nor did Gary know when they'd air the story, or indeed whether they'd air it at all.

Yet he didn't have to wait long to find out—and neither for that matter did his boss, Jack Welch, who flipped on the TV for some channel surfing on the evening of Friday, March 14, 1997, and was dumbfounded to find himself staring at his underling, Wendt, on ABC's 20/20 program, railing before the world against feminism and his estranged wife. Welch couldn't believe what he was seeing. Wendt looked like a moron. He was bringing shame on the whole of GE.

It was the start of the weekend, and rather than pick up the phone and begin screaming at the man, Welch bided his time. The GE chairman had been scheduled to attend an executive conference at GE's Six Sigma campus in Crotonville the following Tuesday, and so for that matter had Wendt—and what Welch had in store for his subordinate was something the GE Capital executive would never forget.

When Tuesday rolled around, Welch spotted Wendt among some executives at the Crotonville gathering, and steered him into an empty room and closed the door. Then turning on him the GE leader began to scream: "You've disgraced this company! I told you not to get GE involved, but you did. I want you out of here!" Then Welch turned about and walked out, and though it would take just over another year and a half before the rupture would ripen into Wendt's actual departure, his career at GE at that moment was effectively over.*

〰〰〰

Ron Perelman as well faced a gal problem at this time—in fact, the same gal problem, with the same gal, he'd been facing for the last four years: Patricia. Whatever he gave her was never enough. Whatever he did for her could never make her happy.

Two years earlier, in the autumn of 1995, he bought her an estate in Connecticut that should have been enough to make the Queen of Siam blush. The forty-three-acre spread was laid out around a 10,000 square foot mansion that had once been owned by Broadway songwriter Richard Rogers.† Next door sat a 5,000-square-foot "cottage,"

---

*During Wendt's final year and a half at GE, the business press reported rumors of strained relations between Welch and Wendt, but specific reasons for the tension remained elusive. When Wendt finally departed in December 1998, the *Wall Street Journal* quoted sources as saying that much of the tension related to Wendt's refusal to make cuts in GE Capital's back-office operations, which Welch had been pushing for. In fact, the tension derived more fundamentally from the intensifying clash of these two large egos. One example: A November 1997 cover story in *Fortune* entitled "GE Capital, Jack Welch's Secret Weapon," for which Wendt had been interviewed extensively, and for which he had sat for a cover portrait to illustrate the story. The article directly credited Wendt and GE Capital for a "surprising amount" of Welch's success, and described the Wendt operation as an "energy source, radiating growth through a mature—some might say lackluster—conglomerate." Elaborate graphs and statistical research bolstered the point that GE Capital was indeed the principal reason for GE's perceived value on Wall Street. The story also contained some astonishingly frank statements by Wendt regarding Welch, whom Gary freely admitted not to like. Remarkably—and at what appeared to be virtually the eleventh hour—the cover photograph for the article was switched from Wendt, who is quoted extensively throughout the story, to Welch, who is quoted only once.

†The main home was the same size as Jack and Jane Welch's Georgian colonial, located a little more than a mile away. Yet Patricia's estate contained nearly seven times as much property.

so he bought her that too. The combined plots came complete with guest accommodations, bridle paths, tennis courts, greenhouses, and a pool.

Patricia called the whole thing her "Leave It to Beaver house," and threw a pillow at him. So he got angry and the next thing you knew they were at it again.

By now Ron had had it, and seeming to know no other way to respond, he'd begun to fight back by waltzing around a whole new group of blondes other than his wife. And if nothing else worked he could always show up at some trendy new nightspot like Moomba, and try to look hip as a balding midlife businessman amidst screen darlings half his age.* Maybe it was Ron's way of showing the world—or perhaps just Patricia—that no bimbo from the Democrats was going to slow him down.

In fact, if that was Ron's game, he soon improved on it, since before anyone knew it he began squiring around a politically connected shiksa blonde who seemed almost to be Patricia's doppelganger. Maybe she was Ron's way of saying, "Bimbo Democrats? They're a dime a dozen."

---

* Ron's ticket of admission to Moomba had not been his chairmanship of Revlon but his friendship with Hollywood producer Keith Barish, an investor in the club. Both Barish and Perelman had summer homes in the Hamptons, and so for that matter did other investors who had put up money to get Moomba going. Among the better known such individuals: art dealer Larry Gagosian. The spark plug who ignited the club's fame as a happenin' place was a young publicist named Lizzie Grubman, whose contacts in the recording industry had come by way of her father, Allen, a well-known entertainment industry lawyer. Nearly the whole of the club's original core of backers and promoters suffered notable reverses of one sort or another thereafter. Barish's restaurant chain, Planet Hollywood, collapsed into bankruptcy in October 1999. The names of both Barish and Gagosian surfaced briefly and in peripheral roles in the ImClone scandal in 2002 after they were linked to investments in an offshore company run by Sam Waksal, ImClone's founder. Waksal thereafter went to prison after pleading guilty to insider trading charges in the ImClone affair. Lizzie Grubman made headlines of her own when she drove her SUV into a crowd of night clubbers in Southampton, New York, in the summer of 2001 and then left the scene.

Eleanor Mondale. Ron's first post-Patricia squeeze was Eleanor, his way of saying, these blonde Democrats, they're a dime a dozen? When Monica Lewinsky learned that Eleanor was visiting with the President in the Oval Office on a Saturday morning she threw a hissy-fit at the White House's northwest gate. Then when President Clinton learned what Monica had learned, he threw a fit, too. But the *New York Times* couldn't figure out why Dick Morris seemed clueless. Couldn't they spell toe fetish? (*Photo credit:* Lawrence Schwartzwald/Splash News.)

Her name was Eleanor Mondale, the twice-divorced daughter of former Vice President Walter Mondale, and she had had been struggling to position herself as more than just that—to which end she had lately secured a perch as an on-air reporter for the CBS *This Morning* show.

Yet, Eleanor's real impact came through best in more up-close-and-personal settings. Her quick wit and protean good looks gave her a repertoire that ranged from the vacuous sincerity of a Miss America beauty contestant ("Plays castanets; wants to end world hunger") to the desperation of a "Threesome Wanted" ad from the Personals pages. It was a skill-set that made her the center of attention whenever men were around. So, with the same showmanship and flair that had made his involvement with Patricia such a hit with the gossips, Ron now began turning up around town with Eleanor. One date led to the next, and on the evening of Tuesday, October 21,

1997, Ron took her to dinner at New York's super-expensive Le Cirque 2000, and spent the entire meal either squeezing her—or being squeezed by her—under the table, oblivious to the stares of the nearby diners.

In fact, one of the onlookers happened to be a reporter for the *New York Post* named Braden Keil, who knew a good story when he saw one. Just to make sure, he followed the couple when they left, and from a discreet distance observed what happened next, as the story got even better.

"It was really hilarious," Braden said later, describing a scene in which Eleanor—blonde, voluptuous, and at least half a head taller than Ron—had him pinned up against a tree in the restaurant's outside courtyard, where the two were locked in passionate and writhing kissing and groping.

It was too late to make the next morning's edition of the *Post*, but on Thursday morning, there it was, in the newspaper's *"Page Six"* gossip column: Ron and Eleanor were now officially an item. And once they had been certified as such, subsequent sightings began to pop up everywhere. Barely two weeks passed before they were spotted again—this time for a Washington, D.C., dinner at the home of Senate Democrat John Kerry of Massachusetts, engaged in what the *Washington Post* described the next day as "nuzzling" over cocktails. It seemed Ron's way of saying, "Patricia? Patricia *Who?*"

It is in the nature of the rich to hold themselves in special esteem. But the price of self-regard can be high, as Ron was soon to discover, for love, like war, is no fairer than it is predictable. By squiring Eleanor around town for lip-lock photo opportunities in the tabloids, he had unwittingly written himself into the developing Monica Lewinsky scandal, in the walk-on role of billionaire boob from out of town.

To begin with, Eleanor appears to have had some side action of her own going on, even while Ron was showing her off at places like Le Cirque 2000. The other man? On all the available evidence (except Eleanor's own eventual denials), it was none other than the president of the United States, Bill Clinton*—who of course had some side action of his own under way in the person of Monica Lewinsky.

Rumors of Clinton's involvement with Eleanor had been circulating for the past year and a half, tracing back to a morning in March 1996 when the president was spotted jogging with Eleanor through Washington's deserted streets, ringed round by Secret Service agents, while the First Lady and the couple's daughter, Chelsea, were on a trip to Bosnia.

Three months later, in June, Eleanor resurfaced as a presidential gal-pal, this time for a Democratic Party fund-raising event in Los Angeles, hosted by Hollywood studio chief Lew Wasserman. An after-hours gathering of about a dozen individuals from the fund-raiser, including the president, actress Barbra Streisand, and Eleanor continued on at Wasserman's home until well after midnight. The *Washington Post* reported that Barbra Streisand was livid throughout the whole of it because "Clinton only had eyes for Eleanor." The next morning, and with only a couple of hours' sleep, Clinton and Mondale were observed jogging along Santa Monica Beach, once again surrounded by Secret Service agents.[7]

It all added up to one of the messiest situations imaginable, for whether Clinton and Eleanor were in fact romantically involved, Clinton in particular had reasons to keep the details secret—and they went far beyond his relationship with his wife, Hillary. After

---

*On October 3, 1998, the House Judiciary Committee of Congress released 4,600 pages of evidence gathered by the Office of Independent Counsel related to the investigation of Clinton. Included in those documents was an interview of July 16, 1998, in which Eleanor Mondale told OIC investigators that she had visited with the president in the Oval Office in December 1997 and, implausibly claimed that she and Clinton had spent the time discussing an "unnamed ex-boyfriend who the president did not like." See the *Seattle Times* (October 3, 1998), p. A3.

all, as Bill well knew, his reputation alone would have made their denials noncredible. Even worse, the resulting publicity could have easily caused the loopy Lewinsky girl—who had lately begun acting more than a bit uppity anyway as far as Clinton was concerned—to go completely off the reservation and maybe even start talking to others about their little arrangement.

Into the middle of all this had now wandered Perelman, showing the world by the arm candy at his side that he was still a player and still in the game. Yet, all he was really doing was gratuitously entangling himself in what would soon erupt as the biggest sex scandal in American history.

18

HUGS AND KISSES AND BOUTS OF NOSTALGIA

From all these various directions, the secret worlds of Al Dunlap, Ron Perelman, Jack Welch, Gary Wendt, and various of their wives and lovers had all been hurtling toward each other for months now—and in December 1997 they collided, one after the next.

From his walled and guarded estate in Boca Raton, Florida, Big Al Dunlap had been wrestling all autumn with the situation at Sunbeam, and in late October he hired the Morgan Stanley & Co. investment firm to help him figure out what to do.[1]

One way out was to sell the company. But what if no one wanted to buy it?

Of course, there was always the opposite solution: to *buy* a company (or maybe more than one company) and then merge them all together and create a whole new business, with new financials.

One thing led to the next, and toward mid-December Big Al found himself looking at a possible deal with New York billionaire

Ron and Patricia info-swap with Jack Welch's go-to-guy, Bob Wright. From GE Financial, Wright moved on to become Welch's eyes and ears at NBC. (*Photo credit:* Marina Garnier.)

Ron Perelman, who, it was said, owned a camping company called Coleman Co. that he might want to sell (at the right price) and that Big Al might find a nice "fit" for his Sunbeam situation.

In this way, the aides of the two men began to draw them together, as arrangements were made for a relationship sit-down. The date: December 18, in Palm Beach. The agenda: To discuss a way that Dunlap might acquire Coleman Co. in return for some Sunbeam stock, thereby making Perelman an investor in Sunbeam, while giving Dunlap control of Coleman (which of course Dunlap could then consolidate into Sunbeam, thereby transferring Coleman's revenues and cash flow to Sunbeam itself).

Meanwhile in Connecticut, the judge in the *Wendt v. Wendt* divorce case at last rendered his verdict. The date was Wednesday, December 3, and to the astonishment of Gary, the delight of Lorna, and the amazement of corporate wives everywhere, he ruled that Lorna was indeed entitled to half Gary's estate from her years as his wife because she had been 50 percent responsible for the fact that he'd accumulated the money in the first place. At ABC News's 20/20 program, the producers quickly dusted off the Wendt story they'd run the previous March, and dropped it into the lineup for the next 20/20, which happened to be Thursday, just twenty-four hours away.

By Friday morning, the Wendt story was front-page news across the country. "Lorna Wendt: Court Battle a Lesson for CEOs" roared the *New York Post*. "Ex-Wife of G.E. Exec Wins Landmark Settlement," thundered the *Miami Herald*. The *Pittsburgh Post-Gazette* even managed to mix up the parties in the suit, producing a headline that made it sound as if Welch himself had been the loser: "G.E. CEO's Divorce."

The next morning was Saturday, December 6, and even as the Wendt story was dragging GE through the headlines and enraging Jack all over again, yet more action was unfolding in Washington. The scene was the Northwest Gate of the White House and the time was approximately 10 A.M. when who should walk up bearing a collection of gifts for the president but Monica Lewinsky.[2]

Monica had seen Clinton briefly the night before at the White House Christmas party and left him a note saying she'd be back with some presents. Now here she was, bearing a sterling silver antique cigar holder, a tie, a coffee mug, a "Hugs and Kisses" box, and a book about President Theodore Roosevelt. She was planning to leave the parcels with the president's secretary, Betty Currie, who had told her at the Christmas party that Clinton would be busy with lawyers and unable to see her.

The situation had not been going well with the president lately— at least so far as Monica was concerned. Prior to the Christmas party, she had not seen Bill since mid-November when she'd managed to exchange a few words and a quick kiss with him in a stairway as he was leaving for a state dinner.

Prior to that, Monica had to think back nearly nine full months, all the way to the end of March—not long after she'd placed that Valentine's Day ad in the *Washington Post*—when "Handsome" had last been so willing to let her help him in her special way. Since then things had gotten so . . . *complicated.*

Monica's big mistake had obviously been letting herself be transferred out of the White House in the first place. At the White House, she'd been working in the Office of Legislative Affairs, handling the mail. But someone had apparently gotten the idea that she'd been spending too much time around the president, and in April 1996, she'd been reassigned to a job at the Pentagon. At least Bill hadn't been behind it. Monica was sure of that much because when she told him she was being reassigned, he told her not to worry and that he'd arrange for her to be brought back right after the November elections. But he never did, and now she wasn't so sure.

After that March 1997 meeting, Monica hadn't heard from Bill again for nearly two months. All of April went by, and no summons to the Oval Office. Then, nearly all of May, too. Finally, on May 24, the president's secretary, Betty Currie, summoned her to the Oval Office. She had arrived bearing gifts of various kinds, which she gave the president in the pantry. Then Bill said they were history, and he was breaking it off. Boom, just like that. She was devastated. Was that all she had meant to him?

Days went by, and then weeks, and from the president not a word. Finally, on July 3, she'd sent him a letter, saying she felt he'd been using her and that he'd promised to bring her back to the job at the White House and hadn't done it. She said she was thinking about telling her parents everything. At 9 o'clock the next morning, the president had her in the Oval Office, railing at her for threatening him in that way, and especially in a letter! But Monica was nearly hysterical already because she knew something that even the president didn't know, and that could blow up in his face any minute. It seemed that a person named Linda Tripp had become her friend at the Pentagon, and that Linda had been telling her things. Things like *Newsweek* was apparently planning to write a story about him and how he'd groped someone named Kathleen Willey right here in the White House. Stuff like that.

After that, things with Bill began to get *really* complicated. Two weeks later, he'd called her back to the White House, wanting to know more about this Tripp person and the *Newsweek* matter. At one point, he'd even asked her if she'd told Tripp about their own little arrangement—he and Monica, that is . . . *that* little arrangement. Of course not, demurred Monica, though she had in fact done exactly that. After all, who was Monica supposed to talk to if she couldn't talk to Bill? Besides, Linda was so understanding. She was just always there when Monica needed her (unlike Bill).

In the months that followed, she felt buffeted by conflicting messages from all directions. In August, Bill and the First Family went to Martha's Vineyard for vacation, where he'd played golf with his pal Vernon Jordan and somebody they both apparently knew, who ran GE—a Jack Welch.* Yet Bill had apparently been thinking about her even up at the Vineyard because, after he got back to Washington, Betty Currie called Monica and said to come over to the White House because she had some presents that the president had picked up for her when he and the First Lady had been in Martha's Vineyard. That was some of the good news. But it also turned out that the very job she'd been hoping to get that would take her back to the White House had mysteriously been eliminated. (That was some of the bad news.)

---

* It is a good indication of the general public's relative lack of awareness regarding who Welch was that as recently as the summer of 1997 the *New York Times* misidentified him as "Jack Lynch" in an August 24, 1997, caption of a photograph showing him playing golf with President Clinton on Martha's Vineyard, and subsequently ran a correction two days later on August 26.

Good news, bad news. It just went on like that. (What's a gal to do?) And by and by, she'd finally accepted what appeared to be the case: He was done with her. But what about *her* rights in all this? Actually, when you got right down to it, maybe she was done with him, too, the creep. In fact, if you wanted to know the truth, maybe she'd had it with the White House, and the government, and all of Washington, D.C. What she wanted to do was get away from all of it— move to New York and land a fancy and glamorous job where they'd treat a girl right.

On October 6, she got through to Betty Currie and told her what she wanted, and Betty said it would be no problem because the president had already said they'd be able to get her a job at the United Nations just like that [sound of snapping fingers goes here].

But the job never developed, and four days later she got through to the president and they started bickering over whether he was doing enough to help her. The next day he summoned her into the Oval Office again—a place where she hadn't been for months—this time apparently to keep her stroked for damage control purposes. But Monica was onto him by now, and she quickly seized control of the situation. Remembering his connection to Vernon Jordan, who seemed to have all sorts of business ties in New York, she threw out his name: Maybe he could help her get a job. The president nodded, seemingly in agreement, and Monica left.

Jordan's involvement on Monica's behalf brought the first forward movement on the job hunt front, and two weeks later she was sitting down for an interview with the U.S. Ambassador to the United Nations, Bill Richardson. Four days after that, and she had an actual job offer in her hand.

But the job didn't particularly interest her, and besides, Monica was in the big leagues now, and everybody knew that when you got to the Bigs you didn't have to swing at every pitch. So two days later, she called on Vernon Jordan personally and handed him a "wish list" of various places she might want to consider.

A whole month had now passed since that meeting, and so far nothing further had come of it. Had she overplayed her hand? There was really no way to tell, but as she approached the Northwest Gate to the White House, gifts in hand for the president, Monica wasn't about to be brushed off a second time.

Inside the guard booth at the gate stood some uniformed Secret Service officers. Telling them that she had gifts to drop off for the president, she waited while the officers attempted to locate Betty Currie. Since she was nowhere to be found and it was cold outside, they invited Monica to come and stand with them inside the guard booth.

Eventually, one of the officers did get a message to Currie. But learning that it was Monica who wanted to see the president, she told them that the young woman would have to wait for at least another forty minutes because the president already had a visitor with him in the Oval Office.

In the period that followed, many things transpired—though few subsequent events would prove more interesting than what was taking place in the Washington Bureau of the *New York Times*, where editors were finishing up work on the first of a massive two-part story by two reporters—Richard L. Berke and John M. Broder—that was designed to take readers inside the private world of the president of the United States. The purpose: to explain the sense of listlessness and malaise that had taken over the president in recent months.

From dozens of interviews—including some with various of Mr. Clinton's closest friends and advisors inside and outside the White House—the two *Times* reporters had pulled together a baffling portrait of Bill Clinton. He was a leader whose first term in the White House had been marked by eagerness, energy, and an all-around zest for life, but who now seemed, at the start of his second term, suddenly bereft of big ideas, filling the void with aimless soliloquies about subjects such as golf.

It was a grim picture indeed, and the two reporters seemed at a loss to explain where its root causes might lie, or to give hope for the future. They cautioned that the portrait of a "listless, distracted Chief Executive" was not the whole story, and that behind his sudden and escapist-seeming obsession with golf could lie a "more complex reality." They pointed to his growing maturity as president, and his awareness of the realities and limitations of government. They found parallels in a sense of drift that took over the second terms of other U.S. presidents, such as Dwight Eisenhower. They drew encouragement from the sense that by "frequently indulging in bouts of syrupy nostalgia," Clinton was allowing himself "more time for reflection." When they asked him why advisors such as Dick Morris, who had orchestrated his re-election campaign, now detected a kind of mellow lethargy seeping into everything he did, the president answered, "Beats me."*

In fact, any *Times* reporter wanting to clear up the mystery of the president's behavior had only to head for the Northwest Gate to the White House that very moment, where an extraordinary scene was about to unfold. Monica Lewinsky, who was waiting in the guard booth for the Oval Office visitor to depart so that she could be ushered in, heard one of the officers in the booth say who the president's visitor actually was. It was not one of his "lawyers," as Betty had claimed. It was not the head of state of any nation either, nor even the Democratic leadership of Congress, or any

---

*In fact, Clinton knew perfectly well why Morris said what he did, and why Morris could claim a particular sensitivity to the president's malaise; the campaign strategist had been forced to resign his post as a White House political advisor in August 1996 after tabloid newspaper reports linked him to a $200-per-night prostitute who was quoted as claiming Morris had a "toe fetish."

Cabinet member. President Clinton's visitor instead was none other than his old bicoastal jogging gal-pal, Eleanor Mondale, who according to her subsequent statements on the matter, had dropped by to discuss an "ex-boyfriend who the president did not like."

In the scene that followed, none of the Secret Service officers seemed able to recall exactly what Monica said, save that she was "livid." Storming out of the booth, she headed down the street to a pay phone, and getting Betty Currie on the line, began to shriek. "You lied to me!" then slammed down the phone.

A minute or two more and the president as well knew what had happened, and he, too, started to shout, demanding to know who had told Lewinsky that the Mondale woman was in the office with him, and insisting that the person be fired on the spot.

By the time Monica got back to her apartment, she had calmed down enough to phone the president yet again. This time she intended to demand the truth. To her astonishment, Betty Currie actually put her through. Yet, no sooner was she on the line with the president than Clinton began to rage at her for "making a stink." What had been going on between Eleanor and him was none of her business, he declared. But in fact he was wrong, and in no time at all it would be the whole world's business. For Monica and Bill—as well as many others—it was the beginning of the end.

~~~

Two weeks later and the spotlight swung back to Ron Perelman. The date was December 18, and Ron was on his mission to meet with Dunlap. The objective: Work out the terms under which Ron might be able to swap his ownership of the Coleman Co. for some of Dunlap's Sunbeam stock.

Ron had acquired Coleman back in 1989 by pushing his way into the middle of a management-led leveraged buyout and topping an offer by the Wichita, Kansas, company's own management with a bid of $545 million. Then, once having gotten control of the company, he piled it high with debt, and in 1992 sold an 18 percent stub-end of the company back to the public.

Unfortunately, with Coleman's balance sheet now weighed down with debt, the company's ability to generate profits had been undermined, and by the start of 1997, its stock was still selling for no more than it had been a half-decade earlier.

In Dunlap, Ron seems to have thought he saw a way to get rid of the problem: Stick Dunlap with it.

The fact that Big Al was a loudmouth and a bully really didn't matter. The man's money was still green, and so far as the market was concerned, he seemed for the time being to hold a hot hand: Once Dunlap was associated with a company that needed a turnaround, its stock price almost always went up. So why should it be any different for Coleman? If Ron sold his stake in Coleman to Sunbeam, he'd get back Sunbeam stock in return. And since the Coleman stock ought to go up just because Dunlap now controlled it, the shares ought to pull Sunbeam's stock up right along with it.

Yet even as Ron and his aide, Howard Giddis, were leaving the MacAndrews & Forbes offices in New York to take the Gulfstream to Palm Beach, a far bigger problem than Dunlap's chainsaw was heading right at them. And for that Ron could once again thank his Washington, D.C., Mister Fixit, Vernon Jordan.

With the whole Monica mess ready to explode, the president had reached out for Jordan, and on December 11 the two men had met, and Jordan had told him he'd undertake to get the girl a job in the private sector—to which end he placed phone calls to a New York public relations company called Burson-Marsteller where he was reasonably well wired in, and to a second New York company where his wires ran right to the beating heart of the business: Ron Perelman's private holding company, MacAndrews & Forbes. After getting Ron's personal lawyer, Richard Halperin, on the line, Jordan arranged for a

job interview for Monica a week hence on the 18th in New York—
the very day that Perelman was leaving for Palm Beach and his meeting with Dunlap.

Though Ron could hardly have realized it at the time, the two
meetings of December 18, 1997, were like daggers pointed at his
heart. In Palm Beach, his meeting with Dunlap was destined almost
instantly to morph into the costliest and most ruinous deal of his
life. Meanwhile in New York, his most trusted advisors were busy
entangling him (and themselves) in the sex scandal of all time.

Ron's immediate concern was of course the meeting in Palm
Beach, which got off to a rocky start when Dunlap offered $20 per
share in Sunbeam stock for Perelman's Coleman shares, and Perelman countered with $30.[3] Within minutes it was clear that neither
side was going to budge, and the meeting immediately degener-
ated into furious and foul-mouthed yelling, at the climax to which
Dunlap stomped from the room snarling, "Fuck you, and fuck your
company."*

---

*Obviously approaching the breaking point, Dunlap played a round of golf several
weeks later at the Boca Raton Resort and Club, where another golfer encountered him
after hitting a golf ball into a lake at the 14th green. When the man reached the lake he
found Dunlap already standing at the water's edge, a metal golf ball retriever in one
hand, and a golf ball in the other. Not knowing who Dunlap was, and believing that he
might have mistakenly recovered the wrong ball, the man asked Dunlap what brand
markings it bore. In a subsequent police report, the man stated what happened next:
"Dunlap looked at the ball and then threw it into the deep area of the lake where the ball
could not be retrieved." When the golfer asked him why he had done that, Dunlap "became angry and put one end of the golf ball retriever into one hand and the other end of
the retriever in the other hand." Then, said the police report, Dunlap pressed the metal
bar against the man's throat, and forced him to his knees, then walked away, saying, "You
don't know who I am." The golfer reported the incident to the police, Dunlap denied the
assault and countered by accusing the golfer of shouting obscenities at *him* and trying to
provoke *him* into a fight. See Boca Raton Police Department, Incident Investigation Report, Case No. 1998-007520 (February 1, 1998).

Meanwhile, back in New York the Monica Lewinsky problem now affixed itself to Ron like gum on his shoe. The first job interview had led nowhere, but Vernon Jordan wouldn't give up and another round of phone calls ensued, leading to a re-interview for the young woman on December 30. This was followed after the holidays by a third visit, on January 8 of the New Year, 1998. This one too led nowhere, so Jordan now intervened directly with Perelman, and yet another round of interviews was set up for the next day, January 9. It was a war of attrition, and in the end Ron surrendered and the Lewinsky person got her job offer, for something at Revlon.[4]

But something seemed wrong about the whole situation. Just why did this little twenty-three-year-old nobody have someone like Vernon Jordan behind her? What was this all about? It didn't take Ron (or anyone else) long to learn the answer since Monica's good friend at the Pentagon, Linda Tripp, had been secretly taping her phone conversations since the previous September. And just three days after Monica had landed her job at Revlon, Tripp went to federal investigators and gave them her secretly taped conversations with Monica.

In no time at all, reporters at the *Washington Post, Los Angeles Times,* and *ABC News* had her name as well, as did Internet news man Matt Drudge, who'd actually been the first journalist of any to get onto the story—as well as to get Monica's name before the public. Drudge thus reported over the weekend of January 17 and 18 that a former White House intern named Monica Lewinsky had surfaced in the Whitewater matter and that sex with the president might be part of the story. On Wednesday morning, January 21, the *Washington Post* and *Los Angeles Times* finally reached print with the story as well, and by the next morning, the name Monica Lewinsky was the lead story on all the networks and cable news shows, as well as the top story in nearly every daily newspaper in the United States.

Before the day was out, Revlon had withdrawn its job offer, but it was too late to get the stink of the situation off Ron. Wherever one looked, the arrows to toyland all seemed to point directly at Perelman: the Webster Hubbell matter, the Eleanor Mondale entanglement, the ties to Vernon Jordan . . . even his bizarre marriage to the Duff woman, who herself was rumored to have ties of some sort with Clinton. And at the end of all that, *Monica, too?*

It is, of course, possible that none of this fazed Ron in the slightest, and that he just went about his business, day in and day out, as America's worst scandal since Watergate threatened to drag both himself and his company into the middle of the impeachment of the president.

It is possible, to be sure, but it seems highly unlikely, since it took all of twenty-four hours before the names of both Revlon and Perelman had become permanently bolted to the story, and by the end of the following week he had already sworn out his first affidavit for investigators.

Yet, if he thought that by insisting he didn't really know anything he would somehow be saved from further involvement, he was mistaken, for investigators in Washington were already drawing up a subpoena to force him to answer questions under oath. And looming ahead, closer and closer, was that other problem that would soon be cutting him to ribbons—the one they call The Chainsaw.

19

BIG AL AND RON EXIT FIGHTING

Perelman and Dunlap both had a common interest in wanting to do a deal, and because both felt they could get the best of the other, the two sides stayed at it. By March, Dunlap was back at the table, ready to pay Perelman's asking price of $30 per share. And at $30 per share, Perelman was ready to shake hands, just as he had been all along.

Too bad for Ron, for in what surely must be a Wall Street record of sorts, it took exactly ninety-six hours—from March 30 to April 3, 1998—before the wheels and fenders started to pop off the Sunbeam-Coleman transaction and Ron began to realize he'd been had. After that, it took scarcely two more months before Ron's nemesis, Big Al Dunlap, was fired from Sunbeam, and the Enforcement Division of the Securities and Exchange Commission began to build a fraud case against him.

For a man who had spent nearly forty years in a furious and ego-driven struggle to reach the top in American business, Big Al's self-destruction proved both ignominious and swift—and astonishingly complete. He was the first of the Great Bull Market's most celebrated

CEOs Gone Wild to go from hero to zero in barely the blink of an eye, but he would not be the last.

In the end, it was the Coleman-Sunbeam deal that triggered his fall. And though the deal itself was publicly announced on March 2, the transaction was not actually completed until March 30. By that time, a number of notable developments had occurred . . . all of which wound up conspiring to paint Big Al in the most self-serving and deceitful light imaginable when it came time to apportion blame for Sunbeam's bankruptcy and ruin.

On March 7—five days after the announcement of the deal—Sunbeam filed a financial report with the Securities and Exchange Commission, making clear that Big Al was determined to pick up his fair share of the spoils whether the deal proved a success or wound up bankrupting both companies (which is what eventually happened). To that end, the company announced that it had given Big Al a revised employment contract, through which his base salary of $1 million per year had been doubled, to $2 million. He also picked up $15 million worth of Sunbeam stock that he could sell immediately, plus $14 million worth of stock options that he could also sell immediately, as well as $30 million more of options over the following three years. All in all, the revised deal amounted to a potential $61 million payday for Dunlap, with the cash payable retroactively to early February when an agreement in principal between Big Al and Ron had first been reached.*

---

*March 7 was an important date in another sense, too, since the financial report—known technically as a Form 10K—that Sunbeam submitted to the SEC on that date bore Big Al's signature as the company's chairman and CEO. The document became a cornerstone of the SEC fraud case against Dunlap alleging that the Sunbeam CEO engaged in a scheme to defraud his company and its shareholders by using improper accounting techniques covering the whole of the 1997 reporting period contained in the audited numbers of the 10K. See Securities and Exchange Commission Litigation Release 17710 (September 4, 2002).

In fact, the company's vaunted turnaround—for which Big Al was now apparently rewarding himself—had been a mirage from the start, concocted out of force-feeding barbecue grills, electric blankets, and other Sunbeam consumer products into the distribution pipeline and booking the shipments as having generated revenues when the company hadn't actually received the cash.*

If Ron had been less distracted by his multiplying problems on the Monica Lewinsky front, he undoubtedly would never have gotten involved in Sunbeam in the first place. Yet now he was stuck with it, and had handed over his control of Coleman to become the second largest shareholder in a fraud-soaked business that accounted for 15 percent of his entire net worth. And no sooner had he done so than the company he acquired blew up in his face.

When Sunbeam had good news to spread, Big Al could typically be found boasting about it in a company press release. But on March 19, Sunbeam issued a press statement that it didn't attribute to Dunlap or to anyone else: that for a reason vaguely described as "changes in inventory management," the company would not be able to meet the first-quarter sales expectations that Wall Street analysts had set for the company.[1] The reality behind that statement was, of course, that Sunbeam had stuffed its distribution channels to the bursting point with merchandise, and the entire pipeline was now backing up right onto the company's loading docks.

---

*Anyone looking at the March 7 10K financial report could have seen the obvious problem. Reported revenues jumped by nearly $184 million or 15 percent over the year-earlier level, along with a dramatic $110 million net profit at the bottom line. But the company's cash flow had completely collapsed, from positive cash flow of $14.2 million in 1996, to negative cash flow of $8.2 million in 1997, while "Account Receivables" (money owed to the company) soared to $82 million—an amount that all by itself accounted for 75 percent of Sunbeam's apparent return to profitability.

Hearing this, investors began dumping Sunbeam's shares in a panic, and by the end of the day, the stock had dropped 10 percent in price, ending the month at $44 per share—down 16 percent from its all-time high of $53 only a few weeks earlier. But worse was to come. Just three days into the month of April came another Chainsaw stunner—this one disclosing that Sunbeam would probably not do much better in the current quarter than it had done in 1996, before Big Al had even arrived.[2] This announcement knocked another 20 percent off the stock, driving the price down to $35 per share. Three weeks later came the first of what was destined to become an avalanche of shareholder lawsuits accusing Al and his crew of orchestrating a fraud.

Where was Ron Perelman through all this? One good indication of the big problem on his plate came on the very day that the much-dreaded class-action law firm of Milberg, Weiss, Bershad, Hynes and Lerach filed a lawsuit for securities fraud against Sunbeam and the company's stock began its final and ruinous plunge into single digits. While that was taking place, Ron was giving a deposition to government lawyers about Monica Lewinsky's job offer from Revlon.

By the end of the following week, Sunbeam's stock price had slipped another $10, to stand at $26 per share. As May began, Ron was looking at a loss of more than $300 million on this one chainsawed investment in less than eight weeks' time, and it was only the beginning.

On May 11, Dunlap appeared before a large gathering of skeptical analysts in New York to explain why Sunbeam's stock would soon be going back up again. But Dunlap had by now become a one-man demolition derby for his own company, and every time he opened his mouth to reassure investors that the situation was fine, the stock fell more. When a PaineWebber analyst named Andrew Shore, who had grown increasingly critical of Dunlap in recent months, asked whether Dunlap would give back the bonus in his revised contract and work instead for a dollar a year, Dunlap grew furious. After the meeting, he began moving menacingly toward Shore as if he were about to attack him. "You son of a bitch," he snarled, "If you want to come after me I'll come after you twice as hard."[3]

Perelman clearly had to do something, and fast. But what? How does one go *mano a mano* with the one they call "The Chainsaw"?

By the start of June, Ron had come up with at least the outlines of a plan—what looked to be a version of a gimmick he'd used success- fully back in the 1980s. It was known as greenmail, and the ploy in- volved accumulating shares in a takeover target, then agreeing to go away if the company would buy the stock back at a premium over the prevailing market price. Ron had made more than $34 million from that gimmick in a hostile bid for the Gillette company, so maybe a variation on the theme would work again now.[4]

With Sunbeam's stock still holding in the low $20s, Ron could threaten to sue Sunbeam (and of course Dunlap) for fraud unless the company agreed to issue him enough stock options, at some dirt- cheap price like, say $5 per share, so that he could gain control of the company and figure out a way to get his money back. Once in con- trol he'd at least be calling the shots. Well, he had to try something!

It was this plan, more than any other single thing, that seems fi- nally to have pushed Big Al round the bend. Though Dunlap never learned the full details, he caught enough of a whiff of what Ron had in mind that he stood up before an emergency meeting of Sunbeam's board of directors on the afternoon of Tuesday, June 9, and began railing that Perelman was engaged in a conspiracy to drive the price of Sunbeam's stock down even further and take over the whole com- pany. If the board wanted Big Al to continue, it would have to give him a vote of confidence right on the spot.

The board members were dumbstruck, and several left the room thinking Big Al had become emotionally unhinged. Six days later and he was out—though it was hardly the end of the matter.

With Dunlap gone, Perelman installed his own man as replacement. And since he still wanted to be made whole from the consequences of his folly, it wasn't long before he sprang his upside-down greenmail plan on Sunbeam's board. Faced with the choice of either agreeing to Ron's plan or opening itself up to a fraud lawsuit that it knew it couldn't win, the board caved in and gave Ron what he wanted.[5]

To the outside world, it looked as if Ron had pulled another one of his nervy feats of high finance. But the truth was just the opposite because his rescue plan meant he had to throw yet more money into Sunbeam, which had already been irreparably damaged by Dunlap's turnaround strategy for "fixing" it.

By the start of 2001, Sunbeam's balance sheet had been reduced to insolvency, the company's equity was gone, revenues were collapsing, and nothing of any real value remained except the brand name Sunbeam. On February 6, 2001, the company declared itself bankrupt, and filed to reorganize its affairs by wiping out all its common stock and $2 billion of its debts, and replacing the debt with stock in a new company. In the process, the investors suffered losses of between 98.5 percent on their money (for the bondholders) to 100 percent for the stockholders. A year later, Sunbeam emerged from bankruptcy and changed its name to American Household, Inc., and continues in business as of 2004 as a private company.

In the process, Perelman's investment in Sunbeam was totally wiped out. Distracted by the siren call of fame and gorgeous women, Ron saw in Big Al Dunlap an opportunity to free himself of a stagnating investment in Coleman Company and wound up making one of the most spectacularly awful stock trades in Wall Street history, swapping his control of a slow-growing but viable company with a market value of more than $1.7 billion, in return for more than half a billion dollars' worth of stock that began to collapse just ninety-six hours after he agreed to buy it.

And that wasn't all. As the situation at Sunbeam grew worse, Perelman knew he had to do something, and when the board ousted Dunlap in mid-June 1998, Ron seized the opportunity to grab control of Sunbeam's day-to-day operations—to which end he pulled his best operating man, Jerry Levin, out of his job as CEO of Revlon, and threw him into the breach at Sunbeam as Dunlap's replacement.

In so doing, he created the same kind of problem that Jack Welch had created for himself at GE when he pulled his top man at GE Capital—Larry Bossidy—up to the board level as vice chairman, opening up a leadership vacuum at GE Capital. By assigning Levin to the job of running Sunbeam, Ron created a leadership void at the top of the crown jewel of his entire empire, Revlon, and in less than two months the company's stock had collapsed from $54 per share (at the end of July 1998) to barely $12 (by the start of October). In the process, another $2.3 billion flew out the window.

By year's end, Ron's ranking on the Forbes 400 list had slipped from No. 6 to 30, with his vaunted $6.4 billion in reported net worth having been nearly halved, to $3.4 billion. In 1999, another $500 million vanished, and in 2000 so did $700 million more. To be sure, he was still enormously wealthy by the standards of even the ultra-rich, but he was no longer in that rarefied and special world inhabited only by the Richest of Them All.

How much did Ron now count for a celebrity newsmaker? No more than Patricia Duff, whose relentless pursuit of his money in court had chewed through nearly two dozen different teams of lawyers, and was still continuing over various side-issues when this book went to press in early 2004. Through it all, Patricia remained entertaining if nothing else, soldiering on as a gossip column regular

Rockin' Ronster. Dennis Kozlowski played in the Hi Tones, and CEO
Richard Scrushy played in a band, too. What's next, trashing a Motel 6?
(*Photo credit:* Marina Garnier.)

with her unfailing knack for entangling herself in relationships with
Problem Men.

In fact, scarcely had Patricia squared off in court against Ron
than she became the constant companion of a Democratic Senator
from New Jersey named Robert Torricelli. Her timing was perfect.
Almost immediately thereafter, the Senate Ethics Committee "severely admonished" Torricelli for showing "poor judgment" and a
"lack of due regard for Senate rules" by accepting illegal campaign
donations and expensive gifts from businessmen seeking his help in
promoting investment deals in North and South Korea, and Torricelli dropped out of politics.

After Torricelli, Patricia hooked up with an East Hampton socialite businessman named Samuel Waksal, who headed a company
called ImClone Systems, Inc., which claimed to have a breakthrough
drug treatment for cancer. Waksal appeared to be extremely wealthy

Ron shows off what he bagged with his 1999 après-Oscars hitter's line: wife number four, Ellen Barkin. Question: "Are you single, or married, or what?" (*Photo credit:* Marina Garnier.)

and had an impressive collection of fine art in a vast Soho loft where he threw parties attended by various celebrity notables. But much of Waksal's wealth derived from secretly defrauding banks, cheating his own shareholders, and eventually from a failed scheme to trade on insider information regarding his own company. In 2003, he began serving seven years in federal prison on a guilty plea for illegally selling his stock in ImClone Systems on the eve of a damaging government report about the company.*

---

* After listening to Duff unreel her tale of woe regarding her choices in men, the former Democratic Governor of Texas, Ann Richards, offered a comment that seemed to say everything that needed to be said, remarking, "Honey, your picker's broke!"

And what of Ron Perelman? In testament to the maxim that persistence reveals either great wisdom or great stupidity, scarcely was he rid of Patricia than Ron made some news of a familiar sort. It was June 1999, and the scene was the latest annual installment of *Vanity Fair*'s post-Oscars party in Hollywood. All the regulars were there—Julia, Sharon, Demi, and so on. And maneuvering in among them was, as always, Ron Perelman, the chairman of Revlon.

Exactly when he spotted her is not known. But she was probably wearing something slinky and she was probably standing alone. She was actress Ellen Barkin, and of course she was blonde . . . and in the end that may have been all that really mattered, as Ron walked up to her and got right to the point. He asked, "Are you single, or married, or what?" And one year later, in June 2000, they were married.

20

LIFE IS A CABARET

H e had done everything the other CEOs had done—and in fact, a lot more. But to what end? Having presided over one of the fastest growing major companies on Wall Street, showering riches beyond counting on his investors and backers along the way, L. Dennis Kozlowski, chairman and CEO of Tyco International, Inc., seemed to be winding up at the end of the 1990s right where he had begun the 1980s—as America's invisible CEO, even on Wall Street. It seemed so unfair.

Dennis had gone to work at Tyco in late 1975 as the company's assistant controller, reporting to the CEO, a showboating ex-lobsterman named Joe Gaziano. Within a year, Gaziano had acquired a struggling operation known as Grinnell Fire Protection Systems Company from ITT Corporation, and to run it he tapped Kozlowski. Thereafter—just as had been the case with Al Dunlap, who at that very moment was distinguishing himself for his seemingly miraculous rescue of Nitec Paper Company in Niagara Falls, New York—Kozlowski began earning the first of his own campaign ribbons for the seemingly miraculous rescue of a troubled company.*

In 1982, Gaziano died of cancer, and Tyco's board appointed a man named John F. Fort III to succeed him. Fort proved to be the 180-degree opposite of the free-spending Gaziano, both in temperament and business style. Yet, because Kozlowski was still running the Grinnell division, he was able to stay out of the penny-pinching Fort's line of fire. To ingratiate himself with the new boss, Kozlowski even adopted a gimmick that in retrospect seems pure Al Dunlap: He held a dinner for Grinnell executives to announce the public firing of the man whom he judged to be the company's worst warehouse manager during the previous year.†

By 1986, Kozlowski had earned a brief mention for himself in *Fortune's* "People to Watch" section for his work at Grinnell,[1] making plain enough that he would sooner or later be chosen by Tyco's board as Fort's successor. Dennis seemed to sense as much and had already begun accumulating the badges of power that CEOs of the late 1980s were coming to regard as their rightful due. To the wine cellar and the million-dollar family residence, he now added a $250,000 sloop, with which he opened the door to membership at the Corinthian Yacht Club in Marblehead, Massachusetts.[2]

---

* In both cases, the main weapon in the fight turned out to be the mass firings of employees—though in Kozlowski's case there were no subsequent accusations of fraud, as there had been at Nitec, to taint the reputation of the victorious commander.

† See A. Bianco, W. Symonds, and N. Byrnes, with D. Polek, "The Rise and Fall of Dennis Kozlowski," *BusinessWeek* (December 23, 2002), p. 64. One could also see elements of Jack Welch's management style in Kozlowski's approach to employee motivation. Just as did Welch, Kozlowski loathed the idea of written reports, and under the guise of "streamlining" Grinnell's bureaucracy, he did away with 98 percent of them once Gaziano put him in charge of the operation. He likewise instituted a system of executive compensation in which managers received low cash salaries but large bonuses, in the form of restricted Tyco stock, when they met or exceeded annual earnings targets. See *Forbes* (June 15, 1998).

And in just the way that he had become involved with the person who was now his wife when they were both beginning their careers two decades earlier as employees at SCM Corporation in New York, he now added a second office romance to his resume . . . only this time he was already married.

The new woman's name was Barbara Jacques, and she was working as an administrative assistant at Grinnell when she caught Dennis' eye.[3] But no sooner had he been promoted to president of Tyco in 1989 than he began to tire of her, and by 1990 he had moved on to a twice-married waitress named Karen Lee Mayo, whom he had met in a local watering hole called Ron's Beach House.

Thereafter it became possible to catch the first foreshadowing glimpses of the seemingly insatiable greed—and equally insatiable sense of personal entitlement—that would eventually engulf Dennis' life, as he, like Dunlap, Welch, and so many others of their generation, struggled to bury an economically stressed past in a nouveau riche future.

By the time Dennis had been elevated to Tyco's top two jobs of chairman and CEO in the summer of 1992, his annual income was still less than one million dollars per year. Yet, he had already traded in his $250,000 sloop for a custom-built $1.5 million racing yacht. Thereafter, he traded up to a $15 million custom racing yacht that required a crew of nine to sail—after which he moved up yet again, to a made-to-order 150-foot aluminum hull yacht costing twice as much. The vessel was barely half completed when his legal problems overtook him in 2002.

Meanwhile he had taken to squiring Karen Mayo around in public, as if publicly humiliating his wife, Angie, was something to which he was personally entitled. Even as he was doing so, his eye had begun to wander once again. By 1995, he had embarked on his *third* office romance—this one with a Tyco secretary named Mary Murphy. What had begun as an office affair two decades earlier with

Angie had now ballooned into serial cheating involving at least four separate women: Angie, Barbara, Karen, and now Mary.

Meanwhile, the same flow of testosterone that was stoking his out-of-control womanizing had likewise begun powering up his behavior on the business front. Board members who had known Kozlowski to be little more than a cost-cutter now discovered that the man they had placed in Tyco's driver's seat possessed what one director termed "a big pair of balls." But the board also discovered that the more risks Kozlowski took, the more they paid off, as his incessant deal making sent the company's share price higher and higher with each new acquisition.

In fact, Tyco had simply caught the up-slope of the familiar and well-documented reaction of Wall Street to conglomerate mergers in a buoyant stock market, though Kozlowski wasted no time in capitalizing on the moment in any case, ramming through an unheard-of eighty-eight deals, worth a total of more than $15 billion, during his first seventy-two months as chairman and CEO.[4] A top advisor to Kozlowski regarding potential takeover targets later expressed amazement at the pace with which the deals were cooked up—and just how little research actually went into them. "There were times when these deals were flowing through at a rate of two and even three a week," he said, "and the board just wasn't able to keep up. A lot of times they'd have to vote on them before any due diligence was even done. Sometimes things would get so frantic that there wouldn't even be time for an actual meeting of the board, and the votes would have to take place via conference calls."

The effect on Tyco's stock price was astounding, with the shares rising more than 1,350 percent during the ten years that followed Kozlowski's elevation to Tyco's presidency in 1989, or more than three times the rate of gain for the Dow Jones Industrial Average during the same period.

Yet, as hard as Kozlowski tried, he was simply unable to personalize this achievement as his own and thereby elevate himself into the ranks of business renown alongside men like Dunlap (who had yet to self-destruct in the Sunbeam deal) and most of all, Welch.

"He was obsessed with Welch," said one in his inner circle of advisors. "He saw Welch as a member of the Establishment, and he liked to claim that he wanted to stick it to Welch in order to stick it to the Establishment. But I think he was simply jealous of Welch, who came from much the same sort of background that Dennis had come from, and that what he really wanted was to *be* like Welch so that he could get accepted by the Establishment, too."

Kozlowski knew well enough what one of his problems was: To get noticed, he needed to get closer to the action—which is to say, he needed to set up a base of operations in New York. Being named Kozlowski was awkward enough, but who was going to take an interest in him if it meant having to go to Exeter, New Hampshire, to do so? Three years into his job as chairman and CEO, Kozlowski finally acted, arranging for Tyco to open a second headquarters office, this one at a prestigious Fifth Avenue and 56th Street address in Manhattan.

However, his new offices changed nothing, at least when it came to gaining admittance to New York's moneyed world of power and privilege—and one reason was instantly obvious to anyone who stopped by to pay his respects. Crude, tasteless, and unencumbered by the graciousness and sense of style that a more cultured upbringing might have provided, Dennis counted on sheer ostentation to put himself across as a figure to be reckoned with.

Not only did the new offices clash with the image that Kozlowski wanted to project for the company as a "lean and mean" operation, but the elegant decor clashed as well with Kozlowski himself. At six feet three inches and 280 pounds, he was not only the largest living thing in the place, but also easily the hungriest. From 11 A.M. onward, he could be found wandering from room to room munching on huge, greasy slices of pepperoni-and-cheese pizza, the grease and cheese splattering onto the carpets as he passed.

For help in dressing up his act and getting some doors opened, Kozlowski turned to a corporate public relations firm named Dilenschneider & Company. The firm had dealt with numerous large corporate clients over the years, and its chairman, a jovial and gracious man named Bob Dilenschneider, saw Tyco and Kozlowski as a worthy challenge. To gain some quick notoriety for the client, the firm began lining up get-acquainted meetings for Kozlowski to meet corporate leaders at the upper echelons of New York money and finance.

But nothing seemed to click. Sensing that Kozlowski needed a "message"—something that could make Tyco International sound exciting as well as give its CEO some personal panache—Dilenschneider arranged for Kozlowski to give a luncheon address at New York's prestigious Metropolitan Club. But the speech, in which Kozlowski focused on Warren Buffett as his hero, sounded unexceptional and even dull. After all, Buffett was *everybody's* hero, and Kozlowski had offered no new insights into the man at all.

After that, the Dilenschneider team tried presenting Kozlowski to the world as a corporate benefactor, but that, too, accomplished little. Though he wound up making enormous, multimillion-dollar gifts to New York's Lincoln Center for the Performing Arts, as well as gifts to the Metropolitan Opera, his alma mater at Seton Hall, the Whitney Museum, and even the Boy Scouts, nothing generated much more than a polite thank-you.

Then one day in the spring of 1999, Dennis caught a break. Realizing by then that the Tyco man was never going to succeed in "buying" his way into corporate America's hall of fame, the Dilenschneider people decided to attack the problem from the opposite direction. Perhaps Dennis would have better luck working his way *up* the food chain of fame.

To that end, they arranged for a reporter at *Barron's* to interview Dennis. The choice proved astute to say the least. Though *Barron's* was not as well known as *Fortune* or *BusinessWeek*, it was one of Wall Street's most influential sources of news. This was mainly because its reporters and editors worked hard to come up with stories about people, companies, and trends before other more mainstream publications spotted them. Then, when the other publications scrambled to play catch-up, it looked as if they'd gotten their idea for the story from *Barron's*—which was usually the case.

A big, attention-getting cover story about a multibillion-dollar conglomerate that most people had never heard of was exactly the sort of material that *Barron's* craved. And the Dilenschneider team gave it an extra spin that they knew the *Barron's* editors would find irresistible: Dennis Kozlowski as the next Jack Welch.

And that is exactly how *Barron's* played it in a cover story for the April 12, 1999, issue: "Tyco's Titan: How Dennis Kozlowski Is Creating a Lean, Profitable Giant." A mere 300 words into the nearly 6,000-word-long story came the payoff, as the story declared Kozlowski to be "in a class with General Electric's Jack Welch . . ." With those words, everything for Dennis Kozlowski began to change—and change fast.

The story was full of the same personal malarkey that Dennis had been desperately spreading for years—stories about his father, Leo, dressed up in Dennis' fabricated finery as a Triple-A baseball player who became a Newark, New Jersey, police detective . . . and of course stories about Dennis himself, adorned with his own bogus past as a star football and basketball player in high school.

But readers weren't interested in any of that. The only things that really concerned anyone were the comparisons with Welch and GE, which the story hammered home over and over again. There were references to such things as Kozlowski's claimed support of Welch's idea that a takeover target should be first or second in its field or it wasn't worth owning. There was also the "lean and hungry" message that had long since become associated with Welch's business style, as in the story's assertion that Kozlowski had reduced Tyco's headquarters staff to a mere seventy employees, which *Barron's* characterized as "near to the point of anorexia."

In fact, the company was hardly running on starvation rations. In addition to its headquarters in Exeter, New Hampshire, and its other headquarters on Fifth Avenue in New York, the company had added a third headquarters in Bermuda in 1997, and a fourth in Boca Raton, Florida.

And Kozlowski was hardly pursuing an anorexic personal life either. Though the *Barron's* story took due note of the $20 million stock bonus he had recently received for his work as chairman and CEO the previous year, the story betrayed no awareness that Kozlowski's lavish lifestyle was in fact being propped up by the opened checkbook of Tyco itself.

In addition to his growing fleet of sailing yachts, Dennis had lately added a $6 million weekend home on Nantucket, complete with a $15,000 wine cellar—financed through something known among the Tyco brass as the company's "Key Employee Loan Program."

Some $2.5 million more of the program's money went for a waterfront home in Boca Raton, bought by the company from one of its board members. Dennis and Karen used it as their Florida love nest while construction was underway on the couple's "real" Boca home, which was also being built with funds from the Tyco program.

Beyond that came company-paid expenses, incurred by Kozlowski, for $72,042 worth of jewelry, $155,067 worth of clothing, nearly $97,000 in flowers, more than $52,000 in wine, and $60,000 in dues for various club memberships. And there was more, including an apartment in Madrid for one of his two daughters, $246,000 for five sets of diamond earrings from New York's ultra-swanky Harry Winston jewelers, a $4,500-per-month rental apartment for his secretarial girlfriend Mary Murphy plus a new car and $70,000 to start her own restaurant.[5]

The impact of the *Barron's* story on both Dennis and Tyco was immediate and dramatic, as he at last stepped forward in the raiment he had yearned for so long to wear—as not just any old run-of-the-mill business celebrity but Corporate America's new Jack Welch. During the previous twenty-nine years, the country's two largest newspapers—the *New York Times* and the *Wall Street Journal*—had mentioned Kozlowski a total of just seventy-three times. Yet the same two newspapers covered him extensively in fully seventy-nine stories during just the first twenty-four months *after* the appearance of the *Barron's* story,* even as Tyco's stock price soared 67 percent in value during the same twenty-four months. Dennis hadn't yet eclipsed Jack Welch or Al Dunlap as the country's most widely known CEO, but he was on his way.

It was December 2000, and the scene was Tyco International's Boca Raton Christmas party, where Dennis and his current girlfriend Karen Mayo were discussing plans with his former girlfriend Barbara Jacques for a Tyco celebration to dwarf anything the company had thrown before. This time, the guest of honor was to be none other than Karen herself, a person who had no connection with Tyco except for her sleeping arrangements with its chairman and CEO.

At Kozlowski's subsequent criminal trial in New York, his lawyers offered various explanations for what this celebration was intended to accomplish. But the most obvious one somehow never came up— that the real and most basic purpose of the shindig was to remove once-and-for-all from Dennis' shoes and pants cuffs the dirt of Elysian Fields.

Dennis intended to accomplish this by showing that he knew how to treat a lady right. Having finally divorced Angie, he now

---

*By the end of the third year (April 11, 2002), the number had climbed to more than 200, and when the CEO crime scandals of 2002/2003 finally erupted, the total surged past 2,000.

Dennis and Karen Kozlowski. For her fortieth birthday bash in Sardinia, Karen had kind of been hoping for a beach party type theme. But Dennis had already locked in Pliny the Elder, so they compromised and went for Jimmy Buffett, disguised as Elvis Smith. Add the shaved-down guys in the Speedo trunks, and the ice sculpture of David that peed booze out the whizzer, and Karen's big 4-0 promised to be a real bender in Margaritaville. Hey, James, are you still lookin' for that shaker of salt? (*Photo credit:* Bolivar Arellano, *New York Post.*)

planned a secret wedding with his new squeeze, Karen, to be followed, for her fortieth birthday with the birthday party blast of all time—not some mamby-pamby affair at a casino in Atlantic City, Dennis was going all-out on this one, the whole nine yards—in fact, he was going half way around the world, to a private resort on the Mediterranean island of Sardinia.*

---

* By the late 1990s, the bull market had showered so much money on America's nouveau rich CEOs that grossly ostentatious displays of wealth had become utterly routine. As the chairman of Indiana-based Conseco, Inc., a one-time encyclopedia salesman named Stephen Hilbert had grown so rich that he built himself a 33-acre walled estate outside Indianapolis and an 18,500-square foot vacation home in the Caribbean, and began raising thoroughbred horses in Kentucky. By the time his business collapsed in 2001,

Dennis had personally chosen the resort, too—the Hotel Cala di Volpe—in part because he was a member of the board of directors of the Starwood hotel chain, which ran the resort.[6] But if either he or Karen had harbored the slightest doubt that they were going top shelf all the way, a discreetly placed name in the resort's promotional material surely put them at ease. In the pursuit of taste through a dropped name, it is, after all, the luster of the branding that ultimately closes the deal, and the luster in this particular name was all but blinding: "The Hotel Cala di Volpe, designed and developed in 1962 by the Aga Khan."*

For Dennis, the year 2000 had been his best ever, with total cash compensation of an incredible $137 million for his work at Tyco—much of it from having Tyco waive and forgive millions it had lent him under the Key Employee Loan Program—so he certainly could have afforded to pay for the party out of his own pocket, no matter how gauche and extravagant he intended it to be.

But Tyco's shareholders had also enjoyed a good year, with the price of their stock rising more than 46 percent even though the

---

Hilbert had burned through five wives and was onto his sixth, a one-time exotic dancer named Tomisue.

In Alabama, a high-school dropout named Richard Scrushy had begun his adult life as a bricklayer living in a trailer park with his pregnant girlfriend, and was ending up 30 years later as chairman and CEO of one of the Southeast's largest and fastest growing hospital management companies, HealthSouth Corporation. By the time *his* business collapsed, Scrushy owned four mansions, ten boats, a Gulfstream jet, a helicopter, and a bulletproof $135,000 BMW, and played guitar in his own rock band.

In Beverly Hills, a business promoter named Gary Winnick, who had begun the bull market as a junk bond assistant to uber-swindler Mike Milken, now headed a telecommunications company called Global Crossings, Ltd., and by the time Winnick's company collapsed, he was putting the finishing touches on a $90 million Bel Air, California, mansion that was reputed to be the most expensive one-family residence in North America.

* Alas for Dennis and Karen, that was the *other* Aga Khan—the playboy scoundrel Aga Khan—who had arrived in Hollywood at the end of the 1940s and wound up sweeping even Rita Hayworth off her feet. By contrast, the developer of the Cala di Volpe was his ascetic half-brother, Prince Karim Aga Khan IV—about as different a fellow as Abel was from Cain.

market as a whole had topped out in January and been weakening ever since. And that may have been all Kozlowski needed to consider (if indeed he considered anything at all) before deciding to stick the cost of Karen's birthday bash on the shareholders instead of paying for it himself. After all, the idea of having Tyco pick up the tab certainly would have seemed routine by that time anyway.*

Meanwhile—and thanks to the momentum that had developed from the *Barron's* article—opportunities were now multiplying before him in all directions. One of his board member buddies, Frank Walsh, pitched him an idea for an investment in a finance company called CIT Group, Inc. The price was huge—$9.2 billion—by far the biggest deal he had ever considered. And CIT's track record as a lender hadn't been all that great either. But owning a captive finance operation would make Tyco look more like GE (and of course make Dennis look more like Jack Welch), so he went for it. And just to show his gratitude to Walsh for bringing him the deal, he paid him a finder's fee of $20 million.†

And there was more. Dennis was a wheel now, even in New York, so he needed suitable digs if he wanted to throw a party, or just have someone over for drinks. So he signed for a $19.8 million Fifth Avenue co-op, and had Tyco pick up the bill for that too, just as he had the company pay for artwork that he and Karen hung on its walls— like a $5.5 million Renoir for example, and a $3.95 million Monet. Then came the interior decorations and renovations, which ran to another $5.5 million, including a $15,000 umbrella stand in the shape of a poodle, and a $6,000 shower curtain.

---

* Testimony in Kozlowski's New York State trial suggested that initially he had wanted to disguise the event, for accounting purposes, as a "Tyco Electronics Incentive Meeting," and that this was eventually changed to "Chairman's Meeting." *People of the State of New York v. L. Dennis Kozlowski and Mark H. Swartz* (September 2003).

† When a reporter for *Business Week* called for a comment, he said, "Hopefully, we can become the next General Electric," making clear enough what the $9.2 billion expenditure was all about. A year later, Tyco sold the CIT business for barely $2 billion.

And in the middle of all this came an opportunity to upgrade the company's Fifth Avenue offices to something *really* grand. Even better, the new offices were just around the corner—a high-rise looking north across Central Park at No. 9, West 57th Street—and he went for that too.*

In just the last four weeks before leaving for Sardinia, Kozlowski presided over enough such adventures to last a normal CEO six lifetimes. In addition to wrapping up the CIT deal and moving offices, he:

- Completed the $393 million acquisition of a gas mask company,
- Signed a deal to acquire a $1 billion collection of security protection businesses from an Illinois investment group,
- Negotiated a deal to buy a medical products company for $3.2 billion,
- Gave the commencement address at Roger Williams University in Rhode Island,
- Sailed his 134-foot racing sloop, the *Endeavor*, in the waters off Antigua in the British West Indies,
- And married Karen Mayo in Antigua on the deck of the *Endeavor*.

At the end of this frenzied month of May, filled with its onrushing surge of yachts and jets and billion-dollar deals, Dennis and his

---

*For Dennis, the best part of the new office was its location on the building's forty-third floor, which happened to be one floor *above* the international headquarters of the Kohlberg, Kravis and Roberts leveraged buyout fund, widely regarded as the most powerful group of its kind in all of high finance. This drove Dennis wild with delight. "He thought the symbolism was great," explained a colleague who worked with him during the period. "He couldn't get over the fact that every time Henry Kravis looked at the ceiling he'd actually be staring up Dennis' asshole."

wife of one month headed for the airport. Destination: the Hotel Cala di Volpe, four miles south of the village of Porto Cervo on Sardinia's Costa Smeralda.

∿∿∿

It is in the nature of situations such as these for the observer to cringe in anticipation—as when one sees the eighteen-wheeler and the loaded school bus careening down the state highway from opposite directions. Do they see the ice patch at the intersection ahead? It is doubtful. But we do, and it is why we cringe . . . because we know what the drivers do not—that everything is about to change, for all concerned, and forever.

Everyone knew the ice patches were out there. Federal Reserve Board chairman Alan Greenspan had been warning of "irrational exuberance" in the stock market for nearly the whole of the previous four years. But few had heeded his warning that stock prices had risen too far and too fast. Since the summer of 1999, Greenspan had been putting real muscle behind his words, and had raised interest rates six times in a row, and still the band played on.

Bizarre investments began to take on a strange and senseless luster—their arrival heralded in the spring of 1999 by the appearance of a stock bearing the name Channel America Broadcasting, Inc., which streaked across the Wall Street heavens like a digital comet, soaring 1,000 percent in value on investor computer screens in a single day.

Internet chat rooms erupted in excited speculation of further gains to come. Guests went on cable TV talk shows to discuss the stock's bright future as an investment. By the end of its first (and as things turned out, its only) week of trading, more than 70 million shares a day were changing hands, making Channel America one of the most widely traded stocks in America . . . for a week.

Then as abruptly as it had appeared, the stock just vanished, leaving nothing behind to mark Channel America's moment in the sun. In reality, the company had gone out of business more than a decade earlier, and had long since ceased to have offices, employees, products or anything else. All that now existed were its shares, looping through Wall Street like free-floating asteroids—a ghost company in digital space.

Nor were the leaders of even the largest and most prestigious of companies immune from the fever. In Rockefeller Center, the chairman and CEO of Time Warner, Inc., Gerald M. Levin, sold the entire company—one of the largest and most prestigious media conglomerates in the world—to a troubled Internet company called America Online, Inc., that had a history of suspicious accounting and was soon to become the focus of fraud investigations by both the U.S. Department of Justice and the Securities and Exchange Commission.

Across town in New York, Edgar M. Bronfman Jr., the chairman of the Seagram Company liquor and beverages empire—having already invested much of his company's assets in Time Warner, Inc., and much of the rest in the weakest of the major Hollywood movie companies, Universal Studios—now pumped much of what remained into the music business. He then sold the entire grab bag of assets in return for stock in a French company, Vivendi S.A., with its roots in the sewage treatment business.

One thinks of other such moments—other inflection points when men everywhere just tumbled into unreasoning and nutty behavior . . . of Paris in the spring of 1940, perhaps, with the Hun poised at the Rhine, while in the distance you could hear the revelers laughing a bit too loud as they lighted their cigars with 1,000-franc notes. Given the right circumstance, life really can be a cabaret, old chum, come hear the music play.

21

LET'S PARTY LIKE IT'S 1999

Extravagant birthday parties are a great tradition of the moneyed classes, especially among those whose capacity for consumption has developed faster than the sensitivity of their palates.* Yet it is not often that one encounters a more vivid example of what the collective failure of taste and decorum can lead to than the weeklong festivities hosted by Dennis and Karen at the Hotel Cala di Volpe in Sardinia.

The great bull market of the 1980s and 1990s produced many grand genuflections before the altar of one's aging. In the summer of 1989, when financier Saul Steinberg turned fifty, his recently acquired trophy wife, Gayfryd, spent $1 million of her husband's money

---

*Flamboyant weddings are part of many cultures and are characteristic of celebrity-world marriages in Hollywood. The 2000 wedding of Jennifer Aniston and Brad Pitt was reported to cost $1 million, with much of it spent on flowers. The wedding in 2000 of Madonna and film director Guy Ritchie at a rented castle in Scotland was reported to have cost $2.1 million. The November 2000 wedding of actors Michael Douglas and Catherine Zeta-Jones in New York cost a reported $1.5 million.

to throw a birthday party for 250 of their closest friends at the couple's Long Island estate.

Among the intimates were Saul's fellow Wharton alumnus and junk-bond grandee, Ron Perelman, accompanied by his wife of the moment, Claudia. And panning the crowd for familiar faces—or at least recognizable names—one could as well have spotted diminutive leveraged buyout biggie Henry Kravis along with his trophy wife of the period, Carolyne Roehm. Ditto for U.S. Secretary of Commerce Robert Mosbacher, and *his* trophy wife, Georgette.

The party itself, incorporating a theme of seventeenth-century Holland and the world of the Old Masters, featured a custom-built replica of a Flemish farmhouse, complete with ten separate Old Masters "paintings" in which live models moved about inside what looked to be dioramas based on the original paintings. One diorama included a female model posing naked as Rembrandt's *Dana*. Outside, vast stretches of Oriental carpeting covered the lawns, while two nubile twins frolicked as mermaids in the pool. Waiters served beluga whole grain caviar by the bucketful. Dinner was served under an air-conditioned tent the size of a tennis court—the table settings featured treasure chests with pearls spilling out of them.[1]

Three weeks later, this same group of people, plus at least five hundred more, headed for Morocco—now in new roles as among the 750 "closest friends" of publishing magnate Malcolm Forbes. Their mission: to provide trim to Malcolm's efforts to throw a seventieth birthday party for himself that not even Saul Steinberg would be able to match if and when *he* turned seventy.

Like the Steinberg affair, Malcolm's three-day desert do came wrapped in the garb of "entertainment" for the guests, though its real purpose was to burnish the *Forbes* brand-name while helping the proprietor move up another rung or two on the ladder of renown. Understanding that the more money he spent, the more attention he'd get, Malcolm *doubled* the Steinberg outlay, thereby instantly raising the price of a ticket to the world of the hyper-party to a full $2 million. In doing so, Malcolm cleverly managed to turn Steinberg's $1 million in effect into part of the promotional budget for Malcolm's own party, reducing the entire Steinberg affair, and all its attendant publicity, to little more than a warm-up act for the Forbes celebration.

And of course, Malcolm also knew that the more big-name people he could get to accept invitations, the more the press would want to cover the party, creating yet more buzz about the event, which would bring in yet more big-name acceptances. In this way, he succeeded in turning the party into an actual news event, with the Associated Press distributing a list of "accepted invitations" on the AP national wire on the eve of the party.*

The celebrations featured fireworks, bus rides to various sights, 250 galloping Moroccan horsemen, 830 roasted chickens, 150 cooks—and under the starry, starry night, Metropolitan Opera star Beverly Sills singing *Happy Birthday Dear Malcolm*. It was a setting that was certainly more exotic, though in other respects not very much different, from the circumstances under which Al Dunlap had arranged things to receive similar sentiments from his own group of snickering "best friends" nearly fifteen years earlier at Nitec Paper Company in Niagara Falls, New York.

What distinguished Dennis and Karen's efforts from the foregoing—aside from the fact that the Kozlowski effort was paid for with shareholder money and the other extravaganzas were private affairs—was certainly not the scale of the undertaking, which as

---

*Among those who showed up: Betsy Bloomingdale, William F. Buckley Jr., Walter Cronkite, Oscar de la Renta, Doris Duke, James Goldsmith, Katherine Graham, John Gutfreund, Lee Iacocca, Henry Kissinger, Calvin Klein, John Kluge, Rupert Murdoch, Regis Philbin, Joan Rivers, Elizabeth Taylor, Barbara Walters, and of course Ron Perelman.

these things go was almost intimate, with barely seventy-five revelers finally making an appearance. Nor was the cost of the affair especially notable one way or the other. At a total price of $2 million, the party was not much more expensive, when adjusted for inflation, than the cost of Steinberg's $1 million bash twelve years earlier. And it certainly looked like a bargain when compared with the Forbes party.

What distinguished Dennis and Karen's effort—in fact, what set it apart from almost any arriviste lunge for social acceptance one might think of—was the utter earnestness of the effort . . . and the unalloyed completeness of the resulting failure. One thinks of the little boy called Alfalfa in the old *Our Gang* comedies, singing desperately to his true love, Darla.

There he stands (or sits, or sometimes kneels) before her, his hands clutched together and pressed against his bosom. The hands might be holding a wilted flower, a token of his love. The coat is four sizes too small, and the pants are ready for high-water wading. From the top of his head sticks his lard-slicked cowlick. He is a mess. Yet all he knows is his desperation and his need and his hunger for Darla's love. So he cannot even begin to imagine what he sounds like as he sings of his love for her—more shrill and off-key with each note—nor understanding the grimaced and pained expression that begins to spread across her face as he continues. And knowing nothing else to do, he sings louder, and the pained look in Darla's eyes grows more intense and even frightened. Finally, the dog at her feet, Pete, puts a paw over one ear and begins to howl . . . at which point she clasps her hands to her ears and shrieks "Alfalfa, Alfalfa, will you please shut up!"

That is what set Dennis and Karen's Sardinian soireé apart from all the others: the painful earnestness of the entire off-key experience, inflicted on the rest of humankind because a videotape of the affair managed two years later to come into the possession of New York prosecutors in the Kozlowski case. From their outstretched hands, it next moved smoothly and swiftly onto the evening news at nearly every television station in America.

Some of the scenes on the tape were pronounced by the judge in the case, New York State Supreme Court Judge Michael Obus, to be so prejudicial to a fair trial for Kozlowski that they were edited out and never seen by the jury or the public.[2] Among other attractions, for example, the party featured a life-size copy, rendered in ice, of Michelangelo's marble statute of David. A videotaped scene of giggling women at the party filling their glasses with chilled vodka that poured in a stream from the ice sculpture's penis was one such moment that the judge ordered snipped.

Another involved Karen's birthday cake, which had been baked in the shape of a nude female. When the cake was brought out to be cut and served—with Fourth of July sparklers twinkling from its nipples—the breasts themselves exploded. That too was excised from the videotape by the judge, as was a scene of an apparently intoxicated reveler dropping his pants and mooning the camera. Yet, another scene, in which Karen was shown being carried around overhead by two Italian male models in Speedo bathing suits, also hit the cutting-room floor.

Learning all this, we are struck not so much by the shock value of such moments, which is minimal, as by the banality of the whole affair. Having transported themselves to the frontiers of licentiousness, clutching $2 million in mad money and a license to blaze, the resulting failure of the imagination seems astounding. Was this the best they could do—exploding tits and a statue that peed booze out the whizzer? They could have stayed home and watched Tom Cruise have a better party all by himself in *Risky Business*—in particular the part where his parents go away for the weekend and he strips down to his skivvies and socks, pours himself a glass of gin, and starts dancing around the living room to an old Bob Seeger tune. For isn't that what this $2 million effort at a week's worth of full-bore karaoke was all about? Today's music don't have the same soul? Then give 'em some old time rock and roll.

We are struck as well by the marked absence of recognizable names on the guest list, which followed the route of the videotape from the prosecutors to the public. On this list, we find no celebrities. No actors, no sports figures, not even anyone from cable television. Nor are there recognizable names from the worlds of business or Wall Street.

Who's on the list? Well, there's a fellow named James Bartle. He's Tyco's corporate chef. And a fellow named Nelson Cantave. He's the company's personal trainer. And a man named Peter Carrie (a personal friend of the happy couple). And Joel and Paula Curcio (ditto). There's Bob and Debbie DeCostas (more personal friends) and Gary Fagin (the company physician). There's Sparky Kania (a member of the *Endeavor* sailboat's crew) and Nancy Maley (an employee of Tyco's travel agency). And, of course, Woody and Hal Mayo (they would be Karen's parents).

It just went on and on like that until one reached the bottom of the list. Save for a couple of directors, and Tyco's corporate treasurer, and one or two others, that was it. For Dennis's parade into business world immortality, he had lined the boulevard with . . . Debbie and Sparky and Gary and Paula and Nelson and Pete . . . with the company doc and the company cook and the company gym coach and the crew of the boat. The guests arrived for the most part on the afternoon of Sunday, June 10.[3] A reception buffet was waiting, followed by a dinner at 8 o'clock. The next day, Monday, featured . . . well, basically, nothing. It was sort of like free period at camp. You could eat, or swim, or sleep . . . or sleep, or eat, or swim. Tuesday was the same, except that dinner featured the presentation to Dennis and Karen of a large ceramic platter, signed by everyone and thanking them for such a nice time. On Wednesday, there was a scavenger hunt, followed by another eat-swim-sleep cycle, with Thursday blocked out to rest up from Wednesday and prepare for Thursday evening, which was the main event—namely Karen's birthday party. On Friday everybody rested up from Thursday, and on Saturday they all went home.

The birthday party on Thursday evening was held at the resort's golf course clubhouse where—Sardinia being part of Italy, which, of course, was once part of ancient Rome—the clubhouse had been decorated in what Barbara Jacques described during her trial testimony as "a Roman theme."

To that end, some local models—both male and female—had been hired and dressed up in toga-type affairs. The males—mostly dressed in Speedo bathing suits and nothing else—walked around flexing their shaved and oiled pecs at the ladies. The females—dressed in more, but not a whole lot—tried to look demure while going as much as possible for arched-back poses that helped with the front cleavage.

After this came "the music." But it brought with it such a jolting hiccup in the theme of Roman bacchanalia as to make one grab the arm-rails of one's chair, as if watching George Washington lead his men across the Delaware not in the bow of the first boat, but from a speeding Windsurfer.

That is because, on this Night of a Thousand Muscles, the music invited no thoughts of gladiatorial combat, nor even the distant encores of La Scala. There were to be no arias from Puccini on this birthday to end all birthdays, nor even a soundtrack from Fellini.

No, for the finale to end all finales in this grand opera of the imagination, the revelers were to get what really turned on Dennis and Karen more than anything else—right there onstage, live before their eyes in exotic Hotel Cala di Volpe Sardinia—forty-five minutes of the master himself . . . the man who'd gone double-platinum more times than Dolly Parton's hair . . . who'd blown through more flip-flops, and stepped on more pop-tops . . . Unhuh, that's right . . . it's him . . . (Hey, are you still lookin' for that shaker of salt, James?) . . . Jimmy [the music is coming up now] Buffett!

From Barbara Jacques' testimony at the trial one may begin to tease forth how all this happened—how the secret, and apparently conflicting fantasies that Dennis and Karen held as to what adulthood would be like, got resolved into this monstrosity of a birthday party.

The picture is incomplete, but it is a start. And without at least something, we are lost. How else do we get from "birthday-bash-as-Roman-orgy," to its accompanying musical subtext of Jimmy Buffett on his six-string?* The answer is, we don't.

We begin as we must, with the models, watching with our host's intended sense of awe as they walk around in Hollywood versions of Roman togas, circa 1960. The togas are cut high on the thigh and slit becomingly on the side, and one of the models even looks a bit like Victor Mature. Cue the chariots out by the putting green and it would not be surprising to see Judah Ben Hur gallop past, whipping his steed and looking strangely like Charlton Heston.

But what is it with the music! On one level we're watching a Russ Meyer remake of *Spartacus*, and we can go with that. But below the soft porn visuals we hear this, live through the Dolby speakers, from the man himself:†

---

*Buffett was flown to Sardinia and brought to the hotel under the pseudonym of "Elvis Smith," ostensibly to prevent throngs of autograph seekers. It seems just as likely that the real reason was his reluctance to be publicly identified with the affair, which simply did not have a quality caché, even from the start.

†Buffett was popular with other CEO rock and rollers besides the guitar-playing Kozlowski, and was a particular favorite of Ron Perelman, who fancied himself a drummer. In March 1995, Patricia Duff organized a dinner at the Perelman home in Palm Beach for President Bill Clinton, and Buffett attended, leading the group after dinner in a chorus of *Margaritaville*. See E. Bumiller, "700 Days in Society and Politics: Fundraiser Wed to Billionaire Finds Roles Clash," *New York Times* (November 3, 1996), p. 41. For his appearance at Kozlowski's Sardinian bash, Buffett received $250,000 for performing a single, forty-five-minute set of Jimmy Buffett favorites. Buffett's imputed fee of $5,555.00 per minute was cheap compared with what the parents of Perelman's second wife, Claudia Cohen, paid for ten minutes worth of singing by the Pointer Sisters at the couple's

Nibblin' on sponge cake
Watchin' the sun bake

This is like a question in the Stanford-Binet IQ test, in which the sixth-grade student is shown the series of three frames—one containing a drawing of a hammer, the next a drawing of a nail, and the third a drawing of something that looks like it might be a slice of chocolate cake. The student is then asked, "Okay, Skip, which of these doesn't belong?"

That's the problem: We can have ourselves a Roman orgy. And we can also have a bender in Margaritaville. But we cannot have half-naked Roman slaves blowing out their flip-flops, stepping on pop-tops, then shaking their booties at the tourists and hurrying home.

Where was this coming from? The Roman orgy bit was a slam dunk, as any of the guests who arrived on the morning of the first day could see readily enough. There to greet them at the hotel entrance stood Dennis, beaming ear to ear with a female toga-babe draped on each arm.

But what about the jarring sense of time-travel from the visuals to the music? How does one get from Pliny the Elder all the way to six strings and porch swings? Where did *that* come from?

From the trial testimony of Barbara Jacques, who actually organized a lot of what transpired, it would appear that it came from the birthday girl herself. Karen, it seems, had been kind of hoping for a "beach party" sort of theme . . . so much so, that Barbara went out and found a group of boys who "sounded like the Beach Boys" and sent them down to the beach to play during the noon hour on Tuesday. Meanwhile, explained Barbara, Dennis had long since told her to

wedding reception: $8,000.00 per minute. See G. Grig, "Lipstick on His Dollars," *New York Times* (September 26, 1993). For the fact that Claudia Cohen's parents picked up the tab, see Richard Hack, *When Money Is King* (Los Angeles, CA: Dove Books, 1996), p. 43.

book Jimmy Buffett for the party and keep it as a surprise for Karen because, apparently, she adored him too, just like Dennis did.

〰〰〰

A day later and it was over; the $2 million was gone; and by Saturday morning, Sardinia was but a memory. Karen and a dozen of her friends left on the Tyco jet for Florence and some cooking classes at Cucina al Focolare, and by the end of the month, she and Dennis were back in New York, stocking up on Monets, Renoirs, Cézannes, and whatnot—all on the Tyco tab—to distribute around the apartment on Fifth Avenue and in the house in Palm Beach.

But one senses an unreality about all this: the $1.2 million gift to the Christopher Reeve Paralysis Foundation . . . the photo ops with Karen and her million-dollar Palm Beach tan . . . the speeches at the Waldorf. There was something wrong with it all.

For one thing, the CIT group acquisition hadn't turned out to be another Dennis Kozlowski masterstroke at all. The deal was actually proving to be an out-and-out fiasco, and it was starting to drag down the stock. Then came a problem with the board member who had promoted it to him: Frank Walsh. Dennis had paid him that $20 million finder's fee but, yikes, he'd never cleared it with the board.

Then came something even worse: Some paintings that Tyco had bought for the Fifth Avenue apartment had been invoiced as if they had been shipped instead to Tyco's offices in New Hampshire. Before anyone knew it, prosecutors in the office of Manhattan District Attorney Robert Morgenthau had opened a tax fraud investigation. In May 2002, Kozlowski was charged with evading more than $1 million worth of New York State sales taxes, and it was only the beginning—though for Dennis Kozlowski, it was already the end.

In September 2002, Kozlowski was charged with having looted more than $600 million from Tyco and its shareholders since 1995 alone. In October 2003, his trial on the charges began in a New York

State court, and lasted six months before being sent to the jury in March 2004. No verdict had been reached by the time this book went to press.

Meanwhile, new management had been installed at Tyco, the board of directors had been replaced, and the company had closed its New York office and moved to New Jersey. From there, Tyco filed its own $600 million civil fraud suit against their one-time boss, thus ending, in the twilight of his career, any hope that Dennis may have had for dislodging Jack Welch from his throne as the King of American business.

22

THAT PESKY NECK WADDLE

Toward the end of the 1990s, Jack Welch began to acquire an almost mythical aura inside GE. Executives spoke of him in hushed tones, as if the mere mention of his name might somehow be perceived as a sacrilege. He had served as chairman and CEO longer than anyone in the company's history* and the relentlessly rising price of GE's stock seemed to confirm that he was a special leader for a special time.

As the chorus of Welch's acclaim grew louder, his own self-regard increased accordingly. His appearances before audiences took on a stage-managed aura, as if he were a Hollywood celebrity or global political leader. He became a frequent guest host on the GE-owned CNBC cable TV financial talk show, "Squawk Box," where he seemed ready to sound off on any topic. During Six Sigma sessions at the

---

*As with many of Welch's achievements, there's an asterisk on this one. The actual record holder for longest-serving corporate leader at GE was Charles Coffin, who by general agreement built the modern GE that survived intact through the whole of the twentieth century. But Coffin never held the title of CEO, serving instead as president for 20 years, from 1892 to 1912, then as chairman of the board from 1913 to 1922.

company's Crotonville campus, he would hog the stage for hours, fielding questions from the audience, then forcing his answers through his own personal life experience to discover the question's deeper meaning. In one biography, the author speculated that if Hollywood were to make a movie of Welch's life story, the lead role would have to be played by adorable tough guy actor, Robert Duval.[1]

Welch as well began to eye himself through fame's mirror. A cosmetician was hired by GE to camouflage his bald spot by painting filament-fine *tromp d'oeil* hair follicles onto his scalp before TV appearances. He had his smile improved. And he would look disapprovingly at his sagging jowls and turkey-like neck waddle in the mirror and say to Jane, "I've got to do something about this."*

Exactly when it was that Jack began to think of himself as irreplaceable and thus priceless may never be known, though by the late 1990s the evidence that he was coming to such a view was beginning to pile up.

Between the start of his career at GE in 1960 and his mid-1995 heart attacks, Welch had managed to accumulate a total of 2.76 million shares of GE common stock, deferred compensation, and options and rights of various sorts. Altogether, these holdings had a market value of roughly $142 million. Their worth to Welch was considerably less than that because the options and rights, which accounted for 85 percent of the portfolio, carried exercise prices that diminished their value.[†] Nonetheless, he was still one of the richest men in America, with no obvious reason to want anymore.

---

*The subject of Jack's neck waddle surfaced during his divorce from Jane Beasley Welch when Jane confided to a friend that Jack was obsessed with the sagging, gizzard-like skin under his chin, and wanted to have cosmetic surgery to remove it. But, according to Jane, Jack's doctors felt such an operation would be life-threatening given the postcoronary condition of his heart.

†For example, according to GE's 1996 proxy filing with the U.S. Securities and Exchange Commission, Welch was issued 320,000 so-called Stock Appreciation Rights

Yet, this was now the 1990s, and the Great Bull Market had already vaulted the whole concept of wealth to a new level, encouraging CEOs to rethink the rationales for what their labors were worth as well.* When Welch took over as chairman and CEO in 1981, the most highly paid CEO in America was Warner Communications Inc.'s Steven Ross, who pocketed what seemed an utterly unimaginable $22.5 million in 1981 via a one-time gain from exercising stock rights during the year. By 1995, a half-dozen different CEOs were routinely pocketing twice that much—not just in one-time gains but year after year as their base compensation for simply being the boss.†

In 1995, Welch was not yet among them—and half way through the year he was sidelined with his heart problems in any case. But when he returned, he began playing catch-up in a big way. During the following five years, his total stock holdings soared nearly tenfold over what he had accumulated during the previous thirty-six,

---

(SARs) in 1995 at an exercise price of $51 per share. Half the rights were exercisable in 1997 and the other half in 1999. But these SARs were valuable to Welch only if the underlying GE stock that they represented rose in value above $51, and their worth to Welch was only the appreciation above that $51 exercise price. Had Welch thus exercised those rights on the day he left the company, he would have acquired stock worth roughly $86 million, but he would have had to pay approximately $16.5 million to exercise the rights, so his net gain would have been about $69.5 million.

*CEOs everywhere were stunned when a Connecticut court ruled that Lorna Wendt was entitled to 50 percent of her husband's accumulated net worth from his days of working at GE Capital. But by the 1990s, the same CEOs were using the same "percentage of the whole" theories to justify their own compensation deals with the companies they ran. When applied to the soaring stock market values of multibillion-dollar companies, even a fraction of a percent of an appreciating market value could result in compensation deals worth $100 million or more annually.

†The magnitude of the shift in wealth from employees to top management during the Great Bull Market is astounding. According to data compiled by the Institute for Policy Research in Washington, D.C., the average annual income of all CEOs of the companies in the Standard & Poor 500 Index was 42 times that of the average for the companies' employees in 1982. Twenty years later in 2002, the average of the same Index of CEOs had widened to 411 times that of the same Index group of employees. See A. Elstein, "Chief Executives' Pay," in Crain's New York Business (June 16, 2003), p. 29.

eventually reaching more than 21 million shares having a combined market value, at the start of his last year in office, of roughly $1.2 billion. Each annual proxy statement of the board of directors justified the largesse by pointing to the rising value of GE's stock as the "key" reason to be awarding Welch such sums.*

Along the way, Welch also got the GE board of directors to agree to give him an actual employment and retirement contract, which he had not had before.† The contract gave him a postretirement lifetime

---

* Basing CEO compensation on a company's rising stock value became a widely accepted enrichment scheme for CEOs in the Great Bull Market, though the method rewards CEOs for something they did not control (the behavior of the stock market), and was hugely unfair to all other stockholders in the companies themselves since the CEOs were never required to give the money back when the price of the shares went back down. Thus, from 1994 through 2001, each GE proxy statement specifically cited GE's increasing market value, caused by the rising price of its stock, as the "key judgment" of the GE Board of Directors Compensation Committee in awarding Welch annual compensation largesse that eventually made him a billionaire. Yet in the last 12 months of his tenure as chairman and CEO (September 8, 2000, to September 7, 2001), GE's stock price fell by 33 percent, wiping out a third of all the market value gains he had been rewarded for bringing about during the previous 20 years. Yet instead of giving back one-third of his accumulated compensation, Welch departed with yet another $16 million, in cash, for his 9 months of employment during 2001, as well as with all his accumulated options, rights, deferred compensation, and other such benefits.

† This retirement package became a major sticking point in Welch's divorce fight with Jane Beasley Welch. Though the contract had been routinely included as an exhibit in GE's annual SEC Form 10K filings every year since it was signed, the language was general and the press hadn't bothered to focus on the specifics of what GE was obligated to provide him under it. But when Jane produced a financial statement detailing the GE payments, and her representatives pointed it out to reporters in the middle of the divorce fight, the press was dumbstruck. As set forth in the statement, GE had been routinely underwriting tens of millions of dollars yearly in personal expenses for the couple. When public outrage thereafter erupted over the lavishness of the package, Welch wrote an exculpatory letter to the editor of the Wall Street Journal (September 16, 2002), p. A14, in which he tried to claim that his retirement package had been, in effect, forced on him by GE's board of directors. Welch argued that although he had no intention of retiring before the age of 65, the board was worried anyway and offered him an ultra-lucrative retirement deal if he promised not to step down early. Rather than simply turn down the offer, Welch wrote that he worked out a modified version of it that was less costly for GE than what the board had been offering him—an explanation in which Welch in effect blamed the board for pushing money at him that he had already just said he didn't want

consulting deal, at a per diem rate prorated from his salary in 1999. It also granted him unhindered lifetime access to any and all company facilities and services he currently made use of, including GE's fleet of corporate aircraft and corporate apartments.*

But there was more, because Jack's job as GE's chairman and CEO required him to be, in effect, on call and on-the-job virtually around the clock. And GE thus had to pay for the infrastructure—from transportation to communications, from security systems to computer networks—that made this possible.

As Welch's own lifestyle grew ever more impressive and sumptuous, these systems, networks, and support structures grew steadily more extensive and lavish, penetrating deeper and deeper into the diminishing space of his personal life. In the process, they began to take on characteristics of a kind of shadow support system for his personal life itself. And given the way in which Jack's retirement deal had been structured, these outlays too seemed likely to continue uninterrupted for the remainder of his life.†

---

and that wasn't necessary to encourage him to stay on as chairman and CEO, ducking the obvious question of why he thought he was doing anyone but himself a favor by agreeing to take "some" of the money instead of none at all. In the end he surrendered some of the package.

*One reason GE's board of directors was willing to approve Welch's requests was undoubtedly the ultra-lucrative compensation and perks they received for serving as board members. All outside members received base pay of $75,000 annually, plus $2,000 for each board meeting they attended, as well as a retirement plan. In addition, each received 6,000 GE stock options annually, plus, incredibly enough, the right to purchase unlimited amounts of diamonds, at cost, from a GE-owned diamond business. In Welch's last year as chairman, his board members purchased $975,000 of such diamonds from the company. See General Electric Def. Proxy 14A, filed with U.S. Securities and Exchange Commission March 9, 2001, for details.

†According to Jane Welch's financial statement, filed in court as part of Jack and Jane's 2002 divorce case, these corporate outlays were running at $291,667 per month in corporate jet transportation alone. In addition, GE was supplying the couple, free of charge, with state-of-the art GE home appliances, electronics equipment, office supplies, emergency power generators, security systems, gates, walls, and other perimeter

Meanwhile, Welch's professional life had acquired the scope and organizational challenges one might normally associate with the head of state of an economic superpower, which in some sense he actually was. His schedule was now regularly blocked out months in advance. There were golf games with the president of the United States, dinners with the president of the People's Republic of China, and processional visits through Spain and India. Of the 252 calendar workdays of 1998, fully 166 of them involved speaking engagements or appearances for Welch that had been booked as much as a year ahead of time. That left barely a day and a half each week that hadn't already been spoken for.[2]

In this world of grand and scripted gestures, it is doubtful that Welch was more than only dimly aware that the unauthorized biography of him begun six years earlier by the *Wall Street Journal* reporter named Thomas O'Boyle, who had covered GE for much the 1990s, had at last reached bookstores. If anything, Welch would have taken satisfaction in the mixed reviews the book received, and in the dismissive and impatient tone expressed by those who had criticized it. A writer for the *Boston Globe* dismissed the book, entitled, *At*

---

defenses in all six of the Welch family homes. The company was also supplying all the couple's car phones and associated charges, all their satellite connections, all their limousine services, all their computers and Internet connections, all their telephone connections, equipment and charges, all their entertaining expenses, and was picking up every dime spent on an $8 million company-supplied apartment for the couple's exclusive use in the Trump International Hotel on Columbus Circle in Manhattan. In addition, GE was picking up "partial" costs on a broad array of the couple's other expenses, ranging from landscaping and property maintenance on all their various residences and automobiles, to the cost of the GE light bulbs illuminating the interiors and exteriors of each of the homes. (In the spring of 2002, *Talk* magazine editor Tina Brown quoted Welch in a column as saying that he enjoyed standing at the window of his apartment high above Central Park and gazing across the skyline of Manhattan, while thinking to himself, "I've got New York by the ass." See T. Brown, "The Dish on Liz Smith," *Salon.com* [February 6, 2003]. In fact, the vista was not his to begin with but GE's, and it soon enough became clear who had whom by what body part in any case, when Welch's estranged wife, Jane, successfully forced him, as part of their divorce settlement, to buy the apartment from GE for $11 million and then give it to her.)

Any Cost: Jack Welch, General Electric, and the Pursuit of Profit, as not merely "one-sided" and a "hatchet job," but as an out-and-out "ax murder." Most reviewers simply ignored it, which for Welch was surely the greatest satisfaction of all.*

In San Francisco, however, one reader had exactly the opposite reaction. As far as Robert Kunze was concerned, O'Boyle's book not only was fair and accurate but didn't go far enough to paint a complete picture of what it had been like to work with Jack Welch when he had been a fast-rising young executive in GE's Plastics Division. And Kunze was in a pretty good position to judge, since he had begun his own career at the same time Welch had—in 1960—and at the same company, GE, and at the same Plastics Division facility in Pittsfield. And from that perch he had been recruited by Welch to help run the Noryl plastics startup operation in Selkirk.

Not a lot had been heard from Bob Kunze after he left Selkirk for GE International at the end of the sixties, then left GE entirely in 1974, at just around the time his former secretary in Selkirk—Regina Paulsen—had killed herself.

Eventually, Kunze moved from engineering to investment banking and became a partner in the Silicon Valley venture capital

---

*The criticisms were grossly unfair to what was a carefully researched and well-argued critique of Welch's career at GE. Many of the incidents, scenes, and anecdotes one finds in Welch's autobiography, *Jack: Straight from the Gut* (New York: Warner Books), which was published in the autumn of 2001, actually appeared three years earlier—and more vividly drawn—in O'Boyle's book. See, for example, pp. 24–25 of the hardcover edition of Welch's autobiography, in which his one-time boss in GE Plastics, Reuben Gutoff, tries to persuade Welch not to resign, and at one point even telephones him from a highway pay phone to continue to make his case. Compare that to p. 58 of O'Boyle's book, published three years earlier, where the same exact incident is set forth, including the pay phone call from Gutoff to Welch. The scene was clearly important to the direction of Welch's career at GE, and Welch certainly had every right to include it in his autobiography—especially since he himself was part of the scene. But in one incident after the next, O'Boyle set forth Welch's life before Welch himself did, offering a different and more critical view of the same anecdotes, incidents, and research materials Welch and his co-author themselves used. Yet, O'Boyle was either criticized or simply ignored whereas Welch was praised.

firm of Hambrecht & Quist, joining the boards of Ridge Computers, Inc., Calgene, Inc., VISIC, Inc., and several others.

But Kunze harbored a desire to write, and after marrying a literary agent named Betsy Nolan in 1989, he published a book of his experiences in investment banking. He called his effort *Nothing Ventured:
The Perils and Payoffs of the Great American Venture Capital Game*, and it was
well-received by reviewers.

Yet even that failed to scratch Kunze's writer's itch, for he still
had a story to tell from an earlier time. And by-and-by a manuscript
took shape—of what he remembered of the world back East so
many years ago, when his secretary Regina had been the easy girl at
the drive-in for the men of Becker House, and they had used her for
their sport.

Kunze changed the names of the colleagues he'd worked with,
and the name of the company they'd all worked for as well. But in
time, there had emerged from Kunze's hand—under the *nom de plume*
of Wesley Harwich—a *roman à clef* that bore the working title *In the
Hunt*. It was Bob's portrait, as he recalled it four decades later, of life
with Jack Welch.

In the book, Kunze appeared as a young executive named Bob
Nolan, and to the man he remembered as Jack Welch he gave the
name Ralph Barnes. And he chose to introduce readers to their
lives together with an unforgettable scene—the first day on the
job for the two young executive trainees—when suddenly and
shockingly an older man walking down the hallway keels over with
a coronary.

Paralyzed with indecision, Nolan watches from his office, not
knowing what to do, when the new man in the next office, Ralph
Barnes, charges into the hallway, rolls the man over on his back, and
begins to administer mouth-to-mouth resuscitation. Minutes pass in
this way, with no sound but the breathing of Barnes trying desperately to revive this man whose name he doesn't even know.

Whether such an incident occurred in real-life isn't known. But it certainly seems to capture one of the most dynamic aspects of Welch himself—someone able to size up a situation quickly, seize control, and act decisively . . . the man who could, and did, grab the moment and challenge fate.

Yet what happened next was also Jack Welch—heartless, glib, and cynical in the extreme. Nolan watches as Barnes realizes at last that the man cannot be revived and is actually dead, then stands up, brushes his hands off, and says to no one in particular, "Well, he's no good to the company now . . ." and walks back in his office without so much as a second thought.

Of such moments did Kunze tell his tale of life "in the hunt." There were scenes in his novel of doctored lab tests for a new kind of plastic, of huddled and whispered antitrust conspiracies at 30,000-feet in corporate jets over international waters, and on and on. But no scene was more vivid, or more shocking, than the noon hour tableau when Bob Nolan left his office on an errand, at which point an executive from down the hall came in, closed the door, un- zipped his fly, and proceeded to present himself for an oral servicing from Nolan's secretary . . . in the middle of which the office door swung open and who should walk in but the Ralph Barnes character, after which he too joined the regular noontime parade through Nolan's office for secretarial servicings.

How troubled a person was Kunze's real-life secretary, Regina Paulsen? It is obviously too late to ask now because she's been dead for thirty years. And her husband, John—who once pulled her out of a late-night scene around the juke box at the Feura Bush Tavern after a bunch of the boys from Becker House had taken her there to get her liquored up for some fun—can't be of much help either since he died of heart failure not long after his wife killed herself.

On the evidence, none of the executives of Becker House seemed willing even to acknowledge what had happened, let alone accept any responsibility for their own contributory role in her suicide. Not only did GE send no flowers or even condolences to the Paulsen family at the funeral, but the "In Memorium" booklet for Regina's memorial service at the Caswell Funeral Home in Ravena, New York, doesn't contain the name of a single known male GE employee. For better or for worse, Regina had been dropped down the corporate memory hole, and when GE was asked, thirty years later, to provide the dates of Regina's employment, a company spokesman declined to acknowledge that she had even been an employee, citing a company policy against disclosure of such information.

So, whatever may have been his motivation for doing so, no sooner did Kunze read the negative review of O'Boyle's book than he picked up the phone, located O'Boyle's telephone number, and rang him up. When O'Boyle came on the line, Kunze introduced himself, and acknowledging that what he had to reveal might well be of nothing more than academic interest since O'Boyle's book had by now been published, he said, "Mr. O'Boyle, there's more to this situation than you know."*

~~~

On November 1, 1999—the same day that *Fortune* proclaimed him "manager of the century"—Jack Welch announced his intention to retire as chairman of GE in April 2001. Whether Jane had been pressuring him to do so isn't known, but as subsequent events would show, he plainly hadn't wanted to retire, and the announcement had an almost grudging, by-the-way feel about it. Moreover, when an opportunity came up to backpedal on the promise, he lunged for it.

---

*Kunze gave his *In the Hunt* manuscript to O'Boyle to critique, which O'Boyle did, writing a positive short review of it, at Kunze's request, after Kunze explained that he wanted to have it published. Now living in retirement in Australia, Kunze declined several requests to be interviewed for this book.

Meanwhile, he and Jane were now seen less and less frequently together in public, and though neither had yet said anything about it even to their friends, the strains that had been present from the very start of their decade-old marriage had by now opened into an unbridgeable gulf. He didn't like her and she didn't like him, at least anymore, and the less time the two spent together, the better they seemed to like it.

In his autobiography, Jack wrote effusively about what he seemed to regard as Jane's premier quality as a wife and a human being—her talents at golf—which he seemed to think existed principally to help him improve his own game. But those who really knew the truth of the matter—the couple's golfing friends in Connecticut—say Jack and Jane almost never played together, and toward the end were almost never even seen together at their club.

There are many possible reasons to mark 1999 as the beginning of the end for the marriage of Jack and Jane Welch. One could point, for example, to the accumulating strains Jack's job was placing on the relationship. After all, here was a man who had survived two back-to-back coronaries and an angioplasty and quadruple bypass, all within the space of two weeks just four years earlier. Then barely one year later, he found himself in the middle of a murder mystery involving his own wife's father—a situation he wanted no part of and didn't want her to be involved in either.

Though a couple with a deeper understanding of each other's needs might have been able to overcome the stresses created by such a situation, in Jack and Jane's case the problems festered and grew. So it is perhaps not surprising that we detect a subtext of testiness beginning to creep into Jack's autobiography at around this time when the subject of Jane comes up—as each becomes less a human being to the other than a reminder of earlier hurts.

And there is the suggestion as well at about this point, at least from Jane's point of view, that 1999 wasn't so much the beginning of the end as the end itself. It was, after all, at this very point, in the spring of 1999, that Jack and Jane Welch's ten-year prenuptial financial agreement expired, barely a year after the courtroom victory of Lorna Wendt in her divorce from Gary had rocked the whole of the matrimonial bar with the news that, at least in Connecticut, a wife could claim half the estate of her husband no matter how many millions of dollars were involved.

Had Jane been biding her time in the slow lane until the detested prenup expired? She has said nothing on the matter in public and declined repeated requests for interviews for this book. Yet a confidante to Jane during her divorce negotiations with Jack says that the couple's marriage had been in trouble "for years" before any evidence surfaced publicly.

Moreover, when Jack's legal team began filing document production orders to acquire proof of what Jack believed to be his wife's infidelities during trips to Europe, the orders sought any and all records of e-mails, phone calls, and similar types of communications, beginning January 1, 2000—suggesting that Welch had only belatedly realized how badly he'd taken his eye off the ball in the most important "management" issue he actually faced: his relationship with his wife. For whatever reason, he appears to have failed to notice the expiration of his ten-year prenuptial agreement, or to realize what a danger that meant now that his wife had quit his fan club. For all practical purposes, it amounted to behavior no different than turning half his net worth into unmarked $20 bills and leaving them piled up in the parking lot at Kennedy Airport.

In many ways, the winter of 1999/2000 was the season of Jack Welch's ultimate glory—that final career-capping moment at century's end when his every decision was judged to be the right one, and his every utterance was deemed to be profound. In January 2000 the Dow Industrial Average topped out at its all-time high of

11,908 then keeled over and began a two-year-long slide that wiped out nearly half its value. But GE's stock price kept right on climbing, month after month, into the following summer.

Even GE's launch in March 2000, of the so-called "Xtreme football league" on NBC television brought applause—for no other apparent reason than Welch was thought to be behind the idea. The programming, jointly backed by NBC and the World Wrestling Federation, started off slow and went downhill from there, drawing neither sponsors nor viewers, and was abandoned in less than a season. But through it all, GE's stock continued to rise.

But by August, the ride was over. Since January, the Dow Industrials had lost 1,100 points, and inexplicably, GE had risen another 25 percent instead, which was as far as it got. By the time Wall Streeters returned to work from their Labor Day weekend, the stock had topped out.

What caused the sell-off that thereupon ensued? From Wall Street came the answer—at least expedient if not insightful: A full year after Welch had said he would step down in April 2001, Wall Street rose as a chorus of one to explain GE's sagging stock price as evidence that Jack Welch was simply irreplaceable. "Who will replace retiring CEO Jack Welch," asked GE's captive cable TV network, CNBC. Après Jack Welch, le déluge, warned the *Providence Journal*. To the *Boston Globe*, the real question for Americans was not who would be the next president of the United States, but who would succeed Jack Welch at GE.

In October, Welch made what appears in retrospect to have been one last effort to postpone the inevitable, hustling up a bid to acquire Honeywell Corporation after rumors began to circulate that United Technologies was about to unfurl its own bid for the company. Nine months earlier, GE had looked at the possibility of buying Honeywell and deemed it too expensive at $60 per share. But since then, the stock had slipped to the mid-30s, and with United Technologies now apparently pursuing it, Welch decided that GE just absolutely, positively had to have it.

In his autobiography, Welch offers a drama-filled account of urgent meetings of GE's top brass, culminating in the enthusiastic thumbs-up support of his colleagues. But set against the backdrop of earlier and similarly impulsive gestures, such as the ill-fated acquisition of Kidder Peabody & Company, the eleventh-hour rush to grab Honeywell looks to have been powered by a familiar fuel: the ego of Jack Welch. Though the deal was buttressed by all the charts, graphs, and spreadsheets generated during GE's first look at acquiring Honeywell, the possibility of a deeper and more urgent motivation can be found tucked away in two telltale sentences toward the back of his autobiography: "I had planned to leave on April 30, 2001, five months after my sixty-fifth birthday. If we did the deal, I'd have to stay a little longer to see it through."

And how did Jane take the news? Not well, if Jack's account of the dinner at which he broke it to her is accurate. The fateful moment apparently came at an Italian restaurant called Campagna, on 21st Street off Park Avenue in New York. One can easily imagine the tension in the air as Jack "excitedly" broke the news that he wouldn't be retiring after all—this to the wife who, so far as Jack understood things, "had been looking forward to my retirement in April. . . ." Jane, we are told, had also been looking forward to getting to move into a new and "smaller" house than the Georgian estate on Long Island Sound that they presently occupied.

There is an oddly disconcerting moment three days later in the autobiography that suggests just how thick the tension quickly got. In the moment, we find Jack, busily working away on the details of the deal in GE's New York offices, and finally becoming so exhausted that he decides not to go home to Fairfield and to Jane but to stay in New York. What follows is a baroque series of shaggy-dog

The Welch mansion, Southport, Connecticut: large and brick-built. Toward the end, Jack preferred to stay in New York and go to Yankees games. (*Photo credit:* Francis Specker, *New York Post.*)

misadventures featuring contact lenses, hospital emergency rooms, and a taxi driver who can't speak English—all of it culminating in the chairman of GE winding up standing alone on a Manhattan street corner on First Avenue at 3 o'clock in the morning.

Jack offers the following interpretation of that night of strange misadventures: a "bad omen." And if that was all there had been to it, he may well have been right, because the Honeywell deal quickly foundered on antitrust objections raised by the EEC in Europe, and by the following June the effort had been abandoned.

But a "bad omen" hardly captured the full flavor of the parade of embarrassments that the Honeywell deal ushered on stage, rendering Welch, at the very pinnacle of his fame, a global cuckold as his wife began an affair with his best friend's chauffeur while he wound up with, well, let us just say that Jack wound up with Suddenly Suzy.

23

SUZY HOTSTUFF AND THE CASE OF JUAN DANGEROSO

I n many ways, the *Harvard Business Review* was the perfect vehicle for the celebration of American corporatism in the bull market 1990s: slick, pretentious, and self-regarding. And no person seemed more completely suited to the job of being its editor than the brilliant, sassy, and infinitely manipulative Suzy Wetlaufer, whose entire life seems in retrospect to have been a series of positioning gestures to tee her up for the moment when someone might say, "Suzy, I'd like you to meet Jack Welch."

Suzanne Rebekah Spring was born the third of four children to an Italian mother and a German Jewish father. In fact, neither heritage seems to have played much of a role in the Spring household, which looks to have been steeped instead in the camouflaging values of a kind of room-temperature Unitarianism. When Suzy was born in 1960, the Springs were living in Portland, Oregon, where her father,

Bernard, worked as an architect, and her mother, Phyllis, as a painter and sculptor. The family was well off, and there appears to have been some inherited money in the background, though not a vast amount.

Mostly, the Springs seem to have been education oriented and were well enough off to provide private school educations for their children, who in turn appear to have been motivated enough—at least in Suzy's case—to take advantage of the opportunities their educations presented. For Suzy, that first leg up in life came at Philips Exeter Academy, the ultra-prestigious New Hampshire prep school that routinely supplies more incoming freshmen to Harvard, Yale, and Princeton each year than does any other secondary school in the nation.

At Exeter, Suzy played squash, worked on the student newspaper, and was already a senior and heading for Harvard in the autumn of 1977 when she met and began dating a young man named Eric Wetlaufer, who was still a freshman. It was the first of several such unconventional relationships with men that would dog her over the years, and it suggested a personality in Suzy that was at once insecure and needy, yet intensely self-centered, manipulative, and hungry for attention—the kind of a girl who made sure everyone signed her yearbook. "She was a very bright woman, very gregarious," recalled one of her Exeter classmates a quarter century later. "She wanted desperately to be popular, and she was always talking."[1]

At Harvard, Suzy majored in Fine Arts (with a curtsy to mom), but her real interests lay in the socially energized world of the media, and it wasn't long before she had landed a perch as a features editor at the student newspaper, the *Harvard Crimson*. This in turn led to a postgraduation summer as a reporter at the *Washington Post*, followed by two more years as a reporter at the *Miami Herald*.

It was the start of the Reaganaut 1980s and of Miami's late-century renaissance as the American media's art-deco dreamland of drama and vice. So, even as Jane Beasley was graduating from law school at the University of Kentucky and heading for New York to begin that big-time job at the Shearman & Sterling law firm, Suzy was heading in exactly the opposite direction, to begin her career as the kiss-and-tell drama queen of the *Miami Herald* newsroom.

At the *Herald*, her name said it all. Everything that Suzy Spring did—every story she pitched, every idea she pursued—seemed to burst forth in ultra-energized form, full tilt boogey. It was the Suzy Spring Show, brought to you in real-life *SurroundSound*, against a backdrop of South Beach thongs and Cigarette speedboats, with Suzy in the starring role.

"Everything she did was interesting," recalled a newsroom colleague from that time. "She could be driving down the street and it would be interesting."[2]

For Miami's Flashdance queen of breaking news, the danger in this situation was clear: the temptation to make her stories interesting even when they weren't, and a combination of inexperience plus the whispers of Narcissus soon had her doing exactly that. The problem developed when she picked up the spoor of a young Latino who claimed to be a drug dealer and to have been involved in a string of unsolved murders that he offered to tell her about if she promised him confidentiality, which she did. This put the *Herald* in the impossible situation of possessing information about a series of homicides that it had apparently obtained by pledging confidentiality to the killer.

Soon enough, the newspaper discovered that its young femme fatale reporter had been snookered, and that the so-called murder informant couldn't pass a lie detector test about the claims he had made to her. It wasn't long after that before Suzy Excitement was exploring the challenges of finding herself a new job. The search took her back to Boston and a two-year stint in the Boston Bureau of the

Associated Press. During that time, she revived her comforting "younger man" relationship with her prep school heart throb, Eric Wetlaufer, who had gone on from Exeter to Wesleyan University, and from there into investment banking. They were married in the spring of 1985, and she enrolled in the MBA program at the Harvard Business School, seemingly intent on making a run at adulthood from a whole new direction, as an MBA. By the spring of 1986, she had left the Associated Press—and it would seem, journalism as well.

The Suzy Spring Story (which at this point officially morphs into the Suzy Wetlaufer Story) features as its heroine the gal who can (and does) do everything. There is, however, little in her career as Young Supermom that seems off the beaten track followed by other similarly positioned Yuppie wives and mothers in the labor force as the 1980s gained momentum. During this entire period, there is almost nothing of note to report about Suzy Wetlaufer at all, save perhaps the ironic fact that one of her classmates at the B-School turned out to be Jack Welch's eldest daughter, Katherine.

Nor does much of interest seem to have developed for Suzy during her first postgraduation job at Boston's Bain & Company consulting firm, which lasted barely a year before she left to give birth to the first of her four children. And nothing changed thereafter either, as she sank into the groove of a young, upwardly mobile mother in the Boston suburbs.

Between her departure from Bain & Company in 1989, and her arrival at the *Harvard Business Review* in 1996, Suzy made only one, brief walk-on appearance before the public. This came in 1991 when she published a novel titled *Judgment Call*, which prettified the fiasco of her entanglement with the Latino teenager while a cub reporter at the *Miami Herald*. Using the book as leverage to gain some media linage, she even managed to get herself profiled in the *Boston Globe* as a with-it young Bay State gal on the go.

In the profile, there is a revealing moment toward the end, which Suzy presented to the interviewer as the climax to her entire dramatic adventure. It stars who else but Suzy Hotstuff, recalled to the screen for an encore performance in her bodice-ripping role as heroine and star.

In the moment, we find the young Latino swaggering into the *Miami Herald* newsroom and up to her desk. We are encouraged to see the dark flashing eyes and the sneer on the lip of this Juan Dangeroso of the streets. Do you see his hand reaching so casually into the jacket pocket as he approaches? Is he going for his gun?

"I thought he was going to kill me," reported Suzy breathlessly to the *Boston Globe* reporter. But, she continued, young Juan Dangeroso walked right up and sat himself down on the edge of her desk, and in a scene straight out of *Absence of Malice*,* he declared, "I'm through with that life." Then, claimed Suzy, he leaned over and kissed her, and without another word stood up and walked out of the newsroom and out of her life. (Fade to black and roll screen credits as Rick gazes into the yearning and tear-filled eyes of Ilsa. "Here's looking at you, kid . . ." he says, chucking her under the chin, as she replies, "Is that cannon fire or is it my heart pounding?")

━━━

It took nearly half of the bull market 1990s before Suzy Wetlaufer and the *Harvard Business Review* found each other, but when they did, it was love at first sight. In the climate of the times, no publication on

---

*This 1981 crime drama, starring Paul Newman and Sally Field, debuted the year before the newsroom scene described by Suzy to the *Boston Globe* reporter was said to take place. As was the case with Suzy, *Absence of Malice* was set in the sex-and-violence demiworld of Miami, and likewise featured a tough guy with a heart of gold (Paul Newman) and a female reporter (Sally Field), who happened to be working the crime beat for a big city daily newspaper. The movie ends in an emotion-charged scene similar to the one Suzy described for the *Globe* reporter.

earth offered a more welcoming embrace than did the *Review* to the background, talents, and sexually drenched imagination of Suzy Scheherazade.* She was smart, highly educated, hungry for attention, and perfumed morning-to-night in the aromas of phero- mone approachability . . . exactly the sort of person to have no trouble getting even the busiest of CEOs to clear time for her in their calendars—thereby to become subject matter for the celebra- tory profiles that were the *Review*'s stock in trade.

Located on three floors of a five-story building not far from the Harvard campus, the *Harvard Business Review* enjoyed a blue-ribbon reputation derived both from its venerable age (it had been pub- lished continuously since 1922) and from the name of the institu- tion it was presumed to represent: the Harvard Business School. Over the years, the *Review*'s editors had become adept at dressing the articles in its pages in the language of academic detachment, adding a further measure of perceived critical independence to the presentation.

Yet, the reality of the *Review*'s editorial message was more com- plex and much less flattering, for beneath the veneer of critical in- dependence and academic detachment lurked a publication that in many ways functioned as a kind of public relations house organ for American corporatism.

In the main, the *Review*'s articles were turgidly written, poorly edited, and unutterably dull, rarely if ever directing criticism at the performance of even the most deserving of CEOs or their specific

---

*In the legend of Scheherazade, the king of Samarkand, King Schariar, threatens to put to death three thousand virgins in his harem, but is distracted from doing so when the cleverest, smartest, and most imaginative and enchanting virgin of them all, Scheherazade, beguiles him night after night with riveting fantasies of intrigue and sex that she spins from her mind. The stories come to us as Scheherazade's *Book of a Thou- sand and One Nights*.

companies. But literary quality was not what one looked for in a publication that mostly seemed to amount to a coffee table polemic on behalf of Big Business.

A search of back issues of the *Review* during the first half of the 1990s reveals the appearance, toward mid-decade, of the occasional freelance piece bearing the name Suzy Wetlaufer, along with the description "a Boston-based writer"—evidence enough that for all Suzy's claimed interest in business, the tug of a byline still exerted its pull. She was closing in on thirty-five years of age now, she had four children, a home in the Boston suburb of Newton, and a marriage to a man who worked at a hedge fund. But what about Suzy herself? Where was the applause? What had become of the Suzy Spring Show? Somewhere along the line she'd been canceled. But why?

Some combination of such frustrations was surely at work—as perhaps were other frustrations besides—when, toward the end of 1995 Suzy spotted an opening to join the staff of the *Review* as a senior editor and she took it. And in the *Review*'s world of shiny and glib pretense, she bubbled right to the top, becoming executive editor in January 2000, and ascending to the top position on the masthead as editor-in-chief ten months after that, in October 2000.

She was *Suddenly Suzy* again. And just as had been the case in Miami, she was soon starring in every scene, dressing up every circumstance for dramatic effect, as the Suzy Wetlaufer Show returned to prime time. What's more, her supporting cast now took on recognizable names. In place of stories involving sex-and-violence from the streets of Miami, she now regaled her colleagues—who themselves were part of the cast—with tales of romantic liaisons involving Fortune 500 CEOs. She told of being whisked off in corporate jets, to dance shirtless at midnight, in faraway places with strange-sounding names. At unexpected moments, her office would swell with bouquets of blood-red roses, and when her colleagues would murmur about Suzy's newest lover, she'd demur in a way that told them they were right.

In fact, it was all part of her act, for there were no CEO lovers, or trysts in Gulfstream IVs high over the Atlantic, or midnight dancing down the bar in a tavern in Dublin. In one such fantasy, Suzy eagerly encouraged her colleagues to believe she had become involved in a torrid love affair with Jacques Nasser, the ex-CEO of Ford Motor Company while researching and writing an article for the *Review* in the spring of 1999. From that initial contact, Suzy spun out a tale that included having accompanied Nasser to Game One of the 2000 World Series, and to Ireland thereafter for the Christmas holidays where she danced shirtless on a tabletop with Nasser and his brother in a Dublin bar.*

It is a sad story to say the least, and in its way even disturbing. But it is not the complete story, for back in real life, all these tales seem to have begun circulating among her colleagues in the spring of 2000, at just around the time Suzy's husband of fifteen years, Eric Wetlaufer, walked out on her and thereafter filed for divorce, citing the irretrievable breakdown of their marriage.

---

* When Suzy subsequently emerged as "the other woman" in the breakup of Jack and Jane Welch's marriage, *Vanity Fair* profiled her in its June 2002 issue (see S. Andrews, "Romancing the CEO"), reporting the affair with Nasser as an actual fact. But when Nasser was interviewed for this book, he emphatically denied knowing Suzy at all, insisting as well that he had never been to a baseball game in his life and hadn't been to Ireland in more than a decade. The claimed affair with Nasser appears as well in a *New York* profile of Suzy. See L. DePaulo, "If You Knew Suzy," *New York* (May 6, 2002). The DePaulo profile sources several of Suzy's *HBR* colleagues regarding her claims to them of her involvement with Nasser. Interviews for this book confirmed the accuracy of the statements attributed to Suzy's colleagues in the *New York* article. Nonetheless, when the magazine contacted Suzy for a comment, her spokesperson denied any personal relationship with Nasser at all. Suzy declined to be interviewed for this book.

In the wake of his departure, one finds Suzy manufacturing her entourage of imagined CEO suitors. But one also finds her in the arms of a person in real life as well as in her fantasies. And that person turns out to be the same sort of manipulable individual she had reached out for in the past when the need arose: the *much* younger man . . . in this case not a CEO at all but the *Review*'s office copyboy, who was cute and named Joe, and was barely half her age.

"It was sick," said one of her editorial colleagues later. "Here was this copyboy kid, and before anyone knew it he was an item with the woman who ran the whole magazine."

~~~

It was around this time—as the autumn of 2000 gave way to winter, and while Suzy was regaling her colleagues up in Boston with her fantasy life as Jacques Nasser's arm-piece when she was actually getting boinked in real time by the *Review*'s office copyboy—that down in New York Jack Welch was breaking the news to Jane that he wouldn't be retiring the following April after all . . . thereby setting up Jane for some revenge-boinking of her own in Italy by Giorgio, the chauffeur of Jack's boardroom buddy at GE, Paulo Fresco.

Closer and closer they were now orbiting to each other—one in her mind, the other in real life.

In a *New York* magazine profile in May 2002, "If You Knew Suzy," one thus finds Suzy thrilling her colleagues with the made-up news that she had accompanied her big-time CEO lover, Jacques Nasser, to the opening day game of the 2000 World Series. Meanwhile, in Welch's autobiography, we find the man soon to become Suzy's actual CEO lover doing almost identically the thing that Suzy had falsely claimed Nasser had done.

In short, we find Jack breaking the news to Jane in a Manhattan restaurant that the Honeywell deal meant his retirement would have to be postponed—following which we find Jack spending the weekend alone in New York, presumably because Jane has headed back to Connecticut in a snit. So what does Jack do to kill time on a Saturday night? According to his autobiography, he hops the D-train uptown to the Bronx to catch the opening day game of the 2000 World Series, what else! The only person missing from the seat next to him and still needed to complete the picture in real life and make everyone happy? Why Suzy, of course, who was now poised to transition from her make-believe lover named Jacques, to the real one named Jack.

24

SONATA FOR SOUL MATES

Jack Welch retired from the General Electric Company on September 7, 2001, five months after the self-imposed date he had set for himself two years earlier. To the history of American business, he bequeathed a company that was, in many ways, the epitome of what capitalism and free enterprise in the Great Bull Market had been all about.

Refracted through the prism of a twenty-year bull run, GE appeared a triumph of late-century American corporatism, with its stock price rising more than 7,400 percent in value, to a pinnacle that for one glorious moment at century's end made GE the most valuable private enterprise business on earth.

But like much of the rest of American business at the end of the 1990s, the triumph of GE began and ended with the price of it stock; in the Great Bull Market of the twentieth century, it was just that—and that alone—that measured the value of what a company did.

In college and later in graduate school, Welch studied chemical engineering. But at GE his success came instead from the new and infinitely more rewarding discipline of *financial* engineering. And GE's stock price responded because Welch stayed alert for twenty years to every new opportunity that financial engineering presented him to put the shine on GE's equity.

To that end, Welch had been quick to see the opportunity for "human arbitrage" presented by the widening gap in labor rates between the United States and less developed countries. And like other agile CEOs, he began shifting more and more of his company's manufacturing capacity abroad, to countries like India, Korea, China, and Brazil, where trainable labor was available in abundance, and at a fraction of the price of equivalent workers in the United States.

When Welch took over as chairman and CEO in April 1981, GE employed 404,000 workers, with roughly 70 percent of them filling jobs based in the United States, a ratio that continued roughly unchanged throughout the whole of the 1980s. But with congressional ratification of the North American Free Trade Agreement in 1993, the situation began to change, and rapidly, as the numbers of non-U.S. employees at the company began to grow. From 58,000 in 1992 (the year prior to the ratification of the Agreement), GE's non-U.S. payroll passed 72,000 employees by mid-decade even as U.S. domestic employment fell from 173,000 to 150,000 during the same three-year period. By the time Welch retired in 2001, overseas employment had more than doubled from its 1995 level, to 152,000, or 50 percent of the company's entire 310,000 workforce.

Investors applauded the shift because it cut labor costs sharply and improved GE's operating margins without the company having to sell a single new product or service to anyone. On the wings of this applause, GE's stock price rose.

And as did many large companies during the Great Bull Market, GE also became adept at managing the flow of its reported earnings so as to keep the company's net income rising smoothly, steadily, and without surprises, which Wall Street also applauded. One popular tactic: The aggressive accumulation of loan loss reserves inside GE Capital. In this way, GE created what amounted to a kind of rainy-day fund that could be drawn down during periods of weak corporate earnings to bolster bottom-line net income.

The use of such techniques helped Welch rack up seventy-nine consecutive quarters of earnings gains during his years as CEO, a record unmatched by any other CEO of a major public company in the United States.* But by the mid-1990s, the business and financial press had begun to question these practices.† But the investing public hardly seemed to care. The stock market was on fire, and investors had no interest in learning why; they just wanted stock prices to keep rising.

As a result, and over time, critical coverage of GE by Wall Street's analysts simply ceased, leaving the company's problem to grow unnoticed and unexamined by almost anyone, like mushrooms in the dark.

During Welch's first year as chairman and CEO, GE racked $27.2 billion of total revenues and $1.65 billion of net income. Over the next twenty years, revenues grew 362 percent while profits soared at

---

*The streak has been misreported to include "more than 100" such quarters. See A. Gabor, "Anticipating Welch on Welch: Book Planned by GE's Chief Generates Must-Read Buzz," New York Times (November 29, 2000), Sec. C, p. 1. But it actually ended at the 80th quarter.

†See "Managing Profits: How General Electric Damps Fluctuations in Its Annual Earnings—It Offsets One-Time Gains with Write-Offs, Times Asset Sales and Purchases—Accounting for RCA Deal," in the Wall Street Journal (November 3, 1999). See also J. Birger, "Glowing Numbers," Money (November, 2000), for which Welch refused to be interviewed. The story, which characterized GE's earnings growth as a "charade," brought a retort from GE press officials, who dismissed the story as an "unprecedented collection of nonsense." Nearly a year and a half later, after Jeffrey Immelt succeeded Welch as chairman and CEO, Money ran a follow-up story, for which Immelt did grant an interview, during which he acknowledged that GE had indeed become adept at the management of its earnings.

twice that rate, and the analysts of Wall Street broke out their pom-poms and the world applauded.

To generate that 729 percent increase in earnings, GE had acquired literally hundreds of businesses, and to pay for them, the company took on billions of dollars of debt, while issuing more than half a billion shares of new stock and orchestrating five separate stock splits to spread out the company's ownership base into more and more hands.

The net effect was to boost GE's total common stock outstanding by more than 4,300 percent, to nearly ten billion shares, in one of the greatest avalanches of stock onto the public market of any major company in modern times. And with the ownership base thus broadened and diluted, the company's actual per-share earnings in fact shrank—and dramatically—from $7.26 per share of net income in 1981 when Welch became chairman and CEO, to a mere $1.38 per share by the time he retired twenty years later. By this most basic and obvious measure of corporate profitability, GE's ability to generate per share earnings hadn't improved under Welch at all but had in fact been undermined, with earnings per share collapsing by 80 percent during his time at the helm.

In fact, GE was simply one of the more vivid examples among America's so-called large-cap stocks of what had been happening up and down Wall Street throughout the whole of the bull market. Twenty years of declining interest rates had lifted the value of the underlying financial assets whether their ability to generate genuine earnings gains was real or not. On the day Welch became GE's chairman and CEO in April 1981, short-term interest rates were within days of touching 16.3 percent, the highest ever recorded,[1] and the stock market was valuing a dollar of earnings by the 500 largest companies in the country at an average of $9.80. Two decades later, in September 2001 when Welch at last stepped down, short-term rates had fallen to 2.64 percent,[2] the lowest in forty years, and Wall Street was valuing that same dollar of earnings at $21.36. In short, though Welch was hardly the greatest business leader of the twentieth century, he was indisputably the luckiest. He climbed aboard the up-elevator at the start of the longest ride skyward in American business history, and twenty years later he stepped off at literally the top . . . at which point everything beneath him began to wobble and then collapse.

The hardcover edition of Welch's autobiography, *Jack: Straight from the Gut,* had already been shipped to bookstores and was officially going on sale on the morning of September 11 when terrorists attacked the World Trade Center and the Pentagon. The shocks from these attacks added to an array of other problems already multiplying for his successor, Jeffrey Immelt, and which Welch had avoided bringing up in the book. In it, he had said nothing about GE's ominously weakening stock price, which had tumbled by 33 percent during his last year as chairman and CEO. Nor did he note that GE's much-trumpeted streak of uninterrupted earnings gains had come abruptly to an end.* Nor for that matter did he choose to mention the troubles that were already mounting in GE's insurance operations and power systems division.

None of those subjects got discussed by Welch until the paperback edition of his autobiography was issued two years later, when he could point the finger of blame at the economic jolts from the attacks of 9/11—which he did in a seven-page Afterword and the accompanying Acknowledgments.

Much as Chainsaw Al Dunlap managed to erase all mention of his first wife, Gwyn, from his life in his business world memoir, *Mean*

---

*Most of the business press seemed too preoccupied with celebratory reviews of Welch's career to have noted it, but his streak ended in April 2001, when the company reported $2.573 billion of consolidated net quarterly income versus $2.592 in the year-earlier period.

Business—and just as Welch succeeded in reducing his own first wife, Carolyn, to little more than a walk-on role in the hardcover edition of *Jack: Straight from the Gut*—he deleted Jane from any expression of gratitude whatsoever in the Acknowledgments section of the paperback.

In the hardcover edition appear these words: "I first need to thank my wife, Jane, for her patience and love. She's my best friend and confidante. Jane has been more than just understanding as I obsessed over this book."

In the paperback edition, those words disappear and Jane is thanked for nothing. In her place, there now appears—abruptly and

Black-tie soul-mating with Suzy and Jack. From Juan Dangeroso to the song of Narcissus, can love finally flourish for these prime-time flashdancers? (*Photo credit:* Marina Garnier.)

SONATA FOR SOUL MATES 365

out of nowhere—who else but *Suddenly Suzy*, lofted heavenward in Jack's pantheon of intimacy on the wings of his highest accolade of all ("my soul mate"), and festooned with the adoring adjectives that he had previously applied to Jane in the hardcover edition.

Jack's four children from Carolyn—Kathy, John, Anne, and Mark—(described in the hardcover edition as "terrific kids") are also replaced in the paperback edition with a whole new set of four "terrific kids" (*Suddenly Suzy's*).

Jack: Straight from the Gut is not the story of a man's life and career; it is simply a work in progress by a man engaged in the serial reediting of his personal failures. It is bereft of either remorse or shame at the chasm between his life as it was and as he has pretended it to be.

During the two years that followed the news of Jack and Jane's marital troubles, the American press published more than 1,000 stories on the couple's problems—some 850 of which dealt with the "other woman" role of *Suddenly Suzy* Wetlaufer in the affair. Yet a reader of the paperback edition of *Jack: Straight from the Gut* would think the reports must be about some other Jack and Jane Welch, for she is written out of Jack's life with a single sentence: "After thirteen years of marriage, my second wife, Jane, and I started divorce proceedings in early 2002."

By September 28, 2001, little more than two weeks after the attacks of 9/11, Jack was back on the stump, promoting his hardcover edition as if nothing had happened—and in his case at least, nothing had. He had not yet encountered Suzy, who was still a week in his future. But he was the same old Jack, nonetheless, as uncomfortably randy as ever around women—especially younger and good-looking ones, whom he clearly seemed to enjoy making feel ill at ease.

One such person was an attractive magazine writer named Leslie Feller, who had been given a freelance assignment to interview Welch on his plans for retirement. Leslie had prepared exhaustively for the interview, reading every word written about or by Jack Welch that she had been able to locate, including most especially the hardcover edition of his autobiography, which had been on sale for scarcely two weeks.

Yet nothing in the book—or in any of the more than 10,000 articles that had been written about Jack Welch over his lifetime—had prepared Leslie for what transpired as she presented herself before him for her interview prior to a speaking engagement and book signing in Greenwich, Connecticut, home to his one-time boss, Reginald Jones, now in retirement and failing health.

Introducing herself, Leslie smiled politely, and he gestured for her to be seated. Drawing forth a pen and notepad, she began asking her questions, but she quickly grew uncomfortable and with each passing minute, her discomfort grew worse. The problem had nothing to do with either the content of her questions or the quality of his answers; something else entirely was throwing her off her game, and she soon realized what it was. From the moment Leslie had walked in the room, Welch's eyes had panned radar-like to her breasts, where they had locked in on her nipples like a pilot's guidance control system in an F-14 Tomcat. She'd shift in her seat, and Welch's eyes would shift in his head. She'd shift back . . . and the eyes would shift back.

It was creepy, and it got even creepier when she asked him what his outlook was for economic recovery in the wake of the attacks and he answered, with his eyes still locked on her breasts: "You're so cute. I love your face."

Nor was Leslie ready for the subtext that emerged during a separate interview she had set up with Jane Welch. In it, Leslie had been hoping to get some sense of what the couple had planned to be doing in retirement, but it soon became evident that there was going to be more (or maybe less) to this couple's sunset years than the public thought. Almost every question Leslie asked seemed to elicit a rote "good corporate wife" response that featured as well—so subtly that one had to listen carefully to catch it—a quiet but marked little dig at the husband.

Jack didn't like the opera, Jane informed Leslie, so now she went instead with "friends who enjoy it."

Jack didn't pick up after himself, Jane reported. "I mean, he doesn't close drawers," she told Leslie. "Every drawer that he opens is left that way."

And Jack was also a TV pig. "He's definitely a remote control hog," said Jane, announcing that the only way she could sometimes get it from him was to wager control of the zapper on a golf game. "I love it when the bet is for the remote," she declared, knowing that she had by now become a far the better golfer and could invariably win whenever she wanted to.

And then came a remark that brought Leslie up short. Jane said, as if responding to nothing in particular, "I told him that if he sticks with me I'll teach him ballet." *Sticks with me?* There was some question about that?

But before Leslie could pursue it, Jane was on to something else. She was taking Italian lessons, she announced, with her next words ricocheting off some thoughts about Jack's kids. Jane wanted Leslie to understand how they always seemed to turn up whenever she and Jack were in Nantucket. "They freeload," she announced.

Leslie had no way of knowing it, but the Italian lessons and the zapper complaints, and the little digs over ballet and the opera, were all just some of the goblins that had been accumulating for years in Jack and Jane Welch's closet of ghouls—at least since as far back as the murder of Jane's father and maybe even for longer than that.

And Leslie also had no way of knowing, when she snapped her notepad shut and headed home to type up her notes, that in barely three days' time a hand would suddenly appear on that closet doorknob and yank it open, and a lifetime of horribles would come tumbling into view. It would be the hand of who else but *Suddenly Suzy*, who in the first week of October headed for New York, tape recorder and microphone at the ready, to bag the biggest interview of her career, the big summing-up thumb sucker with the legendary Jack Welch.

〰〰〰

Between the time that Suzy showed up at the start of October for the first of her interviews, and the filing of Jack's divorce complaint against Jane in Connecticut Superior Court six months later, Suzy simply took Jack over. Returning to Boston after their initial meeting, she began regaling the crew of the *Review* with her newest conquest, quickly writing Jacques Nasser out of the storyline ("He's getting too needy," she explained to a colleague), and rolling in Jack as the replacement.

Soon enough, Sassy Suzy began sending her sweetie saucy e-mails, in the middle of which she suddenly scooted to New York toward the end of November for a three-hour luncheon with her snookums at the swanky 21 Club restaurant, following which the two—it has been widely reported—got to know each other in the Biblical way.

It was more or less at this point that Jane returned from one of her Giorgio-boinking jaunts to Italy, to discover that Jack and someone named Suzy had been involved in what appears to have been the computerized version of phone sex. To this, Jilted Jane—mindful no doubt that with her prenup by now having expired she just could be staring at the payday of all time—sent a gotcha e-mail of her own back to Suzy, who suddenly saw she'd been screwed.

This was followed by much thrashing about at the *Harvard Business Review* as speculation mounted over Scandalized Suzy's next move. But it wasn't long before Jack himself decided to take charge, and began secretly counseling Suzy over how to handle the situation. His role stayed secret for as long as it took the first *Review* staffer to learn about it, leading to a tip to a reporter in the Boston bureau of the *Wall Street Journal*, and from there to headlines in newspapers around the world.

The eruptions of tit-for-tat media leaks followed as the estranged couple fought to blacken each other's names in what everyone agreed was certain to be the divorce fight of all time.

Yet in the end, it was just the shame of the situation that people seemed to remember. Thanks to the precedent set in Connecticut five years earlier in the divorce of Lorna and Gary Wendt of GE Capital, Jane had a strong case for claiming 50 percent of the family estate accumulated by Jack since the time of their marriage. With Jack thus having filed a financial net worth statement in October 2002 showing that his net worth consisted of roughly $440 million, of which not much more than $15 million or so would have belonged to him prior to the marriage, it was clear that Jane had a strong claim in any court fight to perhaps as much as $200 million, and maybe even more than that. So it seems to have been not much more than a kind of blind and furious rage that nonetheless kept Jack fighting with her through his lawyers for more than the next year.

Why the two sides finally quit depends upon whom one talks to. Exhaustion, surrender, victory, defeat? In the end, what did it matter, save perhaps to stoke the petty vanities of the rich and the greedy. In the Old Testament, the number seven revolves like a great wheel of fate, moving men and nations alike through their lives. And it is perhaps as simple as that, for in Deuteronomy it is written, "At the end of every seven years thou shalt make a release." And in that way, it is perhaps useful to know that it was seven years to the day from that July morning in 1996 when Jane Welch's daddy had been murdered, and her husband, Jack, had all but yawned, that Jane and Jack Welch had made their release and, as it is written in Deuteronomy, settled their fight, with Jane walking off with what sources in the case say was $183 million in go-away money.

〰〰〰

Six months later came another release. After a lengthy period of failing health that led him in the end to the bed in his Greenwich, Connecticut, home, Reginald Jones died on December 30, 2003, at the age of eighty-six. As had been the case with Jack Welch, whom he had chosen to be his successor as GE's chairman and CEO, Jones had risen from humble beginnings to the very pinnacle of business acclaim. The son of an English steelworker from Staffordshire, Jones had come to the United States at the age of eight in 1925.

Like so many of the business leaders who rose to wealth and power in the Great Bull Market of the 1980s and 1990s, Jones had attended the Wharton School of the University of Pennsylvania. He had done so on a scholarship, graduating in 1939 with a degree in economics. On the eve of World War II, he married a fellow Wharton student, Grace Butterfield Cole. She was his first and only wife, and she was at his bedside sixty-three years later when he died. It was the first, but certainly not the only, thing to distinguish Reginald Jones from the generation of Wharton graduates who came after him. And it was only one of many things that distinguished him from the man he chose as his successor, Jack Welch—a choice that in the last years of his life he apparently came to have certain doubts.

At the time that Welch's appointment was announced at the start of 1981, Jones granted an interview to a writer for the GE corporate bulletin, the *Monogram*. In it he offered some thoughts that he hoped would be helpful to Welch in taking up the burdens that now awaited him. He said, "People more or less expect technical competence and economic performance from large corporations. They are looking for something more: some evidence that we are operating from principles higher than mere expediency, some assurance of a moral center. Without that moral center, our public franchise is at risk."

Several weeks later, Jones hosted a reception for Welch at the Helmsley Palace Hotel in New York. The date was February 24, 1981, and the guests included the CEOs of nearly every major American company of the time. Yet, it was a moment that in retrospect wound up humiliating and appalling Jones, planting in him the seeds of doubt that he had in fact made the right choice. Instead of behaving with the dignity and grace that Jones felt to be the obligation of any CEO with responsibility for the lives and well-being of others in his charge, Welch got himself blotto and gave a word-slurring welcoming speech that made Jones cringe.

"I've never been so humiliated in my life," Jones told him the next morning. "You've embarrassed me and the company."

In his autobiography, *Jack: Straight from the Gut*, Welch recalled the scene with a kind of awkwardness that suggested his continuing sensitivity to the matter even twenty years later. As he described the incident, later in the day Jones returned to Welch's office and told him, "Look, I've gotten over 20 calls in the last three hours, and everyone is saying it was the best party they've been to in New York in ten years. I'm sorry, I was too damn tough on you. Everyone had a good time. All I'm hearing are good reports about you and the party. They liked you. I just misread the evening."

But did Jones really say any of that? And if so, why?

In September 2001, in his last known press interview with anyone, Jones discussed that party during a remarkable and wide-ranging interview with magazine writer Leslie Feller. In the course of that interview, Jones explained why he had in fact gone back into Welch's office later the following day, and it had little to do with any so-called chorus of telephoned congratulations from other partygoers the night before.

The fact was, Jones had returned to Welch's office because, frankly, he felt sorry for the man—and rather angry at himself for how he had spoken to him. It wasn't in Jones' nature to be critical and abusive of others, but to lead and encourage them with positive rein-forcement, yet he had been so upset at Welch's gross performance from the night before that he had simply lost his temper.

It was true, Jones agreed, that he had received "three or four" complimentary phone calls about Welch during the day—though hardly a fraction of the twenty-such calls that Welch had quoted him as claiming in his book.

In any case, Jones explained to Leslie that he had returned to Welch's office a second time because he'd mulled over how sharply he'd spoken to Welch during his first visit that morning, and he had seen how the criticism had affected him, almost physically in fact. As Jones put it to Leslie, it was if his words had "hit him right be-tween the eyes." Weighing the result, he had felt the least he could now do was to go back to Welch's office for a return visit and apolo-gize in an encouraging sort of way, which is what he did.

One may wonder whether Welch glimpsed even the dimmest outlines of the lessons in true leadership that Jones had given him during those two visits to his office the day after the party. In his autobiography, Welch wrote of the waves of emotion—from anger and hurt, to fury and self-loathing—that had swept over him in the wake of what was clearly a mild rebuke by Jones during his first visit to the new CEO's office.

There had been no raised voices or yelling on Jones' part—no abusive "you asshole!" put-downs. All it had taken was the man to stand in Welch's doorway—ramrod straight and trim at six-feet-four-inches tall, in a blue suit and white shirt and tie—and utter the words, "You've embarrassed me . . ." for Welch still to be cringing at the memory of it twenty years later—still trying to purge himself from the shame by yet another rewriting of a moment in his life.

Moreover, one may doubt as well whether Welch ever grasped the leadership-by-example lesson that Jones gave him when he came back into his office that second time. "God, I was relieved," wrote Welch in his autobiography. Then referring to the challenges that now lay ahead for him as Jones' successor and GE's newest CEO, he added, "I could hardly wait to get going."

How much further might Welch have gotten in the two decades that followed—how much more might he actually have accomplished—if he'd simply opened his eyes to what Jones had done by walking back in to apologize? One will never know, for he didn't, and the Jack Welch Reign of Terror soon began.

In his interview with Leslie Feller, Reginald Jones said toward the end, "In the history of GE, the retired CEO cuts all ties with the company. He doesn't even keep a seat on the board." The remark underscored how much had changed in the twenty years that had passed. Jones had handed the reins of power to Welch and then, determined to let him do what he thought best with them without any kibitzing or second-guessing from his predecessor, devoted the next twenty years to teaching and to his family, and to his life with his wife, Grace.

By contrast, Welch had prepared for his own retirement by cooking up a complex and ultragreedy postretirement financial deal, in which he got to continue enjoying the perquisites of the corner office, with none of the responsibilities. Then he humiliated himself and his company as well by his ruinous affair with Suzy Wetlaufer, enabling his estranged and furious wife Jane to leak the whole gross business to the press.

On the day of his retirement in September 2001, Welch reigned supreme and unchallenged as perhaps the greatest business leader the United States had produced in the twentieth century. Barely eighteen months later, he seemed ready for prime time as one of the biggest bounders and boobs ever to run a major American

corporation, dragged around by his dong by a disgraced former journalist who'd dyed her hair blond, gotten him to give up golf, and
started him at the age of sixty-eight on Marlboro Lights . . . after
which she, and not he, piped up during a cable TV show interview
to announce their approaching marriage, and to discuss a deal for a
book the two now planned to write.

~~~~

On a cold and clear Saturday in January 2004, a memorial service
was held for Reginald H. Jones at the Second Congregational
Church of Greenwich, Connecticut. More than 300 persons
attended, including children, grandchildren, and his wife Grace.
She had been at her husband's bedside when he had died, and had
written down his dying words and given them to the minister of
their church, Rev. Robert Naylor of the Second Congregational
Church of Greenwich, who had chosen them for his sermon.

Rev. Naylor, had visited with Jones toward the end, as he lay
wasting away from the kind of generalized systems-shutdown that
claims even the strongest among us eventually, and the comments
seemed appropriate to a sermon for they were clearly what had been
on his mind. After all, what does one say as eighty-six years of life
draw to an end except what seems most important? With what do
we leave the audience as the curtain comes down and before the
house lights come up, but that which consumes us at the end?

Of the 313,000 people employed at GE on the day Reginald
Jones died, many did not likely even know who he was. And they
cannot now go to Barnes & Noble to find out either, for Jones left behind no memoir to tell of his time, or what he had tried to do along
the way—no *Reg: Straight from the Shoulder* to mark this CEO's passing.

So Grace had written down his final words, and had prepared
memorial brochures for those who attended the memorial service.
And the minister had taken them for his sermon, and had read them

aloud, for they were what Jones had offered as the bookend to his life. Through the spittle of his final breaths he had murmured, "Leadership requires ethics, morals, and values . . ." and there being nothing more, nor less, to Reginald Jones' life than that, he had smiled at his wife and after that he died.

After the sermon, a receiving line formed. As the line filed past Grace for the mourners to pay their respects, an observer in one of the forward pews could not help but notice the smallish and somewhat stubby-looking bald man in the line, and the younger, blondish lady with the sassy flounce at his side. Yes, it was *Suddenly Suzy*, again—though when Jack smiled at Grace and extended his hand to express his condolences, and he thereupon introduced his companion, Suzy Wetlaufer, the smile on Grace's face turned to stone, and the line continued . . . and Jack and Suzy went back outside and into the cold, to return to Boston and their plans for the future . . . he with his latest soul mate, and she with her newest CEO.

NOTES

Prologue

1. Reprinted with the permission of Scribner, an imprint of Simon & Schuster Adult Publishing Group, from *The Collected Works of W. B. Yeats, Volume I: The Poems, Revised*, edited by Richard J. Finneran. Copyright © 1928 by The Macmillan Company; copyright renewed © 1956 by Georgie Yeats.

Chapter 1: "Is That a Gun in Your Pocket, or Are You Just Happy to See Me?"

1. See D. Jones, *USA Today* (September 12, 2001), p. 17B, which ran a review under the headline "Welch Book Big on GE but Short on the Man." And observed, "Welch doesn't tell enough about himself, the man." The *New York Daily News* reviewer came to the same judgment (September 23, 2001).

2. See J. Welch and J. Byrne, *Jack: Straight from the Gut* (New York: Warner Books, 2001), p. xv.

3. See note 2, p. 4.

4. Interview with the author (2003).

5. For the only known publicly available photos of Grace Welsh, see the two photos that appear after p. 208 in *Jack: Straight from the Gut*, see note 2, p. xv.

6. See note 2, p. 11.

7. See J. Lowe, *Welch: An American Icon* (New York: John Wiley & Sons, 2001, paperback), p. 30, wherein the author writes, "Grace Welch hoped her wonderful bright boy would study to be a priest or physician, but Jack followed his own course."

8. See note 2, p. 11.

Chapter 2: "I Want to Play in the Band!"

1. See D. Sider, "The Terminator," *People* (November 25, 1996), p. 77.

2. See *Pilot's Log*, Hasbrouck Heights Junior/Senior High School, Special 1950 Reunion Issue (May 12, 2000).

3. From an interview with the author (2003). The consultant expressed alarm at the manner in which Dunlap's personality would change over the course of conversations, and he turned down the consulting opportunity. Others have remarked on the same personality trait in Dunlap.

4. See J. J. Ratey, MD, *A User's Guide to the Brain* (New York: Vintage Books, 2002), pp. 290–291.

5. L. Lavelle, "Boy Next Door, Rambo in Pinstripes," *Bergen Record* (November 10, 1996), p. 1; and see note 4.

6. All these characterizations, and more, can be found in J. Welch and J. Byrne, *Jack: Straight from the Gut* (New York: Warner Books, 2001).

7. See J. A. Byrne, *Chainsaw: The Notorious Career of Al Dunlap in the Era of Profit-at-Any-Price* (New York: HarperBusiness, 1999). Byrne was the first journalist to publish an extended, critical look at Dunlap from the point of view of his behavior as an individual as well as a business leader. His book is an outgrowth of articles he wrote for *BusinessWeek*.

8. Interview (September 2003).

Chapter 3: A Course for New Providence, or the Drowning Pools of Narcissism?

1. Interview with a Perelman family intimate (2003).

Chapter 4: GE Loves Me!

1. See M. Potts, "G.E.: Changing a Corporate Culture," *Washington Post* (September 23, 1984), p. G1.

2. The details of Cizek's role in the development of Noryl were provided by Cizek during an interview with the author's research colleague, Donna Bertaccini, and confirmed with others who worked with him on the Noryl project.

3. A. Ludwig, *King of the Mountain: The Nature of Political Leadership* (Lexington: University of Kentucky Press, 2002), pp. 3–4.

4. The incident comes by way of a Welch colleague, John Theberge, who witnessed it for himself.

5. The incident was confirmed, years later, by two guests who attended the party.

6. See "Chemicals for Keeps," in *Chemical Week* (March 23, 1968), pp. 73–77.

7. See M. Nelson, "Thomas Fitzgerald, 67, Former GE Executive," *Newsday* (July 12, 1994), p. A45.

8. See F. Ochberg and D. Soskis, *Victims of Terrorism* (Boulder, CO: Westview Press, 1982).

9. See J. Welch and J. Byrne, *Jack: Straight from the Gut* (New York: Warner Books, 2001), p. 43.

10. See note 9, p. xii.

Chapter 5: Al and Dennis in the Passing Lane

1. The narrative regarding Al and Gwyn Dunlap's marriage are all set forth in Gwyn's divorce complaint. See *Gwyn B. Dunlap v. Albert J. Dunlap,* Superior Court of New Jersey, Union County, New Jersey, April 27, 1965.

2. See D. Sider, "The Terminator," *People* (November 25, 1996), p. 77.

3. See J. S. Lublin and O. Suris, "'Chainsaw Al' Now Aspires to Be 'Al the Builder'," *Wall Street Journal* (April 9, 1997), p. B1.

4. See F. Norris, "The Incomplete Resume," *New York Times* (July 16, 2001), p. 1.

5. In a July 1979 affidavit, Dunlap stated under oath that when he arrived to begin work at Nitec, the company's paper mill "was in mothballs with no employees." He said that he did "one Hell of a good job" in getting it running again. See *Albert J. Dunlap v. Nitec Paper Corporation et al.*, U.S. District Court for the Southern District of New York, 77 Civ. 3056, July 9, 1979.

6. Interview with a Niagara Falls, New York, business executive and member of the City Council, who witnessed numerous such performances by Dunlap.

7. See note 6.

8. B. Gallagher, correction and amplification appended to "Bush Won't State Obvious Truth," *Niagara Falls Reporter* (February 5, 2002), with additional interviews by author.

9. See note 8.

10. The five-box case file was retrieved from the National Archives storage facility in Lee's Summit, Missouri, and reviewed in its entirety for this book.

11. See "Streamlining the Management at SCM," *BusinessWeek* (February 21, 1977), p. 96.

12. See Separation Agreement, L. Dennis Kozlowski and Angeles Kozlowski, 4101 Ibis Point Circle, Boca Raton, Florida (July 10, 2000), p. 1.

13. See PR Newswire (June 28, 1995).

14. See M. Brelis, *Boston Globe* (December 1, 2002), p. G1.

Chapter 6: Foolish Faith and the Case of Suzie Cream Cheese

1. See C. Bruck, *The Predator's Ball: The Inside Story of Drexel Burnham and the Rise of the Junk Bond Raiders* (New York: Simon & Schuster, 1988).

2. See *Institutional Investor* (May 1989), p. D4, which estimated Perelman's wealth to be $5 billion.

3. Ron's previously unreported relationship with Susan Kasen is drawn from sworn affidavits and similar court documents, including extensive international surveillance reports of Perelman and Kasen by private investigators hired as part of the sealed litigation in the Perelman divorce action.

4. Mention of the Bulgari bracelet incident has appeared in the press occasionally over the years. See Susan Antilla, "Off Hours, a Man of Society," *USA Today* (April 17, 1989), p. 5B.

5. The extensive role of private investigators by Faith in the divorce against Perelman appears in court documents obtained by the author from retired lawyers and other participants in what is now a 20-year-old case. See *Perelman v. Perelman and Kasen*, Supreme Court of State of New York, NY County, 32734/83.

Chapter 7: Question from the Chairman: How Much Do I Weigh?

1. Jones died at the age of 86 on December 30, 2003, in Greenwich, Connecticut, after a long illness. The information regarding his views of Welch, and all the quotes and thoughts attributed both to him and to Welch in this chapter come from a wide-ranging, insightful, and unpublished interview conducted with Jones by magazine writer Leslie Feller in September 2001. Feller provided the author with the tapes and transcriptions of that interview for this book.

2. For a fuller discussion on Cordiner's bizarre approach to management, see N. Tichy and S. Sherman, *Control Your Destiny or Someone Else Will*, 2nd ed. (New York: HarperBusiness, 2001), pp. 55–57.

3. See *BusinessWeek* (March 16, 1981), p. 110.

4. The anecdotes concerning Welch's management activities as a Sector Executive from 1978 to 1981 come from confidential interviews with those employed in executive level positions at GE's Fairfield headquarters during the period described. Many of these stories have

long since acquired the status of GE corporate lore, and it has proven impossible to locate direct eyewitnesses.

5. Welch's downsizing campaign was extensively chronicled in newspapers. See in particular, T. Lueck, "Why Jack Welch Is Changing G.E.," *New York Times* (May 5, 1985), Sec. 3, p. 1. The campaign is discussed as well in Welch's autobiography and in various biographies of him, including N. Tichy and S. Sherman, *Control Your Destiny or Someone Else Will,* 2nd ed. (New York: HarperBusiness, 2001); J. Lowe, *Welch, An American Icon* (New York: John Wiley & Sons, 2001); and in numerous magazine articles. Notable among them: "Trying to Bring G.E. to Life," by Ann Morrison, *Fortune* (January 25, 1982), p. 50.

6. See "Layoffs Announced at Defense Systems Plant," Associated Press (May 13, 1988).

7. See F. Biddle, "Defense in Retreat," *Boston Globe* (May 7, 1989), p. A1.

Chapter 8: Stretch Role Time for Gary and the Preacher's Daughter

1. See, for example, P. Petre, "What Welch Has Wrought at GE," *Fortune* (July 7, 1986), p. 42.

2. See in particular pp. 239–249 where Wendt's ouster is characterized as almost a collegial parting of the ways.

3. Details of the childhoods and married lives of Lorna Jorgenson Wendt and Gary Wendt come from their divorce file in *Wendt v. Wendt,* Superior Court of Connecticut, Judicial District of Stamford-Norwalk, 1998.

4. In December 1986, Welch sued his wife, Carolyn, for divorce in Connecticut Superior Court, Stamford, Connecticut, filing a net worth statement that listed a net worth of roughly $17.5 million, not counting approximately $6.5 million of federal income tax liabilities. The case was sealed at the plaintiff's request and remained so for the following 16 years. In 2002, the file was successfully unsealed by Welch's

second wife, Jane Beasley Welch after Jack filed for divorce from her. The unsealed file was obtained for this book.

5. See J. Welch and J. Byrne, *Jack: Straight from the Gut* (New York: Warner Books, 2001), pp. 146–147, where he expresses just those desires.

6. See D. Margolick, "The Tao of Jack," *Vanity Fair* (October 1, 2001), p. 350.

Chapter 9: Fitzy Comes Out of the Closet

1. J. Sterngold, "Kidder's Road to Acquisition," *New York Times* (May 5, 1986), p. D1.

2. From an interview with an executive at GE headquarters who relayed the story as told to him by Bossidy.

3. Interview with Grossman.

4. Variations on the Grossman dinner appear in K. Auletta, *Three Blind Mice: How the Networks Lost Their Way* (New York: Random House, 1991) and in Welch's autobiography, *Jack: Straight from the Gut.*

Chapter 10: Champagne Kisses and Caviar Dreams

1. See *BusinessWeek* (February 27, 1984), p. 60.

2. See A. Sloan, "A Manager Rescues the Money Movers," *Forbes* (December 17, 1984), p. 50.

3. See W. Flanagan, "The Unmarried Penalty," *Forbes* (October 27, 1980), p. 172.

4. See J. Yenckel, "Men Facing Up to Plastic Surgery," *Washington Post* (November 5, 1981), p. C5.

5. See E. Taylor, *My Love Affair with Jewelry* (New York: Simon & Schuster, 2002).

6. See A. Sloan, "Pyramid Power," *Forbes* (January 27, 1986), p. 30.

Chapter 11: Jack Meets Celebrity's Dark Side

1. See W. Kiechel, "The Boss Is Coming to Visit," *Fortune* (August 22, 1983), p. 227. The story sketched out, in a bemused way, the panic that would invariably spread through any plant or field operation at the news that Welch was coming for a visit. The writer suggested that the best one might hope for from these encounters was for the boss to come away reinvigorated with a sense of his own omnipotence.

2. See "Who's Who in the New Corporate Elite," *BusinessWeek* (January 21, 1985), p. 78.

3. See A. Lee, *Call Me Roger: The Story of How Roger Smith, Chairman of General Motors, Transformed the Industry Leader into a Fallen Giant* (Lincolnwood, IL: Contemporary Books, 1988).

4. Associated Press (May 1, 1985).

5. See "Charisma Back in Vogue," *Financial Times* (December 7, 1984).

6. Details of the twentieth anniversary celebration come from printed contemporaneous accounts, GE promotional materials, participants in the event, and a member of the organizing committee.

7. See T. O'Boyle, *At Any Cost: Jack Welch, General Electric, and the Pursuit of Profit* (New York: Knopf, 1998), p. 76.

8. Details regarding Welch's net worth and the monthly living expenses of his wife come from financial documents filed under seal in their divorce proceeding and subsequently unsealed in the course of Welch's second divorce a decade and a half later. See *John F. Welch Jr. v. Carolyn B. Welch*, Superior Court, Judicial District of Stamford, December 17, 1986 (FA 87 0085243 S).

9. See U.S. Census Report: Number, Timing and Duration of Marriages and Divorces in the United States (June 1975), Table J.

Chapter 12: The Shiksa Goddess of Wall Street

1. See A. Gerhart, "A Passion for Power; She Had Beauty, Wanted Influence, Married Money, and Now Patricia Duff Has Nothing but

Trouble," *Washington Post* (August 10, 1999), p. C01; and J. Conant, "Working Girl," *Esquire* (September 1994).

2. Details of Patricia Duff's childhood and adolescent years are to be found in the Duff/Perelman divorce file: *Anonymous v. Anonymous*, New York State Supreme Court, County of New York, Index. No. 310754/96; Consultation Report of Donald G. Dutton, PhD (April 10, 2000), pp. 3–6.

3. See note 2, Consultation Report of Donald G. Dutton, PhD.

4. See D. Shah, "Beauty and the Billionaire," *Los Angeles* (December 1996), p. 62.

5. See M. Williams, "Dangerous Beauty," *Vanity Fair* (August 1999), p. 132.

6. See M. Shain and A. Scaduto, "Inside New York," *New York Newsday* (August 19, 1994), p. A13.

7. See note 1, Conant, p. 144.

8. See B. Hoffman, "Revlon King Leaves Gossip Queen Wife," *New York Post* (August 16, 1991). The *Post*, where Claudia once worked as editor of its famous "Page Six" gossip page, was uncommonly well-informed on the couple's travails and was the first to break the story that their marriage was in trouble.

9. For further details on Medavoy's career, see E. Katz, *The Film Encyclopedia*, 4th ed. (New York: HarperResource, 2001).

10. The Donald G. Dutton Consultation Report (April 10, 2000), pp. 3–6, contains extensive discussion of Duff's desire to have a child and the anxiety that overtook her once it became clear that Medavoy was not interested in cooperating.

11. See in particular the Affidavit of Patricia Duff (April 11, 2000), pp. 4–5, *Anonymous v. Anonymous*, New York State Supreme Court, Index No. 310754/96.

12. See note 11, p. 3.

13. See note 11, pp. 5–6.

14. See *Geraldo*, "Hollywood Heartaches and Heartbreaks" (April 26, 1994). Don Johnson's behavior at the Perelman party and the following day

on the radio is discussed at length and was the subject of much press coverage when Melanie Griffith thereafter served him with divorce papers.

15. The 21 Club dinner at which Clinton spoke by telephone is covered in D. Wise, "The Redemption of Michael Milken," *Washington Post* (April 22, 1994), p. G1. The story makes mention of the Sinatra event upstairs later in the evening but does not identify Perelman as having attended. His presence at the Sinatra affair is captured in a separate story. See M. Shain and A. Scaduto, "Inside New York," *Newsday* (April 21, 1994), p. A13.

16. The details of Vernon Jordan's approach to Barry Schwartz, the subsequent hiring of Webster Hubbell, and the dating of the check, are all contained in the *Report to Congress by the Office of the Independent Counsel*, Part C., Webster Hubbell's Billing Practices and Tax Filings (September 11, 1998).

Chapter 13: Jane Beasley and the Spoor of an Older Man

1. See "Al Dunlap's Disgrace," *Australian Financial Review* (July 21, 2001), quoting David Brandon, then head of a Consolidated Press Holdings subsidiary, and now CEO of the United States's Dominos Pizza restaurant chain.

2. D. Kansas, "Scott Paper Selects Outsider Dunlap to Succeed Lippincott as Top Executive," *Wall Street Journal* (April 20, 1994), p. B10.

3. See note 2.

4. Dunlap's entire restructuring plan is set forth in Scott Paper Co.'s 10K annual financial report, filing with the U.S. Securities and Exchange Commission in April 1995 for the calendar year 1994.

5. See J. S. Lublin and A. Markels, "Management: How Three CEOs Achieved Fast Turnarounds," *Wall Street Journal* (July 21, 1995), p. B1.

6. See J. S. Lublin and S. Lipin, "Scott Paper's 'Rambo in Pinstripes' Is on the Prowl for Another Company to Fix," *Wall Street Journal* (July 18, 1995), p. B1.

7. See "America's Disappearing Middle-Class," *CBS Evening News* (August 8, 1996).

8. See J. Welch and J. Byrne, *Jack: Straight from the Gut* (New York: Warner Books, 2001), pp. 147–148.

9. Interview with author (2003).

10. See S. P. Sherman with J. Lieblich, "GE's Costly Lesson on Wall Street," *Fortune* (May 9, 1988), p. 72.

11. See note 8, p. 227.

12. See W. M. Carley, M. Siconolfi, and A. K. Naj, "Major Challenge: How Will Welch Deal with Kidder Scandal?" *Wall Street Journal* (May 3, 1994), p. A1.

13. See L. Jereski and M. Siconolfi, "On the Ropes: Kidder Peabody Gets Infusion from GE, But Problems Mount," *Wall Street Journal* (June 15, 1994) p. A1.

Chapter 14: Marvin Hamlisch Meets the World of Six Sigma

1. The comment first appeared in Dunlap's business memoir, *Mean Business: How I Save Bad Companies and Make Good Companies Great* (New York: Times Books, 1996). It instantly became a classic Dunlap one-liner, appearing in more than 50 newspaper and magazine profiles of the man in the following months.

2. "Merger Mania Causes Major Hardships for Displaced Workers," *CBS Evening News* (October 6, 1995).

3. See J. S. Lublin and A. Markels, "Management: How Three CEOs Achieved Fast Turnarounds," *Wall Street Journal* (July 21, 1995), p. B1.

4. The litany of Gary's complaint's are set forth, in detail, in the judge's ruling in the *Wendt v. Wendt* divorce case. After reviewing them all, he ruled that Lorna was entitled to half the family assets accumulated during the marriage.

5. See J. Welch and J. Byrne, *Jack: Straight from the Gut* (New York: Warner Books, 2001), p. 185.

Chapter 15: Ceo in Banjo-Land

1. S. Waxman, "Top Editors Quit; Movie Magazine Premiere Staffers Refuse Corporate Order to Kill Column," *Washington Post* (May 10, 1996), p. D01.

2. The scene was described by the Louisville, Alabama, Chief of Police, Mack Houston, in a detailed interview with the author's research colleague, Donna Bertaccini, on July 27, 2003. Houston declined subsequent requests for additional interviews.

Chapter 16: Big Al Goes AWOL

1. Official date of his resignation: March 14, 1994. See *Report to Congress by the Office of the Independent Counsel*, Part C., Webster Hubbell's Billing Practices and Tax Filings (September 11, 1998), p. 1.

2. See note 1.

3. Sunbeam Corporation Proxy (August 29, 1996).

4. N. Deogun, "Sunbeam Inspires Investors to Grab Stock as Some Watch in Disbelief," *Wall Street Journal* (July 22, 1996), p. B4.

5. See "U.S. Labor Secretary Reich Implicitly Criticizes Sunbeam Lay-offs," *Agence France Presse* (November 14, 1996).

Chapter 17: Ron's Next Democrat

1. See J. Byrne, "Who Is the Real Chainsaw Al?" *Business Week* (December 2, 1996), p. 40. Byrne went on to turn his coverage of Dunlap into a book on the man, and later assisted Jack Welch in writing his own autobiography, *Jack: Straight from the Gut* (New York: Warner Books, 2001).

2. See O. Suris and J. S. Lublin, "Sunbeam CEO Dunlap Explores Sale of Company or Launching Acquisition," *Wall Street Journal* (April 7, 1997), p. B2.

3. See J. S. Lublin and O. Suris, "'Chainsaw Al' Now Aspires to Be 'Al the Builder'," *Wall Street Journal* (April 9, 1997), p. B1.

4. See "Sunbeam Earnings Triple," *Miami Herald* (April 24, 1997), p. 7C.

5. See J. Waresh, "It's a Dog-Eat-Chairman World," *Palm Beach Post* (September 4, 1997), p. 1A.

6. Channel-stuffing is financial fraud, and on May 15, 2001, the U.S. Securities and Exchange Commission charged Dunlap with exactly that in the Sunbeam case. The SEC complaint accused Dunlap and his aides of using illegal accounting techniques to inflate the price of Sunbeam's shares, from $12.25 when he took over as chairman and CEO, to a March 1998 high of $52. On September 4, 2002, regulators announced that Dunlap, without admitting or denying the allegations, had agreed to entry judgments "(1) permanently enjoining [him] from violating the antifraud, reporting, books and records, and internal controls provisions of the federal securities laws; (2) permanently barring [him] from serving as officer or director of any public company, and (3) requiring [him] to pay a civil penalty of $500,000." See *Delistings, Withdrawls, and Enforcement Proceedings, SEC Digest Issues 2002–170 thru 2002–173* for week ending September 6, 2002.

7. See L. DePaulo, "The Woman Who Made Monica Cry," *Ottawa Citizen* (February 12, 1999), p. A17.

Chapter 18: Hugs and Kisses and Bouts of Nostalgia

1. See R. Waters, "Chainsaw Al May Sell Revived Sunbeam," *Financial Times* (October 24, 1997), p. 27.

2. The narrative action and imputed thoughts involving President Bill Clinton and Monica Lewinsky, and the actions and statements of Secret Service members, White House guards, and Presidential Secretary Bette Currie are derived from the Starr Report. See, Referral to the United States House of Representatives pursuant to Title 28,

United States Code, § 595(c) submitted by the Office of the Independent Counsel on September 9, 1998.

3. See P. Sellers, "Exit for Chainsaw," *Fortune* (June 8, 1998). A lengthier description of this meeting appeared a year later in J. Byrne, *Chainsaw: The Notorious Career of Al Dunlap in the Era of Profit-at-Any-Price* (New York: HarperBusiness,1999).

4. The sequence of events through which Monica Lewinsky wound up being offered a job at Revlon is fully detailed in affidavits and narrative in the Starr Report. See the Report of the Office of the Independent Counsel, Docs. (September 21, 1998; October 2, 1998).

Chapter 19:   Big Al and Ron Exit Fighting

1. See "Sunbeam States First Quarter Revenues May Be Lower than Street Estimates," *Business Wire* (March 19, 1998).

2. See "Sunbeam Corporation Lowers First Quarter Sales and Earnings Expectations; Names Lee Griffith President of Household Products Business," *Business Wire* (April 3, 1998).

3. Both *BusinessWeek* and *Fortune* published accounts of the meeting, including the quote attributed to Dunlap. See J. A. Byrne, "How Al Dunlap Self-Destructed," *BusinessWeek* (July 6, 1998), p. 58; and P. Sellers, "Exit for Chainsaw: Sunbeam Investors Draw Their Knives," *Fortune* (June 8, 1998), p.30.

4. See J. P. Newport, "The Stalking of Gillette," *Fortune* (May 23, 1988).

5. See M. Brannigan and E. J. Pollack, "Perelman Strengthens Sunbeam Grip in Accord," *Wall Street Journal* (August 13, 1998), p. A3.

Chapter 20:   Life Is a Cabaret

1. See A. Kupfer, "People to Watch," *Fortune* (June 9, 1986), p. 110.

2. See J. B. Stewart, "Spend! Spend! Spend! Where Did Tyco's Money Go?" *New Yorker* (February 17, 2003), p. 132.

3. The details of their relationship appear in Ms. Jacques's testimony as a witness for the prosecution in the case of the *People of the State of New York v. L. Dennis Kozlowski and Mark H. Swartz* (September 2003), pp. 2101–2522.

4. See S. N. Chakravarty, "Deal-a-Month Dennis," *Forbes* (June 15, 1998), p. 66.

5. When Murphy, whose job was "administrative assistant," left the company in 2000, her final year's compensation for 1999 had totaled $765,747.00. Details of all these transactions, and more, appear in the testimony of Barbara Jacques and Mary Murphy, *People of the State of New York v. L. Dennis Kozlowski and Mark H. Swartz* (September 2003).

6. See note 5.

Chapter 21:   Let's Party Like It's 1999

1. See E. Sporkin, "Marriage with a Midas Touch," *People* (May 7, 1990), p. 150.

2. See B. Ross and B. Hutchinson, "Tyco Jurors View Video," *New York Daily News* (October 29, 2003), p. 5.

3. The details of the festivities, including the itinerary, are drawn from the court testimony of participants, in the case of the *People of the State of New York v. L. Dennis Kozlowski and Mark H. Swartz* (September 2003).

Chapter 22:   That Pesky Neck Waddle

1. R. Slater, *Jack Welch and the GE Way* (New York: McGraw Hill, 1999).

2. See R. Badowski, *Managing Up: How to Forge an Effective Relationship with Those above You* (New York: Doubleday, 2003).

Chapter 23:   Suzy Hotstuff and the Case of Juan Dangeroso

1. See *New York Daily News* (March 21, 2002).
2. See note 1.

Chapter 24:   Sonata for Soul Mates

1. See U.S. Treasury Bill secondary market three-month rate, as quoted by the U.S. Federal Reserve, monthly historical data.
2. See note 1.

INDEX